THE FRENCH AGAINST THE FRENCH

THE FRENCH AGAINST THE FRENCH

COLLABORATION AND RESISTANCE

by Milton Dank

J. B. Lippincott Company
Philadelphia and New York

First edition

PRINTED IN THE UNITED STATES OF AMERICA

U.S. Library of Congress Cataloging in Publication Data

Dank, Milton, birth date
The French against the French: collaboration and resistance.

Bibliography: p.
1. France–History–German occupation, 1940-1945.
2. World War, 1939-1945–Collaborationists–France.
3. World War, 1939-1945–Underground movements–France.
I. Title.
D802.F8D28 940.53′44 74-10735
ISBN-0-397-01040-0

To My Wife and Daughters

Author's Note

This book tells the story of France under the German occupation of 1940–1944—those four most tragic years of recent French history. Its aim is to tell what happened to a highly civilized people when faced with the agonizing decisions necessary for survival.

The narrative begins with the fall of France in June, 1940, and the establishment of the Vichy government of Marshal Pétain. It closes with the post-liberation purge of Vichy ministers and the collaborationist milieu of writers, actors, journalists, and businessmen. In between is the painful—and often bloody—tale of an isolated society suffering four years of Nazi occupation, four years that the French still refer to as the "time of shame." France was not the only defeated and occupied country, but it was the only one in which collaboration with Hitler was official policy and in which tens of thousands of the occupied eagerly served the conqueror against their fellow countrymen.

The reader who wishes to know the sources of the quotations will find them listed in the reference notes at the back of the book. Also included are a fairly extensive bibliography, a chronology of events both inside and outside France during World War II, and brief biographies of the leading personages.

My wife and our daughters not only encouraged me to write this book but sustained me with loving support throughout—especially in those dark hours that every writer knows. It is only right that this book be dedicated to them, for it is the direct result of their faith in me. For what they so unselfishly suffered through, they have—as always—my love and my gratitude.

Special thanks are due to Mrs. Ray Lincoln, who first championed the partially completed manuscript at Lippincott; her unwavering support and editorial judgment during the writing of the rest of the book were essential to its completion. I also wish to thank Mrs. Beatrice Rosenfeld for her editorial assistance in the final stages of manuscript preparation.

Mrs. Jacqueline Leventhal not only corrected many of the translations but provided invaluable insight into the psychology of the French during the occupation—a period through which she herself lived.

Contents

Illustrations

"Victory . . . defeat . . . these words have no meaning. A victory weakens one nation, a defeat arouses another."
—Antoine de Saint-Exupéry (*Night Flight*)

"Being condemned to death is the only thing that really distinguishes a man, for it is the only thing that cannot be bought."
—Mathilde de la Mole in Stendhal's *Le Rouge et le noir*

"Imbeciles! I am dying for you!"
—Valentin Friedmann to a German firing squad

"I have often felt . . . how difficult it was to speak of those [occupation] days to anyone who had not lived through them. . . . Now, after nearly twenty years, I cannot recall the truth. . . ."
—Simone de Beauvoir (*The Prime of Life*)

"[The ideal historian] thinks neither to praise nor to blame. . . . It is not his job to excite hate or love, to improve hearts or minds. Whether the facts are beautiful or ugly is not important; he is not responsible for people's souls. His only duty and desire is to shorten time, to put the reader face to face with the objects, to make him a contemporary of the personalities and of the events he is describing. . . . Now let the moralists come and pontificate on the portrait he has drawn; his job is done. He yields his place to them and leaves."
—Hippolyte Taine (*Essay on Titus Livy*)

Prologue

June, 1940.

Beneath a summer sun and cloudless skies, the torn fragments of the French army—"the greatest army in Europe"—retreated along the dusty roads south of Paris. Mingling with a frantic mass of civilian refugees were remnants of companies, regiments, and divisions that had just suffered the worst defeat in French military history as they struggled toward the Loire in the desperate hope of making a stand. Cut into smaller and smaller groups by the constant pressure of German tanks, units without cohesion, without orders—some without officers—shuffled wearily along the roads, their backs bent with fatigue under the heavy military greatcoats.

The roads were a tangled jam of everything that could move: trucks, cars, garbage wagons, bicycles, hearses, carts, fire trucks, baby carriages, wheelbarrows, even taxis from Paris—the famous taxis of the Marne in reverse. All had been pressed into service in this headlong flight to escape the armored fist that always seemed to be but a few kilometers behind them.

Terror and resignation. Unknowing, unthinking, obeying some blind instinct for survival, seven million refugees and two million soldiers clogged the roads in one gigantic bottleneck, slowly moving south.

During the last week in May, the Belgians and the Dutch were the first to flee, quickly followed by the French of the northern *départements,* some still with painful memories of the German occupation of the last war. As the pitiful columns moved south, village after village emptied, fields were left unharvested, cows left unmilked, homes left unlocked and deserted to be pillaged by those who came later. The dark angel of the Grande Peur* touched town after town, sending the inhabitants fleeing mindlessly down the roads south.

* "The Great Fear." At the outbreak of the French Revolution in 1789, a similar wave of panic and hysteria led to the flight of peasants in certain areas of France.

They piled their possessions into any vehicle that could roll—loaded mattresses, furniture, radios, cats, dogs, birdcages—and fled.

On June 11, the day after Italy had declared war on France and the Reynaud government had left for Cangé, Paris was proclaimed an open city. The notice was posted on the same walls that, twenty-six years earlier, had borne the cold uncompromising words of General Gallieni: "I have received a mandate to defend Paris against the invader. This mandate I shall carry out to the end." This time, Paris was not to be defended; the official limousines, the trucks loaded with government files, and the taxis left the city headed south.

On the thirteenth, the gasoline and oil tanks in the suburbs were set afire, sending a foul-smelling shroud over the dying city. Paris was deserted to her fate: of five million Parisians, only 700,000 remained—the rest were on the roads toward the Loire.

The next day, Hitler's victorious troops entered an abandoned Paris. By 9:45 A.M., red-and-black swastika flags flew triumphantly from the Arc de Triomphe and, shortly thereafter, were raised on the Chamber of Deputies, the Senate, the ministries, and the Hôtel Crillon. Amid the shrill wailing of fifes and the roll of drums, a victory parade marched down the Champs-Elysées. Most Parisians ignored the gray-green conquerors, staring straight ahead as they passed on the streets; but there were some who crept out hesitantly to speak timidly to the enemy, to admire their uniforms and equipment, to curse the war and to praise the defeat.

To some Frenchmen, the shame was overwhelming and not to be suffered: Thierry de Martel, a prominent surgeon, and Joseph Meister, the Alsatian concierge at the Pasteur Institute, killed themselves. (Meister, as a ten-year-old boy in 1887, was the first to be cured of rabies by Pasteur.)

Three days later, newsboys shouted "*La Victoire!*"—"Victory!"—but it was only the name of a single-sheet newspaper, the first to reappear in the conquered city.

Outside of Paris, the despair of the panic-stricken mobs grew hourly. There were scenes of unselfish aid given to the sick and elderly mixed with incidents of the worst type of petty avarice. Near Chartres, a nurse reported that a peasant shouted to the crowd of thirsty refugees about his water tap: "All right, get out your money. Ten sous a glass, two francs a bottle!"* In the city itself, the youthful prefect, Jean Moulin, waited calmly at his post as ordered. Three years later, the Germans would torture him to death.

Meanwhile, madness reigned on the roads of France. Here and their isolated army units tried to make a stand, to fire a shot "for

* Sources for this and subsequent quotes are given in the Reference Notes at the end of the Bibliography.

honor's sake," only to find the attempt frustrated by civilians fearful of German reprisals. When the bridges at Blanc were mined in preparation for their demolition, the veterans of 1914–1918, wearing medals won at Verdun, Champagne, the Marne, and a hundred other battlefields, marched out and ripped away the fuses. The townspeople at Poitiers threatened to tear down the barricades hastily erected by a French infantry unit, and, under a white flag, the mayor surrendered the town to the advancing Germans. More than one officer who was determined to stand and fight was shot down by his own men "to prevent a massacre."

At the hospital in Orsay, the nurses gave fatal injections of strychnine to several elderly incurables; the alternative would have been to leave them to the Germans. At Orléans, on the sixteenth, two bridges were hastily blown up, killing an unknown number of refugees; for some unexplained reason, a third bridge was left untouched and was promptly used by enemy tanks. German and Italian planes ranged the skies unmolested, bombing and strafing the dense refugee columns. The dead were left in the ditches along with burned-out trucks, cars without fuel, and the litter of abandoned matériel.

On June 17 at thirty minutes past noon, the quavering broken voice of a Marshal of France, the eighty-four-year-old Philippe Pétain, announced over the radio that France had lost not just a battle, but the war as well:

> *Français!* At the request of the President of the Republic, I assume as of today the direction of the government of France.... I give to France the gift of my person to alleviate her misfortunes.... It is with a sad heart that I say to you today that the fighting must stop.

Clustered about the radios in the local cafés, the bewildered refugees and soldiers—exhausted, hungry, and despairing—greeted the announcement of their defeat with a vast sigh of relief. Those few units that were still fighting threw away their guns and marched off wearily to the German prison camps. Although the armistice would not be signed for another five days, there seemed to be no point in getting oneself killed when the war was lost.

The Battle of France was over—after only six weeks of blitzkrieg—and four years of a tragic and bloody occupation that still divides the French people had begun.

1

"Maréchal, Nous Voilà!"

At first, Jean Moulin could not see in the dark farmhouse. It was late at night and the pocket torches of the two German officers cast only the feeblest light into the far corners of the room where the bodies had been dragged. There were seven of them, seven fetid shapeless masses carefully arranged on the dirt floor; it was impossible to tell either age or sex, but the gaping wounds in chests and stomachs showed clearly in the flickering yellow light.

"This is what your black soldiers have done," the tall blond lieutenant insisted, "a massacre of women and children."

Painfully, the prefect of Chartres stepped closer and examined the gruesome scene. Yes, there were women and children. His head still ached from the beating the two German officers had given him earlier in the *préfecture,* and there was a salty taste of blood in his mouth, but the horror of the death that had so suddenly taken the innocent civilians of Saint-Georges-sur-Eure blotted out the pain. Conscious of the fact that the Germans were watching him closely, he went from body to body, observing, checking for papers, examining the wounds.

"Will you sign?" It was the brown-haired German with the long nose who asked the question.

Moulin straightened up from his compassionate study of his dead fellow countrymen. The question was still there: would he sign the piece of paper, the *protocole,* acknowledging that Senegalese soldiers had raped and murdered, had been guilty of this terrible massacre? When he had refused earlier that day, they had beaten him with their fists, screaming insults and threatening to have him shot on the spot. There was something almost maniacal in their behavior; they seemed to believe that his signature on the *protocole* would be the definitive proof of the guilt of the black colonial soldiers. No doubt their hatred of the Senegalese went back to the French occupation of the Ruhr in the early twenties when they had accused General Mangin of demanding German women for the sexual satisfaction of the African troops.

"Will you now sign?" the lieutenant repeated.

Jean Moulin shook his head. "It is clear that these poor people have been dead for several days. They were probably killed during your bombardment of the fifteenth. I cannot dishonor the French army by attesting to a lie."

The blond officer stepped forward and smashed his fist into the side of Moulin's face. The *préfet* reeled and stumbled under the blow. From his position in the doorway, a soldier moved forward and knocked him to the floor with a sharp blow with his rifle butt. For a while, they amused themselves by kicking him from point to point in the room, alternating with slaps, punches, and blows with their torches.

Finally, tired of their brutal play, they dragged the Frenchman to a nearby hut, kicked open the door, and threw him inside. Stumbling forward, Moulin put up his hands weakly to protect himself from falling in the blackness of the small room. He felt his fingers sink into something soft and wet, something with a strange musky odor that almost made him faint.

The light of the torch showed him the horror on which the Germans had thrown him: it was the trunk of a young woman, decently dressed, stretched out on the kitchen table, her mouth half-open as if she had died calling for the help that did not come. Her legs were amputated at the knees as if by a surgeon's knife. Her arms were bloody stumps.

"Does that look like the result of artillery?"

Moulin rubbed the side of his face where the blood was beginning to cake. "I will not sign," he said weakly. "There is no proof that the Senegalese were responsible."

The two Germans cursed and dragged him back to the car. All the way to Chartres, the slaps and beatings continued, but the prefect, sunken into a stubborn silence, endured the blows; after a while, it seemed to him that he did not feel them as much. To this thoughtful, artistic, and reserved Frenchman, that was a fact to be mulled over.

Not far from the *préfecture,* the Germans had requisitioned a private home and converted it into a temporary prison. Later, they would make good use of the widespread French prison system and its submissive officials, but in June, 1940, they preferred to guard their prisoners themselves.

There was a Senegalese *tirailleur** in the empty room into which Jean Moulin was pushed. "Since we now know your love for the blacks, we thought to please you by allowing you to sleep with one." The two German officers laughed uproariously at this sally and left, bolting the door behind them.

* Literally, "sharpshooter"; here a French North African infantryman.

"In the darkness, the good Senegalese gave me his place on the only mattress and stretched out a little further off. I passed him the covers for the ground was littered with bits of glass from the windows which had been shattered during the bombardment.... I know that today I have gone to the limit of my resistance. I know that tomorrow, if it begins again, I will end up by signing," Moulin later wrote.

The thought that he would so dishonor himself and his country by signing the *protocole* was devastating. Jean Moulin's father, a professor of history, had instilled in his son the love of France and of republican principles which would be the mainstays of both their lives. Professor Moulin had seen his father, a land agent, imprisoned as a republican after the conservative revolution of May 16, 1877. His son was never to forget that such principles as the Rights of Man must periodically be paid for in very harsh coin.

Jean Moulin was born in Béziers, in the sunlit Mediterranean province of Hérault, on June 20, 1899. He was a small, puny, nervous child whose schoolwork suffered from his inability to concentrate and the hazing of his classmates. Nothing very remarkable has been recorded of his early years other than a precocious interest and ability in drawing. Mobilized with his class in April, 1918, he was surprised by the armistice while still in training in Alsace. Saved from the carnage of trench warfare, he inherited neither the rabid nationalism of the majority of the veterans nor the extreme pacifism of the few who had felt the horror of the war in the very essence of their being. Neither a chauvinist nor an antimilitarist, Moulin kept that quiet devotion to republican France that he had learned as a child.

After the war, he took a law degree at the University of Montpellier near his home and began his rapid rise in the French prefectoral administration.* After serving as subprefect in several *départements,* he was *chef de cabinet* (a combination of office manager and private secretary) to Pierre Cot, minister for air in the Daladier, Saurraut, and Blum governments. His friendship with Cot was a close one which survived the strains put on it by the latter's political twists and turns from 1940 to 1943. Moulin did not insist on strict adherence to a political creed, or for that matter to a party, among his friends; he only wanted them to love France as he did.

During that fatal June of 1940, Jean Moulin, now prefect of Chartres, watched the terrified masses of refugees clog the narrow streets around the renowned cathedral, moving frantically in their flight south to what they thought was safety on the Loire. By the four-

* The *préfet* is the civil administrator of one of the ninety-five *départements* into which metropolitan France is divided. Appointed by the president of the Republic and assisted by an elected council (*conseil général*), he is responsible for the execution of the laws, appointment of minor functionaries, collection of taxes, police measures, etc.

teenth, the town was deprived of gas, electricity, and telephone service; the police, the firemen and their fire engines, even those responsible for feeding the civil population had joined the exodus. Soon only 800 citizens out of 23,000 were left. The Germans shelled the town on the morning of the fifteenth, setting one-quarter of it afire; with the fire equipment rolling south to the Loire, there was no one to fight the flames. For a time, there was no water, as a frightened waterworks official closed the mains before fleeing the city.

To Moulin, there was only one concern: to feed and shelter *les Chartrains,* to bury the dead, to keep the city alive, and to meet the German army with the dignity worthy of a Frenchman even in defeat. Defying all regulations, he issued free gasoline so that trucks could bring food from the countryside, confiscated all food supplies and stored them in large piles in the *préfecture,* broke down the doors of the deserted bakeries and recruited passersby to serve as interim bakers (there is no record of the quality of the bread in Chartres for this period); when possible, he fed the refugees who still streamed blindly through the shattered town.

When the Germans arrived, the prefect stood stiffly in the door of the *préfecture* with a priest on one side and the mayor of Chartres on the other. France, anticlerical *and* Catholic, was waiting for the barbarian hordes.

It was the next day, the seventeenth of June, that the two German officers arrived in his office with the *protocole.* Jean Moulin refused to sign. As he later described his dilemma:

> Run away? Impossible. I can hear the regular pacing of the sentinels not only in the corridor, but also in front of our only window.
>
> Still, I cannot be an accomplice to this monstrous scheme which could only have been conceived by raving sadists [*sadiques en délire*]. I cannot authenticate this outrage to the French army and dishonor myself [in so doing].
>
> Anything but that; anything, even death.
>
> Death? . . . Since the beginning of the war, like thousands of Frenchmen, I have accepted it. Since then, I have seen it close up many times. . . . It does not frighten me.
>
> A few days ago, if I had died, there would have been a gap in the ranks of the Resistance.
>
> Now I have fulfilled my mission, or, rather, I will have fulfilled it to the end when I will have prevented our enemies from dishonoring us.
>
> My duty is clearly indicated. The Boches will see that a Frenchman is also capable of doing away with himself [*se saborder*]. . . . Once resolved, it is simple to do what one believes necessary to fulfill one's duty.

In the darkness, with a sliver of glass held firmly, Jean Moulin cut his throat.

At first light, the German guard saw the prisoner sprawled on the mattress, his prefect's uniform soaked in blood. Moulin was rushed to the hospital where the doctors operated frantically and saved his life. Although the Germans tried to keep the whole affair quiet, the news quickly spread through Chartres and the townspeople felt a surge of pride at their prefect's heroic gesture.

When he finally returned to the *préfecture*, Jean Moulin continued to resist the German demands, fighting stubbornly step by step against the requisitions, the curfew, and the German refusal to expedite the return of the townspeople who had fled. All this time, he was bombarded with government orders for the removal of those mayors and minor officials who were either ardent republicans, Freemasons, or known to be anti-German. These orders Moulin refused categorically to put into effect. For this obstinacy he was removed from office by the angry minister of the interior, Marcel Peyrouton; it may have been a coincidence, but the revocation reached Chartres on November 11, 1940 (it had been published in the *Journal officiel* on November 3, 1940). It was the German commander in Chartres who said the words that fitted the occasion: "I congratulate you on the energy with which you were able to protect the interests of those for whom you were responsible and *the honor of your country.*"

With an *Ausweis* (permit) given by the Feldkommandant, Moulin crossed the demarcation line into the unoccupied zone. Determined that resistance was the only honorable course, he requested permission to leave the country; it was immediately refused and a telegram was sent to all frontier posts warning that he was not to be allowed to cross into Spain or Switzerland.

With the help of friends in the administration, he obtained false demobilization papers made out to one Joseph-Jean Mercier (he was careful to keep his own initials) with which he was able to procure a passport. In Marseilles, he revealed his true identity and desire to reach England to the American consul, H. S. Fullerton, who promptly gave him a visa to the United States (which enabled him to cross the Spanish frontier). On October 20, 1941, he arrived in London, a white muffler tightly wrapped around his neck to hide the ugly scar on his throat.

In his briefcase was a report on the feeble beginnings of the Resistance in France; in his mind was a concise plan for the unification of the many small dissident groups; and in his heart was a grim determination to return—at any cost—to the underground struggle.

* * *

In front of the Hôtel du Parc in Vichy, the crowd gathered early, fearing to miss the great event. Intimidated by the two Gardes Mobiles with their black leather jackets, crash helmets, and bayoneted rifles, they stood quietly except for an occasional murmur as they greeted friends and passed on the latest rumors . . . "the Marshal is going to Paris to see Hitler" . . . "the government is moving to Versailles" . . . "I heard a minister's secretary say . . ." Everyone had a horror story of the defeat and the exodus to share; with a shiver, they related the stories of the bombings and strafings of the refugee columns that had clogged the roads; the tanks crushing the human mass trying desperately to flee; the towns that fired on the soldiers trying to defend them.

Inevitably, the conversation turned to the new regime and to speculation on the new ministerial appointments, for swelling the crowd of townspeople and tourists were those who had gathered here to either improve or protect their fortunes. Since the first of July when the new government had moved to Vichy from Bordeaux, the town had been inundated by those who had favors to seek, who courted influence, or who naturally flowed to the seat of power. Here could be found many officials of the defunct Third Republic all too ready to curry favor with the new regime; publishers and journalists anxious that their secret subsidies be continued; businessmen worried over the cancellation of lucrative contracts; job-seekers of all descriptions; and the brightest stars of stage, screen, and radio eager to enhance their reputation and prestige by appearing at the new font of influence. They crowded into Vichy by the thousands, sleeping if necessary on the divans in the hotel lobbies or on the floor of the casino. What was important was to be there when the decisions were made, jobs distributed, and contracts awarded; to whisper in this ministerial ear or that one what forms their gratitude would take for present benefits. They filled the streets and the little parks of Vichy with their incessant goings and comings, schemings and maneuverings. Now they gathered before the hotel to do homage to the supreme symbol of the power they worshiped.

The weather was idyllic this July of 1940: sunny blue skies and a soporific warmth flooded the valley of the Allier, that gentle stream flowing through the new capital of the French State—*L'Etat français*, the official name of Pétain's government, which was more commonly referred to as "Vichy."

There was a sense of optimism that seemed to deny or, at the least, to denigrate the crushing defeat of the French armies and the humiliating armistice that had just been signed. "There were many smiling faces that one would have liked to have seen sadder," was the comment in the eyewitness account of Henri du Moulin de Labarthète, the head of Pétain's office of civil affairs.

Even the town itself—this mountain spa for the cure of sluggish bourgeois livers—was not thought of as "*sérieuse.*" Who could imagine a "National Revolution" to regenerate France taking place among these frivolous baths with their gilded cupolas and minarets? Besides, it was well known that Vichy was a temporary expedient, that the government would be back in Paris (or possibly Versailles) as soon as the armistice terms were clarified and certainly before a peace treaty was signed. Until then Vichy was the compromise choice for the temporary seat of government. Southern towns like Marseilles or Perpignan would have suggested the possibility of flight to North Africa and a continuation of the war. Other suggested sites had been rejected as the fiefdoms of certain politicians of the discredited Third Republic who had played too prominent a role in the parliamentary quagmire that had led to the defeat (such as Edouard Herriot*). It was true that Pierre Laval held sway at Châteldon, only ten miles south of Vichy, but that was different: the Marshal "trusted" Laval and, in fact, owed to him his present position and power, for it was Laval who only two weeks before had persuaded the Republic to commit suicide.

At the stroke of noon, the two guards at the entrance to the hotel snapped to attention, white-gloved hands touching rifles in a military salute. A deep respectful silence fell on the crowd. From the shadows of the lobby, a man walked slowly into the bright sunlight. An old man dressed in a gray suit, a soft hat, and carrying a cane. Erect, proud, distant. A man who only weeks before had made "a gift of his person to serve France." With a slight motion of his hand, the Marshal greeted his admirers.

Henri Philippe Bénoni Omer Pétain, Maréchal de France, was eighty-four years old when he took power in the darkest days of modern French history. Born on April 24, 1856, fifteen years before the proclamation of the Third Republic, he was to outlive it by five years. The defender of Verdun and the commander of the French armies in the last years of World War I, he rose to the heights of military glory in a France that worshiped its successful generals as few other countries do. He ended his days as a state prisoner in a fortress prison on the Ile d'Yeu, degraded and despised for treason. Between the heights and the depths, he was to know adulation such as few men have experienced and was to be swallowed in a wave of invective and contumacy such as even fewer have known. Between the idolatry and the contempt, the man himself was to be lost: it was as if his portrait had been painted by two artists, one who adored and one who hated his subject. "Savior of *la Patrie,* Father of the People" . . . "valet of Hit-

* One of the leaders of the Radical Socialist party and three times the premier, Herriot was for many years mayor of Lyons. In 1940, he was president of the Chamber of Deputies and voted for Pétain.

ler, charlatan, murderer" . . . countless words have been poured out by partisans and opponents alike both during and after the occupation and the war. At times, it is impossible to see the man beneath the obscuring mass of words. It is as if a portrait had been painted in glorious golds and reds, then smeared with the blackest of mud through which the figure can be only dimly seen.

At eighty-four, Pétain had the strength of a man of sixty and the heart of a thirty-year-old. He was happy to demonstrate his youthful vigor for the photographers by lifting a six-year-old child on his cane held horizontally. Much has been written of his inability to stay awake at conferences and even of his "senility," but almost everyone who met him during the years of Vichy testified to his alertness, his lucidity, his grasp of the most complex affairs. It is clear that the rumor that he would sign any paper put before him was the same story told of another elderly war hero, Field Marshal von Hindenburg.

He had a robust appetite for a man of his years, enjoying the pleasures of the table in a manner that astonished his guests; yet he took little wine and no alcohol or cigarettes. He slept at least eight hours a night, and no crisis was permitted to interfere with his rest. This habit was one he shared with his old enemy Joffre, and it seems to be characteristic of French general officers.

Although he was hard of hearing in his left ear and had a tendency to catarrh during the winter, his health was never to be a problem during his years in power. He came from a long-lived peasant family and was destined to outlive his two "dauphins," both of whom were to die by French bullets.

According to du Moulin de Labarthète, the Marshal was above average in intelligence, but his mind was more logical than creative, given to inductive reasoning based on shrewd peasant sense. His education at St.-Cyr had given him the rudiments of a classical education: a great deal of Latin and a smattering of Greek. To this had been added the barest touches of English and German, and the mathematics an army engineer would need. His taste in music was deplored by his closest associates: he adored light operettas, whose tunes he knew by the hundreds. His feeling for art was no better: he would go into raptures over the ugliest colored lithographs in shop windows. Of literature he knew nothing.

Although a nominal Catholic, Pétain's attendance at mass was confined to the most important feast days. Having for so many years posed as a "republican" general, he probably found it difficult to discard the anticlericalism which was such an essential part of that role. Unlike Joffre, who made a great display of eating meat on Friday, Pétain observed all the forms, and his relationship with the Church and the Vatican was excellent during the years of Vichy. Later, the

Church—particularly certain high prelates—was to regret the closeness of its ties to Vichy.

The Marshal's fondness for young women was one outstanding characteristic that was to cause a great deal of talk and much trouble for Madame la Maréchale. Nor was this a weakness of his old age, for it is reported by his aide-de-camp, Major Bernard Serrigny, that when Pétain's appointment as commander of the besieged garrison at Verdun came to his headquarters in February, 1916, a frantic search for the new commander finally located him in a hotel room near the Gare du Nord in Paris. "Outside the door," Major Serrigny later wrote,

> I quickly recognized our great leader's yellow shoes with their reinforced tops which that evening were standing so pleasantly next to a charming dainty pair of completely feminine slippers. The mystery was solved. It was love.... According to what the general told me the next day, the young woman who shared his bed that night burst into tears when she learned of the heavy task that her lover was soon to assume. She was so affectionate and ardent that the memory of that evening remained forever in the general's mind.

In 1920, the young lady became Madame Pétain.

The Marshal's reputation for amorous dalliance caused no loss of respect from the French; his delight in surrounding himself with pretty young women alarmed his wife and his staff, but his frankness on the subject pleased the public. To a friend, he admitted that "What I love best is infantry and making love." Gay, even droll, with a sense of humor that ran to off-color stories, he loved to have amusing guests at his table. His manner was simple and direct; the same language was used for peasant delegations and the heads of state. Simple, serene, sovereign—these were the virtues attributed to him by his closest associates.

Yet this grandfatherly savior with his broad white mustache and piercing blue eyes was not all of one piece; there was another Philippe Pétain with roots deep in the past. There was the crafty peasant from the Pas-de-Calais who had been the oldest man in each grade as he slowly moved up through the army hierarchy; the elderly colonel preparing for retirement in 1914; the advocate of the unpopular theory that "gunfire kills" and of the superiority of the defensive at a time when military doctrine called for the offensive without limit (the horrible "*offensive à outrance*" that almost destroyed the French armies in August, 1914); the adored hero of Verdun who halted the 1917 mutinies by a combination of soothing and firmness; the disappointed general who had seen Foch picked as generalissimo of the Allied Armies in 1918; the minister of war in the Doumergue cabinet of 1934; and the influential senior member of the military advisory council between the wars whose blindness to the importance of tanks and aviation in modern warfare and of the weakness of the Ardennes defenses was a factor in the French defeat.

Behind the avuncular façade was a cold suspicious nature that showed itself in sarcasm, spite, and ingratitude. Neither the oldest of friends nor the closest of collaborators was exempt from his almost paranoid fear that he was being constantly betrayed, that important matters were being deliberately kept from him. When du Moulin de Labarthète joined him as head of his civil cabinet at Vichy, Pétain greeted him coldly: "I trust no one. I don't trust you any more than the others. But I know you. I can attach a name to your face. That's already a lot." For a man accustomed to ruling through a staff, the individual was nothing; only the function counted and then only how well it was performed. At Vichy, the Marshal's ingratitude was proverbial; one by one, he dismissed members of his official family from whim, from expediency, or to placate the Germans. "I sacrifice no one," he told du Moulin, "but no one is indispensable to me."

There was one man who, if not indispensable, had been very close to Pétain, a man whose career he had pushed as he had pushed no other. A junior officer in his regiment whom he had mourned when his "death" at Verdun had been falsely reported.* A man whose unpopular theories of modern warfare Pétain had listened to politely, although skeptically; he had even twisted arms to allow them to be presented as lectures at the Staff College. A man who in 1938 had dedicated his book, *La France et son armée,* to "Monsieur le Maréchal Pétain, who wished this book to be written and who directed with his advice the wording of the first five chapters and thanks to whom the last two are the story of our victory."

That man was Charles de Gaulle.

It was this same book and the manner in which it was published that first split the two men. Pétain protested to the publisher that this history of the French army had been written at his suggestion, along the lines laid out by him and by a member of his staff, who now refused to efface himself in the best tradition of junior staff officers and was proposing to put it out in his own name. After an acrimonious correspondence, the publisher refused to suppress the book and de Gaulle haughtily declined to change the dedication. Later, in London, he would say, "He has never forgiven me for putting my name to *La France et son armée,* although in fact I was its author from the first to the last line. . . ."

* Pétain cited the young company commander as "well known for his intellectual and moral courage . . . led his men in a furious assault and fierce hand-to-hand combat. . . . He fell in the fight. An outstanding officer in every respect."

The love–hate relationship between the two men, who were to symbolize acceptance and rejection of the defeat and the armistice, was to have an important effect on the events of the next four years. Shortly after de Gaulle's famous radio speech from London—"France has lost a battle, but not the war"—he was ordered to return to his post; the message was relayed to him by the French military attaché in London. When he failed to respond, Pétain ordered him court-martialed. On July 4, 1940, de Gaulle was sentenced to four years in prison for "leaving France between May 10 and June 30, 1940, without orders." In light of Free French activities to rally dissident elements, this verdict was considered inadequate, and, after failing to have it overturned by the Court of Appeals, the Vichy minister of war, General Colson, on July 12 ordered him tried for treason and desertion in time of war. This time (August 2) the verdict was satisfactory: death *in absentia* and confiscation of all property. Pétain later wrote: "This verdict was required by the need for discipline, to set an example, in order to stop the exodus of French officers out of the country, but it is clear that this verdict *in absentia* can only be in principle. It has never been my thought that it would be imposed." Unfortunately, the date of this memo is August 11, 1944, when it was obvious that de Gaulle had won; as an indication of Pétain's true feeling toward his ex-protégé it is highly suspect.*

The leader of the Free French movement in London shrugged off the condemnation, but showed in private conversation how deeply he had been hurt by the malice of his old commander. "Old age is a shipwreck," he once said to a few intimates,

> and with it weaknesses are monstrously magnified . . . he is eighty-four. . . . If only he had gone in time. But at his age, you don't go, you hang on. He's in the grip of senile ambition and ambition is the last passion of the old. . . . In the country's most disastrous days, he displays merely his limitless pride. . . . I have taken up a position against him and it was very hard for me, very hard; but it was a national necessity.

For de Gaulle, there was no hesitation between the France that he revered and the old Marshal, whom he had once loved. For him, Pétain was dead and buried among his soldiers at Verdun, honored for his courage and leadership during that great crisis of another war. The man who now stood at Vichy and wrapped the disgrace of the armistice in the glorious cloak of a Marshal of France was a senile imposter, the simulacrum of the victor of 1916, an aged ambition-ridden fraud. It was against this sham that he, de Gaulle, was fighting; he was convinced that the honor of France demanded it.

* Despite legend, Pétain was not the godfather of de Gaulle's son, Philippe.

To the men of Vichy in that tragic autumn of 1940, the ex–brigadier general Charles de Gaulle and his handful of followers were of little importance. Indeed, de Gaulle's call to resistance was heard by very few and heeded by even fewer—in spite of the claims made in 1944 when it seemed that almost all of France must have been listening to the BBC on that day. With the penchant for historical analogy that characterizes French political life, the Free French were compared to those royalists who had fled after 1790 to gather in Coblentz and plot against the Republic. The analogy was far from perfect, since the antirepublican conspirators were now in Vichy and at the head of the government. It was only the verdict of the court-martial that condemned de Gaulle and the rantings of the press against the "*émigrés à la solde*" (venal emigrants) that brought him to the attention of the public. As Laval shrewdly pointed out, condemning de Gaulle to death was the greatest service that could be done him.

Besides, the political situation did not permit the luxury of concentrating on one fugitive senior officer. There was a whole parliament to be condemned, a Republic to be denounced and dispelled. What was a de Gaulle compared to such prizes ripe for the fires as ex–Premier Paul Reynaud, ex–Minister of the Interior Georges Mandel, Léon Blum, who had headed the Popular Front government in 1936, and the defeated General Gamelin? France defeated would demand scapegoats for the shame that had been thrust upon her, and the men of Vichy were gleefully preparing to supply the victims for the purge. In any case, it would please the Germans.

Meanwhile, there was a government to be formed in place of the "old whore" who had been kicked out; that meant ministerial chairs to be fought for, as well as the thousands of minor posts, prefectures, undersecretaryships, commissioners of this and of that. The town of Vichy was flooded with place-seekers, grabbing lapels and whispering promises into influential ears; ex-functionaries of the Third Republic vowing eternal loyalty to the new regime; men of the Fascist Right come out of hiding to rejoice in the new dawn; the hangers-on who naturally crawl to the seats of power waiting for the crumbs to fall from an overloaded table. Du Moulin commented bitterly on those who begged him for jobs in the autumn of 1940—and who did not pardon his failure to provide them until late in 1943 when the tide turned.

The problems that faced the new government were staggering: three-fifths of the country was occupied by the Germans and Italians; millions of refugees were unable to return because of the collapse of transportation; almost two million soldiers—the heart of the work force and family life—were on their way to prison camps in Germany; in August, the Alsace-Lorraine of 1914 was annexed to the Reich in violation of armistice terms (French protests were ignored); the staggering sum of four hundred million francs (ten million dollars) per day was set to pay for the costs of the occupation.

Supinely, Vichy yielded to the ever-increasing German demands. The Marshal's government conceived its role to be one of satisfying the victor until after England's defeat, when a reasonable peace treaty could be expected as payment for her complaisant posture. Limiting herself to mild protests "for the record" against the most blatant violations of armistice stipulations, Vichy set out to destroy the last vestiges of the hated Republic and to impose the new morality and dogma of *L'Etat français.*

"They have given me power, in fact, all power," Pétain noted happily, "more than Louis XIV ever had." In quick succession, between July 10 and 14, he issued four acts over his signature alone: The first, naming himself chief of the French State, started with the royal "We, Philippe Pétain . . ." The second gave him all legislative and executive power, as well as the right to propose the new Constitution of the French State. The third act prorogued the two chambers of the Republic indefinitely, while the fourth named Laval (who was now vice-premier) as his successor in case of death or disability.

Was Vichy a legal government or a usurpation of power in the midst of a great defeat? Even today, that question is fought over in articles, books, and newspapers by partisans of both sides as well as constitutional lawyers. The crucial question is whether the National Assembly, in giving power to Pétain, intended to abolish the Republic. The vote of July 10, 1940, clearly mandated "all powers to the government *of the Republic* under the authority and signature of Marshal Pétain in order to promulgate, by one or several acts, a new constitution of the French State [italics added]."

All of this was within the bounds of the Constitution of 1875 and the framework of republican law; the possibility that the Constitution might be amended *by vote of Parliament* had been foreseen. But this new Constitution was never prepared and certainly never submitted for approval to either a legal assembly of national representatives or to the people themselves. Instead, by fiat, Pétain consolidated all legislative and executive power in his own hands, substituted "*L'Etat français*" for "the Republic," and named his successor.

"We, Philippe Pétain, chief of the French State . . ." More power than Louis XIV, the old man had gloated. He could have added more adulation, more praise, more adoration than Napoleon returning triumphant from Italy.

To the French in that disastrous summer of 1940, the Marshal was more than the new head of the government; he was the living link with past military glory. Overwhelmed by the rapidity of the defeat, stunned by the crushing of their army, they clung in shame to the khaki uniform with its seven stars which reminded them of the victories that had been theirs not too long ago: of the Marne, Verdun, Alma, Austerlitz, and Valmy. Into their adoration of the Marshal, they poured not only their love of France, but a plea to the god of war for an ultimate revenge. For the present, Pétain was the father who would protect them from the worst; this was the soldier who could talk to the Germans as one soldier to another and would prevent the "Polandization" of France. True, three-fifths of the country was occupied, two *départements* in the northwest were attached to the German army administration in Belgium, and Alsace-Lorraine was annexed to the Reich, but in the unoccupied zone—the Germans forbade calling it the "free" zone—Pétain stood, solidly erect, his blue eyes confident, gathering about him all Frenchmen to remake a new France. The France of Vichy's "National Revolution" would forever dispel the chaos of parliamentary squabbles and maneuvering, that game of ministerial musical chairs, the plotting and "*combinaisons*" (intrigues) of the politicians of the Third Republic which had been responsible for the shameful defeat and the present tragic state of the French people. It was not only the men of the Right who greeted Pétain and the overthrowing of the Republic—if a plebiscite had been held in August, 1940, all observers agree that Pétain would have been approved by ninety-nine percent of the vote. Even the most ardent supporters of the Republic not only voted all power to the hero of Verdun, but called on the people to gather around the "sacred person" of the Marshal and help him in his task of renewing the nation. Men like Léon Blum, Herriot, and Reynaud cast themselves at the feet of the saintly Maréchal in a massive *mea culpa;* it was only later, much later, that they began to have doubts.

The cult of the Marshal grew swiftly. Everywhere his picture was to be seen; lithographs of the grandfatherly face appeared in store windows, behind official desks, on plates, flags, vases. A new song was written, dedicated to the love that the people bore for him: "*Maréchal, nous voilà!* . . . Marshal, here we are, we your children, standing before you. . . ." Delegation after delegation came to Vichy to worship at the shrine of St. Philippe: war veterans, his soldiers of the past; schoolchildren with their small bouquets of flowers; peasants with work-gnarled hands, who were flattered by his simplicity and directness; politicians, generals, matrons, all arrived to stand in the Presence and to hear the words: "We will work together for France."

The gifts poured in until du Moulin de Labarthète protested; the Marshal agreed mildly: "What will we do with another silver tea service?" Still, he refused nothing, not even the ribbon-bedecked sheep that seemed to be the standard gift of agricultural delegations to the shepherd. With peasant thriftiness, he sent them to a farm he had rented near Vichy.

Meanwhile, the government struggled desperately to establish its authority in what was left of "free" France. The "National Revolution" demanded sacrifices; the people demanded the punishment of those responsible for the humiliation of the defeat; and the Right screamed for the heads of its enemies. Above all, there was Hitler with his implacable demands. All of these had to be satisfied.

Pétain's first cabinet contained a number of leftovers from his predecessor's, such as Paul Baudouin and Yves Bouthillier, who held the portfolios of foreign affairs and finance respectively, but this only served to give a sense of continuity to the new regime and to camouflage its real aims. The other appointments were more indicative of the policies that Pétain intended to follow: the English-hating Admiral François Darlan headed the navy; Raphaël Alibert, a pronounced reactionary and an old friend of the Marshal's, was minister of justice; Maxime Weygand, the defeated commander-in-chief who was whispered to be a royal bastard,* remained in charge of national defense; and, most significant of all, the vice-premier was Pierre Laval.

On July 1, 1940, as the Pétain government was in the process of moving to Vichy, Laval's car broke down just outside the town, an ominous sign to the superstitious vice-premier. He walked across the bridge into Vichy, a stocky figure of average height, a round fleshy yellow-complexioned face with heavy jowls, thick lips, drooping eyelids. His hair was sprinkled with gray and his broad mustache stained with nicotine. One could instantly recognize the features which allowed cartoonists to depict him as a toad with his hair brushed *à la Adolf*. He invariably wore a dark suit and a white necktie, which was his talisman; as a poor young lawyer, he had worn it because it was washable. He carried a cane on one arm and a large briefcase under the other; the inevitable half-consumed Gauloise cigarette dangled from the corner of his mouth.

This was Pierre Laval, who—next to Pétain—was the most controversial figure of the Vichy regime. The Marshal could appeal to past military glory, to Verdun and the victory of 1918, or to the adoration of the French people who had turned to him in this great crisis. Laval could appeal only to their hatred, for he was despised and distrusted from the beginning to the end.

The history of Pierre Laval is the history of the Third Republic

* According to Weygand's birth certificate, he was born on January 21, 1867, in Brussels and his parents were unknown. His expenses were paid by the Belgian royal court until his entry to St.-Cyr. He was rumored to be the son of the Empress Carlotta (daughter of King Leopold I of Belgium), whose husband, the Archduke Maximilian von Hapsburg, was shot in Mexico by the Juaristas on June 19, 1867. Hitler once referred to Weygand as "that Hapsburg bastard."

between the two wars. Born in Châteldon on the twenty-eighth of June, 1883, he first came to public notice shortly before World War I as a flashy lawyer and Socialist deputy (representing the working-class district of Aubervilliers). In August, 1914, his name appeared on the notorious Carnet B, a list of potential subversives who might be harmful to the mobilization effort and who were to be arrested at the outbreak of war. Presumably his name was put on the list because he was the lawyer for the largest labor union in France, and because of his well-known pacifism. In any case, despite the urgings of Clemenceau and Poincaré, the men on Carnet B were not arrested; as the Paris *préfet de police* later said, the suspects "marched off to war to the tune of the regimental bands."

After the war, Laval played the game of parliamentary "musical chairs" with consummate skill, gradually withdrawing from the Socialist party when such an allegiance was harmful to his ambitions. His first cabinet was formed on January 27, 1931, with Laval as premier and minister of the interior, the formidable Aristide Briand as foreign minister, André Maginot (who gave his name to the ill-fated defense line) as minister of war, and, as minister of colonies, a short round-faced man with slanted eyes named Paul Reynaud.

After less than fifteen months, Laval yielded power to the man who had succeeded Maginot as war minister, André Tardieu, and returned to the opposition. After the bloody riots of February 6, 1934, he led a delegation to the president of the Republic, Albert Lebrun, demanding the formation of a government of national reconciliation and peace; it was in the subsequent Doumergue cabinet that he first met the prestigious war minister Marshal Philippe Pétain—a meeting that was to cast a long shadow on later years.

Laval's second cabinet ran from June 7, 1934, to January 22, 1936, without solving the ever-critical problems of the franc and of French security against Germany. The worsening world financial situation ruined any hope of stabilizing the first problem, and his attempts to solve the second through an understanding with Mussolini were defeated by French distrust of both Italian and German Fascism. The Popular Front government of Léon Blum that followed was an unstable conglomeration of Left and Left–Center parties united in an anti-Fascist program that supported the Spanish Republicans in the civil war, in defiance of Italian and German support for Franco.

Angered by his ejection from the seat of power, though still a deputy, Laval moved closer and closer to the French Right; his proposed Italian alliance a shambles, he now placed his hope in avoiding war on coming to an understanding with Hitler. As early as July, 1935, while still premier, he had sent Fernand de Brinon, a germanophile journalist who was to play a prominent role during the occupation, to Berlin to request an interview with Hitler. Nothing came of this mission, but, with the supreme self-confidence which was his outstanding quality, Laval continued his efforts to bind France to an agreement with the Reich.

On October 4, 1938, he abstained when the Chamber of Deputies gave an overwhelming vote of confidence to Daladier on the Munich agreement (by which the French premier and the British prime minister, Chamberlain, had desperately sought to buy peace from Hitler by surrendering to him the Czech Sudetenland). Since he had not made the agreement, he could not approve it, and yet he could not bring himself to vote against it. When war came, he reverted to the pacifism of his youth. "It's begun," he told a friend on the day that Germany invaded Poland. "There will be millions of dead bodies."

Still believing that the war might have been avoided if his diplomacy had been followed and taking credit for the fact that Italy did not immediately honor her alliance with Germany, Laval's attitude during the period of the *Drôle de Guerre*—the "Phony War"—was ambiguous. While outwardly insisting that the war must be pushed to a successful conclusion, he continued his search for a negotiated peace, even at the expense of English interests. His anglophobia was notorious; England, he felt, had sabotaged his efforts to win over Mussolini and therefore was responsible for his wandering in the wilderness.

When the German attack crushed the French armies in May and June, 1940, Laval came into his own. In the midst of chaos and with the government crumbling under the defeat, with the country stunned and bewildered by the rapidity of the catastrophe, he was the one man with both a plan and the audacity and knowledge to make it work. Twenty years of parliamentary maneuvering had given him the insights into the levers by which the National Assembly could be persuaded to commit suicide, for nothing less than the abolition of the Republic would satisfy him. Its willingness to do so did not surprise him; his contempt for the deputies was surpassed only by his scorn for the republican form of government that permitted such nonentities to kick out a man of his worth. "This Chamber has spewed me out," he said with relish. "Now I am going to spew it out."

In spite of last-minute attempts to preserve the republican form of government, while granting full powers to Pétain to rule by decree and to propose a new Constitution—attempts that Laval pushed aside contemptuously—the terrified deputies voted for Laval's proposal giving all powers to Pétain by a vote of 569 to 80. They thereby gave the death blow to the longest-lasting regime in France since the Revolution. Delighted, Laval thanked them "in the name of Marshal Pétain . . . [and] on the behalf of France." He would have done better had he listened to and pondered over the anguished cry that escaped from one of the senators after the vote had been announced: "All the same, long live the Republic!"

Republican sentiment was to die hard in France in spite of the overwhelming vote of unworthy men. Born of another German defeat in 1871, it was nourished in the blood of the Communards, was given a constitution in 1875—and had survived the Dreyfus Affair and the brutal bloodletting of World War I and the governmental instability and scandal of the twenties and thirties. Even while it seemed about to perish forever, a senator stood against the frightened mob and shouted his allegiance. In London, there was another, a soldier, who in his youth may have been a follower of the reactionary Charles Maurras, an aristocrat by nature if not by birth, disdainful of the parliamentary quagmire, who nevertheless denied that the Republic could die.

Two men—Marcel Astier, senator for the Ardèche, and Charles de Gaulle, temporary brigadier general and late undersecretary of state for war—were the first *résistants.*

The vote was legal and constitutional. Even the absence of the Communist deputies cannot be blamed on Laval and Pétain; they had been arrested and imprisoned by Daladier at the outbreak of the war in retaliation for the Stalin–Hitler pact. Why then were the elected representatives of the Republic so willing to jettison their traditions, their beloved republican forms to which they had paid such tribute for so many years?

Fear, Léon Blum said at Pétain's trial, fear of the Rightist gangs in the streets of Vichy, fear of General Weygand's soldiers at nearby Clermont-Ferrand, fear of the German troops close by at Moulins. Perhaps it was also the fear of losing their jobs, their privileges, their stipends; fear of the wrath of the people who would hold them responsible for the disaster that had befallen France. As Blum so eloquently put it, "During those two days, I saw men change and become corrupt . . . as though they had been plunged into a poisonous bath . . . you could see before your eyes all the courage and loyalty which you knew to exist in some men melt away, crumble and disappear."

So it was behind the glory, the prestige, and the honor of the eighty-four-year-old Marshal of France that the frightened deputies cowered on July 10, 1940, begging him once more to repeat the miracle of Verdun, save France—and them.

The will to resist had vanished, leaving only the fervent desire to surrender; Clemenceau and Foch gone, Bazaine* reappeared.

* Marshal Achille Bazaine headed one of the French armies in the Franco-Prussian War. He allowed himself to be herded into Metz and later surrendered without a fight. Convicted by a court-martial of negotiating with the enemy and surrendering before necessary, he was sentenced to death, but reprieved. He later escaped from imprisonment and died in exile. However, as Colonel Groussard pointed out, Bazaine did not have a Verdun to his credit.

The appointment of Laval as vice-premier—which occurred only after he had indignantly refused the lesser post of minister of justice—was not popular with either the men about Pétain or the country. Somehow the Marshal's glory and his promises of a "National Revolution" for the reconstruction of France were tarnished by his association with the man a writer called "the Arab of the Third Republic." Weygand was even more caustic about the appointment: "I never expected that the marriage of a Marshal of France with the Republic would produce Pierre Laval as its offspring." But, then, Weygand was possibly oversensitive about irregular progeny, and Pétain was far from being wedded to the Republic.

From the beginning, Laval's goal was to integrate France into Hitler's New Order, to reassure the Germans of the French desire not only to cooperate but to accept the defeat and thus to ensure a peace treaty most favorable to France, preferably at the expense of England. To accomplish this, he had a few trump cards left, the navy and the French colonies among them. The armistice terms would have been much harsher if Hitler had not feared that the French navy would sail for British ports and that the colonies would split with metropolitan France and continue to resist. With England still to be invaded, he could not afford this, so the French warships were to be disarmed in French ports under the supervision of an armistice commission. The ultimate fate of the French empire was deliberately left vague for the future peace treaty.

Although Paul Baudouin was the nominal head of foreign affairs, it was Laval who took the initiative in seeking high-level contacts with the Nazi leaders (something he had first done in 1935 with the abortive de Brinon mission to Berlin). From his office on the second floor of the Hôtel du Parc, he was in an excellent position to observe and control the traffic between Baudouin's office on the first floor and the Marshal's spartan quarters on the third. Diplomacy was not only Laval's forte, it was his obsession.

His first concern was to prove to the Nazis that France could be a trustworthy and loyal ally. When the Germans expressed interest in the French-controlled Bor copper mines in Yugoslavia, Laval put pressure on the owners to sell the mines at a very advantageous price. The Belgian gold reserves, having been put in French banks at the outbreak of the war for safekeeping and later sent to North Africa, were ordered by Laval to be returned to France, where the Germans promptly confiscated them.

But these gestures of goodwill did not lessen German suspicions of French intentions; there was always the lurking feeling that unless constant pressure was kept on Vichy, the idea of *revanche*—revenge—would soon appear. The instruments of maintaining this squeeze were at hand: the French prisoners in German prison camps; the frightful occupation costs which could be raised unilaterally (as was later done); the demarcation line between occupied and unoccupied France, an ugly scar that ran across the center of France from the Swiss frontier to Tours and then south to Spain (see map, page 43) which could be opened or closed to essential traffic; the hostages taken in the occupied areas to guarantee the good conduct of the inhabitants—the available levers were numerous.

All France, Laval knew, was to be considered a hostage to ensure "collaboration"—a word that was variously defined during the fifty months of the occupation, its meaning shifting with the changing German demands, the requirements of Vichy policy, the fluctuating military situation, the ideological positions of the occupied, who either favored the Nazi cause or fought against it (even in defiance of their erstwhile Vichy governors). In the beginning, it was flaunted as a proud banner by a few, accepted as a necessity by many; later, it was stigmatized as treason, and the "proud banner" all too frequently became a shroud.

The first step toward collaboration was taken less than three months after the armistice at an obscure rural railroad station named Montoire.

The main railroad line from Paris to Hendaye on the Spanish frontier runs through the little town of Montoire-sur-Loir, about 125 miles southwest of the capital. Only slightly damaged in the fighting in the Touraine in June, 1940, it was lost in obscurity, one of a thousand such secondary stops, its people content to have escaped from the worst of the holocaust that had crushed the French armies. But in October, 1940, the town was the center of a world-shaking event that sent diplomats all over the globe rushing to their atlases.

On October 22, Pierre Laval was summoned to the German embassy, rue de Lille, in Paris; he was told to bring an overnight case and not to discuss his destination with any of his associates. Assuming that he was finally to have the meeting with von Ribbentrop* he had been requesting, Laval arrived at the former mansion of the Beauharnais family as ordered and was quickly led, bag in hand, to a waiting limousine by Otto Abetz. Abetz at that time was the representative of the German Foreign Office to the Militärbefehlshaber in Frankreich (the German Military Commander in France), but his close ties to Hitler and Ribbentrop, his prewar activities on the Franco-German committee with de Brinon, and his well-known francophilia (his wife was French) made him the unacknowledged German representative to Vichy.

There was little conversation during the trip, and Laval was still

* See Dramatis Personae.

in ignorance of their destination until they had passed through Châteaurenault. Suddenly, Abetz turned to him and said, "I could not tell you earlier, because I was not authorized, but it is not only Monsieur von Ribbentrop that you are going to see, but also Chancellor Hitler." "*Ah! Merde!*" was Laval's startled reply. His face was "pale with pride and with pleasure" at this unexpected honor.

The Montoire station had been cleaned in preparation for this momentous meeting: the sidewalks had been scrubbed, fresh sand scattered about the entrance way, the white walls and green shutters of the station washed, and the platforms painted. A black carpet had been laid from the entrance through the station to the first platform; from there, a red carpet borrowed from the church led to the second platform, where a heavily armored train, bristling with antiaircraft guns and with all shades drawn, arrived at 7 P.M. This was Hitler's special train, which had the code name *Erika*—his headquarters on wheels. In addition to his office, conference room, and private apartments, there were living quarters for his numerous staff.

Hat in hand, Laval climbed into the restaurant car, bumping into Hitler in the semidarkness. With a laugh at the contretemps, they shook hands and went into the salon where conferences were usually held. Their meeting lasted an hour and a quarter, each man speaking in turn and in the most complete generality. Laval opened the discussion with a résumé of his past attempts to secure good Franco-German relationships, calling on Dr. Paul Schmidt, Hitler's interpreter, to testify to his meeting in the late 1920s with Chancellor Bruening. Hitler interrupted to remark dryly, "I know all about that, otherwise you would not be here." Actually, he did not like to be reminded of events that had occurred prior to his coming to power in 1933.

The talks covered a number of points: French help in the battle against England, the future peace treaty, the fate of the French colonies (Hitler was deliberately vague on this point but promised compensation to France for any losses at England's expense). "We felt the same way," Laval wrote in a report, "and we ended by talking a new language: European."

Hitler—who was en route to see Franco—requested a meeting with Pétain on the twenty-fourth, a request to which Laval eagerly agreed.

On his return to Vichy, Laval enthusiastically told the Marshal the results of his interview and informed him that Hitler had requested a meeting at Montoire for the next day. The Marshal's reaction to this unexpected summons has been variously described as halfhearted, reluctant, indifferent, favorable, and even proud; in any case, he not only agreed to the meeting, but granted Laval's wish that Baudouin, the foreign minister, should not be present. Whatever his reasons for taking only the head of his civil cabinet and his doctor with him—

"above all, no generals"—it is unlikely that it was through confidence in his vice-premier, Laval.

Late that night, du Moulin de Labarthète went to the Marshal's bedroom to warn him against the ill-prepared unexpected meeting with the Führer and begged him to postpone it. Pétain shook his head, saying, "Laval told me it would offend Hitler and that we would pay dearly for it.... We are not free.... Besides, there are precedents. Has no one ever spoken to you of Tilsit?"*

They left Vichy the next morning shortly after seven; it was raining and quite cold and du Moulin de Labarthète, alone in the third car with faulty windows that could not be completely closed, shivered from the cold and from the fear of the elderly Marshal's making some horrible blunder in front of the Germans.

At the demarcation line near Moulins, a company of German troops were drawn up to be reviewed. One can only guess at Pétain's thoughts as he walked slowly down the line of stern young faces half-hidden beneath the steel helmets—the victor of Verdun inspecting the sons of the enemy soldiers he had beaten. As they crossed into the occupied zone the German commandant, General Schmidt ("They are all named Schmidt," Pétain observed gloomily), joined them for the trip to Montoire. At Tours they were entertained by the *préfet,* who took the occasion to point out to the Marshal that the decoration promised him for his outstanding devotion to duty during the defeat had not yet arrived. Abetz and de Brinon arrived from Paris; after coffee, Pétain took his customary siesta.

At 4:40 P.M., just as the rains stopped, the cars set out again for Montoire. Passing through Châteaurenault and Vendôme, they turned onto a smaller road lined with German troops presenting arms. Finally, they reached Montoire and drove through the deserted streets (the townspeople were confined to their homes) to the railroad station. Before the entrance, an honor guard of Hitler's bodyguards stood at attention and, to one side, a military band played the French and German national anthems as Pétain and Laval stepped from the car. A giant of a man, the German protocol chief, Graf von Doernberg, came forward and escorted the French party through the station, across the first track to the second where Hitler, Ribbentrop, and Keitel were waiting in front of their train.

As the Marshal walked up to him, Hitler took two steps forward and held out his hand. "I am happy," he said, "to shake the hand of a Frenchman who is not responsible for this war." Pétain, casually shaking the proffered hand, apparently thought that he was being

* This was a reference to the meeting of a victorious Napoleon and a defeated Czar Alexander I on a raft on the Niemen River, July, 1807, to conclude a peace treaty.

asked about his trip, since his response was, "Very good, thank you." The flashbulbs exploded in the semidarkness and the handshake that was to have such terrible repercussions was recorded for history.

"In the dim light of the lanterns illuminating the platform of the little station, it was difficult at first glance to distinguish the victor from the vanquished," said Doctor Schmidt, the interpreter present at the meeting, many years later. "The two men shook hands silently without a smile. . . ." He denied that the Marshal had misunderstood Hitler's words of greeting, insisting that he himself had translated them. "The Marshal's tone was purposely slightly haughty. . . . I had the impression that he did not like us. It was not the tone of a vanquished man, but of a Marshal talking to a corporal."

In spite of his show of courtesy, Hitler was in a bitter, suspicious mood. The previous day, he had met with Franco at Hendaye in an effort to convince the Caudillo to allow German troops passage through Spain for a joint attack on Gibraltar. The immediate reward was to be German food and arms; the ultimate reward, satisfaction of Spanish claims to French Morocco. The wily Franco, aware of the weaknesses with which his country had emerged from its civil war and convinced that Hitler had failed in his attack on England, refused to be drawn into the struggle. He was well prepared to answer the German demands, since he had received a warning of Hitler's plans from Pétain himself. Pétain had received the information from the Japanese ambassador to Vichy, Renzo Sawada, who had picked it up in Berlin during the signing of the Axis military alliance.

Angry at this ingratitude from an ally, Hitler was now prepared to consider "collaboration" with France, especially if the French could be induced to join him in an attack on England. The successful defense of Dakar against the joint British–Free French attack of September 24–25, as well as the published statements of both Pétain and Laval, convinced a reluctant Hitler that the French might be a reliable ally; the result was Montoire.

Seated about the conference table, which was covered by a green cloth, the four men (assisted by Schmidt the interpreter) quickly turned to the business at hand. Hitler opened with a few polite phrases. "I would have preferred, Monsieur le Maréchal, to have made your acquaintance at another moment . . . a less grievous time in the relations between our two countries." Pétain thanked him and assured him that, in spite of the sadness that he felt in passing through the occupied zone, he was happy to meet him and to see the understanding that Hitler was showing with respect to the difficult situation in which he (Pétain) found himself. He pointed out that his task was all the more tragic since he had opposed the war and now had to pay for the mistakes of his predecessors. He alluded to the suggestions of conciliation that had come from the Hitler–Laval talks: on this question, it might be possible to make up for the time lost before the war. However, he insisted, insofar as it was in his power, he would do everything possible to guarantee the integrity of the French empire.

Irked by this high tone from the leader of a defeated people, Hitler proceeded to point out

> a historic fact: war was imposed on Germany in spite of my efforts to avoid a new bloody conflict and without Germany having made the slightest claims on France. France rejected all my peace offers and France declared war on me. France was beaten. I do not doubt that if Germany had been beaten, France would have made her suffer much more than she did in 1918. It is therefore providential that destiny placed me at the head of my country and of the German army in this war and that I could save the German people from this catastrophe. . . . No nation can declare war lightly without in the end assuming the consequences of that act. So France must pay the costs of the war.

Hitler paused to allow Schmidt to translate. The Marshal, "sitting very erect despite his great age, dignified rather than submissive," stared straight ahead, seemingly indifferent to the translation.

England is beaten, the Führer continued, and only the bad weather has prevented the Luftwaffe from finishing the job. Sooner or later, she will sue for peace. She is putting her hope in an intervention by either the United States or the Soviet Union, but Germany has a treaty with the Soviets and the Americans will not be armed before 1942; by that time England will be either occupied or in ruins. As for an American landing in Europe, it is a complete illusion. By March, 1941, the German army will have 230 divisions plus twenty armored and twelve motorized divisions. With its allies, Germany will be a military power that no nation can conquer.

Either England or France must pay the costs of the war. Since England is the most guilty, it would be only fair that she should pay all; but if France hesitates to join the struggle there may be a compromise peace between England and Germany that would leave the whole burden of the war costs on France. This, according to Hitler, was the crux of the matter: would France join the attack on England by protecting her African empire and regaining the parts of Central Africa which had already gone over to de Gaulle?

To this, the Marshal answered evasively, pointing out that although he agreed in principle to common action with the Axis powers he could not bind himself without consulting the government. In any case, he hoped that the peace treaty would not be an oppressive one "which would not allow the harmonious organization of relations between their two peoples."

Hitler persisted in attempting to persuade Pétain to commit himself against England: "What will France do if England attacks her again?"

Without hesitation, the Marshal replied that his country had suffered too much both morally and materially to throw itself into another conflict.

"If France does not wish to defend herself and still harbors sympathy for the English," Hitler threatened, "she will lose her Empire at the end of the war and will have peace terms imposed on her as hard as those which will be imposed on England."

Staring straight at the Führer, Pétain replied coldly, "In all of history, a peace of vengeance has never lasted."

At this tense moment, Laval hastily interrupted, fearful that Hitler would blow up and walk out. Soothingly, he stressed the importance of the German offer of collaboration and how it was in line with their first conversations. "Thanks to the Führer's offer, France is no longer before a wall without an exit. She wants to show her good will by cooperating with Germany in every way but militarily. It would in fact be difficult to declare war on England; public opinion would have to be prepared for the idea and, according to the constitutional acts, the consent of the National Assembly would be necessary."

As Laval went on about the devotion of the French people to peace, how they had gone to war against their will, had not really fought—"as shown by the great number of prisoners"—how he personally had worked for an accommodation between their two countries, and how important an "honorable peace" would be to end the rivalry of centuries, Hitler slumped sullenly into his chair. After his failure to secure Franco's help in an attack on Gibraltar, it was certainly not in his interest to antagonize Pétain and to prevent any possibility of French aid in the battle against England. In a calmer tone, he reiterated the advantages to France of fighting at his side. "Blood spilled in the common struggle," he said, "would bind us together much more than treaties."

But the Marshal stubbornly refused to commit himself to war against France's ex-ally. "It would be useful," he persisted, "if the French government might know how Germany visualizes the final peace treaty so that France might clearly know its fate."

Now it was the Führer's turn to be evasive. It would not do to mention German and Italian plans for parts of the French African empire, annexation of Alsace-Lorraine, or the war costs. "The final peace treaty cannot be envisaged until after the defeat of England."

Clearly, it was a stalemate: to Hitler's insistence on discussing French aid in the battle against England, the Marshal persistently offered to discuss the ultimate peace terms, the return of the prisoners, the demarcation line, and the "crushing" occupation costs.

In the restaurant-car, where von Doernberg had politely ordered him, du Moulin de Labarthète sat moodily at a table loaded with rolls, butter, tea, mineral water, roast beef, and sausage, listening to Dr. Ménétrel and Hitler's physician, Morell, discuss the health of their patrons; the two doctors had made the interesting professional discovery that both Pétain and Hitler suffered from low blood pressure. At a nearby table, de Brinon, "looking like an undertaker's assistant," chatted with a German officer. In the corridors, aides ran back and forth on unexplained errands.

Suddenly, a bell rang loudly. The interview was over.

It was dark on the platform as the final courtesies were said. Escorted by Hitler, Ribbentrop, and Keitel, the Marshal made his way slowly through the station to his car; the national anthems were played again, the Leibstandarte Adolf Hitlers presented arms. Once again, unsmilingly, the Marshal and the corporal shook hands. Turning to Keitel, Pétain thanked him for the manner in which he had conducted the armistice negotiations, then, without offering to shake his hand, entered his car accompanied by Ménétrel, de Brinon, and General Schmidt. Laval, who was dying for a cigarette (smoking was forbidden in the presence of Hitler and Pétain), ducked into the second car with Abetz.

Du Moulin de Labarthète found himself in the third car with a German officer who proceeded to inform him of the reasons why Montoire had been chosen for the fateful interview. "You see, the railroad station is very close to a tunnel and the train could retire into it in case of an alert."

"An alert?"

"Yes, English planes."

"That's true," du Moulin de Labarthète said sarcastically. "We had forgotten about *them.* . . ."

As a gift from Hitler in honor of the interview, General Schmidt granted two requests by the Marshal: the release of his friend, General Augustin Laure, from a German prisoner-of-war camp and the chance to visit such a camp at Amboise. Unfortunately, the Amboise camp was filled with Annamite (Vietnamese) laborers who had never even fought and who did not speak French.

So ended the inconclusive interview at Montoire which was to be proclaimed by the French newspapers (particularly the collaborationist press in Paris) as the beginning of a new era in French–German relations and a golden moment in the founding of a New Order in Europe.

In London and Washington, it was denounced as a new step in the enslavement of France; *The New York Times* on October 25 claimed that Pétain had ceded Alsace-Lorraine to the Germans and the French Riviera to the Italians. King George VI sent a personal letter to Pétain warning him against "giving direct aid to our enemy"; the Marshal's answer pointed out that the brutal English attack on the French navy at Mers-el-Kebir,* their unsuccessful assault on Dakar, and the seizure of French colonies in Central Africa were not the friendly acts of a former ally. Although the French government would not reply in kind, he insisted, it was determined "in all honor to see that the vital interests of France were respected."

Was the Marshal engaging in a "double game"—the famous *double jeu*—with which so many of his partisans have credited him? Was he in fact convinced that, despite Hitler's boasts, England might still win the war and that he therefore kept his commitment to the New Order deliberately vague? Or did he really believe that a German victory was inevitable and that the only hope for France was to find the best place possible in the Nazi scheme for a new European community, one worthy of a nation with so glorious a past? It was clear that Montoire was inconclusive; Hitler failed to bring Vichy into the attack on England despite his threats of an ultimate peace treaty that would deprive France of her empire and saddle her with onerous war costs. The Marshal had coldly insisted that a treaty of reprisal would not last forever.

In October, 1940, no reasonable Frenchman could believe in a British victory. There was a certain amount of conceit in the thought that if the German army could in six weeks defeat the finest army in Europe—the French—then surely the few divisions left in England could not hold out against them. Even the magnificent English navy would fail under the blows of the Luftwaffe, and a German landing on the English shore was only a matter of time and the weather. And yet . . .

And yet, even as Pétain and Hitler were talking in the railway car at Montoire, a Vichy representative, Professor Louis Rougier, was negotiating with Winston Churchill in London. Despite an explosion

* On July 3, 1940, a British task force under Admiral Somerville arrived at Oran. An ultimatum was sent to Admiral Gensoul commanding the French Atlantic squadron anchored at Mers-el-Kebir: either join us in the fight against the Axis, sail with reduced crews to a British or French West Indian port, or be sunk. Gensoul cabled Darlan for instructions, omitting to mention the alternative of sailing to Martinique or Guadeloupe; he was ordered to resist any aggression. The French squadron was crushed in fifteen minutes, all ships being disabled except the battle cruiser *Strasbourg* and three destroyers which escaped the bombardment. Over sixteen hundred French sailors were killed or wounded. At the same time, French warships in English ports were seized and those in the harbor of Alexandria were blockaded. Churchill was determined to put as much of the French navy as possible beyond the reach of Adolf Hitler.

by the angry Churchill the next day when the newspapers reported the Montoire meeting, it was possible for the two men to agree on a *modus vivendi* between Vichy and London. Having weathered the fury of the Churchillian tempest with rare aplomb, Rougier departed with a written agreement pledging England to restore French integrity and sovereignty after the war, to refrain from seizing French colonies that were faithful to Vichy, to permit food to reach metropolitan France from her African colonies through the blockade, and to terminate the attacks on Pétain by the BBC. In turn, the French government pledged not to try to recover those colonies which had gone over to de Gaulle, not to allow the Nazis to use the French colonies as military bases, to permit the French empire to return to the war against Germany whenever the British and their allies were strong enough to land there in force, and to sabotage the French fleet rather than allow it to fall into the hands of the Axis.

Nor was this the only contact between Vichy and Britain. Secret conversations between Jacques Chevalier, undersecretary in the ministry of public education, and the Canadian chargé d'affaires in Vichy, Pierre Dupuy, led to an agreement similar to the one that Rougier had negotiated; in addition, it provided for the "maintenance of an artificial state of tension between the two countries" to conceal the secret accord from the Germans.

Across the Atlantic a special French military attaché was meeting with President Roosevelt on the Presidential yacht on the Potomac. Captain René de Chambrun was uniquely qualified for the mission confided to him: as a direct descendant of Lafayette, he held American citizenship as well as French; his mother was the former Clara Longworth. Pétain was an old family friend who had appointed his father as his liaison officer to General Pershing during World War I—and he himself was Pierre Laval's son-in-law.

Such impeccable credentials could forecast only success. In return for a public statement by the Marshal in favor of democracy and American rearmament, Roosevelt agreed to send food to France in spite of his fears that the Germans would seize it even in the unoccupied zone.

What then was the true meaning of Montoire to the Marshal? In a letter to Weygand dated November 9, 1940, he wrote that "the situation of our country requires that we maintain a prudent equilibrium between collaboration with the Germans (which is inevitable on the economic level) and the English and American inducements. . . ." If this was his thinking, then, it was doomed to quick failure as a policy for the resurrection and salvation of France. Hitler and Laval had their own concepts of a realistic collaboration, and Pétain was to find himself being led into depths from which he could never recover, following

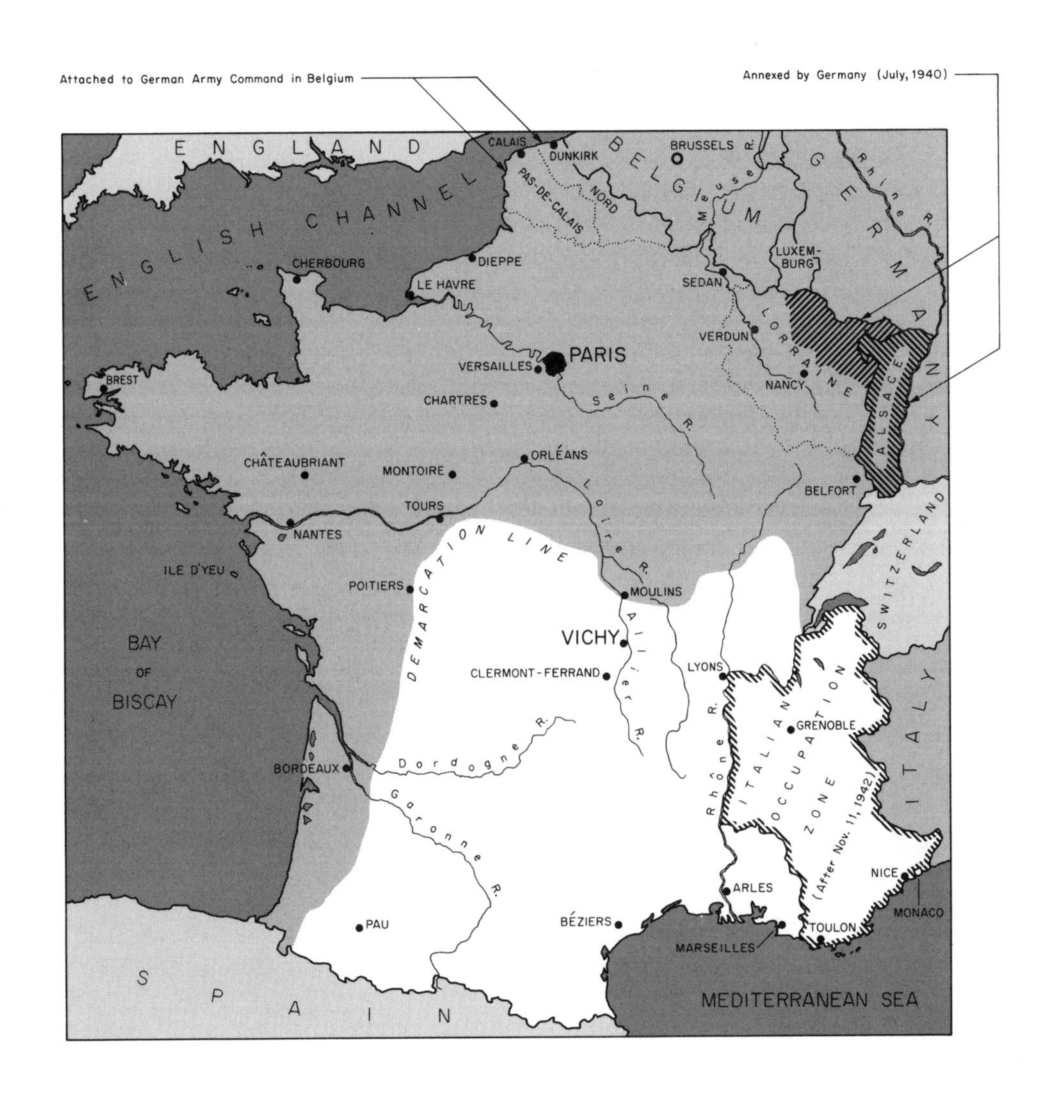

OCCUPIED FRANCE 1940-1944

the fatal word "collaboration" into the abyss and dragging his beloved France with him.

True, not all Frenchmen were unwilling to look collaboration squarely in the eye and to declare themselves fervently in favor of a German victory and a place for France in the New European Order. Above all, there were certain groups in Paris. . . .

2

The Face of Collaboration

Under a foreign military occupation, collaboration, either passive or active, is by stark necessity required for survival; the laws of land warfare are merciless in dealing with acts of sabotage and other resistance. In 1940, the shocked and stunned French people, their self-esteem brutalized by the magnitude of the catastrophe, huddled under the paternalistic cape of the Victor of Verdun and abandoned all to the Father who would protect them from the storm. The only groups who welcomed the occupation were the money-hungry opportunists, that large group of men who had never "made it" before the war in politics, journalism, business, the theater, or radio, and the mediocrities who now sought their revenge on "them." Apart from these and certain prewar Fascist groups—who saw the defeat as a triumph of their political beliefs in the superiority of Fascist doctrine—the average Frenchman and Frenchwoman instinctively withdrew into the family circle for warmth and protection. They adored Marshal Pétain, blindly believing in his omnipotence; they relied like children on his ability to treat realistically with Hitler to get the best deal for France and to punish those responsible for the disgrace of the defeat. Insofar as they consented to the Vichy government, they were also "collaborators."

To the French Fascists, however, the catastrophe of May–June, 1940, was the beginning of a "new dawn." It had been more than six years since their last attempt to bring down the Republic and to convert France into a Fascist state. They considered Vichy the culmination of all their frantic efforts since the terrible night of February 6, 1934, when they had shed their blood in the streets of Paris while trying to storm the Chamber of Deputies.

In the middle of the Place de la Concorde, an overturned bus burned fiercely as the angry mob rushed through the darkness toward the bridge over the Seine. Howling for blood, they pressed against the barricades behind which several hundred police and Gardes Mobiles nervously fingered their rifles. Four times the mounted riot police charged the square, slashing about them with sabers; four times they were forced back by a rain of stones, paving blocks, bricks, and chairs from the nearby café terraces. The air was filled with the screams of the wounded, the vitriolic curses of the rioters, and the shouted commands of the police calling for the mob to disperse. With the street lights shattered by well-aimed stones, it was pandemonium in a darkness broken only by the wavering light of the burning bus and the flicker of fires through the windows of the navy ministry next to the Hôtel Crillon. The Fascist gangs—frustrated in their attempts to storm the navy building by a handful of resolute sailors armed with pistols—retaliated by flinging lighted rags soaked in oil through the smashed windows.

Across the Seine, in the Palais Bourbon, the seat of the Chamber of Deputies, the representatives of the Republic shivered in terror before the fury that screamed for their deaths ("Throw the deputies into the Seine!"). Newly installed in his seat as premier, Edouard Daladier, who had just taken the reins of the government from the faltering hands of Camille Chautemps (hopelessly compromised by the Stavisky scandal* that had brought the Rightist gangs into the street), found himself at the center of the storm. Not only his government but the Republic itself depended upon the steadfastness of a handful of police—police whose loyalty was suspect, whose courage had never been tested, and whose willingness to check the fury of the mob and possibly die for parliamentary democracy in the attempt could never be counted on. Sullenly, the short stocky "Bull of the Vaucluse" slumped in his seat, watching his supporters and foes alike slip away through the back doors to safety in the dark streets of the Left Bank.

Suddenly, the staccato sound of shots was heard in the Chamber. The police were firing on the rioters! The explosion outside was matched by an explosion of furious invective and battle among the remaining deputies. Clawing his way madly across the crowded room, the right-wing deputy Jean Ybarnegaray (later to become minister of youth and family in Pétain's cabinet) tried to get his hands on Daladier's throat. Georges Scapini, who had been blinded in World War I, stood like some sightless Cassandra, screaming, "You are a government of assassins!" Scapini later served as Pétain's special envoy for French prisoners in Germany.

In the Place de la Concorde, the bodies lay in circles of blood in the darkness. Slowly, on foot and on horse, the police moved into the bullet-torn square, driving the furious demonstrators before them.

* Stavisky, an international swindler, "committed suicide" in his luxurious château on January 9, 1934. He died, according to the satirical newspaper *Le Canard Enchainé,* of a "revolver shot fired at point-blank range."

Missiles were still thrown, horses and men still ripped by razor blades at the end of long sticks and firecrackers hurled under the jittery horses. But the mob was forced back into the side streets and slowly dispersed. The insurrection was over; the Republic was saved.

Thus on February 6, 1934, an attempt to overthrow the parliamentary Republic of France was narrowly defeated at the cost of sixteen dead (including one woman who was watching from the balcony of the Crillon) and 655 wounded. The eerie battle in the night had seen such political opponents as the Rightist Croix de Feu (Colonel François-Casimir de la Rocque's war veterans) and the Communists fighting side by side against the republican forces. The Republic had survived the bloody assault in 1934, but never again would it feel secure against the threat of French Fascism, with or without help from the Left.

The rise of French Fascism was no isolated phenomenon on the Italian or German model. Although its growth dated from the end of World War I and its leaders drew their inspiration from the totalitarianism and National Socialism of Mussolini and Hitler, its sources date far back into French history. They included revulsion at the France which still drew its ideals from the Great Revolution; a revolt against the materialism of the day; and a reaction to the parliamentary blundering that had drained France of its youth in the savage bloodletting of the trenches in 1914–1918. There were always those who dreamed of the return to a social order headed by a king and a nobility that would be recognized as the elite. Among the latter was the tall, bearded poet–philosopher, Charles Maurras, and the monarchists of L'Action Française.

To Maurras, the defeat of 1940 was a "divine surprise," the end of the "whorish" Republic, and the finish of "*la France babillarde*"—the France that talked too much and did nothing. The seventy-two-year-old editor and leader of L'Action Française welcomed the crushing of his country, seeing in the catastrophe the end of his foreboding that France, the real France, would continue to be ruined by the fearful consequences of the Great Revolution. Liberalism, anticlericalism, parliamentary government, Freemasonry, Jewish influence, alliance with England—all these had been castigated by his brilliant pen and caustic wit in the editorial columns of his newspaper.

From the time of the Dreyfus Affair, when Maurras had played a prominent role in the campaign against revision of the court-martial verdict and had flayed the Dreyfusards as "half-breeds" in the pay of Germany, he had led the French Right in its violent attacks on the weak Republic. Initially anti-German, he had fought against the declaration of war in 1939, saying it would benefit no one but the terrible Stalin. No faith was to be put in England's support, he cried, and

France alone would bear the shock of Hitler's armies. Anti-everything; calling for the resurrection of France through the undoing of the results of the French Revolution; demanding the return of the monarchy (the Orléans pretender, the Duc de Guise, was waiting in the wings), the destruction of the futile Third Republic, and a rule by the elite—these elements of Maurras' philosophy strongly influenced his readership among the army and navy officers whose higher ranks were overwhelmingly antirepublican. For a while, even the young Captain Charles de Gaulle was bemused by the simplistic views of the causes of French weakness expounded by L'Action Française.

The "divine surprise" that Maurras felt when the Nazis entered Paris was increased by the armistice, Pétain's ascension to power, the dismissal of the two Chambers, and the proclamation of the new "French State." To the French Rightists, as Céline wrote, the Victor of Verdun was "the new king of France," and the new aristocracy was beginning to gather about him in Vichy. Montoire added to their happiness, as did the purge of Freemasons and Jews in the administration, the army, navy, and the teaching professions.

There is a certain innocence about Maurras's delight in the fall of the parliamentary regime, a collapse that he had demanded for so many years. In his exultation there was the innocence of a wayward child whose persistent dream has finally been realized. Cut off from the sinister rumblings of the true Fascist parties by his deafness, and blinded to the realities of Hitler's New Order by his own brilliance and absorption in the concept of "France Alone," he seemed almost an anachronism in those days of paralysis and indecision—a bearded and top-hatted old gentleman who was still shouting in the streets that Dreyfus was a traitor and should be shot. His influence at Vichy was negligible (Pétain spoke to him only four times in as many years), and he quickly found himself pushed into the backwaters of the collaborationist movement by the lusty brawling Fascist toughs whose leaders were men like Jacques Doriot and Marcel Déat—true French Nazis whose aim was to integrate France into Hitler's New Europe. To such Neanderthal types, Maurras was a bleating intellectual chauvinist who could safely be left to the future French S.S.

The most important Fascist party that France produced was the turbulent Parti Populaire Français (P.P.F.), led by Jacques Doriot. Not only was it the sole party of the militant masses, based on a stern party discipline and a consistent ideology, but it could boast of the dynamic leadership of a man who saw himself as the Führer of a France second only to Germany in the New Europe. Discarding the outdated monarchist and nationalist dreams of Maurras, the P.P.F.'s homegrown brand of antirepublicanism and anti-Semitism was designed to appeal to the broadest spectrum of French society.

Doriot himself had charisma. Tall, round-faced, and stocky, he was a superb orator, at his best in front of the tremendous audiences that flocked to the Vel d'Hiv and the other large Parisian halls on the summons of the party. Strangely enough for a man who aspired to lead Fascism in France, he had started life as an ardent Communist.

In 1920, at the age of twenty-two, he had joined the Communist party and had begun a spectacular rise as a militant Leftist. His gift for oratory was quickly manifested in stirring appeals to the workers of Aubervilliers and Senlis to rise against their capitalist oppressors. In the chaotic postwar years, as the reaction grew to a fever pitch against the conservative elements that had led France to the slaughter of Verdun, the Somme, and the Champagne, the exciting dark-haired Doriot became a favorite of the party. By 1924, he was a member of the Central Committee of the party and the director of the Communist Youth; on a trip to China, he met the young Chou En-lai. Even so eminent a Communist leader as Zinoviev pointed him out in 1924 as a coming man. The Russian purge trials of 1936 spared Zinoviev the pain of knowing how accurate his prophecy had been.

One of the youngest deputies in the Chamber, Doriot made a name for himself by his tirades against French colonial policy. During the Rif rebellion under Abd-el-Krim (1924), he sent an audacious telegram of congratulations to the Rif leader; this created a furor in the Paris newspapers and earned the *enfant terrible* the enmity and lifelong suspicion of the then war minister, Maréchal Philippe Pétain. It was a hatred that was to leave many marks during the years of Vichy.

Doriot's break with Communist doctrine and discipline occurred in 1929 over a question of cooperation with the Socialists on the common problems of the rights of the workers. Moscow, at the Sixth Congress of the International, had ordered that the Socialists be treated as class enemies and that no joint efforts were to be undertaken with them. Quickly and without discussion, the leaders of the French party fell in line—but not the independent and fiery Doriot. He protested loudly and in print at what he felt was a betrayal of the masses; unfortunately, he made the tactical error of minimizing the Trotskyite menace and found himself shunned by the top brass. Forced to expiate his faults by self-criticism, he withdrew sullenly from the leadership and started to cast about for a new basis of political support. However, he was not expelled from the party; instead, he was reelected to the Chamber as a Communist, and he even became mayor of the Red stronghold of Saint-Denis.

It was in the bloody events of February 6, 1934, that Doriot found the key to the political changes that he had been seeking. On that day, the party had sent its militants into the streets to fight alongside the Croix de Feu and the other antirepublican leagues against the regime. The hope of profit from the disorder and the overthrow of the government was one reason for this strange alignment; the other reason was a desire to exhibit a display of force against what was called the "Social–Fascism" of the Socialist party. It was this attitude that Doriot could not stomach, for he still believed that the Socialists were allies in the war against Fascism—a doctrine he held as late as 1937.

Soon it became impossible for the party to ignore the heresies of the popular young leader. When he refused to recant, he was expelled (June 27, 1934). One month later, in another switch in its tortuous policy, the party signed an agreement on "unity of action" with the Socialists. This was both a first step in the formation of the Front Populaire and a declaration of war on the Fascist leagues.

But adoption of Doriot's policy still left him in exile, and his bitterness against the party and its vindictive leaders grew constantly until it consumed him. Pride, ambition, and the enthusiasm of his followers all turned him into a most virulent anti-Communist. There may have been more than a little calculation in this turnabout, for denunciation of "rule by Moscow" was certain to find a large believing audience in bourgeois France. In his weekly newspaper *L'Emancipation,* Doriot castigated his former comrades in the most violent terms; on April 4, 1936, he wrote: "The Communist party has become a propaganda society in favor of a foreign nationalist regime."

Strangely enough, the Parti Populaire Français was originally founded among the Communists of Saint-Denis, most of whom were rebelling against the rigid party discipline and were frustrated by the widespread unemployment of the thirties. To them, the dynamic Doriot was the leader who would crush the pretensions of both Communism and capitalism and free France from bondage to both Moscow and the "Two Hundred Families." They followed the stocky young man in the green suspenders as he moved further and further from the Left, denouncing the Franco–Soviet pact and calling for negotiations with Germany to ensure the peace. His hold over them was absolute.

The workers of Saint-Denis were not the only ones to believe in the mission of Jacques Doriot. Among his earliest supporters were two of the best-known young writers in France: Pierre Drieu La Rochelle, author of three sensitive novels on the French soul, and Bertrand de Jouvenal, satirist and journalist *par excellence.* Another early adherent was the ex-Communist Paul Marion, who directed economic policy for the P.P.F. All three were to play prominent roles during the occupation.

As was to be expected in the superheated political milieu of the late thirties, the Communists reacted violently to the attacks of the man who had been one of the rising young stars of the party. "The renegade Hitlerian Doriot" was one of the kinder epithets that the party newspaper *L'Humanité* used.

In his accelerating move toward a Fascism that borrowed some of the trappings of the Italian and German models, Doriot clung to a philosophy that was Socialistic, nationalistic, and peculiarly French. That it brought him into line with the older antirepublican and anti-Semitic leagues (such as de la Rocque's Croix de Feu and Le Françiste of Marcel Bucard) was a development which, if unfortunate in that it diminished his independence, was also inevitable.

The Fascist trappings that adorned the P.P.F. were necessary to a new political party that wished to appeal to the youth and to a people to whom ceremony and the symbols of glory were second nature. The flag was designed to commemorate the Fête de la Fédération, which was celebrated in 1790 during the enthusiasm of the French Revolution; the salute was a very close copy of the Nazi salute but was defined as "the gesture of an officer ordering his soldiers to follow him." There was even a party hymn glorifying the Leader: "Listen to Doriot who summons you, Child of France, to the noblest goal."

From the beginning, the P.P.F. was a great success; by March, 1937, 130,000 members who had paid the one-franc monthly dues filled the Vel d'Hiv to applaud the matchless oratory of an inspired Doriot. Sixty-five percent of the members of the new party were workers, and of these 35,000 had left the Communists to follow the shining star of Jacques Doriot. *L'Emancipation,* the party weekly, had a paid subscription of 200,000.

The one element that was initially missing in the National Socialism of the P.P.F.—racism—was added in July, 1936:

"By their tyranny and their intolerance, the Jews, Socialists, and Communists . . . are giving birth to . . . an anti-Semitism which was nonexistent before their rise to power. If grave troubles arise for them, they have only themselves to blame."

Anti-Communism, anticapitalism, and, finally, anti-Semitism: these were to be the three main points of the political program of the Parti Populaire Français.

Under the urgings of the Left, the Popular Front government of Léon Blum decided to take action against the P.P.F. and Doriot's newly created Front de la Liberté, which in their eyes was a direct threat by a federation of the Fascist Right to the power of the Left. In May, 1937, the minister of the interior, Marx Dormoy,* removed Doriot from his post as mayor of Saint-Denis for "administrative reasons."

Never one to shirk a fight, Doriot also resigned as municipal councillor of Saint-Denis and appealed to the electorate for a new mandate. "The battle will be harsh," he wrote. "They have thrown down a challenge to us. We pick it up."

He lost the election by a decisive margin to the Communist candi-

* Marx Dormoy was murdered by *doriotistes* on July 26, 1941 (see *Le Temps,* August 26, 1941, page 2).

date, Fernand Grenier (who later represented the party in de Gaulle's Free French movement in London). The inhabitants of Saint-Denis had let him down. Doriot then resigned as deputy (the third post he had held in Saint-Denis), boldly holding that "when a man no longer represents the majority of his constituents, he must withdraw. . . . It is true that no parliamentary rule obliged me to resign from parliament. Honor, on the other hand, makes it an absolute duty."

Now he would appeal to the country for the mandate denied him by the fickle workers of Saint-Denis.

This appeal, which was a challenge to the coalition of the Left, took the form of an expansion of the Front de la Liberté—the converse of the Popular Front. Except for de la Rocque and his Parti Social Français, the major Rightist groups subscribed to the fervent anti-Communism of the new Fascist alliance. Among the men who rallied to Doriot in 1937 were many who were to play prominent roles in the tragic days of the occupation: Pucheu, Suarez, Henriot, Bonnard, and Xavier Vallat. The first three were later to pay with their lives for the errors of their political choice.

The slow drift of the P.P.F. toward "international Fascism" was accelerated by the crisis of Munich in September, 1938. Hitler's demand on Czechoslovakia conflicted with French guarantees to the little state that had been created by the Treaty of Versailles. In the turmoil of those autumn days, French nationalism—never deeply buried in a people who had invented the word "chauvinist"—rose considerably; the fears that had inhibited action at the time of the occupation of the Rhineland now combined with French fears of German desire for revenge. There was a popular outcry in the press against yielding once more to what appeared to be an insatiable Führer.

But Doriot would not be moved from his new alignment with Fascism. "In order to save our honor and the peace in spite of Moscow's agents, there must be a realistic peace in Czechoslovakia"—this he published in *L'Emancipation nationale* fifteen days before the French premier and the English prime minister, Edouard Daladier and Neville Chamberlain, flew to Munich and surrendered to Hitler's demands.

The Chamber of Deputies ratified the Munich agreement by a vote of 535 to 75, but the quarrel within the P.P.F. was too deep to be mended by a Fascist victory. Resignations tore the party apart; not only de Jouvenal, but a reluctant Drieu La Rochelle (still calling himself a Fascist) deserted Doriot. They were quickly followed by Pierre Pucheu, Paul Marion, and many others.

The Parti Populaire Français quickly disappeared as a political force of the Right. It would arise again after the overwhelming defeat of 1940, which was the unsought-for triumph of the Fascism and the

Fascist ideals to which the members of the party had proclaimed their allegiance for ten years.

Among the many activist groups of the extreme Right that proliferated in France in the thirties, the most sinister in reputation and the most bloody in fact was the Comité Secret d'Action Revolutionnaire (C.S.A.R.). A perverted offshoot of L'Action Française, it was in fact—under the leadership of Eugène Deloncle—a terrorist underground organization aimed at the overthrow of the French Republic.

It borrowed from its implacable enemies, the Freemasons, all the ceremonies and symbols of a secret organization, including a few cabalistic and magic signs unknown to the Grand Lodges. There was an initiation ceremony, complete with a vow to die before revealing the secrets of the group, a handshake, and mystical passwords by which to recognize fellow terrorists. All of this has the sound of a high school fraternity pledge and undoubtedly appealed to the small boy that lurks in many grown men, but the C.S.A.R. was far from an innocent group of malcontents and dreamers. Not only did it have its allies in the higher ranks of the army through a member of Pétain's staff, the perpetually dissident and turbulent Commandant (Major) Georges Loustaunau-Lacau,* but it is known to have been responsible for a number of bombings and at least four murders (including that of two Italian anti-Fascists, in return for which the C.S.A.R. earned a shipment of small arms from Mussolini).

In November, 1937, the Cagoule—the C.S.A.R. action squads—was broken up by the French police under the direction of the minister of the interior, the ever-vigilant Marx Dormoy; however, the terrorism of the extreme Right, of which the C.S.A.R. was the main arm, awaited only the defeat and the benevolent forbearance of the occupying power to burst forth again in some of the bloodiest incidents of the occupation period.†

Collaboration was also to be a business, and a very profitable one, for those whose conscience—or lack of one—allowed them to serve the Germans for personal gain rather than ideological conviction. There was no lack of such men in France during the occupation, for the tra-

* Loustaunau-Lacau not only represented La Cagoule—the Hooded Ones, as the C.S.A.R. action squads were known—in the upper echelon of the army and to Marshals Pétain and Franchet d'Esperey, but after the defeat he played a prominent and brave role in the Resistance as a member of the ill-fated group "Alliance." He was captured by the Gestapo and suffered terribly in a German concentration camp until his release in 1945. A broken man, he testified at Pétain's trial as to his contacts with the C.S.A.R. For the details of his truly amazing career, see his *Mémoires*.

† On July 10, 1940, Eugène Deloncle in a letter to his wife: "I write to you today full of joy in the midst of my sorrow. The Republic is no more. Today I saw those puppets kill themselves."

dition of being paid (and paid well) for "patriotic" services is a long one, and the most mercenary motives could frequently be found behind the ostensibly pure devotion to the "cause of poor suffering France." Two men with long histories of being "bought" who were to play prominent roles under the occupation as collaborators of the worst type were Jean Luchaire and Fernand de Brinon.

Tall, handsome, graying slightly at the temples, and with the appearance of a successful insurance executive, Jean Luchaire had an open pleasant personality. A handshaker and a back-slapper, he had moved along the back alleys of the parliamentary morass of the Third Republic before the war, always short of money and always finding the minister, political party, or industrialist who was willing to pay for a favor or an article in his newspaper, *Notre Temps*. Completely without political conviction, he could quickly adapt to any line that promised a profit. So openly corrupt was he that many leading figures professed to find him attractive simply for a self-confessed venality that contrasted sharply with the hypocrisy of so many who were being bought "under the table."

His pro-German stance was well paid for by Nazi funds slipped to him by his friend Otto Abetz, the francophile who married Luchaire's secretary, Suzanne Bruyker, thus sealing a friendship that was to pay vast rewards in the years after the French defeat. For Luchaire, loyalty to integrating France into Hitler's New Order was a vehicle which permitted him to indulge in the habits which claimed his true loyalty—dining in the finest restaurants and keeping expensive mistresses. His daughter, Corinne, a well-known film actress, bemoaned the fact that "Papa's" political success led him into such costly foolishness, "which otherwise he would never have been able to afford."

De Brinon was not handsome. Short, stocky, balding, he had a nose worthy of Cyrano and a devotion to money that even Luchaire envied, for it seemed to be an end in itself. There was a rather intriguing inconsistency in his actions before the war: leadership in the Franco–German committee, visits to Nazi Germany to talk with Hitler and to promote "peace," a close friendship with Abetz—all this must be contrasted with the widely known fact that he was living on subsidies from the Rothschilds and Lazard, prominent Jewish bankers. Indeed, de Brinon's ties to Jewish financial circles in Paris were strengthened by his marriage to a Jewish divorcée—wealthy of course—who had to be created an "honorary Aryan" during the occupation to save him from embarrassment.

Fiery Marcel Déat also played an important role in collaborationist circles. An Auvergnat like Laval, Déat was ambitious, totally unscrupulous, and talented. The editor of *L'Oeuvre*, he wrote an editorial at the time of Munich entitled "Die for Danzig?" which had a profound effect on the wavering French people. Anti-Vichy from the beginning, his political philosophy was based on a Fascism of the Left and not the Right, and it was to lead him into an attempt to justify the worst excesses of the occupation period. "He wants to be a leader; he will be one in German if he cannot be one in French."

"We were alone, without a German in sight. We could have escaped a hundred times.... We questioned the soldiers of the Wehrmacht using the only German word that we knew: '*Lager*' [prison camp], and they pointed out to us the road to follow." In these words, the young writer Robert Brasillach described the bitterness and humiliation of the defeat.

To the thirty-one-year-old lieutenant, the surrender was a crushing blow. Born in 1909, he had been too young to endure the life in the trenches that so many men only slightly older had undergone, but World War I had left an indelible impression on the sensitive, brooding boy. His father, a career army officer, had been killed "on the field of honor" in 1914, and young Robert never escaped from the feeling of guilt that he had been spared and left out of the one terrible experience that seemed to unite the young men of the immediate postwar years. There was often in his more romantic writings the idea of the action that purifies, the blood that cleanses—ideas that led him later to Fascism.

As a student at Louis-le-Grand and at the prestigious Ecole Normale Supérieure, he always knew (and his teachers and fellow students always accepted) that he was destined to be a writer; for him, there could be no other career. Deeply interested in politics, he was attracted to L'Action Française and the teachings of Charles Maurras by their emphasis on glory, the army as the sword of the nation, and the idea of "*France seule*"—France alone. It was the bloody insurrection of February 6, 1934, and hostility to the subsequent Popular Front government with its coalition of the Left that moved him toward the Fascist Right. By the late 1930s, the two most talented exponents of Fascist doctrine in France were Brasillach and Drieu La Rochelle, both early literary successes and both graduates of L'Action Française.

Brasillach looked like a choirboy with his round, childish face, high forehead, full sensuous lips, and black horn-rimmed glasses. In his awkward, ill-fitting uniform, his brown hair carefully parted in the center, there was no mistaking what he was—a romantic, a sensitive observer of the follies of his fellowman, and a thinker.

Mobilized as a lieutenant in September, 1939, he was given a staff job with a regiment in the Maginot Line. Buried under concrete during the "Phony War," he worked on a book, largely autobiographical, explaining the thoughts and experiences of those young men who had just lived through the years between the two wars.

When the German attack began on May 10, 1940, he was still writing feverishly. His regiment took no part in the battles in Belgium and at Sedan. Encircled without having fired a shot, he was taken prisoner with his entire unit and sent along the humiliating road to a German prison camp. There was no thought of escape among the French prisoners; it was felt that they would be quickly released since "they had not fought at all." Besides, haunted by the terrible casualties of the earlier war, they were secretly relieved that a holocaust had been avoided even if France was shamed.

Behind barbed wire in Germany, suffering the cold and hunger which were the common lot of the defeated, Brasillach continued to write for the Fascist Parisian newspaper, *Je suis partout,* which still carried his name on the masthead. Finally, after nine months of captivity, a direct request to the Germans on the armistice commission at Wiesbaden secured his release in April, 1941. As Jean Guéhenno noted in his journal: "The price of his liberation was a book . . . in which this Frenchman courageously denounces, on Hitler's behalf, the weaknesses of France."

In strange contrast to the politicians who came to Fascism through conviction in the ultimate triumph of the National Socialist dogma, to the intellectuals such as Drieu La Rochelle and Robert Brasillach who followed it as the "wave of the future," and to the venal men who sought only to profit from it, Joseph Darnand was a Fascist because he was an unshakable French nationalist and a man of action. With an impressive record for aggressive combat patrols on the western front, he had worked at a garage in Nice while fretting at the inactivity between the wars. It was the bugle call of February 6, 1934, that brought him back to the battle, convinced that France was once more in danger. He joined one Rightist group after another, always discontented at the lack of action; from L'Action Française to Croix de Feu to P.P.F., with a side excursion into the C.S.A.R.,* he wandered like a lost soldier looking for the thick of the fight. He was to find it finally in the struggle against the "terrorists" who were threatening his Vichy masters and cooperation with the Germans. He would end as the leader of the despised Milice (the French Fascist militia) and an officer in the French Waffen S.S. (French volunteers who fought in German uniforms on the Russian front), still looking for a battle worthy of him—even if the enemy was French.

Unlike many of the other collaborators, there was nothing in the background of Georges Suarez to suggest that he would finally play

* Darnand was arrested with Deloncle when the C.S.A.R. was broken up by Marx Dormoy; both were released at the outbreak of the war.

such a murderous role during the occupation. A veteran of the 1914–1918 war, he had started a brilliant career in journalism as the Vienna correspondent of the Havas Agency, and he later contributed to a number of French newspapers, mostly of a conservative bent. His biographies of Georges Clemenceau and Aristide Briand displayed an ardent nationalism that certainly precluded any thought of Fascism. As late as 1939, during the *Drôle de Guerre*, his anti-German sentiments were made plain to his readers.

Leaving Paris when war was declared, he did not return until November, 1940, when Montoire put an end to his wait-and-see attitude. It is likely that he was one of those journalists and writers (so common at that time) who could not bear to see their writings interrupted, their books cease to appear. More important than the humiliation of *la patrie* was that their name should appear as a by-line in the lead article of a prominent newspaper or on the title page of a book that the critics would undoubtedly acclaim.

In December, 1940, he became editor of the Paris daily *Aujourd'hui;* there was a rumor that his post had been secured for him by the influence of Otto Abetz. If true, then Abetz was an excellent judge of character, for Suarez quickly established himself as a convinced pro-Nazi. During the fifty months of the occupation, he wrote and published some of the most violent and vituperative articles attacking the Third Republic (particularly the *Front Populaire*), de Gaulle and Gaullist sympathizers, the Resistance, the Jews, and the Freemasons. Alongside these attacks were to be found idolatrous praise of Adolf Hitler and his New Order. His appeals for a unity based on an authoritarian regime and an end to the disorder of parliamentary government was the program and the excuse given by many collaborators to justify the speed with which they had changed coats.

In his labors at *Aujourd'hui,* Suarez was joined by the less talented Paul Chack, who was to be a mainstay of anti-Bolshevik activities in occupied Paris.* A former naval officer and the author of several books on the glories of the French navy, Chack hated the English for having a more glorious naval tradition and the Americans because of their lack of discipline in 1917–1918 when not in the front lines. The British attack on the French fleet at Mers-el-Kebir which killed 1,200 French sailors, the aborted Anglo–Free French assault on Dakar, and the pro-English attitude of Washington all served to confirm him in his prejudices. It was to serve these prejudices that he aided the Germans, finally rivaling in vituperation the vicious attacks of Suarez and such men as Brasillach and Drieu La Rochelle of the Fascist newspaper *Je suis partout.* Chack

* He was president of the *Comité d'Action Antibolchevique* and organizer of the exposition *Le Bolchevisme contre l'Europe.*

was sixty-five years old in 1940 and his was a carefully cultivated hatred for those who had prevented France from attaining the preeminence in the world to which an obvious intellectual and moral superiority entitled her. That that place could now only be subservient to Nazi domination seems not to have concerned him. It was to be a fatal error.

Foremost among those French journalists who worked in the area of radio propaganda was Philippe Henriot. A former deputy from Bordeaux, he was a graduate of the Sorbonne, a teacher and journalist who had worked for both of the notorious anti-Semitic sheets, *Gringoire* and *Je suis partout*. Physically, he was tall and thin, not handsome but possessed of a compelling personality that fascinated everyone who met him. He seemed to burn with an inner fire that could come out only in his words. His effect on the audiences of Radio Paris during the occupation was extraordinary; he never let the fact that he had only one lung hamper him or his electrifying broadcasts. Clever and persuasive, he was the most dangerous and the most able of the "radio traitors," putting into the shadows such men as Hérold-Paquis and Ferdonnet, whose ravings over the German radio before the declaration of war had earned them the contempt of the French population.

Henriot was known for his extraordinary wit and presence of mind. He was once present in the Chamber of Deputies when Edouard Herriot placed his hand on his heart and announced, "Gentlemen, I prefer to have my hand on my heart rather than in someone's wallet." To which Henriot immediately responded, "But sir, you have two hands!" Such was his influence in collaborationist circles that in January, 1944, the Vichy government felt compelled to name him minister of propaganda, in succession to Paul Marion, who had held the post since August, 1941.

One of the speakers of the Free French Radio in London, named Lesage, denounced Henriot in these terms: "There are, thank God, some Frenchmen who have escaped the denunciations of Philippe Henriot and who can testify that he lives in terror of retaliation by patriots, lives in terror under the protection of the Vichy police and the German army.... German agent, denouncer of Frenchmen, accomplice of the Gestapo, it happens that you've never murdered anyone because you are too cowardly to do it yourself—you have it done for you."

Outraged, Henriot leaped to the microphone to answer the attack. "I know nothing more vile or more abject than your profession.... I asked who you are. You answered, a Frenchman... like a lot of your compatriots. Lesage is a pseudonym and if this pseudonym hides a Frenchman I shall be very surprised.

"Tremble in front of you? But you know well that if we trembled we would be silent, but if we were silent the stones would cry out with anger and indignation. . . . You kill? So be it, but try not to insult your victims . . . it betrays you, Lesage. Your conspiracies, your furies —what a confession of your impotence. You are certain that your allies will win. . . . In spite of that, you must still have the blood of some poor devils who are nothing but simple average Frenchmen doing their daily tasks: a stationmaster, a retiree, a mailman . . . you say they are traitors. Be serious, Lesage! . . . Today you have replaced the vote by the submachine gun and you have the advantage of often encountering men without arms. . . . Is that what you mean by patriotism? Is that what you mean by courage? Is that serving France? And you say to me that *I* am a traitor!"

Henriot's hold on his radio audience was undeniable. Even those who remained stubbornly anti-German, while venerating the Marshal and hoping for the social reform promised by the National Revolution, were fascinated by his spellbinding oratory. Next to writers and artists, the French respect their orators most; it is a tradition that stems from the tribunal of the Convention during the Great Revolution of 1789 when men like Danton, Saint-Just, and Robespierre held their audiences enthralled.

There were conviction and sincerity in his speeches. So overwhelming was the vehemence of his words that (as Henriot himself once said of Léon Blum) "it was impossible to know at what point they passed from truth to error."

What then was the meaning of "collaboration"? To the "new men" of the prewar Fascist parties, it was the vindication of their struggle against the Republic, the demonstration of the superiority of Fascist doctrine and the chance for vengeance. To the officials in Vichy, it was the minimum of cooperation with the Germans—particularly in the economic sphere, which they felt was inevitable—for the maximum gain: return of the prisoners, reduction of the crushing occupation costs, the elimination of the demarcation line, prevention of a Nazi annexation of Alsace-Lorraine, etc.

More cynical than most, Drieu La Rochelle—who as an intellectual was incapable of refraining from criticism of the Fascism he adhered to—defined collaboration as "some Germans who do not believe enough in Hitler charged with indoctrinating some Frenchmen who believe too much in him." To the man in the street who never believed what the German-controlled newspapers printed: "Collaboration? That's 'give me your watch and I'll tell you what time it is.' " Later, the jokes were to become more bitter.

Collaboration was survival. To the vast majority of Frenchmen,

Vichy was the legitimate government, the successor of the discredited Republic. To the legalistically minded French, this was a very important issue, as Winston Churchill pointed out in a speech in the House of Commons:

> The Almighty in His infinite wisdom did not see fit to create Frenchmen in the image of Englishmen. In a state like France which has experienced so many convulsions—monarchy, convention, directory, consulate, empire, monarchy, empire, and finally republic—there has grown up a principle founded on the *droit administratif,* which undoubtedly governs the action of many French officers and officials in times of revolution and change. It is a highly legalistic habit of mind, and it arises from a subconscious sense of national self-preservation against the dangers of sheer anarchy. For instance, any officer who obeys the commmand of his lawful superior, or of one whom he believes to be his lawful superior, is absolutely immune from subsequent punishment. Much therefore turns in the minds of French officers upon whether there is a direct, unbroken chain of lawful command, and this is held by many Frenchmen to be more important than moral, national, or international considerations. From this point of view, many Frenchmen who admire General de Gaulle, and envy him in his role, nevertheless regard him as a man who has rebelled against the authority of the French state, which in their prostration they conceive to be vested in the person of the antique defeatist, who to them is the illustrious and venerable Marshal Pétain, the hero of Verdun and the sole hope of France.

There was a difference between collaboration as defined and acted upon in the occupied and unoccupied zones. In Paris, which was the center of the active collaborationist movement (whose goal was to integrate France into the Nazis' New Order), were to be found not only the ardent collaborationist newspapers, but the headquarters of the Fascist parties led by Doriot, Déat, and Marcel Bucard. These were men who had a stake in an ultimate German victory and who denounced Vichy and its supporters as being "wishy-washy" in their desire to cooperate with Hitler. On the other hand, in the unoccupied zone centering about Vichy and relatively undisturbed by the German army of occupation, the "collaborators" wished to do only what was necessary for the survival of France. With unshakable faith in Pétain as the symbol of past military glory and the leader of the National Revolution that would rejuvenate the country, they believed in yielding as little as possible to German demands, particularly in the field of military action against their former English ally.

It was a great shock and disillusionment to the majority of the French people, but a great joy to the Paris collaborationists when, a few days after meeting Hitler at Montoire, Pétain spoke on the radio: "I am today embarking on a path of collaboration . . . this collaboration must be sincere . . . until now I have spoken to you as a father; today I speak to you as a leader."

After Montoire, those who collaborated because they thought it necessary for the survival of France were forced to align themselves more or less unwillingly with those who collaborated because of their belief in an ultimate German victory. As the war went on and the legend of the invincibility of the German army faded, the distinction between the two groups of collaborationists faded. To their opponents in London and in the metropolitan resistance, there would be no distinction; the purge was to deal brutally with both.

The entry of the Germans into Paris on the morning of June 14, 1940, was unmarred by any hostile demonstration; the few citizens who watched their triumphant parade through the nearly deserted streets were too crushed by the suddenness of the defeat to react. Also, there was something stultifying about the wave after wave of immaculately dressed tall healthy Teutons, the impressive bulk of their armored vehicles, the flapping of the numerous red-and-black flags with their crooked-spider insignia, the deafening beat of hobnailed boots on the *pavé*. A girl ran out to present a small bunch of flowers to a German officer who had stopped in front of a café near the Avenue Montaigne. With measured contempt, he threw them to the sidewalk and ground them under the heel of his boot.

The stores which had been closed and shuttered when the owners had fled the city slowly reopened for "business as usual" during July and August, as people slowly trickled back to Paris from the dusty roads of the exodus, cursing themselves for believing the rumors of German rape and murder. What followed was an orgy of buying, as the Nazi troops who had for so long sacrificed butter for guns flung themselves on the well-stocked counters of the famous Paris boutiques, purchasing not only the shoes, stockings, *haute couture*, and perfumes for which the French capital was so justly famous, but also gorging themselves on the bread, cheeses, butter, and wines. Soon it was all but impossible to see a German soldier walking through the streets without the familiar parcel under his arm. The bitter French whispered the story of two British spies who had been immediately arrested in the Métro in spite of their faultless German, impeccable Nazi uniforms, and identification papers, simply because they were carrying no packages!

The German military administration—the Militärbefehlshaber in Frankreich—quickly established itself in the elegant Hôtel Majestic, requisitioning a number of other first-class hotels and outlying villas for its members, and began its work of integrating the French people, industry, and resources into the Nazi war effort. Posters appeared on the walls in the major cities showing a smiling German soldier, bareheaded, his tunic unbuttoned, holding and feeding a French child while two other children looked up at him with awe. The caption read "Abandoned population, have confidence in the German soldier!" Sound trucks roamed the streets playing military marches intended to either soothe or intimidate a people that the older Germans remembered too well from 1914–1918 to be capable of violent emotional outbursts in the name of *la patrie*. The suddenness of the French collapse had startled and baffled those who still recalled the stubborn willingness of the French soldiers to die at Verdun and a hundred other battlefields of the earlier war. In the back of their minds was always the worry that it was some sort of Gallic trap, a trick to draw them deeper into France, until—as at the Marne—the bugles would blow, the stained flags would be unfurled, and the "defeated" French armies would spring again to the attack. Can one really defeat the "greatest army in Europe" in a mere six weeks?

Collaboration was an idea that came later in the occupation—in spite of the joy that the French Fascists showed at the defeat. At the outset, the lessons learned in a conquered Poland were to be applied to teach the potentially unruly French their role in the New Order. Nor were these lessons to be taught by the German army alone, for there were other forces in the Nazi state anxious to share in both the booty and the administration of a defeated province.

Among the thousands of military vehicles that poured into Paris during the German entry on June 14, 1940, no one paid any attention to a group of three cars with false license plates that rolled inconspicuously through the streets. Stopping in front of the Hôtel du Louvre, the twenty men in the uniform of the Geheime Feld Polizei (G.F.P.—German military police) requisitioned rooms for a long stay. Although their presence in Paris was illegal and would soon produce a vigorous protest from the army occupation authorities, these twenty men, all carefully chosen for their knowledge of the French language, geography, and customs, were confident that they would be needed.

Their leader was a tall slim man with an emaciated face and cold eyes. A long thin nose and a wide mouth which showed a twisted sardonic smile dominated a face with a high forehead that gave him the look of an intellectual.* Though he had the appearance of a scholar, his subject was the murderous repression of conquered peoples. His name was Helmut Knochen and his rank was Standartenführer (Colonel) S.S. He was the commander of the Sonderkommando of the

* He was a doctor of philosophy from Göttingen who had written his thesis on the English playwright, George Colman.

Gestapo that—in spite of army protests—had slipped into occupied Paris.

Because of its terrible reputation during the Polish campaign, the Gestapo had been forbidden by Hitler (under pressure from the German generals) to play any role in the administration of the occupied lands in the west; this, however, was a humiliation that Himmler could not tolerate. He ordered his deputy, Reinhardt Heydrich, to find a way to circumvent the order and Heydrich turned to his best man in these matters, Knochen. So, the Sonderkommando of specialists in French affairs, disguised in G.F.P. uniforms, lightly armed and using cars with false plates, was formed and slipped into the line of march of the victorious German army outside of Paris.

The morning after their arrival, Knochen sent several of his men dressed in civvies to the prefecture of police to seize the files on Jews, Freemasons, German refugees, Communists, and "other enemies of the Third Reich." No protest was made by the officials to this unauthorized seizure, which was in violation of the armistice and of the rights of French citizens. The only records that escaped the methodical Gestapists were those which two farsighted police officials had sunk in a barge in the Seine.

At the same time, Knochen proceeded to reestablish contact with French agents of the Gestapo who had been recruited since 1936 from among the members of the French Fascist gangs. The cooperation between the German and French Gestapos for which France was to pay such a terrible price in blood and pain had begun.

When discovered by the real G.F.P. near the end of June, Knochen quickly reached an agreement with the Militärbefehlshaber in Frankreich on the scope of Gestapo operations in France. Under pressure from Berlin, the army reluctantly agreed to allow the Gestapo to remain and conduct searches for enemies of the Reich—provided that all searches, operations, and arrests were disclosed to the G.F.P. This was a policy that Knochen found easy to accept and, under the powerful protection of Himmler and Heydrich, to ignore. He had only contempt for the polished gentlemen of the Abwehr (German Military Intelligence) and never doubted that they would need his help to suppress French resistance.

The resistance that Knochen and his men were preparing to destroy simply did not exist as an organized force. Stunned by the suddenness of the defeat, French opposition was confined to tears at the sight of the huge swastika flags and a tightening of fists as, helplessly, the French watched the victors parade in triumph down the Champs-Elysées. But these futile gestures were a beginning, for there were Frenchmen and Frenchwomen who could not accept the stark reality of their situation. There were those who remembered and repeated the words of Foch: "A man is not defeated until he is prepared to admit defeat."

The forces that would not, in spite of all logic, admit defeat were gathering.

3
The First Resistance

Jean Texcier was disgusted. It was bad enough that Paris in this July of 1940 was still empty from the exodus, that everywhere one saw only shiny black boots, huge swastika flags, and German soldiers acting like ordinary tourists, their cameras aimed at all the historic monuments. That could be tolerated; that was a temporary consequence of the defeat, but the actions of his fellow countrymen made him furious: the men who were being sociable with the Wehrmacht; the young women, always so eager for something new, who were attempting conversations in the cafés. On the sidewalks, the newsboys sold papers that already were boasting of the benefits of the defeat and announcing cynically that France was rid of its true enemies—Reynaud, Daladier, and Blum, among others.

On Bastille Day, 1940, there appeared clandestinely an "Advice to the Occupied," written by Jean Texcier and secretly circulated by his friends. In it, Texcier pointed out the proper conduct for his compatriots in their inevitable dealings with the gray-green occupiers. There were thirty-three separate bits of advice, of which the following are typical:

1. The newsstand dealers offer them maps of Paris and conversation manuals; the buses pour them out in unending waves in front of Notre Dame and the Panthéon; there is not one of them who does not have his little camera screwed to his eye. However, have no illusions about them: *these are not tourists!*
2. They are conquerors. Be correct with them, but do no more than they ask. . . .
3. You do not know their language or you have forgotten it. If one of them speaks to you in German, shrug helplessly and . . . walk on. . . .
6. If he asks you for a light, offer him your cigarette . . . (one never refuses a light—even to his worst enemy). . . .
9. Your haberdasher thinks it a good idea to write on his shop

window: *Man spricht deutsch* (German spoken). Patronize the shop next door, even if the owner appears to be ignorant of the language of Goethe.

10. If you see a whore in a business conversation with one of them, don't get upset. This guy will get what his money is worth—which is nothing. And remember that three-quarters of the French would not be more tactful with this broad than that blonde from the Black Forest. . . .
12. If you have to talk to one of those bronze sentinels who guard the Kommandantur,* don't take off your hat as I have seen you do. . . .
14. Reading French newspapers has never been advised for those who wish to learn how to express themselves correctly. Nowadays, the Paris dailies don't even *think* in French. . . .
22. I know a philosopher who has found a curious way of consoling himself [for the presence of so many German soldiers]: "We have taken too many prisoners," he sighs. . . .
30. You grumble because they make you return home precisely at 9 P.M. . . . Don't you understand that that is to allow you to listen to the English radio? . . .
33. It's useless to send your friends to buy this "Advice to the Occupied" at the bookstore. No doubt you have only one copy and wish to keep it. All right, make some copies and your friends may copy theirs in turn. It's a good occupation for the occupied. . . .

In the beginning, not all of the nascent resistance movements were anti-Vichy. Until Montoire, many patriots believed that the Marshal was playing a "double game": yielding as little as possible to German demands and waiting to bring France back into the fight. Given Pétain's overwhelming popularity, it would have been difficult—if not impossible—to recruit men for an organization that was not only anti-German, but anti-Vichy as well. Many groups, particularly those founded by army officers, claimed to be the secret arm of Pétain's struggle against the occupants.

One such group, which would later become the famous *réseau* (network) "Combat," owed its beginning to the bold and energetic Captain Henri Frenay, an escaped prisoner of war who had walked over five hundred miles through the rugged terrain of the Vosges Mountains to reach the unoccupied zone. Posted to the garrison at Marseilles, he started to contact other army officers whose goal he knew agreed with his—resistance to the Boches. Because of the success of the French army in holding off the numerically superior Italian divisions after the Italian declaration of war on June 10, 1940, morale

* The seat of the German Military Command in France in 1940 was the Hôtel Majestic.

in the south and southwest was relatively high. Frenay quickly set up a number of small cells whose avowed aim was to resist the armistice and to prepare for an armed return to the war.

Frenay's statement of his goals was succinct: "I consider that our first job is to get rid of the Boches. It is my intention to organize a secret army which, when the time is ripe, will strike the Germans in the back."

The response was enthusiastic and the Mouvement de Libération Nationale (Movement for National Liberation) swelled in numbers. From his studies in military intelligence, Frenay was aware of the need for security in clandestine activities (an awareness that was only too rare among early resistants and for the lack of which they were to pay a brutal price in blood and pain). He divided the group into closed cells of six members whose leader alone knew their names; five such cells were headed by a man who knew only the cell leaders. Thus, in case of arrest by the Gestapo, losses could be minimized.

Word of Frenay's organization reached Jean Moulin, who (in early 1941 before his departure for England) was assembling his report on the nascent Resistance. The two men met briefly in Marseilles to compare notes on the future organization and goals of the dissident groups; they discussed the lack of arms and money, and agreed that only General de Gaulle could serve as a rallying point to unify the scattered resistance cells. Moulin announced that he would leave as soon as possible to inform the general of the present situation in France.

When Frenay was ordered to Vichy, where his post in army intelligence was to be perfect for his clandestine activities, he found not only the French armistice army deep in anti-German work, but an old friend, Bertie Albrecht,* who was to become his second-in-command. Before leaving Marseilles, he had issued a manifesto (every truly French group—even the underground ones—must have a stirring statement of its goals; it is *de rigueur*) which ended with the plea: "May Marshal Pétain live long enough to see our work crowned with success!"

On August 20, 1940, a tall stocky French officer, newly escaped from the prison hospital at Chalôns-sur-Marne, stood under a chestnut tree on the Champs-Elysées and watched the German military band, drums beating and fifes shrilling, goosestep down the broad boulevard from the Arc de Triomphe. His face was calm; no casual passerby could have guessed the violent emotions that gripped him as

* Bertie Albrecht was thirty-seven in 1940. Married to a rich Dutch businessman and the mother of two, she was a social worker in the Women's Unemployment Bureau at Vichy and a fearless member of Frenay's group, Combat.

he watched the hereditary enemy parade victoriously through the streets of his beloved Paris. He, too, was a man who would not consent to his country's dishonor. A strange man, unpredictable, ironic, often moody; a man who had served Pétain and had learned to both love and hate the aged Marshal; a career officer who detested the Third Republic and who had had a link with the terroristic Cagoule; a man torn by his hatred for the morass of parliamentary maneuverings that had weakened France and had then plunged her into a war she could not win. Yet, he could not admit, he would not admit, that the real France could ever die.

Georges Loustaunau-Lacau was born in Pau, the capital of Béarn (which has given France such soldiers as Bernadotte and Bourbaki, and a king such as Henri IV, the Vert Galant). His father's house at Number 8 rue d'Orléans was located between the Caserne (Barracks) Bernadotte and the Palais de Justice, which he later took to mean that "war and prison would divide my life."

All *Béarnais* claim to be descended from the amorous Henri IV, whose dalliances with the local peasant girls were a source of pride to his subjects. Indeed, they boasted that Béarn had really annexed France, since Henri, originally a Protestant leader, had been crowned in 1589 (as a Catholic). The switch in religion had been justified by the cynical remark that "Paris is worth a mass."

After a year of studying for the entrance examinations ("Don't worry, young man. The army needs officers so badly that we're even taking the *marmottes*"—the bottom of the candidate list), young Loustaunau-Lacau entered the military academy of St.-Cyr in October, 1913. Nine months later, the new cadets marched off to war "in parade uniform without the slightest regret." In the rolling hills of Alsace, in the forests of the Ardennes, they died bravely in their white gloves and plumed shakos in the frightful headlong attack (*offensive à outrance*) that was the only French concept of strategy in that bloody August of 1914. The carnage of those autumn days that led up to the battle of the Marne was to leave an indelible mark on the French mind. It was to prevent a similar bloodletting that those weaknesses in military doctrine (the superiority of the defense, the Maginot Line, etc.) arose that made the crushing defeat of May–June, 1940, inevitable.

For four years the young St.-Cyrian went through the holocaust of the trenches. Contemptuous of the senior officers, proud of the ability of the *poilu* (French G.I.) to endure the most incredible hardships, to fight on, and to keep his faith in France and in victory, he led them into the slaughter, knowing that it was all senseless and convinced that the war would never end. When three of his men were killed by a stray shell while peacefully eating under a tree, he cursed

God for the stupidity of the whole thing. "We must not prejudge His designs," the battalion chaplain said weakly. "There are no designs," was the retort, "there are only three widows and six orphans to feed."

When the war ended, Loustaunau-Lacau was a twenty-four-year-old major, exhausted in mind and spirit. He thought briefly of leaving the army, but his early training and the need for a career which would lead to an honorable retirement stopped him. Slowly, he recovered his peace of mind and interest in living. After going through the Ecole Supérieure de Guerre (War College)—where one of his classmates was Captain Charles de Gaulle, newly returned from a German prisoner-of-war camp—he served in the occupation army in Germany and in the Rif campaign against the Moroccan chief Abd-el-Krim.

In March, 1935, he reported to Pétain's office on the Boulevard des Invalides for duty as an aide. It was his friend Captain Bonhomme* who introduced him into the sanctum sanctorum where Pétain, seated behind the desk he had inherited from Foch, greeted him with a benign, "Ah, there you are."

As Loustaunau-Lacau later wrote: "Foch had the appearance of a petty official, Joffre of a grandfather, but Pétain looks like a Marshal of France." It was his hands that the major remembered best during this first interview: the astonishing beauty and youthfulness of the hands of a seventy-nine-year-old man.

The interview started well as they chatted about mutual acquaintances; Pétain was constantly amazed that the generals who now held such important posts were not the men of that name that he had known years ago, but their sons. Finally, the Marshal explained his ideas of how Loustaunau-Lacau was to perform his functions. Pétain himself wrote very little, preferring that all military papers, articles, reports, and so forth be prepared under his direction by his staff. But he had very definite ideas on style and demanded that the writer's style match his in every detail (Charles de Gaulle, who had held the post last, had performed admirably in this role until he began to take pride in his literary creations and to publish them in his own name).

"Here's what I want," the Marshal explained. "One central idea that sustains the text from beginning to end. Few paragraphs but these proportioned to their importance. As for sentences: subject, verb, complement . . . no adjectives . . . even fewer superlatives . . . no added words to hide the poverty of the thought . . . always remember that the semicolon is illegitimate. . . ."

The young major stirred uneasily. "One could content oneself with just the title, Monsieur le Maréchal!"

* Bonhomme served as Pétain's aide-de-camp until January, 1944, when he was killed in a guerrilla trap. Speeding along a country road at night, his car struck a rope stretched across his path; it had been set for bigger game.

There was a long pause while Pétain stared at the embarrassed Loustaunau-Lacau with a cold eye. Then, unperturbed, he continued the lesson on the literary style appropriate to a Marshal of France, but he had not forgotten the impudence. The interview over, he walked the young major to the door, shook his hand and said firmly, "Don't forget that here irony acts from the top down."

The years on Pétain's staff introduced Loustaunau-Lacau to the army's role in French politics. Deputies, members of the government, business leaders, influential editors all came to the Boulevard des Invalides to talk to the Maréchal. That fighting gamecock, Marshal Franchet d'Esperey, was still alive (although quite ill), but to the French the Maréchal could only mean the man who had won at Verdun and who had compassionately ended the 1917 mutinies.

The antimilitarism of both the Popular Front government (of Léon Blum) and the Communist party was considered a serious threat by the High Command. With or without Pétain's approval, Loustaunau-Lacau set up a secret purge group known as the Centrale Corvignolles to counteract the Communist menace in the French army. Loyal officers ferreted out what they claimed to be Communist cells in each military district, army corps, air base, or armament factory and reported the names of the "Reds" to headquarters in Paris; then, with the help of loyal officers in the personnel bureau, the cells were broken up by judicious transfer and dispersal of its members. The Corvignolles network was widespread and included such exponents of armed action against the Communists as retired Air Force General Duseigneur and Marshal Franchet d'Esperey. It was the latter who introduced Loustaunau-Lacau to Eugène Deloncle of the C.S.A.R. (the Cagoule).

It was in d'Esperey's office that Deloncle revealed to the major his plans for a coup d'état to overthrow the Republic and prevent a Communist takeover; but Loustaunau-Lacau feared that this would only favor Germany, and the German menace was becoming clearer every day. There was a stormy exchange until the old Marshal, slapping the desk with one of his crutches, shouted, "Together, gentlemen, for France!" Finally, the *cagoulard* and the major agreed on the minimum of cooperation: exchanging information on the Communist threat.

This tenuous tie with the C.S.A.R. led to Loustaunau-Lacau's being forced out of the army in March, 1938, when the Cagoule conspiracy was exposed and Deloncle and Darnand arrested. Daladier was more than happy to strike a blow at Pétain by kicking out a member of his staff, particularly one known for his antiparliamentarian attitude and his nationalistic pro-army stance.

But the major was not to be silenced. Through newspaper articles and personal contacts, he continued to sound the alarm on both the

German and Communist threats. Nor did his close relationship with the old Marshal cease, for in August, 1939, Pétain (then ambassador to Spain) sent Loustaunau-Lacau to see Laval in Paris to test the political pulse and sound out the situation. Laval was delighted at the contact and offered a scheme to get rid of Daladier (whom he referred to as "a dunghill and a bastard") and bring in a Pétain government; he even had a preliminary list of possible ministers in his pocket. There could be no doubt as to who would be the strong man in this new regime under the cloak of the aging Maréchal. Pétain, still distrustful of the wily Laval, took no action on this proposal.

With the declaration of war on September 3, 1939, Loustaunau-Lacau began his campaign to return to the army. It took a full month of beating on ministerial doors and collaring senior officers before permission was granted for him to return to active duty. Flushed with patriotic ardor, he hurried to his post with the Deuxième Bureau (Military Intelligence) of General André-Georges Corap's 9th Army, which was defending the Meuse line in the Ardennes sector. But he was not forgotten by his enemies in Paris. Daladier (then minister of war) canceled this assignment and had him sent to a line regiment (the 123rd) for duty in the Maginot Line. No doubt, he felt that this was a safe place to park such a turbulent and potentially subversive character, but, unwittingly, he did his enemy a very great favor. It was Corap's 9th Army that was to bear the brunt of the massive German attack through the Ardennes in May, 1940; it was these divisions that broke and ran at Sedan, opening the fatal hole for the German armored columns, the wound through which in six weeks France bled to death.

French intelligence having failed to warn of the German preparations in the gloomy woods of the Ardennes, the attack on the Meuse was a complete surprise. Daladier had inadvertently made certain that Loustaunau-Lacau shared none of this blame.

At Vitry-le-François, Joffre's old headquarters in August, 1914, Major Loustaunau-Lacau led his battalion in a gallant but futile attack on a German tank column. Severely wounded by machine-gun fire, he was captured and sent to the hospital at Châlons-sur-Marne, where news of Pétain's request for an armistice reached him. Tormented in mind and body by the humiliation of his country, he worried most about France's fate in the hands of the aged Marshal, whom he had seen so often staring blankly at the papers on his desk, unable to work. It was that hint of senility that had caused the major mentally to tag the old man "closed due to old age."

By quoting nonexistent armistice terms that supposedly required the release of reserve officers over forty-five, he persuaded the baffled hospital commandant to free him. The deception was uncovered the next day, but by the time the Gestapo picked up his trail he had crossed the demarcation line into the unoccupied zone.

At home in Pau, he slowly recovered his strength and tried to determine where his duty now lay. His mother tried to persuade him to give his total loyalty to the Marshal. "If you had heard him on the seventeenth of June with his tearful voice . . ."

"Soldiers are not made for crying, but for fighting, Mama."

"You're not going to start fighting again?"

(Obscenity.)

"My God!"

By mid-September, his decision was made: resistance to the Germans no matter what Pétain demanded in the way of collaboration with Hitler. It was France that mattered, eternal France whose fate could not hang on the outcome of a single battle. He had not heard de Gaulle's call to resistance on the BBC, but along with many Frenchmen and Frenchwomen, peasants, prefects, army and air force officers, shopkeepers, mechanics, throughout the whole spectrum of French society, it was the "*refus*"—the refusal to allow France to die—that was the beginning of what was to become the French Resistance.

It was on the Centrale Corvignolles—the network of army officers he had set up to fight Communism—that Loustaunau-Lacau planned to base his resistance groups. That meant that he would have to contact his friends in the Army High Command to pick up the threads of the organization that had fallen apart upon his arrest in 1938. Once resolved, he moved quickly; by the end of September, he was in Vichy, where he rented the Hôtel des Sports, the only hotel that had not been requisitioned for a government office, as his headquarters.

Vichy disgusted him: the air of optimism, the smiling triumphant faces, even the red-and-gold façades of the hotels and baths seemed to mock a mourning France. No sooner had the Vichy newspapers announced his arrival than he had three unwelcome visitors: Charles Maurras came to remind him of his duty ("The Marshal is the flag itself"); Jacques Doriot boasted of the new strength of the P.P.F. in Paris; and the excitable terrorist, Eugène Deloncle, arrived to complain about the informers who were tracking him around Vichy and to confide that he did not like the Boches any more than before, but "we must make use of them." How he planned to do this was his secret.

Pétain was more than cordial to his former subordinate, appointing him as his delegate to the new amalgam of the many prewar veterans' organizations (Légion Française des Combattants), which Vichy planned to use as a propaganda and spy network throughout France to make sure that the Marshal's wise thoughts and policies were made known and enforced even in the smallest village. Under the cover of his role as *délégué général*, Loustaunau-Lacau traveled widely through the unoccupied zone, making contact with his old friends of the Corvignolles network, instructing them in the new policy of resistance, delegating responsibility, and making plans for action when the time was ripe.

Under the impression that the major was interested solely in aiding escaped prisoners and those demobilized soldiers who had been cut off from their families in the occupied zone, Pétain (who was known for his peasant stinginess) made the grand gesture of offering 25,000 francs (about $550) for the good work. Loustaunau-Lacau laughed in his face: "I need that much every day!" Pétain blanched and said no more of such outrageous extravagance.

The organization based on the old Corvignolles network was not the only resistance movement that was stirring in Vichy. The widespread feeling of shame that many of the army officers felt at the defeat, even when they did not feel personally responsible, led many to grope around to find friends with similar feelings with whom they could plan the coming "revenge." One such group was founded by the head of Pétain's bodyguard, Colonel Georges Groussard, and his friend, Heurteaux, vice-president of the Légion. One of their earliest recruits was a man who was to play a prominent role in the liberation of Paris and who would, twenty-five years later, rise to be prime minister to a president of the Republic who played no role at all in the underground struggle: Jacques Chaban-Delmas was the recruit who was later to become the premier; Georges Pompidou was the man who would become president.*

Groussard, in the second edition of his memoirs, grumbled that Chaban-Delmas (who was never known for his modesty) was an "honorable *résistant* who took great care that no one forgot it."

Of all the places in occupied Paris likely to give birth to a resistance movement, the Communist working-class districts with their revolutionary tradition or the turbulent student quarters of the Left Bank, surely the least likely was the prim science-oriented anthropological and ethnological museum, the Musée de l'Homme, in the stately Palais de Chaillot.† Who could believe that among the academic types so engrossed in their studies of the races of Man there would burn a patriotic fervor so bright and so consuming that only active resistance to the enemy would make it bearable?

To Boris Vildé, a naturalized Russian émigré, France was not only

* President Georges Pompidou died on April 2, 1974. One of the leading candidates for the presidency of the Republic was Jacques Chaban-Delmas, mayor of Bordeaux and deputy. He lost to Valéry Giscard d'Estaing, Pompidou's finance minister, who—at eighteen—had fought for the liberation of Paris.

† Erected for the Exposition of 1937, the Palais de Chaillot is across the Seine from the Eiffel Tower.

his new homeland, but a religion—an altar which was being desecrated by the gray-green Vandals in the streets. This religion he shared with his superior, Professor Paul Rivet, his colleagues, Anatole Lewitzky (also a naturalized Russian), Germaine Tillion, Yvonne Oddon (the librarian), and others, all strongly anti-German and—surprisingly for good French bourgeois—anti-Vichy. Their first pamphlet (September 25, 1940) was mimeographed, and several thousand copies quietly dropped in mailboxes, on post-office counters, in subway trains, or slipped into goods displayed in the department stores. It carried the title "Vichy Makes War!" and castigated Pétain for resisting the Anglo–Free French attempt to recover Dakar on September 23.

A large number of stickers bearing the legend "Vive de Gaulle" were printed on a typewriter with large type; these were plastered all over Paris, in the subway corridors, in telephone booths, and in the public urinals that were reputed to be the trysting places of homosexual collaborators.* The *résistants* took pleasure in following a German truck or staff car until it stopped for a red light and then surreptitiously pasting a call to resistance on the back of the vehicle. It might have been thought of as a childish prank—except that it could be, and later proved to be, fatal.

Boris Vildé was the heart and mainspring of the effort in the Musée de l'Homme. Strikingly handsome, with the piercing black eyes and high cheekbones of the western Slav, his black hair carefully brushed back, he was tireless in his new role. He traveled widely throughout France, recruiting, structuring, testing the feeling of the populace in all parts of the country. The work was slowly changing from propaganda and helping downed English pilots escape to Spain, to gathering information on the location of German army units, especially the Luftwaffe, air-field, and munition dump locations and the effects of British air raids. This vital military intelligence was sent south from Paris in the charge of a young boy, affectionately called "the kid."

On December 15, 1940, the first issue of *Résistance* appeared with the stirring words: "To resist! That is the cry that comes from everyone's heart in the distress that the Fatherland's disaster has left you. It is the cry of all of you who do not give up, of all of you who wish to do your duty." It then went on to warn them against feeling helplessly alone in the struggle, it told them how to seek out other patriots, how to form a *réseau*, and, above all, how to operate securely in the midst of informers and traitors. It was signed "The Committee of Public Safety," which to Frenchmen (who know their history so well) meant that it was to be identified with the committee of the

* ". . . Why are there so many homosexuals among the collaborators? Their joy is that of the inmates of a small town brothel when a regiment passes by."

same name during the French Revolution which included Danton, Robespierre, Carnot, and Saint-Just. It was also a warning that, like the men of the 1790s, they would not be afraid to shed blood, their own or others, for France.

In October, 1940, there appeared in Paris a single-sheet clandestine newspaper with the classical name of *Pantagruel.* Edited by the music publisher Raymond Deiss, whose love of France was all the stronger for having been born in Alsace, it claimed to be a simple information bulletin containing the BBC news, "of which too many people are deprived." Denying any appeal to "a vain struggle against the occupation authorities," it nevertheless reminded its readers "never to forget that the theory of *Deutschland über alles* means that everything and everyone should be crushed, if necessary, to make Germany great." Later, *Pantagruel* was to take a sterner position, castigating Vichy as well as the Germans, and calling for resistance under the banner of de Gaulle.*

The morning of December 24, 1940, was a cold, blustery day, and the Parisians hurrying to work under the steel-gray sky were astonished to see the walls covered with red-and-black posters The bilingual text (French on the right and German on the left) was identical:

The engineer
JACQUES BONSERGENT
of Paris
has been condemned to death by
a German military tribunal
for
an act of violence
against a member
of the German Army.
He was shot this morning.
Paris, December 23, 1940
THE GERMAN MILITARY COMMANDER IN FRANCE
von Stülpnagel

There was a stunned silence in the little crowd that gathered to read the posters, then men cursed under their breath and clenched their fists in the pockets of their overcoats. Wide-eyed, the women covered their lips and wept quietly. They thought of their sons, their husbands, their brothers and fiancés behind barbed wire in Germany,

* Raymond Deiss was beheaded in a German prison on August 24, 1943. The ax rather than a firing squad was used because of his Alsatian birth; he was considered not a French patriot but a traitor to Germany.

at the mercy of men who no longer thought it important to act "correctly." In the horror of the moment, they knew that this execution was only the beginning.

In spite of the stern warning of the flyer beneath the posters in which the *préfecture de police* warned the populace that any damaging of the posters "would be considered an act of sabotage and punished by the severest penalties," most of the notices were soon lacerated. Later that day, when the police had been posted to guard them, people knelt on the pavement in front of the ghastly "certificates of death" and prayed. When they left, there were small bouquets of flowers next to the wall.

It was Sunday, November 10, 1940, about nine o'clock at night that Jacques Bonsergent, twenty-eight years old, left the Gare Saint-Lazare with his newly married friend, Roger Abadie, the bride, and four friends. They had just returned from a wedding reception in the country for the young couple and now marched down the rue Saint-Lazare toward the subway. Paris was dark (someone later remembered that there had been an air-raid alert), but the festive group laughed, sang the forbidden *Tipperary*, and joked about the coming honeymoon.

What happened next has never been made clear. Some say that they blundered into a fight between German soldiers; others that a drunken German would not give way to the young people walking four abreast through the blackness and deliberately crashed into the group. One of the young men (but not Bonsergent) sent the Fritz tumbling into the canopy of a café—from which he came out swinging. At this point, Bonsergent stepped in to save his friend from the blow and started to struggle with the furious noncom. There were shouts, blows, and screams from the women in the confused struggle in the darkness. As other German soldiers came running up, the French scattered, but Jacques Bonsergent, conspicuous by his height, was grabbed and taken under arrest to a nearby military post.

When his friends met on the subway platform and discovered that he was missing, there was not a great deal of concern. No doubt it was annoying and would probably mean a few months in jail for poor Jacques, but certainly no more than that. In the military prison of Cherche-Midi, the young engineer had reached the same conclusion and calmly wrote to his older brother, Gabriel, asking that his boss be informed of his detention and requesting a razor, toothbrush, and a change of clothing.

But the next day, November 11, 1940—the anniversary of the great victory over Imperial Germany—something happened that drastically affected the fate of Jacques Bonsergent. Under the urgings of the

BBC and the nascent resistance elements in Paris, several thousand high-school and college students marched down the Champs-Elysées, flags and banners waving, singing *La Marseillaise* and shouting "Long live France, down with Pétain, down with Hitler!" This was a provocation that the Germans could not ignore. Aided by the French police, they charged into the demonstrators with clubs and rifle butts. Shots were fired and students arrested by the hundreds (the BBC claimed that eleven students had been killed by machine-gun fire,* but this was untrue.

Incensed by this display of French resistance and hostility, the German military command in France decided that an object lesson was needed; the iron fist would have to be taken from the velvet glove . . . and in the prison of Cherche-Midi there was a young Frenchman who had struck a German soldier.

Once instructed, the German court-martial worked quickly. Bonsergent, still ignorant of the fate that had been decreed for him, took sole responsibility for the altercation, refusing to name any of his companions. On December 5, he was condemned to death.

Even when the death sentence was read, the German officer who presented Bonsergent's defense was convinced that it would not be carried out; he assured his client that the sentence was strictly pro forma and that the Führer would undoubtedly grant an appeal for mercy "out of his respect for France." This may indeed have been true, for the Germans had been very lenient with minor acts of hostility toward the occupation authorities up to that time, but another event, more serious and demanding a strong reprisal, took place before the appeal could be acted on, and this sealed Bonsergent's fate.

On December 13, an irritated Pétain, convinced by his entourage that he was being led into a trap, refused Hitler's invitation to attend the return of the ashes of L'Aiglon, Napoleon's son, from its resting place in the Capuchin Chapel in Vienna to the Invalides. At the same time, the old Marshal, suspecting his vice-premier of attempting a coup d'état, demanded and received his resignation despite Laval's denials and bitter recriminations (as related in Chapter 4). This was a double affront to Hitler and one that could not be ignored; clearly the stubborn French were getting out of hand and a demonstration of their helplessness and of German force was called for.

Bonsergent's appeal for mercy was refused.

To his older brother in Lorient, the young engineer wrote on December 22:

* Jean Guéhenno, who witnessed the demonstration, says he heard three volleys of machine-gun fire, but the Paris hospitals report no violent deaths for that day. The Germans closed the Sorbonne and sent the students home.

> They have just told me that my plea for pardon has been refused. I am to be executed tomorrow morning.
>
> . . . I will die the victim of a mistake.
>
> . . . I am accused of having struck some German soldiers on the tenth of November when I only wanted to get between them and the real guilty party.
>
> . . . Above all, don't cry too much for me. I might have been killed at the front.
>
> *Votre petit,*
> Jacques

A German priest heard his confession and stayed with him during his last night while Bonsergent slept. In the morning, mass was said before the long ride to the rifle range at Vincennes.

"I would have preferred to die in battle," Bonsergent said wistfully to the priest. "And would you have been as ready for it as you are today, my son?" asked Abbé Stock.

Jacques Bonsergent refused the blindfold and stood free facing the firing squad. "He died brave, pious, and determined . . . " the priest wrote to his brother Gabriel.

He was the first of thousands of Parisians to fall before the salvos of a German firing squad, an unwilling witness to French resistance and a martyr to his ideal of friendship. When his brother published his death notice in the local paper—"condemned to death by the military tribunal of the army of occupation in Paris and shot on the twenty-third of December, 1940"—the German censor asked that it be published "discreetly." "Do you believe that you shot Jacques discreetly?" Gabriel Bonsergent asked bitterly.

Today travelers in the Paris subway in the direction of Porte de Clignancourt (between République and Gare du Nord) stop at the station named "J. Bonsergent." This is Paris's way of reminding its citizens daily what they owe to others.

When did the Resistance begin? Who first said "no" to the armistice, first refused to admit that France could be lost in one battle?

Two hours after hearing Pétain's radio broadcast of June 17 ("we must stop fighting . . . "), General Gabriel Cochet, the commander of the French 5th Army Air Force, called together his men and ordered them to get ready for resistance. His voice almost unrecognizable from the emotion that gripped him, he warned them of the dangers in the task that lay ahead. "Learn to conceal your actions and your emotions," he emphasized. "I know these Germans . . . " There was no doubt in the general's mind that the struggle would be a long and bloody one. As a former chief of army military intelligence, he knew not only the character of the enemy, but its power to crush opposition as well.

The ambiguity in the Marshal's announcement that he had asked for an armistice was to have terrible consequences. Uncertain as to whether "we must stop fighting" meant that they were required to lay down their arms and surrender, or to continue resisting until an armistice had been granted* and signed, some army units, already locked in battle with the advancing Germans, kept firing. In violation of all rules of warfare, the victorious Nazis treated them as *francs-tireurs* (guerrilla snipers) and shot them out of hand.

Did resistance begin with de Gaulle's broadcast of June 18, as Free French legend has insisted? There is no doubt that this was the first *call* to resistance—"No matter what happens, the flame of French resistance must not be extinguished and will not be extinguished . . ."; there is also no question that, in the midst of the fighting, the exodus, and the confusion, very few people were listening to the English radio (after the liberation, those who claimed to have heard the stirring call and acted on it were legion).

Even those who left France in June and July to reach England and continue the fight did so in ignorance of de Gaulle, his summons, and the presence of the Free French movement in London. The tall, slim, and blond Captain André Dewavrin arrived in England on June 21. The English officers who questioned him "talked a lot . . . about a certain general whose name they could not recall who . . . had made a summons to the French people." Refusing the English pressure to join their Intelligence Service (they were very disparaging about the Free French effort), Dewavrin hurried to London and joined de Gaulle. He was to become the head of the B.C.R.A.† (Free French Military Intelligence) under the name of "Colonel Passy" (which he took to protect his family from reprisals).

Gilbert Renault was working on location in Spain, writing and producing a film on Columbus, when France fell. He immediately returned to France, left his family with his wife's parents, and made his way to Lorient, near Brest. With the help of the port commandant, an old friend, he got passage on a trawler to England, arriving on June 18; he was crossing the Channel and out of touch with events when de Gaulle made his historic broadcast. As "Colonel Rémy," Renault was to head one of the most widespread and successful clandestine networks in France.

* The armistice was signed at Rethondes on June 22, 1940, to be effective upon the signing of a similar agreement with the Italians (June 24). To humiliate the French further, Hitler had the signing ceremony held in the same railway coach and on the same spot where Foch had received the surrender of the German armies in November, 1918. The armistice was signed for France by General Huntziger representing Pétain's government.

† Bureau Central de Renseignement et d'Action.

Should one classify as resistants of the first hour the twenty-six deputies (and one senator) who had sailed from Verdun on June 20, thinking that they were the advance guard of the new Pétain government that would continue the war from North Africa? They did not realize that they were walking into a trap set by their political enemies in Bordeaux who were determined to take France out of the war and to seek an accommodation with Hitler. Seeing an opportunity to avenge themselves on their old opponents of the discredited Third Republic, the men around Pétain permitted the *Massilia* to sail for Algiers with the unsuspecting parliamentarians aboard. No sooner had the ship cleared the port when the twenty-seven passengers were denounced as "traitors"; cables were sent to the authorities at Algiers to arrest them on their arrival. Among the men who were to suffer from this shabby intrigue were such notables as Daladier, Mendès-France,* Georges Mandel, and Jean Zay (the last two were murdered in 1944 by French Fascists).

Certainly among the earliest resisters must be named the humble fishermen of the tiny Channel islands of Senans and Batz. It was at Senans, on June 24, 1940, that the entire able-bodied male population, 130 men in all, set sail for England in the fishing boats upon which their livelihood depended. When the Germans arrived the next day, they found the tearful but proud women of Senans still standing on the beaches looking out to the empty sea. They were all clothed in black, "in mourning for our beloved France."

The sad distinction of being the first of the almost thirty thousand Frenchmen the Germans would put before a firing squad belongs to Etienne Achavanne, who, acting alone, cut the telephone lines between the German field headquarters and the German airfield at Boos on June 20. His sacrifice (he was shot at Rouen on July 6) was not in vain, for shortly thereafter the R.A.F. bombed the airfield, destroying eighteen planes and killing twenty-two German soldiers.

If resistance could only begin with Pétain's broadcast on June 17 or with de Gaulle's call to arms on June 18, is it proper to consider as *résistants* those deputies and senators who on July 10, 1940, at Vichy, voted a resounding "no" to giving full powers to Pétain to promulgate a new Constitution for France? Given the threats of Laval and his antirepublican friends, given the humiliation of the defeat and the complete repudiation of the Third Republic, it was truly a courageous act of defiance. Of these eighty men who would not allow the Republic

* Pierre Mendès-France, who was to be premier after the war, has very movingly told of his experiences in Algiers, his later court-martial and conviction for "desertion," and his escape from jail in Clermont-Ferrand in Marcel Ophuls's brilliant documentary, *The Sorrow and the Pity*, 1969.

and republican principles to die unchallenged, ten would be deported to German concentration camps; of those ten men five would never return and two would be murdered by French Fascists.

Except for the large French Communist party (whose ambiguous role in the first year of the occupation will be expanded upon in Chapter 5), the average Frenchman had no experience in clandestine activities. By nature a garrulous, undisciplined individual, he was accustomed to thwarting authority, disdaining symbols of rank, questioning orders, and insisting on his own political goals when they disagreed with those of the group. None of these traits was useful to the man or woman engaged in underground work against a powerful enemy; many of them proved time and again to be fatal. It was hard to teach a Frenchman to distrust other Frenchmen; his natural instinct was to see any compatriot as an ally against the occupant. The vital need for security, strict obedience to orders and procedures, the need to be constantly suspicious, to be merciless toward traitors and collaborators—all these had to be learned in a painful apprenticeship over the next two years. The prisons, the guillotine, the death camps, and the bullet-pocked walls of Fresnes and Vincennes testified to the fate of those who could not learn the necessary lessons fast enough.

In the very beginning, the Resistance—to the Germans, to the armistice, to Vichy—was an individual thing, or at most a matter of very small groups of close friends or relatives eager to bear witness against the defeat and humiliation of France. Usually, they started by helping French prisoners of war who had escaped from the temporary camps to reach safety in the unoccupied zone or conducting downed English fliers along the quickly established network that got them to Spain. Later, they began to put out propaganda, hastily typed in multiple copies or mimeographed, intended to sustain the morale of the apathetic populace, stir the will to resist, and give the information needed to counteract the lies from the Propagandastaffel (German military news agency) and the Vichy information bureau.

Because it was relatively safer to operate under the noses of the Vichy authorities than those of the Nazis, these little cells flourished mostly in the unoccupied zone: Frenay at Marseilles and Lyons; Loustaunau-Lacau and Groussard at Vichy, and other *résistants* in a thousand smaller towns and villages. Everywhere there was a Frenchman or a Frenchwoman who could not stomach the thought of a German standing on French soil as a conqueror; there the Resistance took root.

Soon the isolated groups, which were like dots randomly scattered across the map of France, began to make contact with each other. Someone in Lyons heard of a clandestine group in Clermont-Ferrand who had a printing press; an emissary arrived at night from Saint-

Etienne with news of a British agent in Nice; the local wine merchant received a guarded inquiry from his supplier in Paris as to "morale" in his area; and so on. Members of the Polish, Belgian, and Czech intelligence services, marooned in France by the defeat, began radio contact with London, using hidden transmitters. Under the outward appearance of stunned shock at the defeat, concentration on personal affairs, acceptance of Vichy leadership, and adoration of the Marshal, France was beginning to stir.

In Paris, as the black-and-red posters announcing the execution of Jacques Bonsergent blossomed on the walls, a bitter rhyme was whispered in the streets:

The Virgin Mary has been evacuated.
Saint Joseph is in a concentration camp.
The Three Kings are in London.
The ox is in Berlin.
The ass is in Rome.
So there will be no Christmas this year.

4
Vichy Plays Its Role

The problems facing the Pétain government in the summer and fall of 1940 were overwhelming: the feeding of the populace in the face of the widespread destruction of bridges, the dislocation of all transportation, and the lack of labor to harvest the crops; the crushing occupation costs (amounting to the 1940 equivalent of nine million dollars every day); the plight of the refugees, many of whom were unable to return home (Jews and Alsace-Lorrainers from the occupied zone in particular); and the millions who had been made unemployed by the exodus and the defeat. The solution to all these problems was complicated by the division of the country into two zones, with the Germans loosening and tightening passage across the demarcation line to put pressure on the Vichy government.

Yet, in spite of the formidable tasks that faced Pétain and his cabinet, they still remembered their "enemies" of the Third Republic. They set eagerly to work to make certain that their "enemies" remembered them.

No sooner had the new government settled in Vichy than it began to issue a series of repressive laws which effectively abolished the Rights of Man, that explicit statement of republican principles which had been written during the time of the French Revolution. For the first time, it was possible by ministerial decree to relieve any government official, functionary, or military officer of his post. The laws also deprived anyone who had left metropolitan France between the tenth of May and the thirtieth of June, 1940 (such as de Gaulle and his tiny band of followers), of French citizenship; they ordered the creation of a special High Court to try the ministers and ex-ministers of the Third Republic who "were accused of having committed crimes or misdemeanors in the exercise of their functions, or who had betrayed their responsibilities" (the first defendants would be Daladier, Blum, and General Gamelin); they instituted a review of all naturalizations and all citizenships granted to foreigners since 1927; and they closed all public offices to anyone born of a non-French father. On the thirteenth of August, 1940, a law prohibiting all secret societies was passed, and all public officials were ordered to take an oath that they did not belong to any secret association. This action was aimed directly at the Freemasons, long considered by the Right to have exercised secret political power under the Third Republic, but it was used even against such innocuous societies as the Theosophists.

On October 3, 1940, the first of a long series of anti-Jewish laws was passed; it was published in the *Journal officiel* on October 18. It has been claimed by apologists for Vichy that this legislation was the direct result of German pressure on the French government, but one can do no better than to quote Xavier Vallat, the first commissioner-general for Jewish affairs, who wrote, "The Alibert law—it is more convenient to indicate it by the name of the Minister of Justice who took the initiative in the matter—owes nothing at all to Nazism."

Also, according to the head of Pétain's office of civil affairs, du Moulin de Labarthète, "Germany was not the cause of Vichy's anti-Jewish legislation. This legislation was, so to speak, spontaneous and indigenous."

The Alibert law contained a number of provisions: it defined as a "Jew" anyone having more than two grandparents of the Jewish "race," or only two grandparents if the person under question had a Jewish spouse. This definition was even stricter than the repressive Nuremberg laws, which required not only that there be more than two grandparents of the Jewish religion, but that the person be presently practicing the Jewish religion. According to the French law, Jews were excluded from holding any public office or any directing role in the state administration. They were excluded from exercising any profession connected with the press, radio, cinema, or theater, and they could not be officers in the army or navy. The proportion of Jews to be admitted to the universities and to the liberal professions was to be regulated by the *numerus clausus* (that is, limited to a small percentage of the total).

To quote the historian Robert Aron, "In French law, as in German law, a Catholic priest of Jewish origin did not cease to be a Jew; while a Jew coming from a family that had been French for generations was still not considered to be wholly French."

According to the unrepentant Xavier Vallat, standing trial after the liberation:

> The Marshal's government did not forbid mixed marriages for Jews. It did not forbid them to have non-Jewish servants. It did not forbid their access to public places. It did not shut them

off in ghettos. It did not limit their circulation on public highways to certain hours. It did not force them to wear distinctive garments. It did not expel them from France.

At his trial, Vallat went on to define anti-Semitism as desirable from both a religious and a nationalistic point of view. He said that it was not desirable that members of a minority cult should have an influence in a Christian country, and that the Jew was an unassimilable and disruptive element in the French community; he proclaimed his "wish to defend the French organism from the microbe which was producing in it a fatal anemia."

Vallat was explicit in listing what Vichy did not accomplish in its anti-Semitic legislation, but what its anti-Jewish laws did do was to exclude the French Jews from public life and from any influence in the liberal professions. It also made it easier for the Germans later to identify them for deportation to the death camps. In light of what subsequently happened to the French Jewish community (see Chapter 12), all the specious arguments presented by men such as Vallat and the other Vichy apologists are horrifying.

In addition to the initial anti-Jewish legislation of October, 1940, the Vichy government repealed the law prohibiting slander or libel against a particular race or religion; this was announced as a return to freedom of the press. It also annulled the Crémieux law, which had granted French citizenship to the native Jews of Algeria.

The German occupation authorities had not waited for Vichy to announce its adoption of anti-Semitic measures. On September 27, 1940, the first German decree stated: (1) Jews who had left the occupied zone were forbidden to return; (2) All businesses having a Jewish manager or owner were to display a sign in their window—in French and German—announcing that the business was Jewish. The sign was to be 20 x 40 centimeters (about 8 x 16 inches), with the words "Jüdisches Geschäft" and "Enterprise juive" (using large black characters on a yellow background). A "Jewish business" was defined as one having more than half its capital belonging to Jews. The decree further ordered that all businesses belonging to Jews who had escaped to the unoccupied zone were to be put in the hands of an Aryan manager.

The sudden appearance of signs designating Jewish businesses in many of the finest shops in Paris gave birth to a number of witty stories at German expense. One of these told of the amorous German flier who followed a particularly attractive prostitute along the Champs-Elysées. He finally approached her and—in very bad French—tried to explain his proposition. She turned on him and in a withering tone said, *"Jüdisches Geschäft!"*

On October 3, 1940, the Germans ordered a census of Jews in the occupied zone to be carried out alphabetically at the commissariat of their quarter. All Paris heard the story of the eminent philosopher Henri Bergson, who, gravely ill and about to be converted to Catholicism, nevertheless sent his resignation to the university and, aided by two friends, went to the police station to register. The wits also related the story of the strange disappearance of the statue of the Virgin Mary and the Infant Jesus from Notre Dame. Upon being questioned, the sacristan explained that they had gone to the nearest police station: "It is their turn to register."

But the French anti-Semites and the native Fascists had not waited for the Nazis to show them the way. As early as August, signs had appeared in the windows of a number of stores, saying, "This establishment forbidden to Jews." Gangs of young Fascist toughs had roamed the streets, smashing the windows of Jewish stores; they were aided by the collaborationist press, which had listed the names of prominent Jews and Freemasons for their special attention. When *Au Pilori,* a violently anti-Semitic weekly, had listed the names of a number of prominent Jewish doctors, some of those named protested that they were able to prove their Aryan quality (if not their sense of solidarity with their Jewish compatriots) and were left undisturbed.

In addition to the Jews and Freemasons, Vichy was quick to vent its spite against the leaders of the Third Republic. In the month of September, 1940, such men as Reynaud (Pétain's predecessor as premier), General Gamelin, Daladier, Mandel, and Léon Blum were arrested and held in protective custody at the Château de Chazeron. It was contemplated that under the new law they would be brought to trial for the failures of the republican regime up to the declaration of war.

The purge in the upper ranks of the administration was severe. According to Aron, 49 prefects, 58 *sous-préfets,* and a considerable number of ambassadors were dismissed from public service. An approximate total of 2,282 civil servants of all grades were purged.

Trapped and helpless in the face of both French and German anti-Semitism, most French Jews submitted to their fate without complaint. But not all—a prominent lawyer, Pierre Massé, wrote a letter to Pétain which is worth quoting:

> Monsieur le Maréchal,
>
> I have read the decree which states that Jews, even those of strictly French ancestry, can no longer be officers.
>
> I would be obliged if you will let me know if I must now go and take away the officer stripes from: my brother, second lieutenant in the 36th Infantry Regiment, killed at Douaumont in

April 1916; from my son-in-law, second lieutenant in the 14th Motorized Dragoon Regiment, killed in Belgium in May 1940; from my nephew, J.-F. Massé, lieutenant in the 23rd Colonial Regiment, killed at Rethel in May 1940.

May I permit my brother to keep the military medal he won at Neuville-Saint-Vaast, and with which he was buried? May my son, Jacques, second lieutenant in the 62nd Battalion of the Chasseurs Alpines, wounded at Soupir in June, 1940—keep his officer's stripes?

Finally, can I be certain that they will not take away retrospectively the medal of Saint-Helena from my great-grandfather?

There was no answer from the Marshal.

In the fall and winter of 1940, the French Jews still had faith in Pétain—or, rather, in France. Many of them had been French for hundreds of years; their families had weathered many such anti-Semitic storms before, particularly during the turbulent days of the Dreyfus Affair, and they could not conceive of being anything—or being considered anything—but French.

They protested their loyalty and devotion to everything French in thousands of letters which poured into Vichy. No doubt, they told themselves, these severe measures were aimed at the foreign Jews: the Germans, the Poles, the Czechs, and that horrible mass of East European Jews who had flooded into France these past years. But they were French, their fathers and grandfathers had fought, bled, and died for France—surely, the Maréchal would protect them.

Those who knew from painful experience the real meaning and ultimate aim of German anti-Semitism, and who had accurately gauged the unwillingness of Vichy to protect them against the conquerors, sold their businesses, changed their names, and went into hiding. Many of them survived.

When the trial of the Third Republic was finally held in February, 1942, at Riom (just north of Clermont-Ferrand), it was an unmitigated disaster for Vichy. Although General Gamelin loftily refused to defend himself, Daladier succeeded not only in discrediting the trials as political (Pétain had already announced that the accused were guilty), but also in flaying the generals who had been called to testify to the lack of preparation for war. When, in the face of accurate statistics, the generals began to stammer, sweat, and suffer loss of memory, Daladier dismissed them contemptuously as "those who were my subordinates yesterday and will be my subordinates in the future."

Who was responsible, Daladier asked, for the failure to use the arms provided and for the faulty strategy employed? Obviously, it was the man who for so many years had presided over the Supreme War Council: Marshal Philippe Pétain.

As the trial dragged on, with Daladier and Blum using it as a forum to attack Pétain and the Germans, Hitler became more and more furious. The perfidious French were not trying their former leaders for having dared to declare war on him—they were trying them for not having been better prepared to defeat him!

Orders were wired to Abetz to demand that the trials be ended, a demand to which Vichy agreed with a sigh of relief. On April 14, the court was adjourned for a "supplemental inquiry."

It never met again.

The defendants were kept in prison until the Germans overran the unoccupied zone in November, 1942, and seized them. Thanks to Vichy's failure to move them to safety in time, they spent the rest of the war in Nazi concentration camps.

When, on May 19, 1940, in the face of the looming defeat, the members of the Reynaud cabinet trooped dutifully to attend a salvation mass at Notre Dame, the Church hierarchy must have greatly relished the sight of these notorious anticlerical ministers kneeling in prayer and bowing before the relics of the holy saints. The quarrel of the Roman Catholic Church with the Republic was a long and bitter one; like so many other divisive factors in French life, it had begun during the 1789 Revolution when Robespierre broke the Church's monopoly on the schools. It became most virulent in the late 1890s, when such political leaders as Jules Ferry and Emile Combes had forced the passing of legislation separating church and state, allowing for seizure of church property and discriminating against religious orders. From that time on, the Church's role in French politics had been a conservative, even a reactionary, one. Its determination to regain its favored position was supported by such Catholic monarchists as Charles Maurras, in his newspaper *L'Action française*.

The church hierarchy's reaction to the defeat was a strange and ambiguous one. Almost emulating the "divine surprise" of Maurras, Cardinal Gerlier, archbishop of Lyons, said on July 30, 1940, "If we had remained victorious, we would probably have remained the prisoners of our errors. Through being secularized, France was in danger of death."

There is no doubt that the Church, particularly the prelates, accepted Vichy wholeheartedly. It was clear that it saw in the new government a chance to restore the power and authority which had been taken from it by anticlerical ministers in the early years of the century. The hierarchy was almost totally favorable to Pétain, nearly to the point of canonizing him. In a message to the Pope by the assembly of cardinals and archbishops, it was stated, "We revere the head of state . . . "; and in speeches before their congregations and in the parochial schools, the clergy identified loyalty to Pétain and his government with loyalty to the Church itself. "Pétain is France and France is Pétain," one cardinal proclaimed.

Pétain welcomed the enthusiastic support of the Church. Although himself a nominal Catholic, he dreamed of restoring Christianity to France, and, "if he had not been stopped in time, he would have crushed the Church under the enormous weight of his favors." The hierarchy of the Church was prominent in all the official government ceremonies, and it held special position and power at Vichy.

Shortly after the armistice, the bishops asked Pétain to undo the work of Ferry and Combes. They asked for a revision of the anticlerical laws and subsidies for religious schools; they wished the catechism to be taught compulsorily in lay schools. Although this was not a return to the Falloux law of 1850 which had put all state schools under the control and authority of the bishops, it was a complete undoing of the anticlerical republican laws of the last sixty years.

The first minister of public education, Georges Ripert, started the work of revision along the lines requested by the Church, but the major impetus came when Jacques Chevalier replaced Ripert. Chevalier clericalized all the state schools and required the lay teachers to give religious instruction; these laws were passed on December 6, 1940. The result, of course, was a bitter conflict between the village priests and the village teachers. To enforce the laws, Chevalier ordered a purge of the teachers, but Jérôme Carcopino, who replaced Chevalier, tried to moderate the severity of the revision. While permitting parochial schools to receive state funds, he proclaimed the "religious neutrality" of the Vichy government.

Pétain, whose personal life had earlier been looked on askance by the Church, since he had in 1920 (at the age of sixty-four) married a divorcée in a civil ceremony, hastened to strengthen his links to the Church. He succeeded in getting Rome to annul his civil marriage and to permit a religious ceremony to be carried out by proxy in Paris. He also asked the advice of the Vatican on his anti-Semitic legislation and was told that the Pope would have no objection to it, provided only that the sanctity of a marriage between a Jew and a Catholic would be respected.

The ardent way in which the Church embraced Pétain and Vichy was to pose a severe dilemma to the many Catholics who were beginning to engage in the Resistance. It was difficult for them to reconcile loyalty to their Church and to their country when that Church proclaimed the highest loyalty to be absolute obedience to the Marshal. In time, however, the close bond between the Church and Vichy began to loosen—first, because of the growing opposition of the French people to the compulsory labor service (which the Church said would be no sin to avoid), and, second, because of the deportation of the Jews, which even the hierarchy deplored publicly and worked against. Still, it was Cardinal Suhard who welcomed Pétain to Paris in April, 1944, a gesture which was to earn him a snub by de Gaulle in August of the same year.

Collaboration was "that uncharted sea," to quote the perceptive Paul Baudouin,* the handsome young Vichy minister of foreign affairs. Angry at having been kept, at Laval's request, from the meeting at Montoire with Hitler, he could nevertheless see quite clearly that "collaboration" meant entirely different things to the Germans and to the Marshal. Where Pétain was trying to buy time by agreeing to a certain level of economic assistance, the Nazis were demanding French participation in the attack on England. But the French would never fight their former ally (as Pétain had told the American diplomats in Vichy), in spite of Mers-el-Kebir, Dakar, and similar British provocations. Not only were the French people still stunned by the defeat, but Vichy was aware through the reports of the prefects of the growing anti-German sentiment. Sick of war and slowly learning the reality of a German occupation, the French, while overwhelmingly loyal to the Marshal, were contemptuous of the men around him (particularly Laval) and distrustful of German aims.

The alliance between Pétain and Laval was an unnatural one. Not only did they differ in background and habits, but the events of the past thirty years had generated a mutual distrust that Laval's courting of the Marshal and his maneuvers to obtain full powers for the new head of *L'Etat français* never dissipated. A senior army officer like Pétain, accustomed to giving orders to a devoted staff that could be depended upon to carry them out without question, could never really overcome his dislike of the shifty parliamentarian who even in the midst of the National Revolution could not help showing preference for his buddies from the old days.

Then there was the constant irritation of the attacks on the Marshal and his associates from the rabid Paris press. In the van of this outpouring of vituperation were the columns of *L'Oeuvre*, edited by Marcel Déat, a close friend and political ally of Vice-Premier Laval. Constantly flaying the Vichy government for its policy of "attentisme" —waiting to see if the Nazis would really win the war—and its failure

* Baudouin, a noted World War I flier and an undersecretary of state in Reynaud's government, was, like General Weygand, illegitimate. As Professor Robert Paxton has pointed out, the Vichy cabinet, which was determined to lead France to a New Moral Order, was headed by a "reformed" roué like Pétain and included two upper-class bastards.

to integrate a submissive France into the New European Order, Déat was considered by Pétain's entourage as no less an enemy than the Germans themselves. For failing to silence *L'Oeuvre* and the other collaborationist newspapers in Paris, Laval was suspected by Pétain and his intimates of wishing to push the old Marshal into the purely ceremonial role of head of state and to assume all power and the directing role in a new ultracollaborationist government.

Nor was this the only grievance that Pétain secretly nursed against Laval. There were Laval's many trips to Paris to negotiate with Otto Abetz—trips of which Pétain, accustomed to complete written reports, received only the most cursory of verbal summaries. There was the constant traffic between the German embassy in Paris and such detested and mistrusted men as de Brinon and Luchaire, who continued the negotiations with the Germans and reported the results only to Laval. Foreign affairs had been taken over exclusively by the vice-premier; it was an area in which he prided himself on his adroitness in spite of the signal failure of his diplomatic enterprises in the thirties. This, of course, earned him the enmity of Paul Baudouin, particularly after Laval had managed to exclude him from the Montoire meeting.

Pétain admitted to his friends that he retained Laval, even though he had quickly lost confidence in him, out of gratitude for his work before the National Assembly in June. But with the sly Marshal gratitude had to be earned constantly. It was a case of "What has he done for me lately?" and the answer, in spite of Laval's almost ceaseless activity, was "Not much." The demarcation line still cut like an impenetrable wall across the center of France and down the Atlantic Coast, preventing the free flow of refugees and commerce; the crippling occupation costs had been set at 400 million francs (about nine million dollars) *per day*, and there seemed no hope of getting them lowered; two *départements* in the northwest had been turned over to the German military administration in Belgium; Alsace-Lorraine was reannexed to the Reich (shortly after Montoire, Gauleiter Joseph Bürckel had started the mass expulsion of pro-French Lorrainers, shipping them in cattle cars to the unoccupied zone)—all these things had occurred in spite of Laval's boasts of his good relations with Abetz and his hints of how terrible things would have been if he had not held high office.

Then there was the matter of the Bor copper mines in Yugoslavia, whose French owners had been pressured by Laval into selling the controlling interest to the Nazis. The Belgian gold reserves which had been entrusted to France for safekeeping at the outbreak of the war were returned to metropolitan France from safekeeping in North Africa to be seized by the Germans. In ordering this done, Laval had bypassed the finance minister, Yves Bouthillier, thus creating another implacable enemy in the cabinet.

For this servile complaisance, Laval had hoped to gain some assurance from Hitler that the French empire would remain untouched by the ultimate peace treaty. The question had been raised at Montoire, where the Führer had given an evasive answer (he had already promised Morocco and Oran to Franco, and Nice, Corsica, Tunisia, and French Somaliland to Mussolini), but Laval had persisted in raising the question time and again, always yielding to German demands and receiving nothing in return but vague promises. Meanwhile, Chad, French Equatorial Africa, and the Cameroons had gone over to de Gaulle.

The French colonies, plus the fleet, were among France's few remaining bargaining points with Hitler, and the loss of even the smallest of the colonies was painful to contemplate. Laval was pushing for French armed action to recover the dissident colonies which had joined de Gaulle. In a meeting with General Walter Warlimont of O.K.W.* Operation Staff on November 29, 1940, Laval bluntly stated that France was prepared to risk war with England by an armed attack to recover Chad. Obviously unaware that the Marshal, through Professor Rougier, had come to a secret agreement with Churchill pledging that no action would be taken to recover the French colonies which voluntarily joined de Gaulle (in return for certain British concessions on the embargo of food from North Africa to metropolitan France), Laval asked that a certain number of officers and soldiers be released from the German prison camps to reinforce the French armistice army of 100,000 officers and men in the military action in North Africa. Military action, however, was a far cry from the economic cooperation which, to Pétain, was the spirit of Montoire. Therefore, when word of Laval's meeting with Warlimont reached the Marshal, he was determined that the vice-premier would have to leave the government.

There was also a great deal of personal antagonism between Pétain and Laval. An old Socialist and pacifist like Laval was not one to defer to soldiers, no matter how exalted their rank. Laval's work habits, his sloppy dress, his failure to report completely and in writing were anathema to the rigid Marshal. Also, his habit of blowing cigarette smoke in the Marshal's face did not endear him to the nonsmoking Pétain. "We, Philippe Pétain . . ."—this monarchic formula was characteristic of Pétain's concept of his position and dignity; one simply did not blow smoke into the face of Louis XIV.

To the men around Pétain, the Marshal's desire to rid himself of his troublesome vice-premier was apparent. It was Finance Minister Bouthillier who took it upon himself to organize the conspiracy. He

* Oberkommando der Wehrmacht—German Army High Command.

secretly contacted those members of the cabinet whom he knew to be favorable to dumping Laval; Admiral Darlan, for one, quickly gave his support: "Count on me. I'll risk it with you." Less than a month later, Darlan completely denied any role in the conspiracy. To Jacques Benoist-Méchin, he said, "I was neither for nor against Laval. Nobody consulted me. That evening [of December 13, 1940, when Laval was dismissed], I went calmly to the cinema, and heard nothing of the affair until the following morning." The other cabinet ministers who agreed to support Bouthillier were more faithful to their word, although there was great fear of Laval, whose furious temper was notorious.

On the morning of December 12, 1940, the plot was set in motion by an unexpected announcement from Berlin. General Laure telephoned du Moulin de Labarthète (the head of Pétain's civil cabinet) to say that the Germans had announced the imminent transfer of the remains of the duc de Reichstadt from its resting place in the Capuchin Church in Vienna to Napoleon's Tomb in the Invalides. The body of Napoleon's son, who had died in his mother's native Austria in 1832, was being returned to Paris by order of the Führer; there it would rest beside that of the father. The Marshal was invited by Hitler to attend the ceremonies, which would take place at midnight, December 14, amid the flare of torches in the *caveau* of the Invalides, one hundred years to the day that the emperor's body had been returned from St. Helena.

There was consternation among the conspirators at Vichy. This sudden decision to return the body of Napoleon's son and the attendant ceremony was seen as a trap. Pétain would be persuaded to attend in person; in Paris, surrounded by the Germans, he would be forced to sign documents naming Laval as the new head of the government with himself as the symbolic head of state. Through their contacts in Paris, word had reached the cabinet that certain German officials were talking about the imminent formation of "a more docile French government."

At 5 P.M., Laval telephoned du Moulin de Labarthète to confirm the arrangements for the Marshal's trip to Paris. He was extremely enthusiastic about Hitler's gesture and hinted that the government would soon be able to move to Versailles, a change that had long been contemplated and that had even been allowed for in the armistice agreement. When du Moulin de Labarthète expressed some reservations about the Marshal's willingness to attend the ceremony surrounded by Germans, Laval bluntly ordered him to tell the Marshal that he was coming immediately to Vichy to accompany Pétain to Paris. The telephone exchange was sharp on both sides (Laval noted that it was "without courtesy"), for Laval was determined that Pétain should come to Paris, and du Moulin de Labarthète and the other conspirators were equally determined that he should not. The crisis had arrived, and with Laval coming to Vichy the next day, the time had come to strike.

At 4 P.M. on December 13, Laval arrived from Paris with de Brinon. He immediately went to see Pétain in the Marshal's office, and flattered the old man with details of the ceremony and a later trip through the occupation zone. The Marshal, who always tended to agree with the last man who spoke to him, was thrilled by the idea of a triumphal tour of such towns as Rouen, Alençon, and Bourges, and agreed to attend, even allowing Laval to talk him into taking only military men with him and none of his ministers.

Du Moulin de Labarthète, who was present at the interview, quickly left and summoned the other conspirators to his office. Present were Admiral Darlan (navy), Baudouin (foreign affairs), Peyrouton (interior), Huntziger (war), Bouthillier (finance), and several others, including General Laure, the head of Pétain's military cabinet. Because of Laval's insistence that no ministers be present in Paris, they were convinced that it was a plot to isolate Pétain and form an ultracollaborationist government with de Brinon, Luchaire, Déat, and Doriot.

Each of the conspirators had a personal reason for hating Laval; but still they hesitated to act, for there was a general fear of what the German response to Laval's dismissal might be. The plotters knew too that, if they failed, Laval's revenge would be a terrible one.

General Laure expressed the thought that Laval was popular in the unoccupied zone, although the others disagreed. But Yves Bouthillier prevailed with his insistence that there was no turning back now. Peyrouton, who controlled the police, took the responsibility for arresting Laval, but he demanded a unanimous vote, which was reluctantly given. It was agreed to hold the scheduled 5 P.M. cabinet meeting to avoid alarming Laval, and then to call another one at 8 P.M., at which time Laval would be forced to resign and then quickly arrested. A committee of the conspirators was designated to inform the Marshal of their plans.

It did not take the committee long to convince Pétain of the necessity for Laval's dismissal and arrest. Faced once again with a forceful group of men, the Marshal switched sides quickly and reiterated his old arguments against his vice-premier. He agreed that the dismissal should take place at the 8 P.M. cabinet meeting, which he ordered du Moulin de Labarthète to call.

The 5 P.M. meeting of the council of ministers went off as scheduled, with Laval in the chair. The vice-premier waxed enthusiastic about the magnificent gesture that Hitler had made in returning the body of Napoleon's son to the French people. The details of Pétain's

OCCUPIED PARIS: German signposts dominate the Place de l'Opéra. In the background is the local Kommandantur (seat of the occupation authorities). (*Wide World.*)

PETAIN AND HITLER SHAKE HANDS AT MONTOIRE: In the center is Hitler's interpreter, Dr. Paul Schmidt, who later wrote, "It was . . . a Marshal talking to a corporal." (*Wide World.*)

PETAIN'S CABINET IN OCTOBER, 1940: (l. to r.) General Huntziger (war); Alibert (justice); Marshal Pétain (premier); Baudouin (foreign affairs); Admiral Darlan (navy); Caziot (agriculture and food); Peyrouton (interior); Laval (vice-premier); Bouthillier (finance); Belin (production and labor). (*Keystone.*)

Opposite: THE COFFIN OF L'AIGLON ARRIVES AT THE INVALIDES: On the one-hundredth anniversary of the return of the body of Napoleon I from St. Helena, the coffin of his son was brought from Vienna to the Invalides in Paris—a gift from Adolf Hitler. (*Keystone.*)

JACQUES DORIOT: The "man in the green suspenders" addresses the faithful of the P.P.F. (*Keystone.*)

FERNAND DE BRINON: Congratulating a newly decorated French officer. Behind him is Colonel Edgar Puaud, commander of the L.V.F. —French volunteers who fought alongside the Germans on the eastern front. In the rear is Joseph Darnand, head of the Vichy Milice. (*Keystone.*)

attendance at the ceremony were discussed and approved. The meeting broke up quickly.* When Laval later learned of the unexpected 8 P.M. meeting, he asked du Moulin de Labarthète for an explanation, but received only a shrug of the shoulders and the information that the Marshal himself had called it.

At 8 P.M., the cabinet gathered once again in the council room. The meeting was a short one, lasting only twenty minutes, but it was nonetheless a dramatic one. Pétain entered and opened the meeting by demanding that all present sign a general letter of resignation, which he then presented to them. Thinking that this was a means of ridding the cabinet of certain ministers to whom he had objected, Laval, unsuspecting, signed the letter. Pétain then took the letter of resignation and left the room for several minutes; when he returned, he announced calmly that only the resignations of Monsieur Laval and Monsieur Ripert were accepted.† Astonished, Laval blurted, "I think that there must be a mistake, Monsieur le Maréchal!" "Oh no, Monsieur Laval, there's no mistake," the Marshal answered smoothly. "I no longer have confidence in you. You have dragged France too far." Pétain went on to complain about Laval's sloppy work habits, his complete acceptance of all the German demands, his failure to keep the Marshal informed on negotiations with the occupation authorities, and the silence with which Laval greeted the attacks that his friends in Paris were making on the Vichy government. Finally, the Marshal said coldly, "I have had enough. I require that you leave the government."

Laval stood up and in a firm voice pointed out the consequences of his dismissal. "You are going to wipe out at a single stroke everything I have done for France during the last three months. The Germans will know that, by sending me away, you are really turning your back on collaboration. They will understand that you are their enemy, that you no longer even respect the armistice. Without thinking, you are throwing yourself into the maddest adventure. Blood will flow. I hope none of it stains you, Monsieur le Maréchal." With this grim warning, Laval left the council room.

Earlier in the day, du Moulin de Labarthète had telephoned to General Fornel de la Laurencie, Vichy representative in the occupied zone, giving him the code message that Marcel Déat was to be arrested in Paris at 9 P.M.‡ When he returned to his room, du Moulin de

* Raphaël Alibert, minister of justice, with all the fervor of a recent convert, hurried to church to seek divine approval of the conspiracy.

† Georges Ripert, secretary of state for public education, was an innocent party to the events of December 13; not only had he previously announced his desire to resign, but the post was earmarked for Jacques Chevalier, the friend of Lord Halifax.

‡ The message was, "La Maréchale [Madame Pétain] passed the demarcation line at 9 o'clock."

Labarthète was horrified to learn that de la Laurencie had obviously forgotten the meaning of the prearranged code message and had not understood the telephone call at all—he believed that Madame Pétain was truly traveling to Paris. Thus no action had been taken to arrest Déat. He immediately telephoned the general and repeated the sentence loudly. This time de la Laurencie understood, and Déat was arrested shortly afterward by the Paris police.

Later that night, Laval paced furiously back and forth in his office at the Hôtel du Parc. He had just been warned by an American correspondent that his chauffeur had been arrested and that all trains and telephone calls from Vichy had been halted. Fearing for his life, he searched his pockets for something with which to defend himself, and came up only with a pocketknife. "I tell you," he said to du Moulin de Labarthète, who had come to his office to keep an eye on him, "they want my skin, and I have nothing with which to defend myself. What bastards!" He was upset and nervous, but du Moulin de Labarthète noted admiringly that he was not a coward. Yet Laval *was* superstitious—and it was Friday the thirteenth.

As Ménétrel (Pétain's physician) and du Moulin de Labarthète were trying to calm him, the door opened and Commissioner Mondanel, who made a specialty of arresting important political personages, entered with an order to take Laval to his home in Châteldon. Suspicious, Laval asked, "Do you have this order?"—"Yes, Monsieur le Président."*—"All right. I believe you. I don't have to read your paper. Just let me have five minutes." Shortly thereafter, accompanied by Mondanel and four armed guards, Laval left the Hôtel du Parc.

Behind them, the hotel was in an uproar. On the second floor, which contained Laval's offices and the rooms of his staff, twenty members of the Groupes de Protection (Pétain's bodyguard) ran through the corridors, entering each room and arresting the occupants. Du Moulin de Labarthète, who had just left Laval's offices, was one of the first to be arrested. He protested that he really belonged on the third floor. "Well, it's not written on your mug," said the young leather-jacketed tough who had grabbed him. "Let's go!" Luckily, du Moulin de Labarthète was recognized by one of the leaders (Méténier) of the Groupes de Protection—a man whom du Moulin de Labarthète described as having "the hands of a strangler and the heart of a shopgirl." This strange character had him freed.

Laval's staff spent the rest of the night huddled in bed with their wives, under the cold watchful eye of a crash-helmeted policeman armed with a submachine gun. No one slept.

* * *

* Laval was vice-president of the Council of Ministers.

Saturday afternoon, word was received in Vichy (still worried by the lack of a response from Hitler to the "palace revolution") that Abetz had obtained the release of Déat by threatening armed action. In an effort to reassure the French people, as well as the Nazis, the Marshal made a radio speech at 7:30 P.M.: "People of France, I have just made a decision which I believe to be in the country's interest. Monsieur Pierre Laval is no longer in the government. Monsieur Pierre-Etienne Flandin is now in charge of foreign affairs. Constitutional Act Number Four, which designated my successor [Laval], is annulled. . . . [These actions] in no way affect our relations with Germany. I remain at the helm. The National Revolution goes forward."

In spite of the Marshal's conciliatory words, Hitler's wrath was still to be feared. Would it mean reprisals on the 1.9 million French prisoners of war? An increase in the already crushing occupation costs? New demands on French labor, materials, and industrial production? In Vichy, they waited fearfully, amazed at their own audacity in daring to provoke the powerful Führer.

Sunday night, December 15, 1940.

Paris, which had buzzed frantically all weekend at the news of Laval's dismissal, was asleep, dreaming of warm rooms and full stomachs. Those few citizens who by necessity were in the streets after curfew wrapped their coats tighter about them as protection against the gusts of snow and sleet. In the darkness and the blackout, there were few indeed who saw the strange convoy that moved slowly along the banks of the Seine toward the Invalides. Preceded by four motorcyclists, a caisson towed by a tractor carried a large bronze coffin draped with a black funeral cloth on which rested several bouquets of roses. Six field guns and a dozen cars followed the royal hearse through the inky night. The silence was eerie; they appeared out of the black night and then vanished into it, leaving the handful of viewers wondering if this was some macabre procession from the banks of the Styx. Only the drone of the motors and the sucking sound of the wheels on the wet streets broke the deep silence. It was midnight.

In the courtyard of the Invalides, the light was dazzling. Two hundred Republican Guards, resplendent in polished cuirasses and plumed helmets, held resin torches that cast flickering lights into the far corners of this citadel of French military glory. From a huge vessel mounted on a tall tripod, incense floated in the icy air. Waiting silently near the gate that led to the esplanade facing on the Place Vauban were several hundred distinguished guests, high government officials, members of the Paris municipal administration, ambassadors, even Pétain's friend, the well-known actor–playwright Sacha Guitry; representing the Marshal and the Vichy government were Admiral Darlan and generals Laure and de la Laurencie. Nervously shivering as much from apprehension as from the cold, they waited for the cortège to arrive. The only sound was the sputtering of the torches under the snowflakes.

Otto Abetz had just left the German embassy on the rue Ulm, after a press conference in which he had carefully praised Laval as the only man the Germans trusted to carry out the policy of collaboration agreed upon at Montoire (in the back of the room, Doriot listened carefully). Abetz had spoken grimly of "certain reactionary changes" and had reminded his audience of French and foreign correspondents that it was England who had exiled Napoleon, whose son's remains were being returned today "to rest forever in the soil of France." He also reminded them that it was the Führer who had planned this generous gesture.

De Brinon, soon to be Vichy representative to the German occupation authorities, had replied to Abetz and thanked Hitler for this gesture "worthy of a great leader and a very great man." The two spokesmen then left for the ceremony at the Invalides.

At 1:20 A.M. the convoy moved slowly into the esplanade of the Invalides. Carried by twenty-four German soldiers, the coffin was moved into the courtyard through the billowing sheets of snow. There, Abetz and General Otto von Stülpnagel, head of the Militärbefehlshaber in Frankreich, made the formal transfer of the remains of Napoleon II, once king of Rome, to Admiral Darlan "on behalf of the Führer." Darlan mumbled his thanks "on behalf of the French state," then twenty-four Gardes Républicaines took the coffin from the Germans and, amid the shrill sound of bugles and the rolling of drums, carried it at a funereal pace into the emperor's tomb and placed it under a tricolor flag before the altar.

Thus, one hundred years to the day that the body of the Emperor Napoleon was returned to Paris from its grave on Saint Helena, the remains of his son—L'Aiglon, the Eaglet—were reverently placed next to the impressive porphyry tomb of the father. It had snowed on December 15, 1840, too, but a million Parisians had braved the blizzard to stand on the Champs-Elysées and shout "*Vive l'Empéreur!*"; bearded veterans of the Grand Army that he had led to victory on a hundred bloody fields and to disaster in the endless icy wastes of Russia had bowed their heads and wept as the imperial catafalque passed.

But this time it was very different. The bronze coffin of the duc de Reichstadt (to give the unhappy Napoleon II his Austrian title) had been sneaked in the dead of night, almost secretly, into the capital—the gift of an Austrian who had humbled the French armies and who held France in his iron grip. Not even the most ardent of Bonapartists who had prayed for this day for over a hundred years would have wanted it under such auspices.

The coffin was banked by dozens of large floral wreaths, one of which carried the inscription "le Maréchal Pétain." There had been another wreath made of pansies and orchids with a red streamer marked with a swastika: "Chancellor Hitler to the duc de Reichstadt," but it never arrived inside the Invalides. Revolted at the thought of the Nazi emblem next to the emperor's tomb, a patriotic Frenchwoman had stolen it earlier in the day and burned it.

Nor were father and son to be left together in the peace of eternity. Unwilling to accept the arrangements made by Vichy and the Nazis, de Gaulle later had the coffin of the son moved from the chapel and placed in another part of the Invalides, next to the marble statue of the emperor in his coronation robes. There it now rests.

In the sumptuous château he had bought in his hometown to celebrate his political and financial success, Pierre Laval spent four anxious days. The house and grounds were covered by the Groupes de Protection, any one of whom would have been happy to "bump him off," and the deposed vice-president knew that his enemies in the Vichy cabinet were capable of giving the order. But he was not forgotten by his German friends in Paris.

On Monday night, December 16, Otto Abetz arrived suddenly in Vichy with an armed S.S. escort. The next day, he met with the Maréchal and expressed "amazement" that Laval was being kept under house arrest in Châteldon. In the most innocent tones, Pétain claimed to know nothing of this and ordered du Moulin de Labarthète to fetch Laval.

The stormy interview between the wily Marshal and the furious Laval shocked even Abetz. "Puppet, windbag, weathercock turning in every breeze"—these were some of the terms the ex–vice-president used to denounce the head of state (according to du Moulin de Labarthète, who was listening at the door). Finally, Laval and Abetz left the meeting room and departed together from Vichy. Later that night, they motored to Paris.

Laval had indignantly refused the post of minister of labor that Pétain had offered him as a sop to the Germans. Now he was out of the government and even more firmly in the ranks of the Paris collaborationists. Abetz was content; Laval in Paris was almost as good as Laval in Vichy. At least now with the spirit of Montoire dead, the French could make no more silly demands for revision of the armistice terms.

The dismissal of Laval and the Marshal's refusal to attend the ceremony at the Invalides affected the fate of more than one man. General de La Laurencie, who had shivered in the snowstorm before the coffin of Napoleon II, was dismissed on December 18 from his post as the French representative to the occupied zone and replaced by the more pliant de Brinon. Pierre-Etienne Flandin, an old parliamentarian and a suspected pro-German,* became Vichy minister of foreign affairs, and, although he served only two months, would be tried before the High Court after the liberation. In addition, to express more strongly Hitler's displeasure at this new independence on the part of the conquered French, Jacques Bonsergent was shot on December 23.

To the average Frenchman, shivering in the winter cold and constantly hungry, the return of the remains of the king of Rome was a matter of complete indifference. While the collaborationist newspapers hailed this evidence of the Führer's good will toward France, the Parisians whispered cynically, "He takes our coal and sends us ashes!"

* He had sent a telegram of congratulation to Hitler at the time of Munich and had opposed the declaration of war.

5
Francs-Tireurs et Partisans

At eight o'clock on the morning of August 21, 1941, the subway station at Barbès-Rochechouart was crowded as the people of this working-class district gathered for the trip to their shops, offices, and factories. After more than a year of the German occupation, they, like the majority of Parisians, were tired, hungry, and under a great strain.* The newspapers that morning carried accounts of further Nazi victories in Russia, including the furious battles around Smolensk; there seemed to be no stopping the victorious German armies. In this part of "Red Montmartre," not far from Sacré-Coeur and the Gare du Nord, the French Communist party was very strong, and pro-Soviet sentiment was widespread. For years, the party had boasted of the strength of the Soviet army under the leadership of Stalin, and yet . . .

0800. Three young men came down the stairs onto the crowded platform. It is unlikely that anyone noticed them, for they looked like three more young workers on their way to their jobs, probably in one of the factories working for German war production. If anyone had been perceptive enough, he would probably have been struck by the smallest of the three youths, the one with the thin face and the strange fire in his eyes. Nervously darting glances through the crowd, he seemed to be keeping himself under control with some difficulty.

Pierre-Félix Georges (known to his comrades as "Fredo") was twenty-two years old in 1941. Intense, jeering, cynical, and very sure of himself, he was a typical former Paris street urchin; however, he was also a veteran Communist militant. Born in Paris on January 21, 1919, he had first worked as an apprentice in an aircraft factory. At the age of seventeen he had served in the International Brigade in Spain as a dynamiter (like Robert Jordan in Hemingway's *For Whom the Bell*

* Jean Guéhenno wrote in his journal on this day: "The atmosphere grows heavier and heavier; it is unbreathable . . . some Jews are arrested, some Communists shot. Every morning new posters invite us to inform and threaten us with death. . . . In this 'revolutionary' neighborhood where I live . . . the people who have been resigned for so long now despair. . . . The news from Russia is bad."

Tolls). Also, like Jordan, he had operated behind the Nationalist lines, on one occasion attacking the rebel staff headquarters with a commando of forty men. Badly wounded in this attempt, he was invalided from the Republican army and arrived home in France in time to be arrested in the roundup of Communist leaders ordered by the Daladier government after the declaration of war. On a train that was transferring him from one prison camp to another, he strangled the guard with the handcuffs that secured his wrists and escaped. For a while he had served in the Marseilles area, distributing pro-Communist propaganda, but soon was ordered by the clandestine Central Committee of the party to come to Paris to undertake a new job.

On a whispered order from Fredo, the second man, known as "Bob," moved to the far end of the platform where, unnoticed, he could cover the other two and later report on what had occurred. The third youth in the group, Gilbert-André Brustlein, was, like Fredo, short. According to the fugitive warrants which were later issued for him, he was five feet four inches tall, with chestnut-brown hair, a straight nose, brown eyes, and an average build. He was described as being usually clean-shaven, but sometimes wearing a small mustache, and walking with his head lowered. On occasion he was known to wear glasses, but today he wore neither the mustache nor the glasses. He was new to this work; until a few weeks ago he had been engaged in putting up pro-Communist posters in the district and writing "Long live the Soviet Union" on the walls of deserted streets. He was very nervous.

Fredo's calm air hid the intensity of the violence that was bottled up inside him. His eyes ceaselessly moved from point to point in the crowd, looking for the prey. He ignored the many German soldiers, ordinary infantrymen for the most part, who were on the platform. They were a familiar sight in occupied Paris, but this morning he was looking for bigger game.

0812. Disappointed and upset, Fredo turned and whispered to Brustlein, "It'll be lousy if one of them doesn't show up." At this moment, a tall young German naval cadet walked down the steps and onto the platform. Unaware of the triumphant look that lighted Fredo's eyes, the German made his way politely through the crowd to the point where the first-class carriages would stop and stood there patiently, his back to the two young men. "That's the one that's going to pay," Fredo muttered. The two Frenchmen moved carefully through the dense crowd until they were directly behind the young Nazi officer. Nonchalantly putting his hand into the pocket of his jacket, Fredo took the safety off the 6.35 (.25 caliber) Belgian automatic that rested there. It was a woman's gun, meant to frighten, not kill; it had been given to him by a friend who had "borrowed" it from his mother. Brustlein also had a gun; it was thought best on an important job like this to have two guns, because the firearms they had frequently jammed.

0817. The train pulled into the station and stopped with a screech. The doors to the white first-class carriage opened and the German naval officer moved forward to enter it. He placed one foot inside the train.

Fredo swiftly pulled his gun from his jacket and shot the officer twice in the middle of the back. The German twisted and fell into the train, his feet dangling on the platform.

Instantly, Fredo ran alongside the train toward the stairs, pointing at an imaginary fugitive and shouting, "Stop him! Stop him!"

For a moment, Brustlein was paralyzed by the noise of the explosions. He stood in front of the body, the pistol hanging limply from his hand; then he turned and ran toward the staircase. On the stairs, a passerby, thinking that a robbery had taken place, grabbed him around the head, but Brustlein twisted loose and ran up the steps, through the automatic doors, and into the street. In a moment, he had disappeared into the back street and was safe.

The frightened crowd stood quietly, staring at the body of Naval Cadet Alphonse Moser, still crumpled in the open door of the train. No one touched him. Soon some German soldiers arrived, took Moser by the shoulders and feet, and carried him off; one of them lifted Moser's white cap from the floor of the train and placed it carefully on the dead man's stomach. No one in the crowd had interfered; no one had seen anything. It was better that way.

A few minutes later, Gilbert and Fredo met in back of Sacré-Coeur. The young veteran was highly excited: "We got even for Titi!"* he exulted.

The twists and turns of the French Communist party between the two wars were enough to confuse even the most ardent and disciplined of its members, but there was one consistent thread to all its actions: the interests of the Soviet Union were always paramount, and came before the interests, even the defense, of France. After World War I, in an effort to inhibit the anti-Soviet actions of the French government, the party was vigorously antimilitarist and voted regularly against all military budgets and all proposals to extend the term of military service, as well as denying even the principle of national defense. It was in line with this general policy that Jacques Doriot, at that time a rising young Communist leader, would send a telegram of congratulation to the leader of the Moroccan rebels. After all, rebellion in Morocco meant that the French army was not available to be used against the Soviets.

* Titi was Szmul (Samuel) Tyszelman, who together with another young Communist militant, Henri Gautherot, had been arrested during a demonstration on August 13, 1941 and shot six days later.

The party stressed propaganda in the army in an effort to lower morale to the point where the sending of troops to fight against Soviet Russia would be impossible; it stressed to the workers in uniform that they had only one enemy: their own bourgeoisie.

The first great twist in this policy came two years after the rise of Hitler to power. In 1935, the Soviet Union called for an anti-Fascist front among the Western democracies. In line with this new directive, the French Communist party now came out in favor of military expenditures, extension of the term of military service, and the general strengthening of defenses against the menace across the Rhine. They joined the Popular Front government in 1936 and were in fact its most dynamic element in pointing out the Fascist menace. The party forced a reluctant Léon Blum secretly to help Republican forces in Spain, while the Western democracies, including France, by an ineffective embargo of all arms, allowed Italy and Germany to aid Franco. In September, 1938, the betrayal of Czechoslovakia at Munich was strongly denounced by the party as a betrayal of the anti-Fascist alliance. By this time, Stalin had decided to gain time by allying himself —not with France and England, who had shown some hesitation to negotiate an anti-German alliance—but with Hitler himself. Characteristically, Stalin did not think it important to inform the French Communist party of this decision.

The signing of the German–Soviet nonaggression pact on August 24, 1939, was a bombshell that split asunder the French Communist party. Caught unaware by this startling alliance between the Socialist Fatherland and the Nazi beast, the French Communist leaders were unable to explain this turnabout in alliances. There was chaos in the party, and soon large-scale defections occurred among militants and sympathizers. Twenty-one out of the seventy-two Communist deputies in the Chamber left the Communist party. The immediate reaction of the French government, stunned by what it considered a betrayal by the Soviet Union, was to ban the Communist newspapers such as *L'Humanité* and *Ce Soir*. When, on September 3, 1939, France declared war on Germany, the Communist deputies patriotically voted for military credits—that is, for war. The secretary of the Central Committee, Maurice Thorez, and other party stalwarts were mobilized and left to join their army units.

On September 26, Premier Daladier struck a crushing blow: he banned the Communist party and ordered the arrest of thousands of the most prominent party members, sympathizers, labor leaders, and others known to support Communist policy. For the moment, he did not touch the Communist deputies in the Chamber (or in the army), since they enjoyed immunity which it would take time to remove. Its leadership decimated by the arrests, the party immediately went underground. Faithful to the propaganda directives issued by Moscow, it denounced the war as an "imperialist" quarrel and demanded a peace negotiated by the Soviet Union. Faithful to its policy of putting Soviet interests first, the party leaders switched from a strong anti-Fascist to an even stronger anti-imperialist, antiwar stand; but many of the rank and file, bewildered by the sudden switch, were unable to follow the party line. Nevertheless, the party's antiwar stand corresponded to the public opinion in France at that time; the majority of the French people were very fearful of the war and hoped for a negotiated peace, even one mediated by the Soviet Union. One can imagine the bewilderment of the party members, the intellectuals, and other sympathizers upon seeing Communist leaders such as Maurice Thorez and Jacques Duclos seemingly standing shoulder to shoulder with Fascists like Doriot and Déat in opposition to the war with Germany.

By the fall of 1939, the Daladier government had succeeded in lifting the immunity of the Communist deputies who had not been mobilized and promptly had them arrested. Fearful that he would in turn be imprisoned, Maurice Thorez deserted his army post on October 4. One month later, a military tribunal sentenced him to six years for "desertion in time of war," but by this time Thorez had reached asylum in the Soviet Union by way of Belgium. On February 17, 1940, a French court annulled his French citizenship.

In the period of the "Phony War," the party organized its clandestine activities, putting out mimeographed copies of *L'Humanité* which denounced the war and castigated the Daladier government for its inhumane treatment of the imprisoned Communist deputies. The Communist leaders also reorganized the party into closed cells of three members, with no connection between them except through the higher echelons; this was to make certain that the arrest of any one Communist would not lead to the arrest of others. This compartmentalization of the party structure and the associated rigid discipline were later to serve them well during the armed struggle.

The cruel treatment of the imprisoned Communists that the party newspaper had denounced was not just propaganda. The sadistic regime to which the Communist deputies were subjected after the Daladier government refused them the special status of "political prisoners" is hard to imagine. Not only were they brutalized by their jailers, but they were systematically starved to the point where several of them died for lack of the food parcels which were readily granted to the rapists and murderers among whom they were incarcerated.

The defeat of France in June, 1940, was hailed by the Communist leaders as a vindication of their antiwar policy. In refusing to accept the German and Soviet peace plans which had been ordered after Poland fell, France, under the direction of the capitalists, the bourgeoisie, and that perennial bogeyman of the French Left, the "Two Hundred Families," had doomed herself to defeat. The suddenness of the catastrophe certainly seemed to make prophets of not only the extreme Left, but the extreme Right as well: Thorez, Doriot, and Déat were all vindicated.

With the German–Soviet pact still in effect, the French Communist party saw no reason why it should not come out of hiding and appear legally under the German occupation. After all, it was the Daladier government which had both banned the Communist party and had declared war on Germany. The party decided to test the waters by an approach to the occupation authorities in Paris to allow the reappearance of *L'Humanité* in the open. The Nazi Propagandastaffel had no objection, but requested that a new name be used and that the hammer and sickle be left off the masthead. As the three Communist negotiators left the Kommandantur, they were arrested by the French police under the old warrant of banishment of the Communist party. They were taken to the *préfecture de police* and questioned for several hours but were quickly released when the Germans learned of their detention. Nothing came of these approaches to the Germans to allow the party newspaper to appear legally, and it continued to be published clandestinely.

For the first year of the occupation, the Communists continued to operate and to publish in a semi-legal fashion, with the tolerance of the Germans. Unwilling to disturb the German–Soviet agreement until Hitler was ready to make his move, the Militärbefehlshaber in Frankreich turned a blind eye to the appearance of the mimeographed copies of *L'Humanité,* provided only that they did nothing to disturb the peace and order of the occupation. But the French Communist party had no desire to attack the occupiers, even verbally. It saved its best invective for its old partners in the Popular Front government (such as Léon Blum and Daladier); it attacked de Gaulle as a reactionary aristocrat who had sold out to the British capitalists and was trying to drag France back into the war. The slogan, "Neither Churchill nor Hitler," was a variation on the earlier Rightist slogan of "Better Hitler than Léon Blum." The party urged the French workers to form closer relationships with the German soldiers; it called for the replacement of Vichy by a government of peasants, soldiers, and workers; it demanded the sweeping away of the capitalists and the "Two Hundred Families," which the Communists said had hurled an unprepared France into a war it was certain to lose. It is obvious that the party leaders were hoping to repeat the Bolshevik experience of 1917, when the military defeat of Russia by Germany had led finally to the establishment of the Soviets.

Although tolerated, even protected by the German occupation

authorities in the northern zone, the party continued to be pursued, arrested, and imprisoned in the unoccupied zone. Vichy was only too happy to take over the pursuit from the Third Republic. Those Communist deputies and militants imprisoned cruelly in the jails of the unoccupied zone found that there was to be no improvement in their living conditions; the slow torture of starvation continued, and there were several more deaths. Finally, in desperation, a Communist prisoner and former deputy named Brilloux wrote a pathetic letter to Pétain, asking that the Communist deputies be permitted to testify against the leaders of the Third Republic in the coming trial at Riom, in return for which they be allowed more food and permission to have their families visit them. In this letter, written on December 19, 1940, Brilloux pointed out that the Communists alone had opposed the war and had demanded peace, an argument that he evidently thought would appeal to the Marshal. After 1945, the party ignored the Brilloux letter and boasted of the appeals by Thorez and Duclos, which they interpreted as a call to resistance; however, the versions of these appeals which were published *after* the war omitted all the references to "imperialist conflicts" and the denunciations of the leaders of the Third Republic and of de Gaulle.

The history of the French Communist party in the first year of the occupation is not one of which it is proud. Its attempts to collaborate—or at least to establish a *modus vivendi* with the Nazis—must be balanced against its later courageous actions in the Resistance; however, even here the party members' willingness to claim all credit for the success of the armed Resistance and to deny any role to the non-Communist elements (who formed about eighty percent of the resistance membership) gained them few friends in postwar France.

The flirtation between the French Communist party and the Nazi occupation authorities came to an end at dawn on June 22, 1941, when the German armies attacked the Soviet Union along a 2,000-mile front. The stunning news was disbelieved at first in Paris (as it was in Moscow), but as soon as it was determined to be real the party swung into action. "The Motherland is in danger!" was the rallying cry, and now the call was for sabotage of war production, strikes—anything to delay the production of war matériel for Nazi Germany. The peasants were urged to restrict their crops and to hold back on deliveries to Vichy and to the Germans. Gone were the denunciations of the Third Republic and of de Gaulle; this was now a "democratic war against Fascism," led by the endangered Soviet Union.

Even more important than the halting of war production was the need to keep those German troops presently in France in position (so that they could not be sent to the Eastern Front) and if possible to see that they were reinforced. The only way to accomplish this was to make France a death trap for the occupation troops.

Three weeks before the assassination of the German naval cadet Alphonse Moser in the Barbès-Rochechouart subway station, a young couple was sitting at an outside table at the Closerie des Lilas at the top of the Boulevard Saint-Michel. It was early in the afternoon of a warm August day, and the man, dressed in a short-sleeved shirt, flannel pants, and sneakers, seemed to be enjoying his drink and light conversation with the attractive plump-faced young woman whose black hair was drawn straight back on her neck. His long thin face was quite animated, and his eyes sparkled under the round metal glasses that gave him an intellectual air as he emphasized a point to his companion. The man was Albert Ouzoulias, who had recently escaped from a prisoner-of-war camp in Austria by hiding under the seat in a train of elderly prisoners who were being repatriated. No sooner had he arrived in Rheims to visit his wife than he was summoned by the party's Central Committee to report to Paris for a new assignment. Three days later, he had a rendezvous at the Closerie des Lilas.

Danielle Casanova was a dentist by profession, but she was also a prominent member of the clandestine Central Committee, which had assigned her to organizing young Communists, women, and intellectuals. She had been selected to explain the new assignment to Ouzoulias, since the other members of the Central Committee at that time were either in hiding or in prison.

What she proposed startled him. He was asked to take over the direction of the armed struggle of the Communist youth against the occupiers. In vain, he protested that he had no experience in this type of work; in the army, he had been a *maître pointeur*—that is, a sergeant responsible for gun-laying in an artillery unit. Danielle laughed. "You will have an adjutant," she said, "a veteran of Spain whom you know very well—Pierre Georges. He has had experience. He was in the unoccupied zone, but we've had him come to Paris."

There was a long discussion about how arms were to be procured. Danielle said that there was already a supply given them by comrades who worked in the Paris sewers. It seemed that for many years the accepted way of getting rid of a weapon that was inconvenient to keep or to turn in to the police (but still had to be disposed of) was to drop it into the Parisian sewers. Many of the guns that the sewer workers found were useless, but some had been cleaned, oiled, and stored away in caches for future use. Unwittingly, the gangsters of Paris had helped to build up the secret arms supply of the Communist party—guns which would now be used against the Nazis.

Later that day, Ouzoulias met Fredo (Pierre-Félix Georges) at the Duroc subway station. They walked across to the terrace of a nearby restaurant and very quickly came to an agreement on how the armed action was to be carried out. The volunteers would be obtained from the existing Communist youth organizations, but they would be set apart and kept distinct from the other Communist groups. Their directive was clear: not only sabotage, but the assassination of German officers. They knew that it would not be easy to persuade young men, inexperienced in this type of action, of the necessity to murder a German officer in cold blood. They decided to call the volunteers together and to explain the need for such a drastic program.

On August 15, a group of campers arrived in the Bois de Lardy (near Etampes, in the south of Paris). They were dressed as campers and promptly installed their tents on a nearby hill; but this was not an outing of Boy Scouts. All the heads of armed action groups of the Communist party in the Paris region were present, and the discussions were not about woodcraft, but about murder. Nor were there bull sessions around campfires; they talked only of the necessity to kill as many German officers as possible.

Inevitably, there were objections to the party directives. The leaders pointed out their inferiority in numbers and the lack of weapons; they protested that they had no experience in assassination, and that the party had always been against individual terroristic action. They complained that the man they killed might be a German Communist, or a worker, and even an officer might be an anti-Nazi teacher. Ouzoulias and Fredo persisted in their argument: the only way to help the Soviet Union was to pin as many German troops as possible in France. This could only be done by armed attack. They pointed out that their comrades, Tyszelman and Gautherot, had just been condemned to death by a German court-martial and would shortly be executed. This must be answered, and only blood could pay for blood. Besides, armed attacks against the Nazis would shorten the war and save the lives of a much greater number of people. "At this moment, internationalism means killing the greatest number of Nazis possible."

Finally, the objections were overcome and it was decided that the directives of the Central Committee would be carried out. There now only remained the methods for putting them into action. The new group was given the name of the "Battalion of Young France"; later, it was to be known as the "Special Organization"; and finally, in 1942, it received the name by which it is best known—Francs-Tireurs et Partisans (F.T.P.).

Still, it was one thing to accept intellectually the party's orders and to understand the necessity for shooting German officers; it was another thing to take a gun, point it at the back of an unsuspecting man, and pull the trigger. There were a certain number of abortive attempts to do just this after the meeting in the Bois de Lardy. Gilbert Brustlein, with two companions, had followed a Nazi officer into the Gare de Lyon. As he pointed his gun at the officer's back, his arm was grabbed by his companions. "It's impossible here!" they cried, and dragged him away. At the Bastille subway station, Tony Bloncourt was about to shoot down a German officer when he hesitated. "I don't know what was wrong with me," he later said. "At that precise moment, I no longer saw a German officer—I only saw a man."

The volunteers for the armed action groups were all young men between the ages of eighteen and twenty, young men who had escaped being mobilized and therefore being captured and imprisoned in Germany. Their experience to that date had been in putting up pro-Soviet posters and scribbling on the walls of the working-class quarters at night. They could understand the need for sabotage of German war matériel, and even guerrilla attacks on German patrols, but the thought of cold-bloodedly shooting down Nazi officers worried and disheartened them.

When he heard of these abortive attempts, Fredo was very unhappy. Grabbing a gun from one of the hesitant comrades (the gun that the comrade had stolen from his mother), he said, "All right, lend me that. I'm going to show you how . . . tomorrow at eight o'clock at the *métro Barbès,* I am going to shoot one of them."

That same night, he went alone to the Barbès subway station and carefully studied the area, noting the positions of the stairways and the exits. In everything, Fredo was thorough.

The German reaction to the murder of Naval Cadet Alphonse Moser was immediate. The walls of Paris blossomed with red-and-black posters:

> On the morning of the twenty-first of August, a member of the German army was murdered in Paris.
>
> Consequently, by order;
> (1) Beginning on the twenty-third of August, all Frenchmen who have been arrested by the German authorities in France . . . will be considered as hostages.
> (2) In case such an act should happen again, a number of hostages corresponding to the gravity of the crime will be shot.

This grim warning was signed by General Ernst Schaumberg, commandant of Greater Paris.

Now it was war in the streets of Paris. The German threat to shoot hostages did not deter the Communist armed action squads; they knew that French revulsion against these barbaric acts would swell the ranks of the Resistance. They also knew that the Nazis would not hesitate to shoot hostages and that, since the prisons were filled with Communists, it would be their comrades who would fall before the German firing squads. They even sensed that for every Nazi officer they killed, fifty or a hundred Communists would be shot. But they did not hesitate. There was no other way to raise France out of its miserable lethargy and bring it back into the anti-Fascist struggle. The attacks continued at an ever-increasing pace.

At Lille, two German officers were killed the day after Schaumberg's warning was posted. The next day, two soldiers fell in the *département* of Nord near the Belgian frontier. In retaliation, von Stülpnagel, the Militärbefehlshaber in Frankreich, ordered the execution of five Communists and three Gaullist agents.*

In their savage drive to kill Nazis, the party did not forget those who had committed the unforgivable sin of deserting to the enemy. Marcel Gitton, once secretary of the party and a Communist deputy, had defected at the time of the German–Soviet pact; now a member of a pro-Nazi group, he was suspected of informing on many of his former comrades. On September 4, 1941, three men walked up to him on the rue de Bagnolet and shot him. He crumpled to the ground in front of No. 18, muttered "The swine!" and died.

On the evening of September 3 in Paris, a German officer, Ernst Hoffman, was badly wounded in the lobby of the Hôtel Terminus by one of Brustlein's group. Three days later, two bullets cut down a German officer named Hauffman as he was strolling on the rue des Perchamps, while in other fashionable quarters of Paris three other German officers fell under the Communist volleys. At the subway station Quai de la Rapée, Tony Bloncourt, who had once hesitated to shoot an officer in the back, fired at a German standing on the opposite platform. However, the recoil of the unfamiliar weapon threw off his aim and he succeeded only in shooting the cap off the head of his intended victim.

On September 10, a fifteen-year-old high-school student named André Kirchen went hunting for his Boche with a borrowed revolver. He finally found him, after much searching, at the ticket window of the Porte Dauphine subway station. André walked up behind the unsuspecting officer, took out his gun, and fired once. The noise was terrible, and he stood there frozen, fascinated by the sight of this body that seemed to be falling, and falling, and never to finish falling. Then he shook himself, ran swiftly up the stairway, and out into the streets.

* One of the Free French agents, Commandant Honoré d'Estienne d'Orves, so impressed the German court-martial by his fearless demeanor that the judges apologized to him for the stern duty that forced them to condemn him.

But it was not only in Paris that the party intended to carry out its armed actions. It was important that the attacks be widespread throughout the occupied zone in order that the German police be widely scattered and unable to repress them. On Monday, October 20, Gilbert Brustlein and Guisco Spartaco were returning to the center of Nantes after blowing up railroad tracks on the outskirts of the city. As they were crossing the Place de la Cathédrale about eight o'clock in the evening, they saw two German officers walking ahead of them. The streets were deserted. "We followed them rapidly, splitting the Nazis to be shot between us. On the sidewalk, we fired; Spartaco's revolver jammed, but mine shot down one of the Nazis, who fell screaming like a pig whose throat had been cut."

This time, the German reaction was immediate and terrible. Over the signature of von Stülpnagel, the posters appeared on the walls of both Paris and Nantes:

> Cowardly criminals in the pay of England and Moscow have killed, by shooting in the back, the Feldkommandant of Nantes (Loire-Inf.) on the morning of October 20, 1941. To date, the murderers have not been apprehended.
>
> In expiation of this crime, I have already ordered that fifty hostages be shot.
>
> Given the gravity of the crime, fifty more hostages will be shot if the guilty parties are not arrested by midnight, October 23, 1941.
>
> I offer an award totaling fifteen million francs to those citizens who contribute to the discovery of the guilty parties.
>
> Helpful information can be given to any German or French police service. Upon request, this information will be treated as confidential.

There were no denunciations of the guilty parties, since the only people aware of their identity were their fellow members in Brustlein's group. The same day that the Feldkommandant was shot down, a German officer went to the nearby camp of Châteaubriant and studied the list of detainees.

To Pierre Pucheu, Vichy minister of the interior, the list of the hundred hostages that the Germans presented to him the next day was horrifying. By a great deal of argument he was able to get the list reduced by half, but even then, of the fifty names remaining, there were at least forty veterans of World War I, many of them decorated for valor. He protested strongly against considering such men as hostages for what was obviously a brutal Communist murder. The

Germans then sent him another list; this one contained, except for six names, nothing but Communists. Pucheu remained silent.

The next day, Wednesday, October 22, 1941, the camp at Châteaubriant, halfway between Rennes and Nantes, awakened to a beautiful autumn day. The sky was blue and empty of clouds.

The night before, one of the gendarmes who guarded the camp had gotten drunk and had whispered to one of the Communist prisoners in Barracks 19 that thirty hostages would be shot the next day. It was clear that most of the hostages would be taken from among the Communists in Barracks 19.

During the day, three German officers had come to inspect the camp and had been shown through it very courteously by the commander, Captain Moreau, and his second-in-command, Lieutenant Touya. During the night of the twenty-second, German soldiers took over the watchposts around the camp.

Late that night, the prisoners in Barracks 19 talked over the situation. Escape was impossible; it was only a question now of knowing how to die well. One of them wondered whether they would be guillotined or shot. "Shot, of course! We are not criminals, but soldiers," another replied indignantly.

"If we are going to die," said a former deputy from Paris, "we might as well have a good meal." He went over and started to cook the rest of their meager rations.

The next day, around ten o'clock, the prisoners could see Moreau and Touya examining the main gate as if to make certain that the German trucks could pass through. The number of guards had been increased.

At 1:30 in the afternoon, Lieutenant Touya, very pale, entered Barracks 19, followed by a German officer, and saluted.

"*Salut, messieurs.* Prepare to leave when your name is called."

The ominous roll call began. "Michels, Timbaud, Poulmarsh, Granet." The next man, Delavacquerie, was not in Barracks 19, but in a different part of the camp. Touya made a note on his list.

There followed a list of ten more names. As each name was called, the condemned man rose quietly and walked through the door. Two of them, Bourki and Laforce, were teachers who were to have been released that day, the charges against them having been dropped. Finally it was done. The lieutenant saluted again and walked out, closing the door between the living and the dead.

The six men who remained looked at each other, stupefied. They were going to live.

The fourteen men who had been condemned were now taken to Barracks 6, where a machine gun had been trained on the door. Lieutenant Touya continued his ominous tour. At each barracks he called out the names, and those summoned were put with the others in Barracks 6. Gardette, who was ill, was taken from the infirmary.

As one survivor reported, "In Barracks 10, Lieutenant Touya called out without hesitation, but with a strained smile, a single name: Guy Môquet . . . and as if without thinking, erect, taller than ever, our Guy moved forward rapidly and assuredly, seventeen years old, still unaware and whose life had hardly awakened to the first dreams of love. . . ."

By two o'clock, there were twenty-seven men in Barracks 6. Now they were each given a sheet of paper, an envelope, and a pencil. It was time to write the last letters to their wives, to their families, to their sweethearts. Each man was alone with his thoughts. A priest, Abbé Moyon, entered. Michels, the Communist deputy from Paris, said to him, "We don't receive you as a priest, but as a man. We are not Catholics, but we are happy to have you here and we thank you for it." They gave the abbé their personal papers, their wedding rings, their photographs.

The letters finished, they began to sing *La Marseillaise*. The prisoners in the other barracks heard them and joined in.

According to an eyewitness who later escaped from the camp, the German trucks arrived at 2:25 P.M. Lieutenant Touya opened the door and began the last roll call. As his name was called, each man rose and walked to the door. The gendarmes searched them, emptied their pockets, tied their hands, and made them climb into the *camions*. Each truck took nine men; they had not stopped singing, and the prisoners who stayed behind made signs of farewell through the windows. In the doorway, Doctor Ténine spoke to one of the German officers: "It is an honor for Frenchmen like us to fall under German bullets," he said. Then, pointing to the young Guy Môquet, he continued, "But it is a crime to kill this kid!"

"Knock it off, Ténine, I'm as much a Communist as you are," said Guy Môquet. Then he walked out and climbed into the truck.

After the trucks were loaded, Lieutenant Touya shook hands politely with the German officer in charge. As the convoy rolled through the village of Châteaubriant, the men were still singing *La Marseillaise* and *L'Internationale*. The townspeople took off their hats in farewell as the trucks passed.

Two kilometers outside of Châteaubriant, there was a sand quarry. Earlier in the day, the peasants who lived in the vicinity had been confined to their homes by the Germans. At the far end of the quarry, three rows of nine freshly cut posts stood starkly in the afternoon light.

The twenty-seven hostages died bravely, refusing to have their hands tied or to use blindfolds. Almost all of them cried, "Long live France! Long live the Soviet Union! Long live the Communist party!" One of them, Timbaud, cried, "Long live the *German* Communist party!" and Doctor Ténine said to the German officer in charge of the firing squad, "You are going to see how a French officer dies!"

But Guy Môquet, who had been so brave in leaving the camp and on the road, lost his courage when he saw the three rows of execution stakes. He fainted and was dragged to the execution post and shot while still unconscious. In his last letter to his family, the boy had written, "Certainly I would have liked to live . . . seventeen and a half years, my life has been short. I have no regrets." His crime? His father was a Communist deputy.

Charles Michels wrote in his last letter to his wife, "You see, darling, how funny life is. Deprived of my seat as a deputy for so-called complicity with Germany, I am being shot today by the soldiers of that country. . . ." Then he added, "If on the way you find someone worthy of you, don't hesitate, dear, remake your life. You're still young. Do not mourn, I am going to die with courage. Pardon the little woes that I have caused you."

Delavacquerie, who had been searched out by the efficient Lieutenant Touya, wrote wistfully: "No longer will we see the happy days return. I will see my lovely Montreuil no more."

Later, as the bodies were being put into the coffins, it was found that one of them was too tall to fit. A German soldier took an iron bar in order to break the legs and force it into the crude pine box. When a French ditchdigger protested, the German shouted, "Communist, not French!"

The butchery of the hostages did not end with the three salvos fired ten minutes apart in the sand quarry outside of Châteaubriant. In the prison at Nantes, twenty-one men were selected: Catholics, Socialists, Communists, and two seventeen-year-old boys. They were shot the same day, in the courtyard of the prison. Forty-eight Frenchmen had died for the murder of Lieutenant Colonel Hotz, Feldkommandant of Nantes. The balance sheet was now set: forty-eight French hostages for one German officer. But the price of the life of a member of the Wehrmacht was to be set even higher. The next day, for the assassination of an officer of the German military administration in Bordeaux, one hundred hostages were shot.

In Vichy, Pierre Pucheu tried to defend himself against the charge that he had selected the hostages that the Germans had executed. "I could not," he said, "let them shoot forty *good* Frenchmen. . . . I didn't pick them out . . . I only let the Germans substitute a second list for the first. . . ."

That evening, on the radio, Pétain pleaded for the French to denounce those guilty of attacks on German officers: "We have put down our arms," he said, "we do not have the right to take them up again to strike the Germans in the back." For a short time, he talked to his intimates of presenting himself at the demarcation line as a hostage; without too much difficulty, they talked him out of such a "theatrical" gesture.

From London, there was a radio broadcast by de Gaulle, disturbed by von Stülpnagel's murderous arithmetic: "It is absolutely natural and absolutely right that Germans should be killed by Frenchmen. If the Germans did not wish to receive death at our hands, they had only to stay at home. . . . Since they have not succeeded in bringing the world to its knees, they are certain to become, each of them, a corpse or a prisoner . . . but there are tactics in war. War must be conducted by those entrusted with the task . . . for the moment, my orders to those in occupied territory are *not* to kill Germans there openly. This for one reason only: at present, it is too easy for the enemy to retaliate by massacring our fighters, who are, for the time being, disarmed."

But the Communists were not listening to either the Vichy or the English radio.

NOTICE

> At dawn on October 21, 1941, one day after the crime that had been committed at Nantes, cowardly murderers in the pay of England and Moscow treacherously shot an officer of the German military administration at Bordeaux.
>
> The assassins have succeeded in fleeing. The murderers of Nantes are still not in my hands.
>
> As a first measure of reprisal for the new crime, I have ordered once more that fifty hostages be shot.
>
> If the murderers are not taken by October 26, 1941, at midnight, fifty more hostages will be shot.
>
> I offer a reward of fifteen million francs. . . .

The murderous war went on: German officers continued to die in the streets; French hostages (chiefly Communists and Jews) were pushed in ever-increasing numbers before the efficient German firing squads. Von Stülpnagel was frantic: threats, rewards, shooting one hundred hostages for every German officer killed, setting the curfew at 5:30 P.M., closing the restaurants, theaters, cinemas, and other places of public entertainment, massive fines on the towns where the assassinations occurred; promises to release a husband, a brother, or a fiancé from the German prison camps to anyone who would inform—nothing stopped the fatal tempo from increasing.

On November 21, Fredo led a commando against the German bookstore on the Left Bank. It was an operation he had prepared for at an earlier date, but on the day selected, "Bob"—who was in charge of the bombs—forgot to set his alarm clock and overslept! But at 7 A.M. on a fine autumn day, all went well; the windows of the bookstore were smashed with rocks and the bombs hurled through the shattered panes destroyed the stock and fixtures. The French police who were charged with protecting this Nazi propaganda center opened fire on the attackers. Fredo's carefully placed protection squad returned the fire, and the police, frightened by this violation of the usual rules of the game, fled.

Fredo, by now in charge of all armed action in the Paris region, pushed the young "terrorists" hard. He was determined to give the Nazis no rest from the murderous attacks.

The day after the destruction of the German bookstore, incendiaries (stolen from the Nazi army depots) were hurled into a hotel at Number 100 avenue du Maine, requisitioned by the Wehrmacht. There were German soldiers killed and wounded. On the twenty-sixth, a guard post, another bookstore, and a hotel were bombed; German casualties increased.

In December, 1941, according to a German army report, there were two hundred and twenty-one separate attacks on Wehrmacht personnel and installations. A furious von Stülpnagel telegraphed Hitler, requesting permission for the following reprisals: (1) the execution of one hundred hostages; (2) the levy of a one-billion-franc fine on the Jews of Paris; (3) the deportation to Eastern Europe of one thousand Jews and five hundred young Communists.

Four days later, Hitler sent his approval. Otto Abetz wrote the press release that emphasized the lie that the hostages were not "Frenchmen," but Communists and spies for British and Soviet intelligence networks. The next day, the word "British" was changed to "Anglo-Saxon," for now the United States was in the war.*

It was not only the ever-increasing number of hostages and German officers who were dying. Reckless and inexperienced in the stern need for security, the young Communists of the action squads soon suffered their first losses. A member of Brustlein's group boasted to his fiancée and showed her his revolver. His girl friend mentioned it to a

* Germany and Italy declared war on the United States on December 11, 1941, in fulfillment of their treaty obligations to Japan.

friend who told his father (a Gestapo informer). The next day, seven young militants were arrested; Brustlein escaped just in time, and his picture and description were published in all the newspapers in the occupied zone with the warning: "Several terrorists responsible for recent attacks have been arrested, but one of their leaders, Gilbert-André Brustlein, has fled. It is a duty to the nation to help capture him!"

The non-Communist resistance groups also suffered grievous losses in 1941. At the beginning of February, the Gestapo surrounded the Palais de Chaillot and arrested three members of the Musée de l'Homme network. Boris Vildé, who was in Toulouse, insisted on returning to Paris to help his friends and was arrested in March. Other embryo resistance groups in both the occupied and unoccupied zones were decimated either by carelessness, naïveté, infiltration by Gestapo and Vichy elements—or betrayed by their faith in a fellow countryman who believed in the Marshal. By the end of the year the little islands of resistance on the map of France began to disappear and the death cells of Fresnes, La Santé, and other prisons began to fill with men and women who scratched "Long live de Gaulle" on walls that bore the fresh inscriptions "Long live Stalin and the Red Army." The brotherhood of pain and suffering was forming within the prison walls.

At two o'clock on the morning of January 1, 1942, four parachutes blossomed in the black sky not far from Arles in the Bouches-du-Rhône *département* of the south of France. Overhead, a twin-engined British plane banked sharply and started its long journey back to England.

It was bitter cold and the mistral, that savage wind that flows down the Rhône Valley, dispersed the three parachutists widely (the fourth parachute carried their radio).

The leader of the group, known as Max, splashed down in an unseen marsh, landing in the waist-deep icy water and losing his pistol and compass. Worse yet, the sandwiches, which would be his only food until he reached safety at his farm, were soaked with the stinking black water. But, despite this, Max was filled with joy. He was back in France; this was French earth; yes, even this miserable bog was French. Shivering from the cold, drenched from head to foot, but jubilant, he cut himself out of the parachute harness and stumbled out in search of his companions.

The scars on his throat hidden by a muffler, Jean Moulin—ex-prefect of Chartres—had returned to the struggle.

6

The Resistance Unites

After digging one hole in which the radio transmitter would be buried and another for one of the parachutes, the three men were startled to see the first signs of dawn on the horizon. Dropped twenty kilometers from the designated landing zone, they had a long walk ahead of them to reach their rendezvous point—Moulin's farm on the other side of Arles. Hastily concealing the remaining parachutes in the thick underbrush, they set out.

Just before reaching the farm (it was now broad daylight), the three men separated to cross the village of Eygalières without arousing suspicion. Moulin went first, followed by Raymond Fassin (who was charged with a liaison mission to the resistance group Combat); the radio operator, Hervé Monjaret, agreed to be last.

As Moulin and Fassin disappeared in the distance and Monjaret was bathing his aching feet in a nearby stream, two gendarmes appeared suddenly and demanded his papers. It was clear that they had been watching the three men for some time and were intrigued by their decision to cross the village one by one. Confident of the appearance of his newly forged papers, Monjaret handed them over, adding a cock-and-bull story of a student and two professors who were studying the scene of several Alphonse Daudet short stories. Suspicious of such literary zeal on a freezing January morning, but confused by the apparent authenticity of his papers, the gendarmes left. Monjaret waited almost an hour before hurrying after his friends, but Max (Moulin) and Sif (Fassin) had disappeared. A week later Laure Moulin, Jean's sister, located Monjaret and brought him to Marseilles.

In the false bottom of a matchbox, Jean Moulin had hidden a microphotograph of his orders:

> I designate Monsieur Jean Moulin, prefect, as my representative and as the delegate of the French National Committee for the

> non-occupied zone of metropolitan France. Monsieur Moulin's mission in this zone is to achieve unity of action by all elements which are resisting the enemy and his collaborators. Monsieur Moulin will report directly to me on the accomplishment of his mission.

It was signed "Charles de Gaulle" and with this, plus the sum of five hundred thousand francs, Jean Moulin had been dropped "blind" into the Vichy zone to unite the fiercely independent, mutually suspicious clandestine groups. It was a task worthy of a Hercules, and it had been given to a gentle, artistic man with a soft, rather hoarse voice (his vocal cords had been damaged by his suicide attempt in June, 1940). But de Gaulle, despite his cold exterior and lack of personal feeling for his staff, was a superb judge of character; he had not only confidence in Jean Moulin, but a rare respect for the man.

In spite of the half-million francs, Moulin lacked almost everything necessary to accomplish his task. The Resistance in France badly needed arms, paper, and printing presses for their propaganda, and ten million francs *per month* to keep their people alive. They were not wholly attached to de Gaulle (in spite of his great prestige) or to the Free French movement. There were many who were suspicious of the tall, aristocratic general, recalling his early attachment to Maurras and suspecting him of monarchist and antirepublican tendencies. This suspicion was accentuated when the Free French broadcasts, beginning in September, 1940, opened with the army motto, "*Honneur et patrie*" (Honor and Country), rather than the republican motto, "*Liberté, egalité, fraternité*" (which was also used by the Freemasons). It would require a strong man indeed to unite the many squabbling resistance groups, so jealous of their independent role and authority in their own areas of responsibility. Often, they attached paramount importance to the policies and the goals of a particular political party and believed that being on the spot in France—and exposed to all the dangers—made them better judges of what was necessary for the underground struggle.

But Jean Moulin, with his laughing, lively eyes, his sweet, open smile, and his appearance of a young adolescent on his way to his first Communion, was equal to this task. There was in him a strength and an authority, a brilliance of mind, and a superb memory which never failed to impress his listeners. Trained in the hard school of the French prefectoral administration, he displayed a firmness, an energy, and a stubbornness which, combined with the obviously seductive nature of his personality, was to win over even the most suspicious of the resistance groups. His was not the cold, authoritarian manner of his chief, de Gaulle, but rather a warm human feeling for the men and women under his command, to whom he had to assign the most dangerous of tasks. He was constantly concerned for them, frequently asking about the safety of their spouses and children. To those who had sheltered him for a few days during his constant travels across occupied and unoccupied France, he would send a bouquet of roses as a sign of gratitude for the risk they had taken.

Still, he was firm and unshakable in his intention to carry out the task assigned to him, to play the role that had been given him in London. In the constant petty bickerings that marked his meetings with the different resistance groups, quarrels over means, supplies, propaganda objectives (some of these groups still believed in Pétain and his "double game") were constant. Jean Moulin listened carefully to all of the arguments, and when he spoke it was with authority and finality. He told them that he knew whom they represented, and that, from lack of means, they were unable to expand their activity; it was obvious that they could not fight alone. Therefore they were going to have to change; they must recognize de Gaulle as their chief, and in return for this they would receive not only financial aid and arms, but the means of communicating with London. He had brought with him a transmitter and a radio operator, and he promised that others would follow. This radio contact with London was all important, for now the Resistance would no longer be isolated in its struggle.

The heads of the different clandestine organizations grumbled and squirmed, but they could not refute the logic of his arguments. It was obvious that the Resistance could not survive, split as it was into so many tiny groups. If anything were to be accomplished, there must be not only unification but coordination, and only de Gaulle in London had the stature to accomplish this. In spite of their misgivings as to the ultimate role that the general might play in the political life of France after the war, they could see no other alternative: it was either the general or the Marshal, and there was no hope for an accommodation with Vichy.

To understand the reluctance of the Resistance in France to affiliate with the Free French movement in London, it is necessary to study the way in which it had grown. In the beginning, in 1940, the nascent Resistance had consisted of scattered groups of friends who found they had a mutual aversion to the armistice, to the presence of the Germans, and sometimes to Pétain and the Vichy government. They agreed to meet frequently, to study the situation, and to determine what could be done and what should be done. These isolated cells had the most diverse membership, for the defeat and the armistice had caused a cleavage in French society which was reflected by the different social origins and political beliefs of the early *résistants*. One group in Paris was led by a retired army officer who was himself very religious, anti-Communist, and monarchist, but his organization was soon flooded with people with different religious orientations (or none at all), with varying political views—and certainly no monarchistic conviction à L'Action Française. They included firemen, priests, petty officials, small businessmen, bookkeepers, even a shoemaker. Another group, also led by an ex–army officer, recruited former officers, non-commissioned officers, industrialists, engineers, railwaymen, and doctors. Boris Vildé of the Musée de l'Homme network had a wide acquaintanceship among university people, scientists, and lawyers; it is in this milieu that he recruited the first members of his resistance group.

In the early Resistance, the complete spectrum of the French prewar political parties was represented, from the far Left to the far Right—except for the Communist party, whose attitude was equivocal with respect to the German occupation until June 22, 1941, when the Nazis invaded the Soviet Union (see Chapter 5). The early Resistance would have welcomed Communist members for their experience in illegal propaganda and clandestine operations, but no member of the party presented himself. No doubt the Central Committee, still in hiding, was unwilling to have the party militants escape from its control.

The first resistance cells were nameless; the labels came later. It was thought puerile, not chic, to adopt some flamboyant tag. There was very little structure to their organization; their leaders rose spontaneously, by common consent, and derived their authority through efficiency or daring. The hierarchy that was imposed upon the resistance movement came much later. There was no specialization in their activities; each group put out its own propaganda, printed and distributed its own pamphlets, gathered information about the German military activities in France, organized escapes of Allied fliers and French prisoners of war, as well as collecting and hiding arms that had been abandoned during the exodus. Later, when a few small groups joined together in a mutual endeavor and found the means of communicating by radio with London, the first *réseaux*—resistance networks—were born.

To the early resistance members, de Gaulle was the man of June 18, 1940, whose radio appeal for resistance (which many of them heard of only many months later) was a rallying point. Proud of their own work, jealous of their own authority, and suspicious of the aristocratic army officer and his "reactionary" entourage, they viewed the French National Committee in London simply as a source of money, arms and propaganda. They were aware of the need to unite in order to be more effective, and contacts between the many small groups had been made on a personal basis in spite of the danger involved. Such contacts, of course, increased the danger of betrayal, of introducing a traitor into more than one group; but it was a question of either accepting the risk or ceasing to do anything useful. Because of the need for more people to gather intelligence on German military activities throughout France, the need for people familiar with crossings of the demarcation line, the urgent necessity for more "safe houses," "mail drops," and secure places from which radio messages could be transmitted to London, the dangers were accepted. Only the fact that these contacts between the early resistance groups were personal contacts between friends explains their ability to survive in the midst of the Gestapo and the Vichy police—this and the silence under torture of those who were arrested. However, inexperience in secret work and the need for security—plus the naïve trust of the French in their fellow countrymen—made it easy for a traitor or a double agent to penetrate a resistance cell and to learn all the ramifications of its relationship with other clandestine organizations. Once the leader had been identified, massive arrests followed; the few survivors then joined another resistance network and continued the work.

Conscious of the dangers and the risks to which they were subjected daily, the early resistance groups were contemptuous of those Free French agents who deigned to give them directives on their work. There were many bitter words about *les embusqués*—the goldbrickers—who, from their comfortable hotels in London, knowing nothing of present conditions in France, pretended to direct the underground struggle. That they did so in the name of General de Gaulle did not make him popular with the early Resistance. As Germaine Tillion wrote: "Among the Resistance in 1940, I knew some who did not become Gaullists until 1942, and others who never became Gaullists. They could not stand the presence of the Germans in France and needed no other motive to act."

This, then, was the situation in early 1942, when Jean Moulin began his work. Of average height, dressed in a nondescript topcoat and soft-brimmed hat, with a scarf constantly around his neck to hide the scars on his throat from his suicide attempt at Chartres, he seemed to lack the authority to deal with the turbulent leaders of the resistance groups. He did not appear to be the sort of man to represent de Gaulle, especially since the general was so widely distrusted and was suspected of having his own postwar political plans inimicable to the Republic. But Jean Moulin was a leader, a man trained in the strict administration service of prewar France, and, what was even more important, he had great charm and a way of dealing with people. With "serene sunburnt face and eloquent gestures," he was to conquer the petty chieftains and change their feudal viewpoint.

His first contact was with Henri Frenay of the Combat network, which by this time had sent its antennae not only throughout the unoccupied zone but, even more dangerously, into the occupied zone. They met in Marseilles, where Frenay, after some initial hesitation, pledged his people to the Gaullist movement. He had long been convinced of the necessity of unifying the resistance groups and had been able to contact and to draw up a working agreement with several of them in the unoccupied zone. The group Combat was the largest and strongest clandestine organization in 1942, so Moulin gave Frenay half of his five hundred thousand francs for immediate expenses. At Lyons, a meeting was arranged with Emmanuel d'Astier de la Vigerie, the fiery ex-navy officer turned journalist who headed Liberation, which drew its main strength from among the Socialist and trade unionist movements. At Avignon, agreement was quickly reached with the movement Franc-Tireur, a Leftist Catholic resistance group.*

Since his initial mission was to unify the resistance groups in the unoccupied zone, Jean Moulin opened an art gallery at Nice under his real name, using pictures from his private collection as inventory. For the formal opening on February 9, 1943, he invited prominent local citizens and the regional *préfet.* One of the local newspapers hailed this event as evidence of the renaissance of art to be expected under the benevolent rule of Marshal Pétain. Actually, the art gallery was an ideal cover for Moulin's activities, for it permitted him to travel widely throughout the unoccupied zone on business.

Using trains, *gazogène* buses (which ran on the fumes of charcoal or burning green wood), and even bicycles, he traveled from city to city, contacting the local resistance groups, explaining the goals and objectives of the Free French movement, and rallying them behind de Gaulle. Although the Vichy authorities were unaware of his trip to London (which he had made on a false passport under the name of Mercier), it was impossible for him to remain unrecognized. After all, he had been the youngest *préfet* in the French prefectoral administration. Everywhere he went he was bound to run into an acquaintance, and, on one trip to Paris, he even unhappily ran into his former wife.

The difficulties in unifying the Resistance in 1942 lay not only in the individualism and feudal thinking of the resistance chiefs, but also in other political and national problems as well. General Benoit Léon de Fornel de la Laurencie, who had been Pétain's representative in the occupied zone until replaced by Fernand de Brinon, was chosen by the Americans as a replacement for the troublesome de Gaulle. In October, 1941, he met with Frenay at Lyons; also present were the U.S. military attaché in Berne, Colonel Legge, and the head of U.S. Intelligence in Europe, *Scott.*† La Laurencie showed Frenay a list of his future ministers, which included such prominent Vichyites as

* Not to be confused with the Communist group Francs-Tireurs et Partisans.

† In his recent book, *La Nuit finira,* Frenay identifies *Scott* as Allen Dulles.

Lémery and Admiral de Laborde. He boasted that the Resistance was following him and that he had the complete support of the Americans. As for the leader of the Free French movement in London, he said nonchalantly, "De Gaulle? Oh, all right, we'll give him an amnesty." From the funds that the Americans so generously supplied him, he gave Frenay 350,000 francs for Combat. The impetuous General de la Laurencie was to be a minor stumbling block to the unification of the Resistance until Vichy learned of his American contacts and had him interned.

A much more serious threat was the Front National, which had been formed under Communist leadership as early as May, 1941, but which received its greatest impetus after the German invasion of the Soviet Union in June. The idea was to have a single organization of the French Resistance covering both the occupied and unoccupied zones, including those groups with attachments to political parties (other than the Communist party) and even those based on certain religious groups. The program of the Front National called for direct action against the German invaders: sabotage of their installations and assassination of Nazi officers. The collection of intelligence was to be left to what was contemptuously referred to as "those people from London." A unified resistance movement covering all of France under the control—even the surreptitious control—of the Communists was a direct threat to the authority of de Gaulle and to his prestige as the announced leader of the total French Resistance.

These were not all of the problems that faced a weary Jean Moulin: no sooner had he landed in France than his planned unification was severely threatened by a serious quarrel which threatened to split the Resistance and to delay unity indefinitely.

In January, 1942, a massive series of arrests of members of Combat in the unoccupied zone was made by the Vichy police; less than a month later, the Gestapo crushed other Combat networks in the occupied zone. The arrests were the result of treason, the traitor being one Henri Devillers, a double agent employed by the Abwehr (the German Military Intelligence, whose headquarters were at the Hôtel Lutétia in Paris). The damage to Combat was minimized by the arrest, by pure chance, of Devillers at the demarcation line by the French police. Devillers tried to bluff his way out, giving names of members of Combat as references, but it was quickly learned that he worked for the Abwehr. Judged and condemned in March, he was hastily shot in April, just before Pierre Laval returned to the Vichy government and was about to demand his release.

Henri Frenay, for whom there was now an arrest warrant outstanding, attempted to gain the release of the imprisoned members of his network by arranging for a meeting with Major Rollin, the director general of the Sûreté Nationale (the French equivalent, roughly, of the FBI). They met in Vichy on February 6, 1942; Frenay was driven to the rendezvous by a member of the Vichy police who was closely allied to the Resistance. On his desk, Rollin had ostentatiously scattered a complete dossier of the Combat network, including many copies of its clandestine newspaper. For two hours the two men sparred, each looking for a chink in his opponent's armor. Rollin claimed that Vichy was the center of the real Resistance, which Frenay ardently denied. To him, Combat, Liberation, and Franc-Tireur were the genuine Resistance, and Vichy was inalterably tainted by collaboration. Rollin proposed that the attack on the Vichy government by the resistance newspapers cease; Frenay countered by demanding an end to arrests and the release of his militants. Finally, Rollin offered to introduce Frenay to a member of the government; since Darlan was traveling, it was to Pierre Pucheu, the minister of the interior, that Frenay was taken.

This strange interview between the Vichy minister, who was so bitterly hated by the Resistance for his role in the execution of the hostages at Châteaubriant, and the man wanted by the Vichy government for "terrorism" was frequently stormy. Pucheu started out by trying to convince Frenay that Vichy was engaged in a subtle "double game" with the intention of bamboozling the Germans and permitting an early return of France into the war on the side of the Allies. He spoke of the preparations which were under way in French North Africa, of the arms which had been hidden by the armistice army, and of Pétain's secret agreements with the English leaders. He ardently denounced the attacks by the clandestine newspapers on Pétain and his ministers, and he warned Frenay: "We know you. We know where you come from, who you are. We are really astonished that a man like you should be at the head of a clandestine organization. After what I have said, I would like you to consider whether your behavior might not backfire against the country."

Frenay answered rudely. "I don't believe so. I believe just the contrary . . . by definition, this policy of the 'double game' cannot be made official. You only show the French people the collaboration side of it. The other side you keep to yourself. You can't show it in broad daylight, otherwise you'd be in prison. So, the good people who listen to you and who are the majority, less a handful, follow you, and because of that, you assume a crushing responsibility. Your responsibility is all the greater since your policy of a 'double game' is a sham, because the Germans will lose the war . . . if you are really only waiting for the right moment to join the winning side, why then do you stick my boys in the can? But in the can they are . . . you'll have to make your point of view and your actions consistent. There's no reason, if you're really playing a 'double game,' to throw these guys in the jug."

After a long, and at times bitter discussion, Pucheu finally said, "All right. I'm going to think about this conversation." Frenay requested him, in any case, to make no new arrests, to which the Vichy minister agreed. Frenay was given a safe-conduct pass; if he should happen to be picked up by the Vichy police, he had only to show the pass and Pucheu would be informed of his arrest and would secure his release.

In spite of the inconsequential results of this first interview, the two men met again on February 14; but it was only a rehashing of the old arguments. Once again Pucheu asked for time to think it over, and the time was set for a third interview, which never took place. After the second interview, Vichy had spread the word that it had reached a *modus vivendi* with the leaders of Combat; there was immediate consternation among the resistance groups. Because of his role in "selecting" hostages for the German firing squads, and because of the repression of the Resistance by the French police, Pucheu, minister of the interior (and therefore in control of the police), was hated more than any other Vichy minister. Any negotiations or agreements with him were felt to be a stain on the whole resistance movement. In particular, Frenay's bitter enemy, Emmanuel d'Astier de la Vigerie, who headed the Leftist Liberation group, was only too happy to irritate the wounds opened in the Resistance by the Frenay–Pucheu talks. Never eager for the fusion of Combat and Liberation, as desired by Jean Moulin, he was only too willing, even anxious, to flay Frenay for his "agreement" with the traitor Pucheu. It was not only d'Astier de la Vigerie, but also resistance leaders from groups other than Combat who reacted violently against any contact with the hated Vichy minister.

The uproar over these negotiations did not make Jean Moulin's task any easier, but, as Frenay pointed out, there was at least one solid result: his men were released from jail.

Even as Jean Moulin struggled with the internal strife within the resistance movement, a crucial event took place in Vichy. Flandin's cabinet had lasted only two months, having given way in February, 1941, to a triumvirate headed by Admiral Darlan. Darlan, who had played a sneaky role in the arrest of Pierre Laval on December 13, 1940, had attempted to tie France even more closely to collaboration with Germany, even going so far as to promise the use of the French fleet in attacks on English ships. He had met on several occasions with Hitler and Goering and had convinced them of his sincerity in seeking to fit France into its rightful role in the New Order. Darlan was ambitious and saw himself as grand admiral of the Greater European Fleet that would grow out of the Nazi New Order. He was also violently anti-British, a fact that is often explained not only by his jealousy of British naval might, but by the fact that his great-grandfather had been killed at Trafalgar in 1806. As head of the government, Darlan had favored senior naval officers for all the important jobs, going so far as to flood the prefectoral administration with admirals; Vichy soon became known as "the Admirals' Protective Association."*

Nevertheless, the Nazis were dissatisfied with Darlan, who was held responsible for Vichy's attitude in demanding strict adherence to the armistice terms, its failure to repress the Resistance in the southern zone, and its various demands for easing the rigors of the occupation. What the Germans wanted in Vichy was not a Frenchman eager to collaborate, but a "European" who would see the benefits that would accrue to France from the New Order and who was convinced of the ultimate German victory. This they obtained on April 17, 1942, when Pétain accepted the resignation of the Darlan cabinet and once again appointed Pierre Laval vice-premier or effective head of the government under the chief of state, Pétain. Keeping for himself the portfolios of foreign affairs and the interior, Laval filled the other cabinet positions with convinced collaborators such as Abel Bonnard (education), General Eugène Bridoux (war), Admiral Gabriel-Paul Auphan (navy), and the ex-Doriotist Paul Marion (information).† To demonstrate his distaste for the National Revolution, he also gave several posts to some of his buddies who were politicians of the Third Republic.

In spite of German expectations, Pierre Laval did not believe in an ultimate German victory, especially with the entry into the war of the United States and the Soviet Union, but he did not think that Nazi Germany could ever be totally defeated. It was his belief that there would be a compromise peace, a negotiated settlement in which France, to its great benefit, would act as arbiter. With his unshakable belief in his own skill in negotiation, he thought that the German victory over Bolshevism (with French military assistance) would be followed by a peace between Nazi Germany and the Anglo-Saxon powers. This peace, he was convinced, could only be arranged by someone with the skill and daring of Pierre Laval.

The heavy losses of the German army in the first six months of the Russian campaign forced the Nazis to draft more factory workers to fill the gaps in the Wehrmacht, even though there was an urgent need for increased war production to replace the losses in planes and tanks. Great pressure was therefore put on France (and the other occupied

* Cardinal Suhard was quoted as saying: "When I die, an admiral will undoubtedly replace me."

† As a consolation prize, Darlan was made head of all armed forces: army, navy, and air force.

countries in western Europe) to send skilled labor to the German factories—voluntarily, if possible; by force, if necessary.

Hitler appointed Fritz Sauckel, Gauleiter of Thuringia, to head the "recruiting." Offices were opened in both zones in France, but the enlistments were negligible. Since French factories were busy turning out planes, tanks, locomotives, and other equipment for the German war machine, and French laborers were building airfields and fortifications for the Nazis, why should Frenchmen go to Germany to do what they were doing so successfully at home for the Reich?

But Sauckel had promised Hitler that large numbers of foreign workers would be recruited—or forced—to work in German factories. The compromise reached by Sauckel and Laval was *"la relève"* (the relief troops): for every three skilled French workers who volunteered for work in Germany, a French prisoner of war would be sent home. For a while, this appeal to the widespread anxiety over the fate of the French P.O.W.'s was successful—240,000 new French volunteers left for the Reich—but this source of labor soon dried up. Then, following German threats to seize workers, Vichy published a decree substituting forced labor (*Service du travail obligatoire*) for the military service required of young Frenchmen.

To avoid being sent to Germany, the young men fled; called *réfractaires* (draft dodgers), they were relentlessly pursued by the Vichy police. Soon the first groups of the young fugitives from the S.T.O. began to gather in the woods and hills, particularly in southeast France. The first Maquis (the word means "the scrubby underbrush," characteristic of the hills of Corsica which had been the traditional hiding place of outlaws) were rebels against the S.T.O., but not yet *résistants*. Untrained and unarmed, they were soon joined in the hills by the officers of the French armistice army, after the Germans dissolved it in November, 1942.

Organized by the Secret Army, supplied with arms (always inadequate to their numbers) by parachute from England or taken from the local police, they stole or counterfeited ration cards for food and requisitioned supplies from the surrounding towns (none too gently from merchants suspected of black-market dealings). By the middle of 1943, they were strong enough to control those areas which were held by Vichy officials, but not those garrisoned by the German army. The battle to drive out the Nazis would wait until the liberation.

The Maquis, as Laval pointed out bitterly, was an army created by Sauckel!

On May 5, 1942, less than a month after Laval's return to head the government, Karl Oberg arrived in Paris. Tall, with sparse fair hair and pink cheeks, he had a slight pot belly which protruded from underneath his black uniform. His title was Höhere S.S. und Polizeiführer (Supreme Head of the S.S. and Police). Like many a successful sales organization, the Paris Gestapo posed for a group photograph in front of its headquarters on avenue Foch, and Oberg stands in the center of the front row, with globular eyes protruding behind thick glasses.

Karl Albrecht Oberg was born on January 17, 1897, in Hamburg, the son of a doctor. He had a distinguished record in World War I, winning the Iron Cross, both First and Second Classes, and ending the war as a lieutenant. After the war, he took part in the Kapp putsch, which unsuccessfully tried to overthrow the young German Republic. He later failed in several personal business attempts. In June, 1931, he joined the Nazi party and rose rapidly in the S.S. and Gestapo. He was described by his subordinates, to whom he was very considerate, as a ponderous, patient, and kindly man—a devoted husband, who doted on his three children. This is also the man who, when a Vichy official came to complain about the kidnaping of Jewish children from orphanages in the unoccupied zone, snarled, "*Ein Jude ist kein Mensch!*" ("A Jew is not a human being!")

Oberg's appointment was a victory of the Gestapo over the German army command in France. The directive that Himmler had gained from Hitler gave Oberg absolute power over "all police matters and reprisals against criminals, Jews, and Communists implicated in attacks against the German Reich or the citizens of the Reich." The Militärbefehlshaber could only give him orders on matters concerning military operations or the security of German armed forces in France, and it was directed that all disputes between the two services would be settled by the Führer himself. In addition, the Abwehr—the German Military Intelligence responsible for counterespionage and repression of the Resistance—was absorbed into Oberg's command, as well as the French police in the occupied zone.

To celebrate this victory over the stiff-necked army generals, who tended to look down upon the proletarians of the party, Oberg's boss, Reinhardt Heydrich, arrived in Paris to preside at the presentation of the new police chief to the Army High Command; this took place at the fashionable Ritz Hotel on May 7. One can imagine the lack of joy with which the army, steeped in the traditions of imperial Germany, greeted the former banana importer from Hamburg, now head of all police functions in occupied France. General Heinrich von Stülpnagel, the new German army commander in France,* was present and managed to hide his anger at the appointment.

Whatever feeling of triumph Heydrich may have experienced dur-

* Heinrich von Stülpnagel had replaced his cousin Otto, who retired in January. This transfer of power was unknown to most Parisians since the name that appeared beneath the execution notices posted on the walls was still von Stülpnagel.

ing this chilly ceremony was short-lived; less than a month later, he was assassinated near Prague by Czech patriots parachuted from England.

Perhaps it was as a tribute to Heydrich (and his methods for suppressing resistance in the occupied territories) that Oberg issued the infamous "Family Hostage Law" (July 19, 1942). Now, not only those guilty of "terrorism were to be held responsible, but if they were to flee after being identified (and did not surrender within ten days), their grandfathers, fathers, brothers, and male cousins would be shot. All female relatives would be condemned to hard labor and all their children under seventeen would be sent to reform schools.

The return of Pierre Laval and the arrival of Oberg were only two more problems for Jean Moulin. The quarrels and recriminations within the resistance movement over the Frenay–Pucheu conversation had not yet abated, and d'Astier was using these as an excuse to delay the fusion of Liberation with Combat and Franc-Tireur. In an effort to bring the prestige of de Gaulle to bear on the hot-headed d'Astier de la Vigerie, Moulin arranged to have him sent to London. He was picked up off Antibes by a British submarine which landed him at Gibraltar, where he took a plane to London. Stubborn and sharp-tongued, d'Astier de la Vigerie was not a success in the circles about de Gaulle. Passy referred to him as an "anarchist in dancing shoes" because of his immaculate dress and radical policies, while Jacques Soustelle (commissioner of information) called him a "pinko Beau Brummel." It was inevitable that d'Astier de la Vigerie's Leftist leanings and the large number of Communists in his Liberation group should cause him to be regarded with suspicion by the traditional, even conservative, Free French officials. When Moulin, fearful of the effect that d'Astier de la Vigerie would have on de Gaulle, radioed "D'Astier represents only himself. Shall I send Frenay?" London answered wearily, "No. One is enough."

Back in France Jean Moulin was slowly making progress. He set up a new propaganda office (the Bureau d'Information et de Propagande—B.I.P.) to coordinate the efforts of both the Free French movement in London and the metropolitan resistance. The first director of the B.I.P. was Georges Bidault, who had been a prisoner in Germany and had recently been repatriated as a veteran of World War I. A professor of history in Lyons, he belonged to Combat and was close to a number of prominent journalists from various resistance groups. Bidault proceeded to coordinate the propaganda themes generated by both London and the metropolitan resistance; this was a job that badly needed doing, especially at a time when some resistance newspapers were still reluctant to speak disrespectfully of Pétain.

Moulin also organized the penetration of the Vichy administration by creating the Noyautages des Administrations Publiques—the N.A.P.—with the goal not only of converting public officials to the Resistance, but obtaining information and intelligence vital to both clandestine action and to the British war effort. The N.A.P. listed outstanding people, chiefly officials, to take over the public administration once the signal was given; it also listed notorious collaborators to be "neutralized" at the same time.

At every point Moulin's attempt at organization and structuring of the different resistance groups was opposed by their leaders. Proud of their work and jealous of their prerogatives, they resented him for standing between them and de Gaulle. They also worried about losing control of their members and therefore their stature, since Moulin was withdrawing their people to staff his auxiliary services, such as the B.I.P. and N.A.P. In response to the rivalry between the different chieftains—a rivalry that was inevitable, perhaps, but still extremely distressing at a time when the enemy stood on the soil of the Motherland and threatened her destruction—Jean Moulin exclaimed, "Gentlemen, think of France!"

This climate of suspicion and recriminations was not eased by the Free French agents sent over from London to work with the different resistance groups. Their lack of appreciation for the work which had been done, for the dangers involved, and for the priority given propaganda over armed action increased the misunderstanding between London and the metropolitan resistance. Too strongly Gaullist in their thinking and resented because of their inability to supply money and arms in the quantities required, they simply added to the squabbling. In addition, the independence of certain resistance groups was regarded by these Free French agents as not only a crime, but treason.

Money was always a sore point. Dependent for all things upon the British, the Gaullists never had enough money available to fund the Resistance in France properly. By 1942 large numbers of people had left their jobs to work full time in the Resistance, and these people had to receive at least a minimum stipend in order to live. Propaganda was very expensive—paper and presses were hard to secure and had to be purchased for exorbitant sums. Rivalries and misunderstandings were rife, since each chief of a resistance group thought that he was being kept in short supply in order to give more money to the others.

On top of all this, Jean Moulin had to face the reluctance of the resistance groups to permit their paramilitary units to be assembled into a Secret Army. De Gaulle wanted the political effort separated from the military, but the resistance chiefs saw it quite differently. They proposed that the Secret Army be made up of volunteers from the resistance groups, and that there be a close liaison between the heads of the Secret Army and the group leaders. Frenay, who quickly put in his bid to head the Secret Army, called it "a military and revolutionary tool . . . liberation and revolution are two aspects of the same problem, and indissolvably tied together."

Fearful that control of the military effort by the political groups would lead to trouble after the liberation, at least to unacceptable political demands on the structure of the future regime, de Gaulle summoned Frenay and d'Astier de la Vigerie to London* in October, 1942, and informed them that he was appointing General Charles Delestraint to head the future Secret Army. The decision was accepted with ill grace, and later the resistance chiefs would try to organize their own military formations based on the Maquis.

After his meeting with Frenay and d'Astier, de Gaulle wrote to Jean Moulin with new instructions:

> *Mon cher ami,*
>
> You are to assume the leadership of the coordinating committee in which the three principal resistance movements, Combat, Franc-Tireur, and Liberation, will be represented. As the representative of the National Committee in the unoccupied zone, you will continue to make all the political contacts that you judge useful. For that purpose, you may use certain of our agents who are directly subordinated to you.
>
> Other than the three large movements put together by the coordinating committee, all other resistance organizations, no matter what their character, should be invited to join their members to one of these groups and to merge their action squads with the units of the Secret Army now being organized. This, indeed, should avoid the proliferation of multiple little groups which would risk working at cross purposes, and which would generate rivalries and create confusion."

In November, 1942, as Moulin struggled with these problems, two events which were to have a critical effect on the Resistance occurred: by the end of the month, the unoccupied zone in which they had operated with relative impunity had vanished and two rivals to de Gaulle had appeared.

Early on the morning of November 8, 1942, 110,000 American and British soldiers started landing from almost three hundred ships at Casablanca, Oran, and Algiers. Operation Torch had been prepared in

* "Upon my return from the Levant and Africa, I found unimpugnable witnesses waiting for me in London—Frenay, the head of Combat, and D'Astier, the head of 'Liberation'—who gave me their reports on action in the unoccupied zone. Their accounts emphasized the will towards organization, and the pressure from the rank and file towards unity, but also the extreme individualism of the leaders, from which their rivalries resulted." De Gaulle, *op. cit.*, p. 42.

great secrecy by the Allies; indeed, the exact date of the landing on the coast of French North Africa was unknown to the French conspirators in Algiers, who, in contact with the American consul, Robert Murphy, had helped plan the invasion. Even General de Gaulle had not been told that Torch was imminent, supposedly because of the fear of leaks from Free French circles.

Originally, the conspirators, who were neither pro-Pétain nor pro-de Gaulle, had offered the command of the French armed forces to General Weygand, who refused, saying he was too old to become a rebel. The extravagantly tall General Henri Giraud, who had made a spectacular escape from a German prison camp and who had refused the insistent demands of both Laval and Abetz to return voluntarily to captivity, was next approached. He accepted the proposition made by the conspirators, provided that he was given the supreme command of all Allied forces, and that there would be a simultaneous Allied landing in metropolitan France. After incongruously pledging his loyalty to Pétain, Giraud left by submarine for Gibraltar on November 5. The same day, by sheer coincidence, Admiral Darlan, commander of all Vichy air, sea, and land forces, arrived in Algiers to visit his son, who was desperately ill of poliomyelitis.

While the Allied landings were facing heavy resistance at Casablanca and Oran, in distant Vichy (where news of the Allied landing had just been received) a letter from President Roosevelt was handed to Pétain. In it the president explained that the landings were intended to prevent a German aggression against the French empire and proclaimed that the United States had no territorial ambitions in this area. To this Pétain replied coldly: "We are being attacked; we will defend ourselves. This is the order I am giving." In spite of this hostile reply to the American president, Pétain secretly wired Darlan: "TAKE WHAT ACTION YOU THINK NECESSARY."

The Marshal was under great pressure from General Weygand and members of his own staff to leave immediately for North Africa to take command of the government there and to return France to the war on the side of the Allies. Fearing the complete occupation of France by the Germans and an imposed government headed by a supercollaborator such as Déat or Doriot, the Marshal refused.

The German reaction to the news of the Allied landings was violent. A message was sent to Vichy demanding a French declaration of war on the United States. Unable to agree to this, but fearful of the results of a direct refusal, the Vichy council of ministers declared that by its attack the United States had broken off diplomatic relations with France. The Germans were not soothed; the breaking-off of diplomatic relations was not the same as a declaration of war. Hitler summoned Laval to Munich.

Fearful of what might await him there, Laval sewed a poison pellet into the lining of his jacket. At Munich, on November 10, he was received icily by Hitler, who immediately demanded landing fields in Tunisia for use by German planes. Laval refused; Hitler insisted that it was Germany's firm resolve to take these landing fields—if necessary, by force. As the French deputy premier left the room, Ribbentrop told him of the German decision to occupy the French free zone.

Meanwhile, in Algeria, Darlan had signed an armistice with the Allies the same day, at 10 A.M. Shortly thereafter, he received a message from Pétain ordering him to resist, and later, in a secret naval code, the countermessage "Act for the best. You have all my confidence." The confusion in Darlan's mind as to the Marshal's true intention led to a tragic series of orders, counterorders, armistices, and breaking of agreements. Before it was over, fifteen thousand French soldiers and as many British and Americans had fallen in North Africa.

At seven o'clock in the morning of November 11, 1942, units of the Wehrmacht crossed the demarcation line in France and began the overrunning of the unoccupied zone. In anticipation of this violation of the armistice agreement, the tiny French army had prepared to resist, and was about to move out to take positions in the open country. They quickly received orders from General Bridoux, the Vichy minister of war, that they were not to leave their garrisons, and they were not to resist the new German invasion. Only General Jean de Lattre de Tassigny refused to obey this order and continued to move his troops in anticipation of a further resistance. However, he was soon arrested by the Vichy police and imprisoned.

Hitler's letter to Pétain announcing the occupation of the free zone was a model of hypocrisy and spite:

> Monsieur le Maréchal,
>
> Since the day when Fate called me to lead the destinies of my people, I have sincerely tried to improve our relations with France. . . . The declarations of war by England and France against Germany on September 3, 1939, had all the more profoundly affected me. . . .
>
> In the hope of once more carrying the war to Europe, England and America have begun to attack and occupy the French territories of West Africa and North Africa. In such circumstances, Monsieur le Maréchal, I have the honor and the regret to inform you that in order to thwart the danger which threatens us, I am forced, in conjunction with the Italian government, first, to give orders to my troops to cross France by the most direct way in order to occupy the Mediterranean coast, and, second, to participate in the protection of Corsica against the imminent aggression of Anglo-American armed forces. Above all, it is the conduct of a French general which has led me to act thus. During the course

of his captivity, he had faked an illness, and because of this he had been given certain privileges which he used to escape.*

As a sop to French sensibilities and outraged sense of honor, Hitler declared in his letter that the Marshal was now free to move his government from Vichy to any other city in France.

In the initial overrunning of the unoccupied zone, the German army very carefully did not try to take the naval base at Toulon. Hitler thought that any attempt to do so would cause the French fleet, then in Toulon, to sail for either North Africa or England. However, this lasted only until the morning of November 27, when a sudden attack by German tanks forced the gates of the naval arsenal at Toulon. Acting on prearranged instructions, the French fleet scuttled itself. The last trump card in Vichy's hand sank voluntarily to the bottom of the harbor.

At the beginning of November, Vichy had been a sovereign government, although subject to the pressures of the occupation authorities. It had had an army, no matter how small, a territory to administer, a fleet, and a powerful empire. It still maintained diplomatic relations with both the Allied and the Axis powers, as well as most of the neutral countries. By the end of November, these were all gone, and all that remained were the representatives of Switzerland and the Vatican in the now meaningless city of Vichy.

Recognizing that Admiral Darlan (although he had been hastily proclaimed a "temporary expedient" by the Americans) and General Giraud both represented threats to the Free French claim to represent the entire French Resistance, Jean Moulin hastened his work of unification. To bolster his claim that the Free French movement represented both the interior and exterior Resistance, the name "Fighting France" (France Combattante) was adopted by de Gaulle. But a change of name was not enough, for it was clear that the Americans intended that either Darlan or Giraud would replace de Gaulle as head of a new French government-in-exile. The antipathy that President Roosevelt felt for the temperamental de Gaulle was well-known, and although Winston Churchill on many occasions had tried to protect his protégé, it was clear that the volatile Frenchman would never be sufficiently submissive to please the American president. The only thing that would preserve de Gaulle's position was a proclamation by a strong united French Resistance that it would recognize him—and him alone—as the head of the effort to liberate France.

On Christmas Eve, 1942, half the problem disappeared: Admiral Darlan was assassinated by a young Royalist fanatic named Fernand Bonnier de la Chapelle. As de Gaulle later wrote:

* This was General Giraud.

This young man, this child overwhelmed by the spectacle of odious events, thought his action would be a service to his lacerated country, would remove from the road to French reconciliation an obstacle shameful in his eyes. He believed, moreover, as he repeatedly said until the moment of his execution, that an intervention would be made in his behalf by some outside source so high and powerful that the North African authorities could not refuse to obey it . . . the hasty and abbreviated trial before a military tribunal convened at night and in private session, the immediate and secret execution of Fernand Bonnier de la Chapelle . . . all these led to the suspicion that someone wanted to conceal at any price the origin of his decision. . . .

In February, 1943, Jean Moulin flew to London. For a month, he conferred with de Gaulle and his staff on the new organization. At the end of March, he returned by a small plane with General Delestraint and Christian Pineau, a delegate from the Socialist Resistance. Moulin carried with him a new directive for the establishment of a National Council of the Resistance (Conseil National de la Résistance—C.N.R.) which would unite the resistance groups in both zones. The demarcation line, although pointless after the German invasion of November 11, 1942, was not finally eliminated until March, 1943.

It took Jean Moulin two months of hard work to form the Conseil National de la Résistance. The closer they came to unification, the more the heads of the different resistance groups balked. First, the larger groups, those whose members were more numerous, demanded more than one seat on the new council, in spite of Moulin's insistence that each group have only one representative. The leaders of the smaller groups feared loss of prestige and absorption by the larger groups. The Communist party arrogantly claimed that it was the only political party in the Resistance, in spite of the existence of Socialist and radical clandestine groups. The presence of Joseph Laniel as a member of the C.N.R. was disputed by certain groups, for he had voted for Pétain on July 10, 1940 (although he later disavowed his vote). Moulin, who had named Laniel himself to the council, took his side firmly, and the incident was closed.*

Finally, on May 27, 1943, in a private apartment on the rue du Four, Paris, the first meeting of the C.N.R. took place. It was composed of representatives of all the clandestine groups, political parties, and trade unions then part of the Resistance. Moulin opened the session with a statement of the aims of Fighting France as defined by de Gaulle: "To continue the war . . . return free speech to the French people . . . reestablish republican liberties in a state from which social justice would not be excluded and which will have a sense of *grandeur*."

* In 1955, Joseph Laniel was premier of France.

Later a motion was proposed that clearly put the French Resistance on the side of de Gaulle in his conflict with General Giraud: "France expects that a real government will be formed in North Africa... and that it will be headed by General de Gaulle, the soul of the Resistance in its darkest days."

After almost three years of German occupation, the Resistance finally was united, albeit weakly. This was the work of one man: Jean Moulin, who, in spite of the many obstacles placed in his path by the petty rivalries of the different resistance chiefs, the antagonism felt toward him by some of the men around de Gaulle, and the ever-threatening German repression, had succeeded in bringing together the scattered Resistance into a single united front against the invader.

As he left the apartment on the rue du Four, his goal finally achieved, Jean Moulin had only a month to live.

7
Betrayal

On April 27, 1943, Jean Multon (alias Lunel) was arrested by the Marseilles Gestapo. As chief assistant to Frenay's second-in-command, Multon was an important prize, and Dunker, the Gestapo chief, spent long hours interrogating him. It took three days to "turn Lunel around." As with many resistance men who broke under threats and blows, Multon's conversion was wholehearted; once having agreed to betray his many contacts in the local Resistance, he set to work eagerly. He searched the streets of the port city, pointing out familiar faces to the German agents who accompanied him. He haunted the restaurants in which resistance people were known to dine, and whenever he spotted a well-known face a simple nod was enough to cause the arrest of another *résistant.* As one of the resistance survivors reported:

"Multon roamed the streets where we used to meet, went straight to the restaurants that we frequented, and gave the kiss of Judas to those that he met there. Now none of us could walk on a street, could leave a railroad station, could get on a train without asking ourselves if we would not meet him, accompanied by his dreaded protectors."

According to a report later made by the Marseilles Gestapo, 125 members of the Resistance were arrested because of Multon's treachery. Of those arrested, five agreed to work for the Gestapo.

Having exhausted Multon's usefulness in the Marseilles area (the Resistance very quickly learned of his treason and stayed out of sight), Dunker sent Multon and another French traitor, Robert Moog, to Lyons, where they continued their deadly work under the head of the Lyons Gestapo, Klaus Barbie. Although Multon and Moog never operated in Lyons, then known as the "Capital of the Resistance," they had met many *résistants* from that town in Marseilles.

Barbie, whose real name was Klaus Altmann, was born in Berlin on October 25, 1915. After studying in the Berlin schools and serving for a short period in the labor ministry, he entered the criminal department of the police in 1936 and from there transferred to the S.S. After the outbreak of the war, he had made a name for himself by his brutal repression of the Resistance in Belgium and Holland, in recognition of which he was transferred to France in November, 1942, and put in command of a special S.S. unit stationed in Lyons.

Multon's first assignment upon arriving in Lyons was to watch a *boîte aux lettres*—a mail drop—which Barbie had learned from an arrested resistance member was used by the elusive head of the group Sabotage-Fer (Railroad Sabotage) to receive messages from other resistance organizations. It was the head of Sabotage-Fer (whom Barbie knew only by his code name, Didot) that the Gestapo chief hoped to trap. It was in the investigation of many train derailments that had caused the deaths of numerous German soldiers that the name Didot had appeared time and time again.

Didot was René Hardy, a young railroad engineer with impeccable credentials as a *résistant.* Stationed in Corsica in June, 1940, he had tried unsuccessfully to raise an insurrection against the armistice and to rally the island to de Gaulle. Later, employed by the French National Railroad in Paris, he managed to create so many traffic jams and to send so many German troop and supply trains astray that he quickly came under suspicion and had to flee. While trying to reach Spain en route to London, he had been arrested by the Vichy police and spent a year in the prison at Toulon. After his release, he was persuaded by Frenay to join the *réseau* Combat as head of its railroad sabotage group. He accepted and soon assembled a network of railroad workers which enabled him not only to supply valuable intelligence on German train movements, but to carry out a number of train derailments. Extremely efficient in his work and highly popular with both his chiefs and his co-workers, Didot was a top priority target for the Lyons Gestapo. It was through the newly discovered mail drop in the rue Bouteille that Barbie hoped to capture him.

Impressed by Hardy's work, General Delestraint, the head of the Secret Army, met him in Lyons in May to offer him a job as head of the transport section (G-4) on the Secret Army staff. At the same time, while Hardy was considering the offer, General Delestraint asked him to draw up a sabotage plan for all French railroads to be put in effect at the moment the Allies landed in France. To accomplish this complicated task, Hardy retired to a country hideaway with his assistant, an engineer named Heilbronn, plus a draftsman and a secretary. Three weeks later, he had finished a report of 150 pages covering thousands of railway stations, assembly points, and crossings—all in code. In the meantime, General Delestraint had returned to Lyons, hoping to have an answer from Hardy on his offer of the staff job. Since Hardy was away, the general set a rendezvous in Paris for June 9 and asked his chief of staff, Henri Aubry, to see that Hardy was informed of the meeting upon his return to Lyons.

Now occurred the first of a series of strange events that would form a chain to destroy Jean Moulin. Aubry, greatly concerned over his wife's health and about to leave to join her, told his secretary, Madame Raisin, to type the message for Didot to meet Vidal (Delestraint) at the exit to the Paris subway station La Muette at 9 A.M. on June 9. What mysterious lapse occurred at this point has never been explained, but Madame Raisin delivered the message for the Paris rendezvous typed "*en clair*"—uncoded! She herself delivered the letter to the rue Bouteille, where Multon was observing the mailbox (according to Hardy, Madame Raisin had told Aubry that the mail drop was known to the Germans, but Aubry had ignored the warning). Why she was permitted to leave without being arrested, or even followed, is another inexplicable fact; in any case, Multon soon had the message revealing the fatal meeting.

Did Multon read the message and then return it to the mailbox? Did Hardy know that he had a rendezvous with Vidal in Paris on June 9? In January, 1947, at his first trial, René Hardy vehemently denied that he had ever seen this message. He told the court that he had abandoned the mail drop when he learned of the arrests in the Marseilles area caused by the traitor Multon. The members of Sabotage-Fer who worked closely with him also testified that there had been no mention made at this time of a meeting in Paris between the head of the Secret Army and their boss on June 9.

Now the deadly coincidences began to pile up: at 10 P.M. on the evening of June 7, René Hardy boarded the Paris train. He later stated (and it was confirmed by the man who waited in vain for him in Paris) that he had a meeting to study the organization of railroad sabotage in the northern zone. His ticket had been purchased for him in his real name by his fiancée, Mademoiselle Lydie Bastien. Occupying the other berth in his compartment was a minor Vichy functionary named Cressol, who was traveling to Germany for the ministry of public education. In the very next compartment were Lunel (Multon) and Moog, on their way to arrest General Delestraint in Paris.

Either on the platform or in the corridor of the train, Hardy spotted Multon, who had been pointed out to him in Marseilles several months earlier, and of whose treacherous activities he had been informed. The traitor also recognized Hardy, whom he knew only as "Carbon," and whispered the startling information to Moog. Hardy, aware that he was in grave danger, approached another *résistant* on the train and, under the pretense of getting a light for his cigarette, whispered to him, "If I am arrested, tell Bénouville that Lunel is on the train." (Bénouville was a prominent member of Combat with whom Hardy had worked closely.) Yet Hardy, although aware that he had been recognized by a traitor, made no attempt to leave the train at any of the intervening halts.

At one o'clock in the morning at the Chalon-sur-Saône station, German police—at Multon's direction—arrested Hardy and the flabbergasted Vichy official Cressol and took them to the local prison.

That Hardy was considered a prize catch was soon obvious. Although Multon had only known him under code name Carbon and had no idea of his true role in the Resistance, he must have suspected that this might be Didot, the chief of Sabotage-Fer. The importance of Hardy in the eyes of the Gestapo was emphasized when Barbie himself arrived in Chalon to take charge of the prisoner and to conduct him back to Lyons. Why would an S.S. Obersturmführer bother to make the trip for an ordinary resistance man who would otherwise have been immediately delivered to him by the German police in Chalon upon his request?

Cressol, who had been able to establish his status as a loyal member of the Vichy government, was released on June 10. At eleven o'clock in the morning of the same day, he saw a handcuffed Hardy being taken to a car for the trip to Lyons.

At 9 A.M. on June 9, 1943, an elderly gentleman was waiting patiently at the exit to the subway station La Muette in Paris. Although dressed in gray civvies, one could tell by his military posture and the rosette of the Légion d'Honneur in his buttonhole that he was an army officer. Occasionally, he would glance at his watch, for, like a good soldier, General Delestraint was prompt in his appointments.

Multon and Moog were also prompt. Walking up to Delestraint, Moog asked, "Monsieur, are you waiting for Didot?"

"Yes."

"He has sent us. As a precaution, he did not come himself, but sent us to fetch you."

Unsuspecting, the general got into the car which was parked nearby. He asked the two men kindly to stop at the entrance to the Métro station Pompe, where two other members of his staff were waiting for him. The French Gestapo agents were only too happy to comply. The three men were then taken to Number 95 avenue Foch, the headquarters of the Paris Gestapo.

Thus, through the incredible lapse in security, General Charles Delestraint, the head of the Secret Army, and the man personally selected by General de Gaulle* for this important work, was captured along with several of his aides. Hardy, however, was undoubtedly innocent of causing this severe blow to the Resistance.

* * *

* As inspector general of tanks in 1939, Delestraint had known Colonel de Gaulle, the French apostle of armored divisions.

What happened at the Gestapo headquarters in Lyons when Hardy and Barbie arrived there on the afternoon of June 10? According to Hardy, he was subjected to an arduous six-hour interrogation which Barbie commenced by trying to get him to admit that he was Didot, the chief of Sabotage-Fer. This Hardy vigorously denied; he told the Gestapo that his name was René Hardy (since he was traveling under his real name, he had all the proper documents to prove this) and that he was the owner of an agricultural machinery business in Garons. (Barbie immediately telephoned to Garons, where the cover story that Hardy had given him was confirmed.) He vigorously denied having anything to do with the Resistance and swore that he was loyal to Vichy. According to Hardy, Barbie swallowed this story, saying, "A tall, blond, long-headed Aryan like you would not help the Jews and Bolsheviks in the Resistance." Laughing, Hardy agreed, saying that he had no desire to aid such people. (He later admitted that he was determined to get out of the mess at any price: "If they had asked me to take an oath to Hitler, I would have done so. I even pretended to be ready to help them, if the occasion presented itself.")

Barbie jumped on this hint of cooperation with the Gestapo. He agreed to release Hardy on the single condition that the young man return each day to his fiancée's home; if he failed to do so, Barbie threatened to arrest Lydie Bastien and her parents and hold them as hostages. Hardy quickly agreed to this condition.

Barbie's version of the interrogation was obtained after the war when he was located in Germany, living in the American-occupied zone. At this time, he was an employee of the United States army counterintelligence corps, and his extradition to France as a war criminal was refused by the American army authorities on the grounds of his "contributions to U.S. national security." Nevertheless, upon the strenuous demands of Edouard Herriot, mayor of Lyons, president of the Chamber of Deputies, and three times premier of France, the American occupation authorities permitted Barbie to be questioned by a French policeman.

According to Barbie, Hardy had immediately admitted his identity as Didot, told of the existence of the railroad sabotage plan, and even reconstructed it from memory. He had also revealed the planned rendezvous with General Delestraint in Paris—and accepted eagerly when Barbie offered him the opportunity to work for the Gestapo. Barbie also claimed that Hardy had told him that Max, General de Gaulle's delegate to the Resistance and the head of the C.N.R., was the ex-prefect of Chartres, Jean Moulin. Hardy was then released with orders to pick up his contacts with the Resistance, to try to locate Max, and to stay in touch with the Lyons Gestapo.

Hardy denied that he had ever agreed to work for the Gestapo. He said that he had been arrested on the train when Moog noticed

Multon's start of recognition. Traveling under his own name with genuine papers and a valid cover story, he had been released because the Gestapo had failed to establish that he was Didot. And it had been Barbie who had told him during the interrogation that General Delestraint had been arrested.

Barbie's testimony has been proved false on many points. Why would Hardy, knowing that Multon knew him only as Carbon, admit that he was Didot, the head of Sabotage-Fer? To admit that he was responsible for the deaths of so many German soldiers in the train derailments was to buy himself a fast one-way ticket to the execution stake. How could Hardy in six hours reconstruct from memory the 150-page report on railroad sabotage covering all of France—a report that contained a thousand or more stations known only by their code numbers? How could Hardy inform Barbie of his rendezvous with the head of the Secret Army (a fact that the Lyons Gestapo had known for some time) when he had abandoned the mail drop in which that fatal message had been left? Finally, how could he identify Jean Moulin as Max when he had never met Jean Moulin? Constantly aware of the strict need for security, Moulin had worked in near-anonymity; only a handful of people could identify him as Max and Hardy was not one of them.

However, one fact is indisputable: René Hardy *was* released by the Gestapo at 11 P.M. on June 10th, 1943. This in itself is very puzzling; the Gestapo was not in the habit of releasing a suspicious prisoner after a short interrogation, particularly one who was important enough to bring the head of the Lyons Gestapo to Chalon, a distance of 110 miles, to conduct him personally back to Lyons. Had Barbie, pretending to believe Hardy's story, released him in order to grab the rest of the Sabotage-Fer network? Or had Hardy been "turned around" by the threats to his fiancée and her family? In either case, René Hardy knew that he was in imminent danger of execution—if not by the Gestapo, then by his own comrades in the Resistance.

By the middle of 1943, three years after the armistice, the Resistance—which had been so proud, optimistic, and even innocent in the beginning—had paid a terrible price in blood for its inexperience. Time and again, Frenchmen and Frenchwomen who were the paid eyes and ears of the Gestapo had infiltrated the resistance networks and, by their treachery, had exacted a ghastly toll in torture, imprisonment, deportation to the death camps, and execution. Even more heartbreaking was the fact that many *résistants,* some the most valiant in their group, had been arrested, and, under torture or the threat of torture, had agreed to work for the Gestapo. The Resistance was pragmatic; it knew that there was a limit to which the human body could be subjected before a man would yield, would do anything to make the pain cease. But it could not afford to be merciful. The inflexible rule was that any resistance member who had been arrested and released by the Gestapo or the German police was invariably suspect. If the member went immediately to the head of his network and admitted that he had been in the clutches of the Gestapo, that he had broken under torture and had agreed to work for the Germans, the usual procedure was to send the suspect "*au vert*"—to some secret hiding place in the countryside, far from his usual base of operation. At the time of his arrest all resistance members with whom he had contact had been warned to change their names and hiding places. His old quarters were watched to see whether they would be raided by the Gestapo; if they were not, the suspect was gradually, with many safeguards, integrated back into resistance work. If the Gestapo did raid the old addresses—well, the Resistance had no prisons in which it could safely keep those who were a danger to it. There would be a midnight burial in some empty field or a hastily filled-in grave in the depths of a forest.

When René Hardy walked out of the Gestapo headquarters in Lyons late on the night of June 10, he was conscious of the danger that he had escaped, but he was equally aware of the even greater danger that he faced. By now he knew that General Delestraint had been arrested in Paris at a rendezvous which he had given Hardy; the chief of Sabotage-Fer knew that if the Resistance learned of his arrest and interrogation by the Gestapo they would never believe that he had not talked and caused the arrest of the head of the Secret Army. This would automatically be a death sentence, even for a man like Didot whose services to the Resistance were outstanding. So when, two days later, René Hardy renewed contact with the members of his group, he said nothing—nothing of the arrest at Chalon, nothing of the interrogation by Barbie, nothing of his pretense of helping the Gestapo. (He later claimed that he also did this in order to carry out a private inquiry as to who was responsible for betraying Delestraint.)

Of the hundreds of members of Sabotage-Fer whose real names and addresses Hardy knew, only one was arrested at this time by the Gestapo. Heilbronn, the engineer who had helped him formulate the master plan for railroad sabotage, had a rendezvous with Hardy at a street corner in Lyons on the afternoon of June 12, two days after Hardy's release. The two men strolled along, talking quietly for a few minutes, then separated, each going in a different direction. One block later, Heilbronn was arrested by the Gestapo. During his interrogation, a Gestapo agent told him that Hardy had betrayed him—a statement which the young engineer never believed. During his imprisonment, Heilbronn was tortured to make him admit that he was Didot!

Perhaps the Gestapo was being very clever in trying to cover a "double agent"; however, this incident would seem to indicate that they had not identified Hardy as Didot.

If Hardy had really been "turned around" during his interrogation, why didn't Barbie use him to destroy the Sabotage-Fer network which was doing such harm to the German army? Was he in fact aiming for much bigger game, such as the head of the Conseil National de la Résistance, General de Gaulle's personal delegate to the Resistance, the elusive Max?

The arrest of General Delestraint was a bitter setback to Jean Moulin. With a single blow the Gestapo had decapitated the organization that Moulin had labored arduously for over a year to construct; his plan for a union of the different paramilitary units, a single army covering the whole of France, now lay in ruins. In addition, he knew that the major resistance groups were still opposed to the idea of a Secret Army under one chief, since they feared losing control of their own paramilitary groups and thereby losing status. The general's arrest was bound to bring these suppressed disagreements to the surface, and Moulin feared that unless a replacement for Delestraint was named quickly open warfare would break out in the Resistance over this matter. But Delestraint had been named by General de Gaulle and had had his absolute confidence. Only de Gaulle could name his successor, and this would take time. In any case it would be difficult to find another senior officer who, in addition to being a good organizer and administrator, would be willing to act in second place to Jean Moulin, a mere ex-prefect.

Since it might be weeks or months before de Gaulle could name a new head of the Secret Army, Moulin decided to name provisionally two inspector generals of the A.S. (Armée Secrète): Raymond Aubrac for the northern zone, and André Lassagne for the southern zone. In addition, as a temporary measure, he proposed to name a Lyons *résistant*, Colonel Schwartzfeld, to continue Delestraint's work. But these decisions had to be ratified by all the resistance groups, especially the major ones. Unfortunately, the heads of the three largest groups in the C.N.R.—namely, Frenay of Combat, d'Astier de la Vigerie of Liberation, and J.-P. Lévy of Franc-Tireur—were all in London. The seconds-in-command to the leaders of the last two groups readily agreed with Moulin's proposal as a temporary measure, but Frenay's chief assistant was reluctant to make any important decisions in the absence of his boss. Knowing Frenay's disappointment at not having been given the command of the Secret Army, his deputy balked at approving Colonel Schwartzfeld even as a temporary chief of the Armée Secrète. Who was this reluctant deputy? It was Henri Aubry, who, in addition to being Delestraint's chief of staff, was also second-in-command to Frenay—the same Aubry who had inadvertently allowed an uncoded message specifying the rendezvous between Delestraint and Hardy to be placed in a mail drop known to the Gestapo.

Irritated by Aubry's obstructive tactics and convinced that valuable time was being wasted, Jean Moulin decided to call a meeting of all those concerned with the reconstruction of the Secret Army. In addition to the two new inspector generals, Colonel Schwartzfeld and Colonel Lacaze (who was being considered for a staff job) would be present. Aubry was also invited to present his objections, or rather Frenay's objections, to the proposal. Lassagne, who was a native of Lyons, was assigned to find a convenient place for the meeting, preferably one which had not been used before. The time of the meeting was set for the following Monday, June 21, at two o'clock in the afternoon.

Lassagne, who was an experienced *résistant,* preferred a doctor's office for this type of rendezvous since the arrival and departure of seven or eight men would not excite any notice or comment. He had two doctor friends whose homes might serve, but until he had contacted them he would not know if they were available, so he told Aubry, "Let's meet Monday, June twenty-first, at a quarter of two, at the *ficelle* [cable railway] at the Croix-Paquet. In the meantime, I'll have settled on the place."

But Aubry was still unhappy about the coming meeting. Suspecting that he would be outvoted, he decided to take someone along with him to the meeting to reinforce his arguments, and to support Frenay's thoughts. It would have to be someone well thought of in the Resistance, a Combat leader whose opinion Jean Moulin would have to respect. Who better than the highly regarded chief of Sabotage-Fer, the man to whom Delestraint had offered the staff job as head of transport? So, by another coincidence, Aubry decided to take René Hardy with him to the clandestine meeting.

On Sunday, June 20, at 11 A.M., Aubry met Hardy near the Morand Bridge, which crosses the Rhône River. Hardy was waiting for him, seated on a park bench. Aubry paid no attention to the rather short, round-faced blond man who was seated next to Hardy and who seemed to be deeply engrossed in his newspaper. Out of a sense of caution, Aubry asked Hardy to walk a little way with him. When they were out of earshot of the stranger on the bench, Aubry told Didot of the meeting the next day in which Max, General de Gaulle's delegate, would be present, and in which the leadership of the Secret Army would be decided. He asked Hardy to accompany him to the meeting and to support him when he presented Frenay's objections; since he himself did not know the location of the meeting, Aubry asked Hardy to meet him at the foot of the cable railway at a quarter to two the next afternoon. Hardy agreed and the two men went to lunch together.

On the park bench, the blond young man carefully folded his newspaper and stared thoughtfully at Aubry's retreating back. He motioned to his bodyguard, who was hidden in the bushes nearby, and the two men walked to their car.

The man on the bench was Klaus Barbie.

(The mystery of the "man on the park bench" is still unsolved. Hardy denied vehemently that Barbie had been sitting next to him when Aubry arrived. "On a beautiful June morning," he said, "there are a lot of people along the Rhône, some even sitting on the benches." But Barbie's presence at the Pont Morand was testified to by his bodyguard, Steingritt, and was even admitted by Hardy's lawyer in his plea to the jury. According to the defense counsel, Barbie arrived at the rendezvous by following Aubry and, hidden behind his newspaper, he [Barbie] had not been recognized by Hardy!

Still, if René Hardy was working for the Lyons Gestapo, why would Barbie risk getting such a valuable agent killed by the Resistance by the presence of the Gestapo chief at the Pont Morand?)

Meanwhile, Lassagne had decided on the meeting place. The previous day, he had lunched with an old school friend, Doctor Frédéric Dugoujon, whose home and office were in Caluire, a northern suburb of Lyons. To reach the doctor's villa, one took the *ficelle* to the Place de la Croix-Rousse, then the Number 33 trolley to the Place Castellane; the doctor's white villa stood on one edge of the square. At lunch, speaking only in a few guarded sentences, Lassagne had obtained the doctor's permission. Doctor Dugoujon had no idea of the purpose of the meeting, nor did he wish to know; in the past, he had lent his former residence to similar resistance meetings.

To inform Jean Moulin of the meeting place, Lassagne sent his assistant, Bruno Larat (known as Xavier); Moulin would bring with him Aubrac and Colonel Schwartzfeld. Larat also informed Colonel Lacaze of the meeting place. As previously arranged, Lassagne himself would meet Aubry at the bottom of the cable railway and bring him to the meeting; he did not suspect that Hardy would also be there.

So, by the evening of Sunday, June 20, 1943, five men were aware of the location of the meeting to take place the next afternoon: Moulin, Lassagne, Colonel Lacaze, Bruno Larat, and Doctor Dugoujon (although the doctor did not know either the purpose of the meeting or the names of the other participants). Four others knew that the meeting would take place and had received instructions on where they were to be picked up: Aubrac and Colonel Schwartzfeld would be brought by Jean Moulin; Aubry would be brought by Lassagne, and—unknown to the others—Aubry was bringing René Hardy.

But were these the only ones who knew of the meeting? Did Klaus Barbie know that a meeting was to take place on Monday afternoon, a meeting in which Max, General de Gaulle's delegate to the Resistance, would be present? If he was unaware of its exact location, did he know that René Hardy would be present and that, if one followed Hardy the next afternoon, one would be led inevitably to a rendezvous with Max?

On Sunday evening, Doctor Dugoujon told his maid that several men would be coming the next afternoon who would give Monsieur Lassagne's name. She was to take them to the bedroom on the first floor and not to his waiting room on the ground floor.

The stage was set; the tragedy was about to begin.

Monday, June 21, 1943.

Early in the morning, Jean Moulin had a meeting on a street corner with his newly arrived assistant, Claude Serreulles, who had exchanged an anxiety-ridden staff job in London—working for the demanding General de Gaulle—for a less dangerous one working with the Resistance in occupied France. He had been parachuted into France on the night of June 16 and had only reached Lyons on the nineteenth. He found a weary and nervous Jean Moulin struggling with the many problems arising from Delestraint's arrest. Moulin, who had expected Serreulles two months earlier, was surprised at his arrival and somewhat suspicious that he had been sent by Colonel Passy and the B.C.R.A. (see page 79), who were none too favorable to Moulin's work. Serreulles had smoothed over this difficulty very quickly, protesting that he had not come to act as a spy for Passy. He was also able to inform Moulin of the formation on June 3 in Algiers of the French Committee for National Liberation under the co-chairmanships of Generals Giraud and de Gaulle.

As they walked along the banks of the Rhône River, Jean Moulin proposed a role in the reconstruction of the Secret Army to Serreulles, and then told him of the meeting to be held that same afternoon. Serreulles was told to be at the top of the cable railway at *one o'clock;* from there he would be taken to the meeting place by a resistance member.

Later that morning, Jean Moulin met with Aubry in another part of Lyons. It was raining hard, and the two men walked slowly along the sidewalk under their umbrellas, conversing in low voices. There was an argument about the delivery of some weapons that had been parachuted to the Resistance. The local *résistants* who had received the weapons had not taken them to the assigned spot, and Aubry had forced them to return the arms to the hiding place previously agreed upon. Moulin reproached him for having acted in an arrogant and high-handed way. The constant pressures and tensions of clandestine work were enough to make the two men edgy, but the additional strain due to the arrest of General Delestraint and Aubry's objections to Moulin's plan for rebuilding the Secret Army made the two men even more short-tempered than usual, and both were quick to take offense. As for naming a new head of the Secret Army, Jean Moulin said that that would be decided at the afternoon meeting.

Every mystery should have a beautiful woman in it, preferably one whose loyalty is suspect and whose role is ambiguous. Mademoiselle Deletraz was young, pretty, and blond, and she had been a member of the Lyons branch of Colonel Groussard's resistance group until she was captured by the Gestapo in April, 1943. Like Multon and so many others, she was "turned around" and for a while served as the bait in what the French called *la souricière*—the rattrap. Placed in an apartment which was known to the Resistance as a "safe house," her job was to open the door and admit the *résistants* who came seeking refuge; inside the apartment, the Gestapo was waiting to gather them in.

On May 28, the Gestapo drove her to Maçon. When they dropped her close to the center of town, they told her to walk to the nearby square, where a woman would be waiting, and to say to her, "Henry is well." In the middle of the town square, Mademoiselle Deletraz saw a white-haired woman with blue eyes and a deep scar over one eyebrow. Walking up to her, she repeated the code phrase. Reassured, the woman smiled and said, "Tell them [the members of Combat] that you saw me." Mademoiselle Deletraz then left to take the train back to Lyons. On the way to the station, she was stopped again by the Gestapo and taken back in their car. Shortly after this, the white-haired woman in the Maçon town square was arrested. She was Bertie Albrecht, one of the first *résistantes*, a gallant member of Combat and Henri Frenay's longtime confidante. Captured by the Vichy police in October, 1942, and sentenced to six months in prison, Bertie Albrecht had simulated madness and had been sent to a psychiatric hospital at Bron, from which she quickly escaped. She had been hiding in Maçon for several months.*

Shortly before noon on Monday, June 21, 1943, Mademoiselle Deletraz, highly excited, entered a French army office in Lyons looking for an officer whom she knew was in the Resistance. Unable to locate him, she confided to another officer (not a resistance member) that she had just left the office of the Gestapo, where she had heard a

* Her fate is uncertain. After the liberation, a death certificate was found in the files of the Fresnes prison. It reported the death on June 7, 1943, of Madame "Berthe Halbrech," née Wild on February 15, 1893, at Marseilles. The report states, "Cause of death unknown."

man named Didot, alias Hardy, tell the Gestapo that there was to be a meeting of the leaders of the Secret Army that afternoon, about one o'clock, and that he—Hardy—was to take part in the meeting but did not know where it would be held. However, the Gestapo had only to have him followed to the meeting place; Mademoiselle Deletraz had been picked by Barbie to trail Hardy to the rendezvous point.

Strangely enough, in spite of her role as a Gestapo spy Mademoiselle Deletraz had maintained contact with her old resistance network. It was to the head of this group that she first went to warn him that the meeting was known to the Gestapo. Unfortunately, the chief of the *réseau* was not at his home, and although she left a message for him he did not receive it until the next day. The young officer she spoke to in the army office warned two of his friends who he knew belonged to the Secret Army. One of them tried to contact André Lassagne through a "mail drop" at the home of a mutual friend, but Lassagne was busy with the details of the meeting and never picked up the message.

It was now one o'clock, and Claude Serreulles was waiting at the top of the *ficelle* for the liaison agent to take him to the meeting. Either there had been a misunderstanding about the time, or else Jean Moulin had made an incredible mistake, for Serreulles was much too early. If it was intended that he meet Lassagne and Aubry and proceed with them to Doctor Dugoujon's house, the two men were not due to meet until 1:45 at the *foot* of the cable railway. In any case, after waiting twenty minutes, Serreulles became nervous and left. He was not to be present at the fatal rendezvous.

At 1:30 P.M., Lassagne made a final inspection of the villa and the surrounding area, then went to meet Aubry at the bottom of the cable railway. He did not seem to have noticed that there were two gross errors in the security plan for the meeting: there was only one entrance to Doctor Dugoujon's villa and no emergency exits, and there had been no provision for a guard or protection unit to watch the outside of the house while the meeting went on. Arriving by bicycle at the agreed-upon rendezvous spot at 1:45 P.M., Lassagne was surprised to see René Hardy standing with Aubry. However, since Aubry had asked Hardy, as the head of Sabotage-Fer, to attend the meeting, Lassagne made no protest and the three men entered the cable car and rode to the top. There Lassagne told them to take the Number 33 trolley and to get off at the Place Castellane in Caluire while he preceded them on his bicycle. When the two men descended from the trolley, Lassagne was waiting and took them directly to Doctor Dugoujon's house. Colonel Lacaze and Larat were already waiting in the bedroom on the first floor.

Outside the villa, on the opposite side of the Place Castellane, a pretty young blonde watched the three men enter the house and then went to report the meeting place to the Gestapo. She still hoped that her warning had been received in time, but she did not enter the villa and warn the men inside.

When she arrived at Gestapo headquarters, Mademoiselle Deletraz was shown a map of Lyons and told to pinpoint the meeting place. Pretending that she could not read the map, she told them that they would have to follow the line of the Number 33 trolley and perhaps she could recognize the house again. In this way she was able to stall for time, hoping that the meeting would break up before the Gestapo arrived. Pretending not to recognize any of the landmarks in Caluire, she was able to gain time before, bowing under their threats, she pointed out Doctor Dugoujon's house. It was 2:45 P.M.; the Gestapo was forty-five minutes late.

But by a sad coincidence, Jean Moulin was also forty-five minutes late. He and Aubrac had met at the Place Carnot at 2:15 P.M. and had gone to the terminal of the cable railway to meet Colonel Schwartzfeld. The colonel arrived fifteen minutes late, so by the time the three men entered the cable train, rode to the top, took the trolley to Place Castellane, and entered the villa, it was 2:45 P.M. If the meeting had been arranged for 2 P.M., why had Jean Moulin set his meeting with Aubrac for 2:15 P.M., and why had he told Serreulles to wait at the top of the cable car line at 1 P.M.? This is a mystery that has never been explained. Possibly Moulin had been mistaken about the time of the meeting and thought that it was arranged for 2:30 P.M., a time at which he could have been at the villa if Colonel Schwartzfeld had not been late. But this still does not explain the orders he gave to Claude Serreulles.

If Jean Moulin had been punctual, the meeting might have been over by the time the Gestapo arrived forty-five minutes late. If he had been even later, he would have seen their familiar black cars in front of the villa and would have escaped the trap.

When Moulin, Aubrac, and Colonel Schwartzfeld entered the house, the maid, who had been told to expect Lassagne's friends at two o'clock, thought they were genuine patients and led them into the waiting room, where five or six real patients were waiting to see Doctor Dugoujon. Upstairs, in the first-floor bedroom, Lassagne, Aubry, Hardy, and Lacaze were still waiting for Moulin's arrival.

It was only several minutes after the last three men arrived that Aubry, looking out of the window from the first-floor bedroom, saw three black cars pull up in front of the villa. Seven or eight civilians in black leather jackets jumped out and rushed into the front door. "We've had it . . . it's the Gestapo!" Aubry exclaimed. Hardy pulled a gun from his jacket pocket, but was quickly persuaded to put it away. The door of the bedroom opened, and the Gestapo entered, led by a short blond man who shouted in excellent French: "Hands up! German police!" The four *résistants* were slapped and thrown violently against the wall; their arms were twisted behind their backs and they were handcuffed. A thorough search was made of their persons. Then the short, blond man said to Aubry, "Well now, *Thomas* [Aubry's alias], you were happier yesterday at the Morand Bridge. I was reading my newspaper, but it was such a beautiful day that I thought I would let you have at least this one lovely morning more since today we would meet again. . . ." It was then that Aubry claimed to have recognized the man who had been sitting on the bench next to Hardy during the rendezvous at the Morand Bridge.

In the waiting room on the ground floor, the same scene was taking place. All the patients—both the real and the false ones—were brutally slapped and thrown against the wall. Before being handcuffed, Jean Moulin was able to take some notes from his jacket and swallow them. As Doctor Dugoujon was pulled from his office and thrust against the wall next to him, Moulin whispered, "My name is Jean Martel." He had taken the precaution of securing a letter from a doctor asking Dugoujon to recommend a specialist in treating rheumatism; this would be the explanation he would offer for his presence in the waiting room.

Opposite the bedroom on the first floor was the dining room, and it was here that Barbie conducted his preliminary interrogation.

All the men in the waiting room were brought up to the first-floor bedroom (several women who were obviously genuine patients were soon released). It was then that Moulin, Aubrac, and Schwartzfeld were aware for the first time of the presence of René Hardy. They were astonished to see him there. Aubrac, who was particularly indignant at this violation of the security rules, also noted that, although all the other prisoners were handcuffed with their arms behind their back, Hardy was being held only by a *cabriolet*. This was a knotted rope which was twisted around his right wrist; the attached handle of the rope was held by one of the Gestapo agents. It would also appear that, in spite of the thorough frisking that all the prisoners had received, Hardy had managed successfully to hide his gun in a secret pocket in the sleeve of his jacket.

One by one, the prisoners were brought into the dining room, where Barbie and another Gestapist conducted the questioning. It was obvious that the Gestapo knew that Max was present at the meeting, but that it did not know which one of the prisoners was the redoubtable delegate of General de Gaulle to the French Resistance. The interrogation was a brutal one. As the prisoners stubbornly maintained their silence, a furious Barbie tore a leg from a valuable table and beat them about the shoulders, back, and head. Still, he was unable to determine the identity of Max.

It was while Lassagne was being questioned that several shots were fired outside the house. He later testified that Barbie and his assistant smiled at each other; neither of them appearing to be disturbed by the shooting. The shots announced the escape of René Hardy.

Hardy had been taken out through the front door, past a guard armed with a submachine gun, down to the waiting cars.

> When my guard tried to make me enter one of the cars [he told an interviewer in 1972], he opened the door with one hand. I shoved him and, hitting him with my free left hand, tripped him, and slammed the door in his face. He fell on the fender, letting go of the *cabriolet*, and I ran. . . . I zigzagged between the trees, and I heard bullets whistling by. I was wounded. . . . I pulled out my gun to fire over my shoulder in order to cover my flight. The Germans, who had a dozen prisoners on their hands, gave up the pursuit as soon as I reached the heights of the Place Castellane. I threw myself into a ditch covered with high weeds to catch my breath. The open fracture of my arm began to hurt. I stumbled down the ditch, then rushed into one of the cross-streets and decided to reach the Saône River by way of the steepest slope, not knowing exactly where I was.

This miraculous escape of René Hardy has several puzzling aspects: the German armed with a submachine gun at the entrance to the villa did not fire, although he had a clear shot at the fugitive; an elderly roadworker standing on the Place Castellane testified that only one of the Germans had fired, not toward Hardy, but against a nearby wall. He also said that the Germans did not search the ditch but quickly came back. According to Doctor Dugoujon, "a child playing at hide-and-seek could have found Hardy in that ditch."

Meanwhile, Barbie had his prisoners taken to his headquarters at the Military Medical School on the Avenue Marcelin-Berthelot. There they were shoved into the basement and lined up against the wall, still handcuffed; then, one by one, they were taken up to Barbie's office for new questioning. They were beaten and threatened incessantly, but the Gestapo still could not learn which one of the prisoners was Max. Late that same night, all the prisoners were transferred to the prison of Montluc and placed in the same cell.

Hardy, in great pain, stumbled along the banks of the Saône. Two passersby helped him to a nearby shelter, then called the police, who questioned Hardy briefly and then took him to the hospital. There, the doctors who examined his wound said that there was no trace of a powder burn, which meant that the bullet must have been fired from a distance of more than a foot. At Hardy's trials—years later—there was conflicting medical testimony on whether the wound could have been self-inflicted. The prosecution claimed that Hardy had shot himself to avoid any suspicion about his escape; the doctors who first treated his wound denied this. A week later, the French police turned him over to the Gestapo, who transferred him to the prison quarters of the German hospital at the Croix-Rousse.

But before he was returned to the clutches of the Gestapo, an attempt was made by the Resistance to murder him. Aubrac's wife, Lucie, on orders from his resistance group, made up a food package containing a small pot of jam which had been saturated with cyanide. To make sure that no one else would taste the jam, Madame Aubrac brought the package herself to the hospital to give it to Hardy. She was too late; Didot had escaped again!

It was from the German hospital, on the night of August 3, that René Hardy performed his second miraculous disappearance. Many years later he described his evasion as follows:

> I escaped by blowing off the padlock which secured the window. There was a guard in the corridor who spent most of his time flirting and drinking with the nurses . . . my room was above the garages, which looked out on a courtyard closed by a doorway and a gate. I jumped out through this window and found myself in the courtyard. . . . I hoisted myself over the gate and dropped down into the street.

All this derring-do was accomplished with his arm still in a plaster cast.

The next day, accompanied by his fiancée, René Hardy left Lyons for the south of France. Because of his previous immaculate record as a *résistant*, not all of the resistance groups were willing to believe him guilty of such vile treachery. After performing some missions in Paris for Combat, Hardy reached North Africa with his fiancée. Henri Frenay, who was now a minister in de Gaulle's cabinet, gave him a job on his administrative staff.

In the prison of Montluc, the interrogations continued without a break. Barbie, frantic at his inability to determine which of the prisoners was the long-sought-after Max, increased the brutality and the tortures. Aubrac had his shoulder dislocated from the beating, and several times was marched out in front of a firing squad in a sham execution. Lassagne, who was also suspected of being Max, was horribly tortured, and Jean Moulin himself was beaten to the point where he was unable to walk and had to be dragged back to his cell by the guards.

Among the other prisoners at Montluc was Christian Pineau, who had returned from London with Moulin and General Delestraint in March. On Thursday, June 24, Pineau was called from his cell by a German noncom, who ordered him to bring his razor. They walked down the stairway together and entered the courtyard. On a bench was stretched an unconscious man guarded by a single German soldier with a rifle slung over his shoulder. Pineau was ordered to shave the unconscious man!

"Imagine my stupefaction, my horror, when I recognized the man stretched out on the bench as none other than Max Moulin. He had lost consciousness; his hollowed eyes seemed to be sunken in his head. There was a filthy bluish wound on his temple. A soft rasping sound escaped from his swollen lips. Without a doubt, he had been tortured by the Gestapo."

Pineau began to shave the unconscious Moulin, trying to avoid the swollen parts of his face. As Pineau later wrote:

> It wasn't a good razor blade—it had been used to cut too much hair—but I managed little by little to shave the upper lip, the cheeks.
>
> Suddenly, Max opened his eyes and looked at me. I'm certain that he recognized me, but how could he understand what I was doing next to him at that moment?
>
> "Drink," he murmured.
>
> I turned toward the soldier: "*Ein wenig wasser.*"
>
> He hesitated for an instant, then took the saucer filled with soapy water, went to rinse it at the fountain, and brought it back filled with fresh water.
>
> During that time, I leaned over Max, whispering some banal words of comfort, stupid words. He said five or six words in English which I could not understand, his voice being so badly broken, so gasping. Then he drank several swallows from the saucer which I held for him and fainted again.
>
> Since no one came to fetch me, I remained next to him, looking at his immobile face as if at a wake, while little by little night fell and the prison lights went on.

The next day, the prisoners were transferred to the prison at Fresnes, just outside of Paris—all except Jean Moulin. By now, his identity was known; perhaps he had admitted it to save his companions from further torture. Too badly hurt to travel by train, he was taken by car to the luxurious villa in the Paris suburb of Neuilly which was kept by the Gestapo chief Carl Boemelburg for the reception of important resistance heads. It was here that Jean Moulin was seen by General Delestraint and André Lassagne. "He was stretched out on a sofa, his skull enveloped with bandages, his face yellow and bruised. He was barely breathing; only his eyes seemed to be alive."

Aware that Jean Moulin was dying, and frightened either of the reaction of their chiefs to the death of such an important prisoner or by possible prosecution as war criminals after the war, the Paris Gestapo decided to ship Moulin to Germany by train. But it was too late—the torturers had been too efficient. According to a death certificate in the registry at Metz, he died in the railroad station of that town on July 8, 1943. A German medical officer certified that the death was due to a heart attack. For some unexplained reason, the body was not taken off the train until Frankfurt and, stranger still, was returned to Paris, where it was cremated at the Père-Lachaise cemetery and the ashes placed in an urn which later carried the inscription: "The presumed ashes of Jean Moulin."

As for the other prisoners of Caluire, they suffered various fates: Colonel Lacaze was freed almost immediately after Lassagne declared that he had never been part of the Resistance; Doctor Dugoujon was imprisoned at Montluc until the spring of 1944, then released; Henry Aubry was in the tender care of the Gestapo until December, 1943—he managed to confuse them with a tissue of lies mixed with just enough truth to fool the Germans without hurting the Resistance. When released, he joined the Maquis in the south.

Raymond Aubrac was condemned to death, but was released by his friends during a daring escape organized by his wife. Colonel Schwartzfeld and Bruno Larat died in German concentration camps. General Delestraint was in the concentration camp at Dachau, where on April 19, 1945, just before the American army freed the camp, he was killed by the S.S. with a bullet in the nape of the neck; to the end, he believed that Hardy had betrayed him. André Lassagne survived deportation to Germany and returned to become senator for his *département;* he died two years after the war.

As for René Hardy, he was arrested in 1945 and tried for the first time in 1947. Under oath, he denied having been arrested by the Germans on the train at Chalon and was acquitted. However, Lydie Bastien, the fiancée who had made the berth reservation for him on that train, found the receipt and located the conductor, whose worksheet reported the two arrests made on that night. Two months after his acquittal, Hardy was back in prison.

His second trial was held three years later, in 1950. Hardy now admitted his arrest, saying that he had lied because he feared the revenge of the Resistance, since he would be unable to clear himself of the arrest of General Delestraint. His defense counsel very effectively discredited the testimony of Mademoiselle Deletraz and Barbie, and the members of Sabotage-Fer vouched for Hardy's impeccable conduct as a resistance leader. In the end, there was a great deal of conflicting testimony. As one witness said, "In wartime the slightest suspicion must be resolved *against* the suspect; in peacetime, if there is the slightest doubt, it must be resolved *in favor* of the suspect." The jury seemed to agree, and Hardy was acquitted for the second time amid applause from the audience.

After the liberation, Klaus Altmann-Barbie went into hiding and then escaped to Germany. As we have seen, he was for a time a member of the U.S. army counterintelligence corps and protected by the corps from extradition to face charges of war crimes made by the military tribunal at Lyons. In August, 1948, he escaped to Genoa, and from there, with Red Cross documents, reached Bolivia. He worked for a time as a manager in a sawmill and later exported raw quinine to Germany. His wife and three children joined him there and he became quite prosperous; he even owned a shipping business, the Transmaritina Boliviana. In 1972 he was discovered by Beate Klarsfeld, a German woman who specialized in hunting down Nazi war criminals. At the present time, he has been arrested by the Bolivian authorities, who are reconsidering the request for extradition by the French courts, which have twice sentenced Altmann-Barbie to death in absentia.

In an interview with an Argentine journalist, Altmann claimed that in 1966 he had returned secretly to France to place flowers on the tomb of Jean Moulin. The newspaperman asked him whether he had done it as penance. "No," Altmann replied, "only because Jean Moulin had been my finest enemy. The toughest. The most worthy."

Who betrayed Jean Moulin and the rendezvous at Caluire? After so many years and with so much conflicting testimony still unresolved, it is unlikely that the truth will ever be known. As for René Hardy, he has been acquitted twice (after spending a total of five years in jail awaiting trial) and, in the end, the judgment of the tribunal must be respected. It may not be the final answer, but at this time it is the only one.

On December 20, 1964, in the presence of the notables of France and following a eulogy by André Malraux, what were believed to be the ashes of Jean Moulin were laid to rest in the Panthéon, where repose the remains of those great Frenchmen whom the nation thinks most worthy of being honored and to whom it is most grateful.

"Before him, there were *résistants;* after him, there was a *Résistance.*"

JEAN MOULIN: "Max," de Gaulle's delegate to the Resistance in France. The scarf around his neck was to hide the scars of his suicide attempt in June, 1940. (*Keystone.*)

CEREMONY HONORING PIERRE GEORGES ("COLONEL FABIEN"): The streamer on the right reads: "Here, on the twenty-third [actually the twenty-first] of August, 1941, the first German officer was shot down by the man who would later become the glorious Colonel Fabien." (*Keystone.*)

Opposite: RENE HARDY: "Didot," head of the railroad sabotage branch of the Resistance, at his second trial in April, 1950. He was charged with betraying Jean Moulin and was again acquitted. (*Wide World.*)

GEORGES LOUSTAUNAU-LACAU: Recently returned from a German concentration camp, the head of the resistance group Alliance testifies at Pétain's trial. (*Wide World.*)

THE GESTAPO IN PARIS: Karl Oberg (left) and Helmut Knochen (right) greet their boss, Reinhardt Heydrich, upon his arrival in Paris, May, 1942. (*Wide World.*)

8
The Ersatz Life

Life went on, but the strain, the anxiety, the worry over the prisoners of war, the execution of hostages, the hunger, the shortages, the cold—all these rubbed raw the nerves of the occupied. Even such a seemingly simple matter as writing to one's family across the demarcation line was complicated. No regular mail crossed the line before March, 1943, five months after the invasion of the unoccupied zone by the German army (who feared British agents would use the postal system to pass information).

Interzonal postcards were introduced in September, 1940, to permit the minimum of information between families separated by the line. (Laval, an astute businessman, arranged that they should be ordered from his printing firm in Clermont-Ferrand.) Only thirteen lines were permitted, and, although one could cross out words that did not apply, if a single word not pertaining to the family was added, the card was torn up:

____________194____

__________ in good health __________ tired __________ slightly, seriously, sick, wounded __________ killed __________ prisoner __________ died __________ no news of__________

The __________ family is well __________ needs food __________ needs money __________ news, luggage __________ is returning to __________ __________ is working __________ is returning to school at __________ has passed examination __________ going to __________ on __________

____

____

____

Fondest thoughts. Love and kisses.
Signed ____________________

Thirteen lines for a mother's grief or a father's despair; thirteen lines for a lover's ardor or the concern of a devoted wife. Death, illness, captivity, desperate want, fear, loss—all in thirteen unchangeable lines. Now the French in the occupied zone realized that they were as much prisoners as their men in the German camps.

The resentment at this and a thousand other petty restrictions: the erratic curfews, the shortages that the French knew were due to German looting, the long hours of waiting in the queues for a handful of vegetables—all these built up a bitter hatred in the French people that fostered resistance. More and more people began to listen to the English radio despite the German threats, and more and more they applauded, openly or in secret, the Anglo-American and Russian victories. As the occupation dragged on and the certainty of a Nazi victory retreated, people began to repeat the prophecy of Sainte Odile (a seventh-century nun, the patron saint of Alsace), who had foretold the defeat of the Germans at the hands of a young French war leader who was an ally of the English. Old differences with their former allies were not forgotten, but the occupied began to realize that those who fought the Germans were fighting for the liberation of France and were their friends. "The French people are not so much pro-English as anti-German . . . if the planet Mars were to declare war on Germany, the French people would soon be pro-Martian," one observer wrote.

One of the difficulties of describing the behavior of the French under the German occupation is the absence of any valid generalization that can be based on social or economic class. For example, the Fascist Parti Populaire Français, headed by Jacques Doriot, drew much of its strength from the disillusioned working class; the bourgeoisie and the upper classes constituted a large part of L'Action Française. At the same time, the ranks of the Resistance were being swollen by members from every segment of French society: Combat, Liberation, and the other resistance networks all included workers as well as members of the middle class and the aristocracy. In the same resistance cell gathering information on German military units, one might find a Socialist metalworker, a radical shopkeeper, an anticlerical schoolteacher, a devoutly Catholic farmworker—all led by a monarchistic ex-army officer.

In the same way, it would be a mistake to try to generalize about the behavior of French youth during the tragic occupation years. As profoundly shocked as their elders by the humiliating defeat, they found themselves in a situation for which neither school nor family life had prepared them. Some of them flocked to the banners of collaboration and became the arrogant, aggressive young followers of Doriot, Déat, and Darnand; others joined the small resistance groups, acting as couriers, gathering information, distributing the clandestine newspapers, and all too often paying for their inexperience in conspiratorial life with prison, torture, and death.

The demoralization of family life had a particularly bad effect on the teenagers, called "J-Threes" in the then-current slang from their ration-card category. With their older brothers, their fathers, and other male members of the family in German prison camps, they found themselves in a strange world of privation, shortages, black-market dealings and an overall atmosphere of doing what had to be done to survive. It was the time of "*le système D*"—which stood for the French verb, *se débrouiller,* which means "managing under any circumstances," "making do," "solving any difficulty regardless of the cost to others." To this general decline in morality, the J-Threes responded with alacrity and ingenuity. Soon it was common to see black-market transactions taking place in the classroom under the complacent eye of the professor: cigarettes, razor blades, soap, and food supplies of all sorts changed briefcases, and twelve- and thirteen-year-old *élèves* walked around with thick wads of hundred-franc notes jammed into the pockets of their short pants. At a time when so many were suffering from the shortage of food, clothing, and other necessities of life, their black-market operations seemed more important and more relevant to daily life than translating Caesar or writing a theme in English.

In addition, the teenagers inherited the nonconformism and the willingness to shock their elders that had long been the prerogative of the students of the Latin Quarter. Early in 1942, there appeared at certain select bars and terraces of the Champs-Elysées groups of extravagantly dressed teenagers, mostly middle class, who proceeded to display their contempt for the conventions and the hypocrisy of their elders. Remarkably similar in dress to the American zoot-suiters of the 1940s, the young men wore very full jackets that came down to the middle of their thighs. Their pants were narrow, with cuffs that gripped the ankle; their shoes were large, heavy, and deliberately unpolished. The round collars of their shirts were held together by a straight stickpin under a linen or wool necktie. Their full bushy hair shone, not from pomade (which had disappeared from the counters), but from salad oil. They invariably wore the sheepskin jackets that the French called *canadiennes;* they seldom took them off and "they preferred [them] wet because they were never truly themselves except in the rain. Obeying one of the rites dear to them, they dragged their feet in the water, soaking their trousers, and exposed their bushy greasy hair to the rain," reported the magazine *L'Illustration.*

Like the boys, the girls wore their hair down below the collar, but theirs was in curls. They wore turtleneck sweaters under fur coats, regardless of the weather, and striped stockings, flat shoes, and very short pleated skirts, and they carried large umbrellas, which remained resolutely closed even in the rain. In contrast with the sloping shoulders that the male affected, the female showed a padded square shoulder.

Their rallying cry was "Swing!" which had been made popular by Johnny Hess and his top tune, "*Je suis swing.*" Their recognition sign was the yell, "*Zazou! Zazou! Zazou!*" and from this came the name given them—the Zazous.

At a time when public dancing was prohibited as being unsuitable for an occupied country, the Zazous danced frantically to the tune of jazz records at their favorite bars. They drank only soft drinks, mostly fruit juices, saving their serious drinking for home parties where getting drunk on gin to the sound of the latest jazz records was considered a part of the Zazou style of life.

Where in the midst of the severe clothing shortages did they find the Zazou dress style they insisted on? At a time when the average housewife was finding it extremely difficult, if not impossible, to find a pair of cheap black stockings, even if she had the coupons, and when men were turning their suits inside out and having them recut, the Zazous were still able to obtain the exaggerated long jackets and narrow pegged trousers of their cult. Some of the money undoubtedly came from doting parents, but most of it was obtained from the same black-market operations which also supplied them with the cloth and the tailor for their suits and dresses.

They were an abomination to the Fascist league and the collaborationist newspapers in Paris denounced them viciously. On several occasions the pro-Nazi French youth of Doriot swept through the bars and terraces where the Zazous amused themselves and provoked fights. To the Doriotist youth, the Zazous with their nonconformist dress, their exaggerated style of dancing, their senseless cries of "Swing!" and "*Zazou!*" were a deadly insult to the New Order. The new emerging France was better served by shoving Jews off the sidewalk and throwing rocks through the windows of Jewish stores.

The Zazous had no political beliefs and no real orthodoxy other than jazz. They laughed at patriotism and believed only in themselves, dancing, and the good life—now. By their nonconformist behavior and exaggerated life-style they exhibited their contempt for their elders, whom they held responsible for the defeat and who had shown a disgusting willingness to suffer uncomplainingly under the occupation. To "shock the bourgeoisie" is an old and honorable French tradition; but when the bourgeoisie and the rest of one's fellow countrymen are suffering under the boot of the invader . . . Still, it was not a total rejection of their country, for during the bloody insurrection that liberated Paris in August, 1944, many of the Zazous were found lined up behind another ancient French tradition—the barricades.

* * *

In the new motto of the French state—"Work, Fatherland, Family" —it was the family that received most of Vichy's attention. Convinced that one of the main factors of the defeat was the small number of babies born, Pétain, himself childless and in the past a longtime bachelor, set out to repair this deficit in the growth of the population. Not only did Vichy favor large families, but divorce was made even more difficult and abandoning one's family was strictly punished. Married women were given more legal rights in disposing of their own property and pregnant women received more food.

Even under the privations and shortages of the occupation years with almost two million men absent as prisoners of war, the policy proved to be successful. Whereas in the prewar years the excess of deaths over births was on the order of thirty thousand per year, and although in 1940 because of the losses in the Battle of France this figure reached two hundred thousand, by 1943 it was almost zero. In a way, this change in the population trend was due to the suddenness of the defeat; a long bloody war like that of 1914–1918 would have cut down the adolescents which the defeat had spared. Then, too, in spite of the grimness of the times, the number of suicides decreased drastically. The French refused to give up hope or to give way to despair; they tackled their daily problems courageously, looking forward to the future with hope. Women were courted, marriages arranged, and weddings took place even in 1944, the worst year of the occupation, even though there were incredible difficulties to be surmounted: nothing could be obtained without ration tickets, neither food for the wedding feast, a gown for the bride, nor a suit for the groom. To go from the church or the town hall to the reception meant taking the subway, not only for the wedding party, but for the guests as well (one ingenious family in Nantes rented a trolley car for the occasion).

Vichy continued throughout the occupation years to encourage marriages, reward large families, and protect the sanctity of married life. A particularly stern penalty was proclaimed for anyone found guilty of seducing the wife of an absent prisoner of war.

Even under the German boot, the traditional French verve and wit remained alive. The following item appeared in the newspaper *Au Travail* for June 1, 1941:

> On the avenue de Clichy about nine this morning, a man clothed only in a jacket, and wearing neither pants nor underpants, was taking a walk. When apprehended, he was taken to the police station.... He had wanted, he said, to protest against the difficulty of obtaining a clothing coupon at the town hall of his district.... "I had only one pair of pants," he added, "and after washing them I put the pants over the railing of my balcony to

dry . . . unfortunately, they fell to the street below and a passerby took off with them!"

Under the most tragic circumstances, with the Germans everywhere and with the Allied bombers overhead, the French could always find something to make the reality a little less grim, the moment a little more pleasurable. "Yesterday, the man who sat next to me in the subway forced me to inhale from L'Etoile to Châtelet the ripened perfume of the camembert he carried with respect in his hand. I felt like asking him for the address [of the black-market restaurant where he had purchased the cheese], because, if the smell was strong, so was my desire to taste it. . . ."

The curfew was normally midnight (although the Métro stopped at 11 P.M.) but was subject to the whim of the occupation authorities. After a rash of assassinations of German officers in the streets of Paris, the townspeople found themselves compelled to remain in their homes from 5:30 P.M. until five o'clock the next morning. They took particular delight in standing outside their front doors until the last second, disappearing inside only when a German patrol turned the corner. But woe to anyone found outdoors after the curfew without the *Ausweis* which permitted certain categories of essential municipal workers to be on the streets. If lucky enough to be arrested by the French police, it meant a long night in a stuffy police station under the suspicious eye of the sergeant until the curfew ended at dawn. If, however, one was arrested by a German patrol, the consequences were much more serious: one stood a good chance of ending up in prison as a hostage. A watch that was slow, a rendezvous at which one lingered too long, or a missed subway connection could bring one to the execution stake.

It was a time of substitutes, of gravelly ersatz soap made out of ground horse chestnuts and slaked lime. Chestnuts were both plentiful and popular: one could crush them along with acorns and roast the mixture to make an ersatz coffee, which could then be sweetened with chestnut juice. A decent ersatz coffee could also be made by roasting wild-rose petals; the resulting "coffee" was often sweetened with the juice of licorice sticks. It was also a time of potato pies, wooden soles for shoes, and dried beet leaves for tobacco.

As the food supply diminished steadily and rations were cut more and more, stark hunger drove many to desperate solutions. Soon the pigeons in the public square began to disappear, and, at the end of October, 1941, several newspapers carried a warning from the police:

Cat Eaters! Attention!

During the present period of shortages,
certain hungry people are not afraid to trap

> cats to make a nice stew of them. These
> people do not know the danger which threatens
> them. In fact, cats whose useful purpose is
> to kill and eat rats, which carry the most
> dangerous germs, can because of that fact
> be particularly harmful when eaten. . . .

As the occupation dragged on and the massive German requisitions increased, the scarcity of food—particularly for the city dweller—became an obsession. There was no hope that the farmers could increase their crops. Lacking labor since their sons and hired hands were in German prison camps, lacking farm animals which had been drafted by the German army, lacking even fuel for their tractors and seed for planting, they were helpless. The harvest decreased from year to year; compared to 1939, only one-half the amount of potatoes was raised in 1941 and a little more than half the amounts of wheat and oats. By the middle of 1944, agricultural production was one-fourth of the prewar figure.

As Vichy struggled ineffectually with the problem of food production and rationing (it instituted meatless Wednesdays, Thursdays, and Fridays), the average housewife continued to stand in the long ration lines for hours, hoping there would be something left when her turn arrived.

To find the needed calories, city dwellers set out daily by bicycle or on the crowded trains (suffocatingly hot in the summer and freezing cold in the winter) to search the countryside for food. Armed with briefcases and suitcases in which they carried the few articles they had to barter—soap, chocolate, razor blades, a new pair of shoes—they scoured the farms within thirty miles of the city, hoping to trade a hundred cigarettes for a few pounds of potatoes or a radio set for a fat goose. The farmers were quickly aware of their privileged status in a time of restrictions and shortages; the price of a pound of peas or six eggs rose quickly. Nor was it enough to simply have found and purchased the food, for on the return trip there was the constant danger of the Vichy economic controllers, the guards at the railroad station exits, and the police at the entrance to the city—all of them alert and quick to spot the bulging briefcase, the poorly wrapped bulky package, or the heavy suitcase. As the government decrees against illegal prices, hoarding, and food smuggling increased, seemingly without bounds, the ingenuity of the French increased in proportion. They became more clever in evading the restrictions, more astute in slipping by the controls, and, finally, more corrupt in their dealings with the government and with one another.

Not everyone suffered equally under the occupation; not only did the avaricious farmers grow rich on the food they concealed from the Vichy inspectors and sold to the hungry city dwellers (or to the black-market restaurants in town), but many French industrialists, under the pretense of keeping their employees at work, found lucrative contracts providing planes, tanks, and other essential materials to the Nazi war machine.

Strangely enough, business was excellent during the occupation: the number of bankruptcies decreased sharply from the prewar years; thousands of new groceries, dairy stores, clothing stores, etc., were opened—and flourished. There was no equality in hunger either; for those who had the money, there was a special category of restaurants where the best of food and the finest of wine could be obtained at a price well above the legal rate, provided only that ten percent of the bill be given to the National Aid for the destitute. Nightclubs and restaurants catered to the newly rich, including those who had made vast fortunes practically overnight on the black market at the expense of their fellow countrymen.

It was the little people, those on small fixed incomes and with little to barter, who suffered most from the food shortage: the retired, the elderly, the prisoners' wives, the clerks, the petty officials. For them, life was a constant struggle to find enough food to stay alive. In 1942 the average daily salary of a minor government employee was 2,000 to 4,000 francs; at the same time the price of butter on the black market (which was the only place where it could be obtained) was 120 francs per pound; coffee was 500 francs per pound. By January, 1943, the price had risen to 160 francs and 900 francs respectively. The daily salary of a minor official or a department store clerk was equivalent to the black-market price of one pound of sugar or ten pounds of potatoes.

In this time of constant hunger, it is small wonder that false ration cards were printed by the hundreds of thousands and that genuine ones were stolen from the town halls. The ration cards sold initially for fifty francs each, but by 1943 the price was 250 francs. For the famished, there was no other way to obtain their daily bread.

Simone de Beauvoir described her preoccupation with food:

> I wandered through the streets, rummaging behind dummy window displays for unrationed foodstuffs, a sort of treasure hunt, and I thoroughly enjoyed it; what a windfall it was if I stumbled on a beet or a cabbage! The first lunch we had in my room consisted of "turnip sauerkraut," which I tried to improve by pouring canned soup over it. Sartre said it wasn't at all bad.

Lucky indeed were those who still maintained a friendly relationship with a relative on a farm. Those were fortunate who had kept their friends in the country when they had deserted the "manure heap" for a tiny apartment in Paris. Packages from a Breton cousin with butter, eggs, cheese, sometimes a plucked chicken or a whole ham, were a godsend to those whose official rations were just enough to allow them to starve. At a time when crows were being sold in the marketplace for ten francs apiece, the people of Paris wondered whether they would soon be reduced to eating the sewer rats as the hungry poor during the siege of 1871 had. People were so starved that they would eat their entire weekly ration in one sitting simply to enjoy the feeling of a full stomach—and not knowing, in any case, what the next day might bring.

The Germans and their French collaborators were not unaware of the hunger and misery of the average Parisian. The German writer Ernst Jünger wrote in his journal on July 4, 1942, that he had dined at the famous restaurant Tour d'Argent: "One has the impression that the people at the tables, eating the soles and the famous duck, are damned satisfied to see below them the gray ocean of roofs beneath which the starving struggle to live. In times like these, to eat well and a lot gives one a sense of power."

Lieutenant Jünger of the Wehrmacht continued to note his impressions of life in occupied France during his period of service there. He was particularly impressed by the letters of condemned French hostages, which he translated for the benefit of the German occupation authorities.

The disappearance of cars from the streets of cities and the roads of the countryside was one of the unusual aspects of the occupation years. The silence in Paris, the emptiness of the streets where one saw only the open touring cars (which were so favored by German officers) speeding along the boulevards, was commented upon by many observers. However, there was one consequence of this which was salutory: the number of automobile accidents and vehicle deaths decreased markedly over the next four years. In two *départements* of France, in 1943, no auto deaths were reported.

With the unavailability of gasoline, except for those engaged in essential services, the taxicabs disappeared from the streets. It was the era of the bicycle, and their numbers quickly doubled and tripled throughout both occupied and unoccupied France. The overweight businessman, the fashion model, the elderly worker all pedaled their way to work and then home. So important were bicycles to the economy and to the life of the people that their prices skyrocketed and thefts of bicycles from public areas were widespread. In the last three months of 1940, 22,000 bicycles were stolen in Paris alone. The cautious Parisian not only chained his bicycle with a lock and key, but in the evening he took it up to his apartment with him. As the occupation went on and spare parts vanished (except at exorbitant prices on the black market), the ingenious French were hard put to keep their bicycles operating, but many managed the feat. Soon it was not uncommon to see tires, worn beyond repair, which were stuffed with grass so that they could still be used.

The number of fiacres—horse-drawn carriages—was insufficient for the needs of the population, so a new method of transportation sprang into use. This was the *vélo-taxi,* which consisted of a two-wheeled cart carrying a bench or a chair attached behind a bicycle ridden by a driver with strong legs. Painted in bright colors and carrying an eye-catching name like "Why Not Me?" they were among the most familiar sights in the streets of occupied Paris. In front of the railroad stations, the theaters, the office buildings, the drivers clustered their vehicles and fought for the passing trade. Prices for even the shortest trip soon ballooned. A woman chose a velo-cab with an eye to the color which complemented her outfit; others by the youth and vigor of the driver. The businessman hurrying to an appointment, the sportsman rushing to the racetrack, or the lover being taken to a rendezvous were all conducted with pride and dispatch by the velo-cab.

Transportation of all types was big business during the occupation—over 1,500 new companies engaged in moving people and matériel were started. The trucks, which brought a large part of the food into the city, and the buses were quickly converted from burning gasoline to *gazogènes.* In this system, which was well-known in Europe, charcoal or green wood was burned in a twenty-gallon metal boiler strapped either to the fender or to the roof of the vehicle; the combustion products were then fed directly into the carburetor. The conversion from gasoline to *gazogène* could be done quickly, and soon the sight of large trucks or buses with the unwieldy metal tanks puffing along the streets and roads was a familiar one.

The prize for ingenuity in devising a new mode of transportation goes to the wealthy Parisian who had his elegant Rolls-Royce cut in two just behind the engine; the two-wheeled rear half was then pulled by one of his racehorses!

The Métro, the famous subway of Paris, performed heroically throughout the occupation. Except during those periods when the electricity was cut off, the subway never stopped running. It was the sole means of transportation for five million Parisians every day, and, although terribly crowded and stuffy, it continued with marvelous regularity to carry them to and from work. The Germans, who traveled free, used only the first-class carriages, and most Parisians made it obvious that they preferred the discomforts of the second-class cars to rubbing elbows with the Fridolins. The walls of the subway corridors were still the best indication of the morale of the Parisians; obscene jokes about the gray-green conquerers and their collaborationist lackeys, patriotic exhortations, vows of political fidelity such as *"Vive de Gaulle!"* and *"Vive Stalin!"* covered the walls until the frightened French police ordered their removal. Even the beggars in the subway played a role in showing the growing resistance of the common people: A German soldier who had lost his way asked one of them to help him find his station. With sincere pity, the old man said, "You know, you're awfully stupid. What the hell did you come here for? It's much too complicated for you!"

In the corridor of the Châtelet station, a blind beggar, his cup filled with coins, played *La Marseillaise* over and over on his accordion.

Who dealt on the black market? Everyone. The housewife, the student, the postman, lawyers, clerks, the concierge—every stratum of French society was represented. The large-scale black market was carefully organized by operators who made fantastic fortunes practically overnight at the expense of their starving compatriots. To smuggle food into the cities from the countryside, *gazogène* trucks with false bottoms, trains with hiding places behind false partitions, even convoys of cyclists were used. So tremendous was the volume of smuggled food that the Vichy economic inspectors who strove desperately to check it were overwhelmed. Newspapers daily carried accounts of the discovery of caches of food in the metropolitan area: hundreds of pounds of sugar were hidden in a grand piano, thousands of pounds of meat in a cemetery vault, and tons of potatoes in an abandoned quarry. From their enormous profits, the large-scale black-market operators were able to secure relative immunity from prosecution, but the little man, the *lampiste,* seized while coming off the train with half a dozen eggs or a pound of dried vegetables in his valise, was dealt with harshly by the courts. In one year alone, there were over 400,000 prosecutions for violation of the food regulations in the *département* of the Seine (the Paris region). A mother who had used the food-ration card of her dead child to obtain a bit more bread was sent to jail.

As the food rations decreased, as the clothing coupons became useless, as the shelves of the stores emptied and the ordinary articles of commerce disappeared, the French turned in desperation to the black market. For those who were troubled by the moral dilemma of dealing illegally, the Catholic Church, recognizing that depending solely on the official food ration was simply a form of suicide, declared that it was no sin to deal in the black market for survival.

This then was the French black market (an expression that first appeared in the authoritative Larousse dictionary in 1942) which sprang up spontaneously at a time when so many of the city dwellers were close to the starvation point. It was a purely French enterprise, and, in spite of its many inequities, in spite of the fact that so many Frenchmen grew rich from the suffering of other Frenchmen, it is still true that it prevented even more suffering and kept many alive who would have died.

The armistice of June, 1940, did not end the war for many French civilians. When German bombings ceased, English bombings began.

As the American bombers joined the R.A.F. in the skies over France, the tempo of air raids increased and French factories serving the Nazi war machine were a favorite target. On March 3, 1942, the R.A.F. hit the Renault works in southwest Paris and, inevitably, the workers' homes in Boulogne-Billancourt. The toll was 623 dead and over 1,500 wounded. Seeing an opportunity for propaganda against British "terrorism," Otto Abetz invited Marshal Pétain and Admiral Darlan to attend the state funeral for the victims. They declined the invitation and sent the ultracollaborationist Admiral Jean Platon to give the eulogy.

In the spring of 1944, the bombings were stepped up as a preliminary to the Allied landings—and aerial machine gunning added to the French losses. Total casualties are difficult to compute, but at least 60,000 French civilians died and 75,000 were wounded by Allied military action: bombings, machine gunnings, and artillery fire.

This is the price the French involuntarily paid for their liberation.

9
In Search of Forgetfulness

During all the great upheavals of French history—even in the shadow of the guillotine—books were written, poems composed, plays and dances performed. The four years of the German occupation were no exception; the people not only survived, but managed to find amusements and distractions to help them forget the harshness of the day.

The incessant search by the French for a few pounds of potatoes or a skinny chicken was accompanied by their pursuit of—if not happiness—entertainment. The French public, particularly the Parisians, severely restricted in its ability to travel because of the absence of gasoline, the necessary *Ausweis,* and the erratic, uncertain train schedules, turned to books, the theater, and the films to help them forget the terrible reality of daily existence. To the Germans, who had always been impressed by French prestige in the arts, and by Paris as a center of intellectual ferment and creativity, the reestablishment of the theaters, cinema, and publishing industries was a primary objective. In addition to the economic spoliation of France for the benefit of the Nazi war effort and German civilian needs, they planned to use their new conquest—and particularly Paris—as a recreation center for their victorious troops.

To sway French public opinion toward "collaboration" in the Nazi New Order, they had made their plans well in advance. Shortly after the German army arrived in Paris, a large crew of the German Propagandastaffel took over two stories of the modern building belonging to the National City Bank at Number 52 Champs-Elysées. The chief of the press section of the Propagandastaffel was the short, fat Leutnant Weber, who as a journalist for the official German news agency (D.N.B.) in Paris before the war had learned the ins and outs of the capital intimately. He spoke French fluently, even knew the latest slang, and he had a number of influential friends in French artistic circles. Weber, although only a lieutenant, gave orders to the captains and majors of the Propagandastaffel who specialized in various aspects of French creative life. From the imposing marble building on the Champs-Elysées, all directives controlling books, newspapers, plays, the opera, films, and even painting and sculpture were issued. Nothing was neglected in a tremendous effort to influence the notoriously skeptical French public, but it was thought important that this should be done through the artistic structure with which the French were familiar, rather than by a superimposed German production of books, films, or plays. It was therefore planned to use French actors, journalists, and writers who, either through vanity, greed, or ideological conviction, could be persuaded to lend themselves to the German propaganda mission. The Germans found such assistants in large numbers; the collaboration of Frenchmen working in the theater and cinema, on newspapers and magazines, was notorious during the occupation.

Because of the average Frenchman's devotion to his favorite newspaper, the Germans planned to reestablish all the prewar dailies with their reassuringly familiar format and to use these as propaganda vehicles. Most of the newspapers had followed the French government in its flight from Paris and chose to remain in the unoccupied zone after the armistice, establishing themselves at Lyons and Clermont-Ferrand. Before their hasty departure, the owners of *Paris-Soir* had given the keys to the building to an elderly Alsatian who was the elevator operator and watchman; they also gave him written authorization to do whatever was necessary to save the building from being requisitioned. Weber had no difficulty in convincing the old man that publishing the newspaper as quickly as possible was the only thing that would save it from being taken over completely by them. Bewildered at his promotion to editor, he found himself seated behind the owner's luxurious desk, directing the functions of a large newspaper: hiring journalists, arranging for the delivery of paper stock, scheduling the press runs, and consulting with the Propagandastaffel and the censors on the news to be printed. Despite the denunciation of his promotion by the real owners from their safety in the unoccupied zone (they considered him a fifth columnist), the new director seems to have done a highly creditable job—which may or may not be a commentary on French newspaper publishers. In one respect the elderly Alsatian was unusual: his honesty. He insisted on returning the difference between the pay for his new position and his old job to the owners!

One week after the entry of the German army into Paris, the counterfeit version of *Paris-Soir* appeared on the newsstands, and the country was treated to the unusual sight of two newspapers with the same title, one published in Paris and one in the unoccupied zone.

On June 17, *Le Matin* reappeared. Its owner, Maurice Bunau-

Varilla, anxious to retain his huge circulation and not unwilling to submit to Nazi directives, had kept most of his employees in Paris and his presses ready to roll. Other popular prewar newspapers that appeared in Paris before the end of 1940 included *L'Oeuvre* and *Le Petit Parisien,* although (as in the case of *Paris-Soir*) the real owners took no part in running the newspapers during the occupation (Déat later took over the editorial direction of *L'Oeuvre*). New titles began to appear, often subsidized directly by the Germans in an effort to influence particular segments of the French public: *La France au travail,* whose slogan was "Salvation through Work," was a counterfeit *L'Humanité* (the Communist party newspaper); it tried to appeal to the workers of Paris and often used many themes and slogans of the Communist party itself. For a while, it succeeded in confusing the workers, but it did not survive the German attack on the Soviet Union in June, 1941. *Le Cri du peuple* was Jacques Doriot's paper and found its readership largely among the members of his P.P.F. party. Jean Luchaire started *Les Nouveaux Temps* as an obvious imitation of the prestigious *Le Temps* and hoped to find his readers among the intelligentsia of the Boulevard Saint-Germain and the Café Deux Magots.

In addition to the dailies, a number of weekly and monthly newspapers and magazines were authorized by the Propagandastaffel. Permission was easily obtained, since the Germans knew that they could always take over a publication if they did not like what it published. Among those with the largest circulation were *La Gerbe,* a literary weekly published by the well-known Alphonse de Châteaubriant (who thought he could reconcile the Nazi racist credo with a vaguely defined Christianity), and two obscenely anti-Semitic weeklies that were published at the express wish of Goebbels: *Au Pilori* and *Je suis partout,* which enjoyed the talents of Robert Brasillach and Lucien Rebatet.

There were newspapers for every segment of society: *Le Journal de la bourse* for the stockbroker and financial community, *La Vie industrielle* for the manufacturer and industrialist, and *Aujourd'hui* for literary circles. All of these were subsidized by the Propagandastaffel, which kept a tight rein on their content not only through a rigid censorship but by controlling the supply of paper, ink, and lead. To capture the minds of the individualistic and suspicious French public, the Germans planned to use every possible means of propaganda, but the newspapers (to which the French were devoted) were always given special attention. With familiar formats, with the names of the columns unchanged, with the articles to which the readers were accustomed, the Germans hoped to convince the public that their press was still free and that what could be read in it about "collaboration," the strength of the German army, the logic of National Socialism, and the perfidy of the English was the thinking of French, not German, minds. This attempt to sell the French press in the occupied zone as "uncontrolled" was often carried to ludicrous lengths: when one newspaper carried a story of some minor vandalism which had occurred the previous night, a German officer of the Propagandastaffel protested vigorously. "Not Vandals, monsieur. Do not use the word Vandals; they are our ancestors!" For the same reason one was not permitted to write of the "Anglo-Saxons" but rather the "Anglo-Americans"—so as not to give offense to an honorable German tribe.

Daily streams of directives came from the Propagandastaffel to the French press "suggesting" certain themes to be developed in their news columns; daily, the editors marched dutifully to the marble headquarters on the Champs-Elysées to submit their copy to the German censors. To make certain that the Nazi world view was correctly expressed in the occupied press, the Propagandastaffel held press conferences twice a week for the French journalists. The latest military summaries as issued by Goebbel's propaganda ministry were read and explained; newsreels of the victorious German army were shown. Finally, certain ideas for explaining these to the French public were expanded upon and subtle pressures exerted to make certain that the interpretation that would appear in the Paris newspapers was the correct one. These biweekly conferences were not unwelcome to the working press, for they were one of the few places in Paris where real coffee and an assortment of fresh pastry could be found. But the Germans did not depend on these for attendance; after the journalists entered the hall, the doors were locked as a protection against "terrorists."

The journalistic life under the occupation was not an enviable one. Not only was the press subjected to a constant stream of directives from the Propagandastaffel, not only was it inspected rigorously by the German censors, but there was always the fear that something you had written would offend the occupation authorities and would result in a direct reprisal. Anyone who attempted to be witty or ironic at the expense of Hitler or the German Reich quickly found himself dismissed or in jail, or both. One can only admire the courage of the reporter of *Le Petit Havre* who, in 1941, wrote:

> As for us, who in fact have imposed upon ourselves the duty of disseminating only information and who have no intention of getting entangled—in the present situation—with any political issue, national or international, who let each man judge for himself, all we want to do, in all objectivity, is to report one fact: Adolf Hitler was born in 1889 at Braunau in Lower Austria and today is his birthday.

The writer was dismissed.

But there were other journalists who lent their pens only too willingly to the Nazi New Order—and not only those who wrote for Doriot's *Le Cri du peuple,* Déat's *L'Oeuvre*, and the scurrilous *Je suis partout*. Vanity, greed, the desire to keep their readers and to see their name in print—whatever the motivation, many outstanding French journalists served the Propagandastaffel throughout the occupation. "I even know some who will betray only so that people speak of them. They are afraid that they will be forgotten, so they awaken Fame as best they can," observed Jean Guéhenno sadly.

Outside of Paris, the regional newspapers in the occupied zone were also submitted to the careful attention of the Propagandastaffel. Since many of them had only small presses with limited circulations and were the only means of livelihood for both the owners and their employees, there was a reluctance to cease publication and move to the unoccupied zone. Also, it had been made clear by the Germans that they could quickly put their own people in to run the newspapers if they encountered any opposition. Therefore, under the urgings of the municipal authorities, anxious to have newspapers that would express French and not German opinion, the small-town papers continued to be published by Frenchmen. Very few of them fell to the bootlicking level of the Paris collaborationist press.

Posters which had for so long been used to heat the Gallic temperament to war, revolution, or electoral battles were also used by the heavy-handed German propaganda machine. As early as June, 1940, in the midst of the Battle of France, the first propaganda poster appeared on the walls of the cities: it showed a bareheaded smiling German soldier feeding three hungry French children and the caption exhorted, "You who have been abandoned—have confidence in the German soldier!" The anti-English (and later anti-American) theme was repeated again and again; in its service some of the most famous names in French history were called from the grave by the Nazis. "I would prefer to give up my soul to God rather than be in the hands of the English!" vowed Joan of Arc from a poster; Victor Hugo was quoted as saying, "The new Europe will be formed from which England and Russia will be excluded. England will be pushed back to the ocean and Tartar Russia into the steppes." Napoleon ("I delivered myself to England . . . by my own choice because I believed in its laws and its public morality. I was cruelly mistaken.") and Montesquieu ("France's help is prompt; but England's is long in coming and uncertain.") were also used in the Anglophobic campaign. To keep alive the memory of the destruction of the French naval squadron at Oran (Mers-el-Kebir), there was a poster showing a French sailor sinking into the sea while clutching a split *tricolore* and shouting, "*N'oubliez pas Oran!*" There were posters exhorting the French to enroll voluntarily for work in Germany, to enlist in the French Waffen S.S. and fight on the Russian front in German uniform; there were posters showing a greedy Franklin Roosevelt and an avaricious Winston Churchill fighting over the French colonies in Africa. One showed a beach littered with dead soldiers and destroyed tanks: "Invasion. The cemetery of the Allies."

The French (always alert to sexual implications) were delighted with one poster intended to recruit French labor for German factories. It showed a smiling young French housewife and was captioned. "The happy days have returned. My husband is working in Germany!"

For four years propaganda posters were used—pleading, exhorting, boasting, threatening—but it was another type of poster that had the deepest effect on French opinion: the infamous red-and-black execution notices that announced the death of *résistants* and hostages.

Adolf Hitler, Charles de Gaulle, Léon Blum, and Charles Maurras—these names appeared on the first list of prohibited books (the "List Otto") issued by the Germans in September, 1940. Considered dangerous for the French reading public and ordered off the counters of the bookstores and off the shelves of libraries were Blum's youthful work *On Marriage*, Maurras's *Before Eternal Germany*, de Gaulle's *Toward a Professional Army*, and the Führer's *Mein Kampf*. To these were added all books by English authors (except for the classics), Polish and Jewish writers, and even biographies of prominent Jews written by Aryans. German refugee writers were particularly proscribed: Thomas Mann, Stefan Zweig, Leon Feuchtwanger, Erich Maria Remarque, and even Vicki Baum were on the list—and Freud, of course, both as a Jew and as an Austrian refugee. Léon Daudet, son of the famous Alphonse, found his book *The Franco-German Drama* was no longer suitable for the public; as one of the mainstays of *L'Action française*—along with Maurras—he must have found this particularly galling. All histories and novels of World War I, all spy stories, all reports and studies of Hitler's Germany disappeared from the bookshelves, as did the works of Malraux and Cardinal Baudrillart.

In the occupied zone, the Germans controlled the contents of the books published, not only through a strict censorship, but by their control of paper and ink. Only those whose themes were considered suitable by the Propagandastaffel could appear in any quantity. Whereas in 1938 French book publishers had used 38,000 tons of paper, in 1941 there were only 20,000 tons available—and by 1943, only 3,300 tons. This led to that familiar phenomenon which appeared spontaneously whenever a particular item was scarce: a black market in books. Many of the works on the List Otto could be bought at highly inflated prices "under the counter"—a retailing technique usually reserved for sexier tomes. A copy of *Gone with the Wind* or *The Rains Came* sold for the equivalent of twenty dollars (which was also the price of a quart of cooking oil).

Still, in spite of the censorship, the List Otto, the severe shortage of paper, ink, and lead, books were still printed and sold under the occupation. Detective stories were devoured and there was a minor renaissance of poetry. Albert Camus's *L'Etranger* and Roger Peyrefitte's *Les Amitiés particulières* appeared to critical raves. There was an upsurge of interest in books which explained the decline of France and the recent debacle: Lucien Rebatet's *Les Décombres* was one of the publishing sensations of 1941. In a brilliant scathing style, Rebatet—one of the feature writers of *Je suis partout*—explained the fascination of Fascism for himself and for other young intellectuals such as Robert Brasillach. He ripped apart the sterile outmoded milieu of L'Action Française with its reactionary monarchistic goals and turned with venom on his former master, Charles Maurras. His description of the early days in Vichy, of the parasites and hangers-on who clustered about Pétain was corrosive. In fact, according to the critics, the only weak passages in the book were those which tried to explain the role of a defeated France in the Nazi New Order.

In *Les Beaux Draps,* the wild man of French literature, Céline, exploded venomously in another of his extraordinary scurrilous diatribes against the Third Republic, the Jews, and the fainthearted French people. Alfred Fabre-Luce, in the first part of his *Journal de la France,* which appeared in the autumn of 1940, presented what is probably the best personal account of the events in France from the declaration of war to the first of January, 1940. The last two volumes, which presented a pro-Vichy collaborationist view of what occurred under the occupation, were to cause the author considerable trouble, including jail sentences under both the Nazis and de Gaulle.

The servility of so many prominent French authors during the occupation is one of the most shameful episodes of that period. Courted assiduously by the Germans, who wanted their propaganda themes presented by the best-known French writers of the day, many of them—out of gullibility, or the desire to keep their names alive—lent their pens to the Nazi cause. Their reward was not only in seeing their books appear or in receiving special privileges, but also in being invited to travel to Germany to give lectures and readings. At sumptuous banquets in Berlin, they were presented as the proof of French collaboration and their visits extolled as a harbinger of the creativity in the new Nazi Europe. Upon their return they were required to submit to interviews by the collaborationist press on their impressions of Hitler's

Germany—and woe to anyone who failed to be extravagant in his praise!

On one of these "star excursions" there were three writers who were members of the prestigious French Academy. One of these "immortals" wrote ecstatically about the reception they had received in the Third Reich; it seems that every morning they had been given not only extra cigarettes, but some pocket money.

When one French editor, Jean Paulhan, refused to publish the important literary review *Nouvelle Revue française* under German direction, the publishing house was requisitioned by the Germans. At first the Germans were temporarily deterred; a sketch by Cocteau above Paulhan's desk had an angel in it which appeared so Semitic to them that they left in disgust. A month later, however, the *N.R.F.* appeared with Drieu La Rochelle as the editor and with articles by such well-known names as Gide, Giono, Jouhandeau, Valéry, and de Montherlant. As can be imagined, there was nothing in the new magazine that would give offense to the Germans and a great deal that they must have read with pleasure. To quote Guéhenno once more, "*Homo scribendi* is not one of the great human species. . . ."

Giraudoux, the well-known French author, died in January, 1944, and there were those who blamed him bitterly for continuing to write and publish during the occupation, for his personal dealings with the Germans—which enabled his books to appear—and for offering *Sodom and Gomorrah* to distract the enslaved populace. As one perceptive observer noted, "The people get not only the government, but the poets they deserve."

To combat the harm done by the collaborationist authors, the Resistance turned to the writers in its ranks. It is true that the clandestine newspapers never ceased to attack the lackeys who served the Nazis with their pens, but in France the printed volume has much greater prestige than the newspaper, so it was decided that books which presented the point of view of those who refused to kneel to the swastika would have to be published. In the spring of 1943, the first volume by Les Editions de Minuit (Midnight Publications) appeared in Paris. A well-made volume of about one hundred pages, printed on good paper and bound in a plain white cover, it was handed surreptitiously from person to person and widely read. The first book was a great success: entitled *The Silence of the Sea*, it attempted to instruct the reader on the proper attitude to have toward the Germans. The plot was straightforward: an elderly Frenchman and his niece have a young German officer billeted in their house. This is no Nazi brute, but a sensitive, courteous young man who claimed a distant French ancestry and a love of all things French. In spite of his many attempts to establish a friendly relationship, the officer is put "in coventry"—the old man and the girl refuse to exchange a single word with him. Month after month, year after year, as the occupation drags on, the terrible "silence of the sea" is maintained in the house. Finally, transferred to the Russian front, the young officer comes to say good-bye and to stammer some embarrassed apologies; as he leaves the room, the niece without turning her head, whispers, "Good-bye." Did she have some secret feeling for the young German or was this just an involuntary civility? The ambiguity is left unresolved, but it is made clear that—to a Frenchwoman—any German, no matter how correct, must be ignored and despised. *The Silence of the Sea* was signed "Vercors," which was the name in the Resistance of Jean Bruller, a cartoonist by profession. Most of the twenty-five volumes of Editions de Minuit which appeared during the occupation were written under noms de plume (or, better, noms de guerre); but one book was openly signed by Jacques Maritain—he was safely in New York—and there was even a translation of Steinbeck's *The Moon Is Down.*

Although the Gestapo never seems to have paid much attention to Editions de Minuit (Jacques Decour was the only one of its authors who was arrested and shot by the Germans), it served an important function, for it bolstered the morale of the wavering populace, so discouraged by the bootlicking of many prominent French writers. Editions de Minuit published many phantom authors, including such outstanding figures as Sartre, Camus, and Aragon ("François la Colère").

The bookstores that the Propagandastaffel opened in Paris (the largest was on the Boulevard Saint Michel) displayed translations of German books and the works of French collaborators but never drew a large clientele. Although attractively designed and lighted, with open counters filled with books, they seemed to draw very few French readers—but more than a few bricks and grenades.

The racetrack at Auteuil was reopened on October 12, 1940, by order of the German occupation authorities, who were eager to offer the Parisians any diversion that might turn them from thoughts of resistance. Although General de la Laurencie, Vichy representative in the occupied zone, refused to attend the opening since the stand usually used by the president of the Republic would be occupied by German generals, French society, eager as usual for any amusement, turned out in droves. It was a highly fashionable opening, full of color and style: the Frenchmen wore their pearl-gray cutaways and top hats, the women displayed *parisienne* chic in their light summer frocks and wide-brimmed flowered hats. The crowd was friendly and the French mixed easily with the immaculately uniformed German "sportsmen," chatting and comparing their bets. There was among the occupied the condescending idea that one simply must teach civilized manners to the Nazi brutes; there had been—in history—examples of "the defeated who conquered their conquerers."

The races were very popular with the Parisian crowd and continued through the four years of the occupation, in spite of all the widespread misery and hunger which, after all, afflicted only the poor and the unprotected. Nothing interfered with the regular running of the races—not even the frequent air-raid alerts. When, on April 5, 1943, several Allied bombs fell into the stands at Longchamps, killing eight people and wounding fifty others, the races were interrupted only long enough to remove the dead and injured. The stewards consulted hastily with the German officers present, then decided that the incident was not serious enough to terminate so important an event. The races went on, and the French and Germans hurried to the betting booths. Under an occupation, not only the occupied but his master must be continually amused.

The cartoonists who for so long had satirized the weaknesses of the men of the Third Republic now found that making fun of politics was a dangerous business. Unable to needle the Germans or Vichy (and unwilling to turn their pens against de Gaulle and the Resistance), they concentrated joyfully on the one subject which was left to them—the black market. Aldebert drew a lampoon of a fat bourgeois couple seated in a black-market restaurant before a large plate of mashed potatoes. Over them hovered the waiter, whispering, "in the potatoes, you will find the goose containing the steaks in which are the thrushes stuffed with mushrooms." In another restaurant scene, the couple is about to order when they note at the table behind them what are obviously two Vichy inspectors, one disguised as a woman. The man then says to his wife, "I think that today I will have the legal single platter. . . ." The collaborationist newspapers also used propaganda to fight against the growing feeling of resistance; one of their favorites was the great patriot Barbi-Chou, drawn as a typically French figure who is vaguely pro-Allied and not too bright. In one cartoon he is seen reading a newspaper called *Rumors*. "So, the Americans are going to land soon in spite of the submarines . . . but how?" he asks. After a great deal of thought and struggling with the idea, he suddenly finds a solution: "Eureka! They will arrive by a tunnel under the Atlantic!" This type of heavy-handed propaganda made very little impression on the sophisticated Parisians, who knew that an eventual landing by American and English troops would take place in spite of all the attempts by the Germans and their French collaborators to prove to them that it could only end in a bloody debacle.

The Louvre reopened on October 29, 1940, although most of its treasures were safely hidden (in the châteaux along the Loire in the unoccupied zone) beyond the avaricious hands of Hitler, Goering, and other German aficionados of art. (De la Laurencie once again refused to attend since the opening was to be sponsored by the occupation authorities.) The Nazi commissioner for the arts in occupied France bore the illustrious name of Metternich, "whose ancestors had been noted for their caution and refinement," but he was helpless in his attempts to protect French art against the greed of the Nazis.

On July 1, 1940, Otto Abetz sent a message to the general commanding German Army B:

> By order of the Führer, the minister of foreign affairs [Ribbentrop] has ordered me to seize the objets d'art in the possession of the state, the towns, and the museums in Paris and in the provinces. In addition to the seizure of objets d'art in the possession of Jews, the most precious articles must be transferred to the German embassy in Paris. I request your help in this work.

French art continued to flourish and French artists continued to paint even under the occupation. In November, 1940, the Autumn Salon opened; and, although several artists refused to exhibit because of the exclusion of all work by Jewish artists, a number of paintings by their less squeamish colleagues were exhibited. Of all the propaganda fields available to influence French thought, the arts were probably least touched by Nazi hands; except for the possible censorship of certain subjects and the refusal to allow the exhibition of any works by Jewish artists, the Germans did not attempt to use painters, sculptors, or musicians for propaganda work. Indeed, they created a very profitable market for French art, buying up everything in sight, particularly the Old Masters, once again using the vast amount of money made available to them by Vichy payments of the occupation costs. Resistance to the Germans from the artists was almost nonexistent (except for the musicians at the Paris Conservatory who put out an underground publication called *The Musician Today*). In the fall of 1941, a dozen of the most famous French painters and sculptors were invited by the German propaganda ministry to visit Berlin. Two of them refused, but the others made the trip and were wined, dined, and exhibited as proof of Franco–German collaboration. On their return, they had to make the usual laudatory comments on the Third Reich, which were eagerly printed in the collaborationist newspapers.

To glorify the "renaissance" of Nazi art, Goebbels sent the sculptor Arno Brecker to Paris, where an exhibition of his huge muscular Teutonic male nudes and gigantic horses was opened, much to the amusement of the Paris public.

As Alfred Fabre-Luce noted in his journal, the opera flourished under the tutelage of the occupation authorities.

> In May [1941], the Berlin Opera, damaged by an English bomb, moved to the Paris Opera to give performances of *The Abduction from the Seraglio* and *Tristan and Isolde.* In Garnier's monument, the collaborators and the few remaining Americans touched elbows with the gray-green uniforms, as in 1814, in another opera house, Madame de Staël and Benjamin Constant sat among the Cossacks. The true believers suspected those music lovers who could not resist the temptation to attend, of Hitlerism.

The conductor was von Karajan.

At the intermission, as the Germans strolled en masse through the corridors, another astute observer noted that the French fell in behind them—in step!

In July, 1940, three weeks after the armistice, the movie theaters in Paris reopened. In the beginning, they were only permitted to show German films and all American and English films were ordered removed. Tyrone Power, Fred Astaire and Ginger Rogers, and Leslie Howard were felt to be unsuitable for the propaganda the Germans wished to impress on the French public. Instead, such films as *President Krüger*, with Emil Jannings, and *Mary Stuart*, with Zarah Leander, were presented in an effort to impress the French with the superiority of German art and creativity in the field of cinema. The German propaganda ministry installed a commissar for films in the occupied zone, Herr Grevin, who reigned supreme over all film production for the four years of the occupation. No director could start a film, no actor or actress could appear in one, without Herr Grevin's written consent. He controlled not only all production and distribution of films, but also the availability of essential props and materials. Very quickly the French film industry accepted the idea that if they were to work and to produce films it would be necessary to do so in collaboration with the German film industry, so a purely technical and commercial collaboration (between the French and German film industries) came into being under the benevolent auspices of Herr Grevin.

By the spring of 1941, the first French productions appeared on the screens. The public was able to see such favorites as Danielle Darrieux in *First Meeting* and Harry Baur in a life of Berlioz called *La Symphonie fantastique*. In 1942–1943, seventy-two major films were authorized and produced as a joint Franco–German enterprise. The French public was largely unaware that the films that they were seeing, which were advertised as purely French productions, were actually completely under German control. "Only the layman could be mistaken about it: all those in the trade knew that French films made in the occupied zone were controlled and exploited by the Germans."

The Germans were very careful not to force their favorite propaganda themes on the suspicious French film public through the ostensibly French productions. They did require that the Paris cinemas show such films as the anti-Semitic *Jew Süss* and the triumphant *Campaign in Poland;* but their experience with the showing of German newsreels (which were the only ones permitted to be screened) had taught them that the French could not be trusted. Particularly in the working-class districts, these newsreels showing German military victories were greeted with a pandemonium of coughs, sneezes, and foot stampings. Scenes of British bombings of German cities were applauded, while similar scenes of German bombings of British cities were jeered. Finally, the frustrated Germans demanded that the light be kept on during the showing of the newsreels and a still was flashed on the screen warning the spectators to "be on their guard against freedom of expression which could cause the person responsible to be arrested and would bring about loss of employment for the staff."

The Germans were also interested in any opportunity to show the "degeneracy" of the French: the film *Le Corbeau* (*The Raven*), which dealt with the tragic results of a vicious poison-pen campaign in a French village, was shown in Berlin as *Une Petite Ville française.*

During the occupation the movie theaters were crowded with people eager for a few hours of forgetfulness, all too ready to lose themselves even in the most ordinary melodrama. *The Night Visitors* was one of the great successes of the occupation—not because it was a work of art, but rather for the one scene showing a great feast in which roast pig, swan, partridge, and other such delicacies were served on large silver platters. The French movie public, famished, went time and again to see this Lucullan dinner and mentally to savor the food.

The inevitable propaganda trip to Germany was made by a dozen of the top French film stars in March, 1942. At a time when the walls of Paris were being covered more and more by the ugly red-and-black execution posters, the artists lined up in front of their train at the Gare du Nord, smiling, happy, and waving for the publicity photos. In the center of this handsome talented group, one may easily spot the lovely face of Danielle Darrieux. In Berlin, their reception was all that they could hope for: formal parties, toasts, tours of the German film studios, eulogies of French–German film collaboration, and the little extras that the occupied had come to expect in the capital of the occupiers.

By the time they returned, twenty hostages had been shot in Paris and the total of the occupation costs passed four billion dollars.

Maurice Chevalier went to Germany, too—but not to be wined and dined at the Hotel Adlon in Berlin. He went to the prisoner-of-war camp at Alten Gabow (where he himself had been a prisoner in World War I) to entertain the French P.O.W.'s, to bring them a breath of home. The Nazis photographed his performance and filled the newspapers and magazines with his picture.

Back in Paris, he sang several times before mixed French and German audiences. "At the Casino de Paris," one journalist wrote, "Chevalier did his singing act before a *feldgrau* audience who had only come to look at the girls' behinds." But the false rumors* that he had collaborated with the Nazis haunted Chevalier for years after the war.

Until the middle of 1943, there had been very little propaganda in the French films, and Jean-Louis Barrault had even been able to produce his powerful *Children of Paradise;* but as victory receded, the desperate Germans began to put the screws on their French collaborators. Soon a series of films was produced and shown which attacked not only the Resistance (portrayed as men more interested in the money they received for their terroristic acts than in ideals) but Freemasons, Jews, and those Frenchmen who straddled the fence. "*Attentisme*"—waiting to see which side would win—was as great a crime in the eyes of the Nazis and their friends as resistance. These films were greeted by French audiences with the same jeers and hoots as had greeted the German propaganda newsreels; soon they could be shown only in lighted auditoriums.

"*Radio-Paris ment, Radio-Paris ment. Radio-Paris est allemande.*" (Radio-Paris lies, Radio-Paris lies. Radio-Paris is German.)

With this daily refrain, the BBC stigmatized radio broadcasting from the occupied zone. It was an opinion shared by the vast majority of the French.

The day after the Germans entered Paris, Radio-Paris returned to the air with a German accent. Most of the programs—intended for the German troops—were given in their language, but the Nazis appreciated the tremendous propaganda value of the radio and were anxious to find Frenchmen who would help them accomplish their goals. From its new offices in the building of *Poste parisien* on the Champs-Elysées, the radio section of the Propagandastaffel let it be known that they were looking for program directors, artists, singers, and musicians. The salaries offered were fabulous, were paid in marks (at twenty francs to the mark), and were guaranteed not to be reported to the Vichy tax office. The would-be collaborators flocked in droves, attracted by the money, the privileges, and the lure of "fame." "The German directors of

* *Life* Magazine (August 24, 1942) printed a blacklist of forty French collaborators, including Maurice Chevalier, René de Chambrun, and Colonel René Fonck (the World War I French ace).

Radio-Paris welcomed them and their choice was not guided by principles significantly different from those used by the directors of the French radio: an appreciation for real talent and sexual desirability [*cote d'amour*]. Sexual desirability was not applied exclusively to female performers. . . ."

Soon the unwary French listener could have believed that Radio-Paris was still in French control. He heard the familiar commentators, the orchestras that he knew so well, and the dramatic and lyric artists that he had appreciated before the occupation. Slowly, the Germans injected their propaganda into the familiar programs; their star was the cultured Dr. Friedrich, whose French was impeccable and who had an excellent grasp of the psychology of the populace. He appealed to their common sense and their feeling for logic; above all, he was "reasonable"—at times even seeming to agree with some of the resistance statements. He pointed out the inevitability of a German victory and the advantages that France could gain in the new Nazi Europe by a proper attitude toward collaboration. His success among the apathetic French was considerable, but, as time passed and the food situation deteriorated, as the occupied found themselves without heat, as the execution of hostages and other repressive measures increased, the French began to see through Dr. Friedrich's subtle words and the spirit of resistance grew.

The two stars of Radio-Paris were Philippe Henriot, whose brilliant flaming oratory was much appreciated by many of his listeners who disagreed entirely with his philosophy of collaboration, and Jean Hérold-Paquis, who had started his career in radio treason even before the war, broadcasting German propaganda to the French from Radio-Stuttgart. Paquis's signature for his twice-a-day editorials was "England, like Carthage, must be destroyed."

As a relief from the lies of Radio-Paris and the inanities of Radio Vichy, the French turned more and more to the neutral Swiss radio (whose broadcasts of all the military communiqués was much appreciated by amateur strategists) and to the clandestinely heard programs of the BBC. So popular were the English broadcasts and so important to French morale that the following joke made the rounds of Paris: Two friends meet on the street. One says, "Did you hear what happened? Last night at 9:20 P.M. on the rue de Clichy, a Jew killed a German officer, cut open his chest, and ate his heart!" "Impossible!" his friend replied. "Impossible in three ways: one, a German does not have a heart; two, a Jew does not eat a pig; and three, at 9:20 P.M., everyone is listening to the English radio!"

On June 9, 1940, with the Germans only forty miles from Paris and the Reynaud government about to leave, the Comédie-Française closed its season with *On ne saurait penser à tout (You Can't Think of Every-*

thing)—"a bit of black humor at the moment when France fell for not having thought of tanks and airplanes."

After the armistice, the theaters hastened to open. The Germans took control of the national theaters in the occupied zone—the Opéra, the Opéra-Comique, and the Comédie-Française—while permitting them, "out of delicacy," still to be subsidized by Vichy. All managers, directors, actors, and plays had to have the approval of the Propagandastaffel and a certain number of seats at each performance were set aside for the German military. All Jewish actors were banned; all plays by Jewish playwrights were prohibited. The Théâtre Sarah Bernhardt was renamed Théâtre de la Cité.

The difficulties of putting on a play under the occupation were enormous: actors and actresses had to cycle to the theater and rehearse in a freezing hall; material for costumes, stage settings, props, furniture—all could be obtained only with ration coupons or on the black market. Even makeup was difficult to find. Nevertheless, the French theater enjoyed some artistic triumphs under the German boot. Before the end of 1940, a new version of *Le Cid* with Jean-Louis Barrault was performed by the Comédie-Française; Giraudoux's *Sodom and Gomorrah,* Anouilh's *Antigone,* Mauriac's *Asmodée,* and Sartre's *No Exit* were all presented to full houses. Sartre's play caused a minor scandal; it opens with a man and two women being thrust by guards into what looks like a prison cell. The audience thought that it was Fresnes prison and that the actors represented resistance members. When it turned out that the setting actually was meant to be the antechamber to hell, the play was strongly criticized. More to the liking of the Paris theater goer was Henri de Montherlant's *La Reine Morte* in which the single line, "The flower of the kingdom is to be found in prison," was eagerly awaited and enthusiastically applauded each night.

The greatest success of the French theater during the occupation was the performance of Paul Claudel's period piece *Le Soulier de Satin* (The Satin Slipper), which was so frequently announced and postponed that *Je suis partout* angrily announced it was being held up until the Allied landings. Actually the postponements were due to disagreements between the playwright and the directors of the Comédie-Française; Claudel wanted his play performed in two parts and the directors wished him to make cuts sufficient for it to be given in one performance. The matter was finally smoothed out by the ever-active Jean-Louis Barrault (who was to direct the play), and Claudel agreed to make the necessary changes. It opened on November 26, 1943, to empty seats, as there was an air-raid alert; finally, the audience filed in and the play, which started at 1:15 P.M., finally ended at 6:40 P.M. It was the great success of the season, and because of the demands for seats three other performances were permitted.

Interruption of theater performances by air-raid alerts was the rule rather than the exception. In June, 1944, a performance of *Cyrano de Bergerac* at the Comédie-Française started at 7 P.M. (since Paris was now on Berlin time, this was 5 P.M. by the sun). There were three alerts in the next hour and a half and the performance was finally stopped.

Strangely enough, English classics were still permitted, both in the theater and on the bookstands. The Odéon was able to remain faithful to its repertoire, which included not only Shakespeare's *Coriolanus,* but the play by Madame Clara Longworth de Chambrun (who was the mother-in-law of Laval's daughter) on the English playwright. The latter, in spite of official Anglophobia, was performed in Berlin as well as Paris in the summer of 1941.

So eager were the French for diversion, and so hungry for amusement, that no form of entertainment was neglected: the zoo, the circuses, the waxworks at the Musée Grevin (from which the figures of Jewish notables and the king and queen of England had been withdrawn), the auction houses where Modern and Old Masters, jewelry, rare books, stamps, and other valuable articles were sold at fantastically inflated prices to the new rich who had made their fortunes from the black market or German war contracts. Convinced by now of an inevitable German defeat, these gentlemen were anxious to hide their money from any possible confiscation after the war, and they buried it in the purchase of paintings at ten and twenty times their prewar prices. A quite ordinary Corot was sold for 1,210,000 francs; six months earlier, a more important painting by the same master had gone for 28,000 francs.

The nightclubs flourished and were filled with gray-green uniforms. On New Year's Eve, 1940, the Lido was presenting *Et voilà Paris* with ten stars, sixty artistes, and the most beautiful models in the world. At the ABC, one could hear Edith Piaf with a supporting cast of twenty-five; the Schéhérazade advertised that it was permitted to remain open all night. For those who wished to show their loyalty to the Allied cause (in complete safety), there was a performance of Shaw's *Saint Joan* at the Théâtre de l'Avenue. For the more intellectual, the Théâtre de Paris featured Charles Dullin (the close friend of Simone de Beauvoir) as Harpagon in Molière's *The Miser,* while at the Michodière, Pierre Fresnay was appearing in Anouilh's *Léocadia,* with music by Poulenc.

Amusement for the occupied, distractions for the hungry. Since bread was lacking, the French were given circuses—for the performance of which other Frenchmen were given not bread, but cake.

10
The L.V.F. and Milice

Hitler's attack on the Soviet Union on June 22, 1941, was greeted with wild enthusiasm by the French ultracollaborationists who had pinned their hopes—and indeed their lives—on a German victory and a Nazi hegemony over Europe. As three million German soldiers moved with devastating swiftness into Russian-occupied Poland, the pro-Nazi French parties dreamed of joining in an anti-Bolshevik crusade and thus binding France even closer to Nazi Germany. For Vichy, it was an opportunity for a real "collaboration" and a chance to win an easing of the armistice terms—and, eventually, better peace terms. To their opponents in the Resistance, it was a German blunder that would inevitably lead to a bloody war of attrition and a quicker Anglo-American victory; the liberation would come that much sooner, with help from the French themselves. Even the vast majority of the French public which was resolutely *attentiste* and pro-Pétain was enthusiastic over the news, happy to see their two deadliest enemies at each other's throat.

The idea of a legion of French volunteers to fight with the German armies on the eastern front occurred to several of the leaders of the pro-Nazi groups, each of whom was quick to claim credit for first thinking of it. On the day of the German attack on the Soviet Union, Jacques Doriot, who was attending a mass meeting of his P.P.F. party in Lyons, said, "France cannot simply be a spectator in the decisive battle which has begun and whose issue will determine the fate of the entire continent."

Just as quickly, Marcel Déat and Eugène Deloncle rushed into print to demand that the French join their German comrades in this life-and-death struggle against the Bolshevik menace.

Soon all of the French Fascist parties sounded the clarion call for the formation of a Légion des Volontaires Français contre le Bolchevisme (L.V.F.). In addition to the three D's (Doriot, Déat, and Deloncle), whose parties counted some tens of thousands of militants and perhaps a hundred thousand sympathizers, there were the smaller

Fascist groups such as the Front Franc of Jean Boissel, the Ligue Française of Pierre Constantini, the Parti Français of Pierre Clémenti, and the Francisme of Marcel Bucard. Their bitter rivalry for leadership of the French pro-Nazi movement was temporarily to be submerged in their enthusiasm for recruiting mercenaries for the Wehrmacht. Also to be found among those who hoped to secure France its rightful place in the Nazi New Order by spilling French blood on the plains of Russia was the ex-naval officer, Paul Chack, whose Committee for Anti-Bolshevik Action clearly gave him priority in the anti-Soviet struggle.

It was obvious that no sizable force of volunteers could be raised, uniformed, or armed without Pétain's consent and encouragement. Indeed, the pro-Nazis hoped that the recruits would be found in the pitifully small army that the armistice had left to Vichy. To determine the government's attitude toward the L.V.F., de Brinon wrote to Admiral Darlan on August 11. The admiral answered that the government was favorable to the creation of a legion of French volunteers and even foresaw "certain political advantages" that it could derive from it. Nevertheless, he declared that Vichy was unable to do more than to comment favorably on the L.V.F., "unless the government and the High Command of Germany inform us officially—and in advance—of their desire to see France represented among the forces fighting Bolshevism. . . ."

Having broken its diplomatic relations with the Soviet Union on June 29, Vichy was more than willing to send Frenchmen to fight on the eastern front, but only if they could obtain a quid pro quo from the Germans, such as reduced occupation costs or the return of French prisoners of war.

Unperturbed by Darlan's equivocal answer, the organizing committee of the L.V.F. went ahead with its plans, allowing the rank and file to believe that the Marshal had approved. On July 8, the first recruiting center was opened at Number 12 rue Auber in a building which had formerly been the office of the Soviet travel agency, Intourist; a number of Jewish shops (which had been requisitioned by the German army) were turned over to the L.V.F. as additional recruiting centers. Meanwhile, the necessary money for all this activity came from the ever-generous Otto Abetz, who looked on the new mercenaries as forming the opening wedge that would eventually bring two million Frenchmen to fight Hitler's battles under German command.

While the collaborationists were overjoyed about French legionnaires fighting shoulder to shoulder with their German comrades on the Russian front, and Vichy was favorable provided only that it received something in return, strangely enough it was Hitler and the German army who failed to show any enthusiasm for the idea. The Führer expected a quick victory over the Soviets and was therefore unwilling to share the glory with non-Germans. Since June, 1940, he had had a very low opinion of the fighting quality of the French and this—combined with his ever-present suspicion of foreign soldiers—led him to drag his heels when the idea of the L.V.F. was first brought to him. It was the "spirit of Montoire" and the propaganda benefits to be gained from a French contingent in Russia, plus his expressed desire to bring Europe together in a common struggle against Bolshevism, that finally swayed him. The German High Command, which could see little value in untrained, ill-equipped troops, was strongly opposed, but it bowed to Hitler's order.

On July 5, Ribbentrop sent a telegram to Abetz saying that it had been decided to use French citizens as volunteers in the struggle against the Soviet Union. Hitler, however, had set three conditions: the initiative must come from the political groups in the occupied zone (that is, Doriot, Déat, et al.); no more than 15,000 volunteers must be enlisted; and Vichy must not make any demands in exchange for this aid.

Two weeks after this "gracious" consent was communicated to the organizing committee, 8,000 French Fascists (about one-quarter of them women) crowded into the Vélodrome d'Hiver, a large glass-roofed sports stadium on the rue Nélaton, to hear their leaders speak on the new anti-Bolshevik legion. Deloncle, who had been named president of the organizing committee, announced the formation of an L.V.F. division to consist of a regiment of heavy and one of light tanks, a regiment of motorized artillery, and an aviation squadron. Doriot proclaimed France's determination to recover the glory of French arms in Russia after Napoleon's disaster there and solemnly swore to go with the first volunteers into combat. Unwilling to be outshone by the dynamic ex-Communist, the other pro-Nazi leaders hastily repeated this oath to follow the L.V.F. into battle (only Doriot and Clémenti would keep their promise). The enthusiastic crowd was guarded by over five hundred of Déat's bully boys, standing in the aisles in their black pants, blue shirts, black ties, and berets, carefully watching for any signs of disapproval. Their presence was not uncalled for, since many windows of the L.V.F. recruiting centers had already been broken by stones.

There were some things that the Fascist leaders did not tell their militants. They let them believe that Pétain had enthusiastically approved the L.V.F. and that Vichy would supply both arms and money. They proclaimed that the French volunteers would fight in French uniform with French arms and under the French flag, when in fact the Germans had specifically prohibited this. (Their argument was that the rules of land warfare require volunteers from nonbelligerent countries to wear the uniform of the army in which they are fighting; it was pointed out that the Soviets did not observe these rules and shot their prisoners regardless of the uniforms they were wearing, but the Germans were adamant on this matter.) It had been announced that the L.V.F. would be commanded by the Alsatian General Hassler, but the general had made some inquiries at Vichy and had decided not to take command of volunteers raised by the purely political Fascist party. In desperation, the organizing committee had turned to the sixty-year-old Colonel Labonne, whose military career had consisted of a long series of desk jobs terminating with his retirement as the military attaché in Turkey. The only good thing that anyone could say about Labonne was that, as an enthusiastic student of Napoleon's career, he was probably familiar with the reasons for the emperor's failure in Russia (later, when he started to emulate the emperor, he was quickly replaced by the hard-headed Colonel Edgar Puaud).

In spite of a tremendous publicity campaign, including appeals in the collaborationist newspapers and a large number of posters scattered about Paris, the French public proved to be not only indifferent but hostile to the idea of Frenchmen dying in Russia for the Germans. If, as Marcel Déat's famous 1938 article proclaimed, it was foolish "to die for Danzig," then to die for Hitler was imbecilic and—in addition—despicable. So few were the recruits that the Fascist leaders had to put pressure on their own party militants to enlist; Déat and Deloncle ordered six hundred of their paramilitary troops to sign up or be kicked out of the party. Deloncle, the ex-*cagoulard,* was simply transferring his prewar anti-Communist struggle to a new arena, but Déat, the ex-Socialist and ex-pacifist, now dreamed only of bloody battles in the east.

The "collabo" press boasted of the three thousand recruits who had signed up in the unoccupied zone and the five thousand who had stepped forward in the occupied zone; but by the end of July barely one thousand volunteers for glory had been enlisted. One recruit for the battles in Russia (where he would win an Iron Cross, First Class) was a second-hand bookseller on the rue Guénégaud; a veteran of both world wars, he yearned for the military glory that had escaped him. "Well, is your husband happy?" a neighbor asked the recruit's wife. "Now he has a Boche helmet!" The glory-seeking bookseller–legionnaire later proved a great embarrassment to his nephew, Georges Pompidou, who from 1967 to 1974 was the eighteenth president of the Republic.

The paucity of recruits for the L.V.F. made it a laughingstock. The Germans sneered at this lack of martial ardor and the French public laughed at the newsreels showing the L.V.F. leaders orating. One of their particular joys was to hiss the egotistical Constantini who, after Mers-el-Kebir, had plastered Paris with posters personally declaring war on England.

Nevertheless, the recruiting effort continued, and to show that it was serious an L.V.F. "committee of honor" was formed: Cardinal Baudrillat, Jean Luchaire, Alphonse de Châteaubriant, the scientist

Georges Claude (the inventor of liquid air who was wrongly suspected of having invented the V-1 "buzz bomb"), and two members of the French Academy, Abel Hermant and Abel Bonnard. The last two (who were expelled from the Académie Française after the liberation) were lashed in a bitter quatrain by Jean Paulhan:

> While Abel Bonnard licks our conqueror's boots,
> Abel Hermant fans him, flowers strewing
> On his stomach or at his feet. Seeing such Abels,
> One wonders what the Cains are doing?

By the end of August, a motley group of less than three thousand men had been enlisted. Ranging in age from eighteen to thirty, they had appeared at the legion recruiting centers with the documents that are so vital to the average Frenchman: proof that he had never been in trouble with the police, proof of military service, a doctor's certificate of good health, and—something peculiar to the occupation years—a certificate of his "Aryanness." There were among the new legionnaires a few idealists who were convinced of the correctness of Nazi doctrine or drawn by their own anti-Communism; there were opportunists rushing to be on the winning side, fugitives from justice anxious to escape the police, and those whom the French call "*les baroudeurs*," the brawlers, soldiers of fortune unfit for a peaceful life who were only happy with a gun in their hands. Some enlisted in the hope of freeing a relative from the German P.O.W. camps and some—unemployed and hungry—for the food, the pay, and a place to sleep.

There were also those who signed up under a false name, took the enlistment bounty, and disappeared; since the L.V.F. was a private enterprise and had no official status (Vichy later made it an official organization "having public utility"), the police refused to pursue them as "deserters." Two-thirds of those who tried to enlist were eliminated by the German army doctors for bad teeth, poor eyesight, and varicose veins.

Their pay was that of the German army: twenty francs a day plus another twenty francs for every day in combat; in addition, there would be a family allotment of 1,200 francs per month. Although they were unaware of it, they were also agreeing to wear a German uniform (with a tricolor badge inscribed "France" on the right sleeve) and to swear an oath of loyalty to the Führer.

On August 27, the first group of recruits to be inducted into the L.V.F. was summoned to Versailles. The Germans had turned over the dilapidated barracks of Borgnis-Desbordes for the use of the L.V.F. and for the first time since the armistice a French flag was displayed on an official building in the occupied zone. An elaborate ceremony was planned and all the pro-Nazi leaders plus Laval (still out of office, but anxious not to be forgotten), de Brinon, and a number of German officers and embassy officials were present. After the usual flowery speeches about the union of French and German troops in the common struggle against the Bolshevik menace, a flag was raised on a central flagpole while the recruits sang *La Marseillaise* (the Germans had forbidden the playing of the national anthem by a military band). Unexpectedly, the Germans invited Déat, Laval, de Brinon, and the others to inspect the troop quarters. The inspection was quite brief, and twenty-five minutes later (about 6 P.M.), they left the barracks, pushing their way through the mob of recruits crowded around the portals.

As they came out into the courtyard, a tall red-headed young man suddenly stepped forward and, before anyone could stop him, fired quickly, five times, at point-blank range.

Laval was hit twice: one bullet nicked his shoulder and the other penetrated his right lung, barely missing his heart. Déat was sent sprawling by a bullet that pierced his stomach and colon. The colonel commanding the barracks and two legionnaires were slightly wounded. While Laval and Déat were rushed to the hospital, the French police broke into the courtyard (from which they had originally been forbidden to enter by the Germans) and rescued the would-be assassin from a furious pummeling by the legionnaires.

Paul-Léon Collette was a twenty-one-year-old former sailor who, before the war, had belonged to Colonel de la Rocque's conservative P.S.F. An ardent patriot, he had been disgusted by the collaborationists and their betrayal of a prostrate France. Convinced that a patriotic deed was necessary to shake the French from their apathy, he had joined the L.V.F. with the single intention of killing a prominent collaborator. Since Laval's visit to the barracks had been decided at the last minute, it was clear that Collette had no advance indication that the ex-premier would be present at the ceremony and had simply fired blindly on the leading members of the pro-Nazi group.

Taken to the police station, he told the interrogators that it had been his intention to shoot a German officer if no prominent collaborationist was present. The police hastily told him to stick to his original story of aiming only at the pro-Nazi French; otherwise the Germans would take over his case and he would undoubtedly be shot. In fact, the Germans tried several times to get possession of Collette on the grounds that his gun was the same type (0.25 caliber) that had been used a week earlier to murder the German naval cadet, Moser, in the *métro Barbès* and that Collette was probably responsible for that assassination. However, when a ballistics check showed that it was not the same gun, the French police refused to turn Collette over, saying that the matter was a strictly French affair. As we shall see in Chapter 12, however, the French police were not so punctilious when the Germans ordered them to arrest and hand over the Jews.

In the Versailles hospital, the X rays showed that the bullet that had pierced Laval's lung had stopped less than a quarter of an inch from the left ventricle of his heart. The surgeons who operated on him decided that the risk of removing the bullet was too great, particularly since Laval was a heavy smoker and there was not much chance of keeping him quiet for postoperative recovery, so they simply cleaned and closed the wound in his chest. Laval's recovery was slow and for four or five days he ran a fever of over 104 degrees; there was a pulmonary congestion "which would have killed anyone with less resistance."

There is no doubt that the fact that a small-caliber weapon had been used by Collette saved the lives of Laval and Déat. Condemned to death on October 1 by a French tribunal, Collette was reprieved by Pétain at the urgent request of Laval, a plea for mercy which Déat reluctantly joined. Convinced that Deloncle was responsible for the assassination attempt (probably on orders from Darlan), Laval was hoping that Collette could be made to talk; in addition, he feared that the execution of a young patriot of the mold of Charlotte Corday would have a bad effect on French public opinion. But Collette had acted alone and no shred of proof of a conspiracy was ever found. In January, 1943, the Germans finally got hold of the young man and deported him to a concentration camp from which he returned after the war.

During his convalescence in the hospital, Laval remarked gloomily to a friend, "I have just received the first two of the ten bullets that are waiting for me. . . ."

Determined to set an example after the *métro Barbès* affair and the attempted assassination in Versailles, two days later the Germans shot Navy Lieutenant Commander d'Estienne d'Orves and his two companions, who had been sent from London on an espionage mission.

Before dawn on September 4, 1941, the first contingent of the L.V.F. left the Caserne Borgnis-Desbordes for a training camp in Poland. Twenty-five officers and 830 men, still dressed in the worn civilian clothes in which they had been inducted, marched in total silence in the dark fog-filled streets of Versailles. There was no one to bid them farewell, no flowers were thrown, no military band lightened their hearts with martial airs. Only a few gendarmes and German sentries watched as they paraded past the historic château and reached the Versailles-Chantier railroad station. There, all the exits were carefully guarded by German field police, not only to protect them against "terrorists," but to prevent any last-minute desertions from the ranks of the mercenaries. In the first company to board the waiting train (coaches for the officers and freight cars for the men) was Sergeant Jacques Doriot, who was keeping his promise to lead his men into battle. The train moved out of the station as soon as it was loaded, carrying the L.V.F. to war.

Four days later, they arrived at Deba, Poland, a German training camp set amid the pines 125 miles south of Warsaw. There were two unpleasant surprises awaiting them: not only were they forced to put on German uniforms in spite of the assurances they had been given, but—assembled on the parade grounds—they were required to take an oath of loyalty to Adolf Hitler. Those who refused to don the *feldgrau* uniform or to take the oath were immediately sent to punishment battalions (where several of them died of the atrocious treatment). The feeling of having been betrayed gripped the legionnaires and the fear that perhaps, after all, the war in Russia would not be over as quickly as the Germans had promised. There might be some tough fighting ahead before they could participate in the victory parade through Moscow. Political rivalries broke out as each man blamed the leader of the other parties for his predicament and cries of "Down with Doriot!" "Down with Déat!" and "Down with Deloncle!" filled the air. But it was too late for recriminations, and the tough German noncoms quickly beat the unruly French into submission. The German infantry training was brutal, crawling through the sand with full pack, marching twenty and thirty miles a day in the unfamiliar German boots, and the exhausted legionnaires soon found they had little time or energy left for fighting among themselves.

In November, the first battalion of the L.V.F. left Deba for the front. Before their departure, Colonel Labonne read a telegram from Marshal Pétain:

> ON THE EVE OF YOUR COMING BATTLES, I AM HAPPY TO KNOW THAT YOU HAVE NOT FORGOTTEN THAT YOU PERSONIFY PART OF OUR MILITARY HONOR. THERE IS PERHAPS NO MORE USEFUL TASK AT THE PRESENT TIME THAN TO GIVE BACK TO OUR COUNTRY CONFIDENCE IN ITS OWN VALOR.
>
> IN TAKING PART IN THIS CRUSADE WHICH GERMANY IS LEADING, THUS ACQUIRING A RIGHT TO THE GRATITUDE OF THE WORLD, YOU ARE HELPING TO PROTECT US FROM THE BOLSHEVIK PERIL: THUS, IT IS YOUR COUNTRY THAT YOU ARE PROTECTING, WHILE AT THE SAME TIME SAVING THE HOPE OF A RECONCILED EUROPE.

With cries of "On to Moscow!" and not forgetting "Down with Doriot, Déat, or Deloncle" (and even "Long live Collette!"), the mercenaries of the L.V.F. marched off to fight alongside their German comrades in the Great Anti-Bolshevik Crusade.

Among the legionnaires marching to the front there were two who stood out by the force of their personalities: a French priest and an ex–war correspondent, both now in the uniforms of German officers with numerous French, English, and even American decorations on their chests.

Monseigneur Count Mayol de Luppé was a monarchist of the old school (his comrades suspected him of hiding the royalist flag in his kit), distinguished, cultivated, and aristocratic. At the age of sixty-seven, he had become the chaplain of the L.V.F. to fight "atheistic Stalinism and to defend both France and the New Europe." He was a propaganda prize of the first order for the Nazis and his photograph appeared frequently not only in the Paris press, but in the German magazine *Signal*—especially after he was awarded the Iron Cross (Second Class) for a minor wound.

Jean Fontenoy was a Fascist Malraux, a pro-Nazi *homme engagé.* It was in China as an Havas correspondent and an editor of the *Journal de Shanghai* that he created the mysterious legend of himself that so intrigued his fellow legionnaires; there were even hints of a passionate affair with Madame Chiang Kai-shek. In 1940, having broken with the Communist party, he fought with the Finnish army against the Soviets and was invalided home with severe frostbite. By now violently anti-Communist, he joined Déat's R.N.P. and later the L.V.F. Posted as a lieutenant commanding the propaganda company, Fontenoy quickly involved himself in the squabbles between the pro-Nazi factions. His hatred of Doriot was well-known and, at times, he feared being murdered by the *doriotistes.* He was instead to die in Berlin in May, 1945, defending the Führer's bunker to the last.

Passing through Smolensk on their way to the battle lines in front of Moscow, the legionnaires discovered two tattered French flags in the Church of the Assumption, banners that were taken from Napoleon's rear guard in 1812. It was an ominous warning of what awaited them.

In spite of Pétain's congratulatory words, the L.V.F. marched off to battle in its ill-fitting German uniforms viewed with contempt by all those Frenchmen whose hatred of Hitler exceeded their hostility to Stalin. The French public was all too aware that the firing squads that were slaughtering innocent hostages were German and not Russian.

Although a fierce propaganda campaign was carried out on their behalf by the Nazis and their French collaborators, the legionnaires of the L.V.F. were never considered anything but a group of venal mercenaries by their fellow countrymen. Yet, there was one virtue that could not be denied them: there was never to be any French blood on their hands. Guilty as they later were of the massacre and torture of Russian partisans, the L.V.F. was never viewed with the same virulent hatred as the Milice—those Frenchmen who were guilty of massacring and torturing French *résistants*. It was the Milice Française (French Militia) which dealt the most brutal blows against those fighting to free France from the Nazi occupiers. In the end, they drew upon themselves such overwhelming hatred that after the liberation to be a "*milicien*" was to be condemned to death.

The formation of the L.V.F. was the joint product of many collaborationist groups—particularly those led by Doriot, Déat, and Deloncle—but the Milice was the work of one man: Joseph Darnand; like his idol Pétain, he was to be both war hero and condemned traitor.

Darnand was carved from a block of native granite: strong, muscular, square shouldered. He was not tall and tended to put on weight (later he displayed a small potbelly), but there was about him an air of authority—and violence—that fascinated even his enemies. His followers worshiped him (and many died with his name on their lips) with a devotion that only the *doriotistes* could match. He was a born leader, often taciturn, obstinate, and even cruel, but his words and his orders were never questioned.

At his trial, the prosecutor paid tribute to his brilliant military record—his decorations, his citations, his wounds—his audacity in combat—then demanded the death penalty for his crimes against France. What could cause a magnificent soldier to fall so low?

Unsophisticated, sentimental, credulous—even timid when it came to ideas—Darnand was unable to distinguish between collaboration and treason. A man of direct action, he followed Pétain's policy to what seemed to be a logical conclusion—long after the Maréchal, himself, had turned back from the brink. Doriot saw the abyss and voluntarily leaped into it because he was ambitious; Darnand, slavishly devoted to Pétain, never glimpsed the chasm gaping at his feet. He fell into it, blindly following his marching orders.

Pierre Laval, who was a shrewd judge of men, probably defined Darnand best: "A fine soldier, but about as much political intelligence as a curbstone."

Born on March 19, 1897, at Coligny, the son of a railway worker, Darnand had been apprenticed at sixteen to a cabinetmaker. The zest for violent action displayed itself when, at age eighteen, he volunteered for the French army in World War I and rapidly rose to the rank of sergeant in the 366th Infantry Regiment. He was always to be found where the action was hottest and soon gained the reputation of a daredevil. He specialized in trench raids, and, in thirteen months at the front, he won six citations and the Legion of Honor, and suffered ten wounds. In July, 1918, he took twenty-seven prisoners in a raid on the German lines; interrogation of the prisoners revealed an impending German attack which was foiled. For this exploit, Darnand received the Military Medal personally from Pétain—an event which led to a lifelong devotion to the Marshal; many of his actions during the occupation arose directly from this dedication to the "Victor of Verdun." There was also a personal letter from the president of the Republic which lauded Darnand as "one of the principal artisans of the victory."

After the war, Sergeant Darnand hoped for a commission in the army, but the class-conscious officers corps, while willing to admit his military virtues, was not about to admit him to the officers' mess. Disappointed, Darnand went to Nice where he later set up a successful trucking business, but the urge to action had never left him. It was in the violent politics of the extreme Right that he saw the best chance for "combat." With a sergeant's respect for authority, he joined L'Action Française, but quickly found himself ill-at-ease in monarchistic salons so filled with the empty talk that the followers of Charles Maurras substituted for decisive action. The Croix de Feu pleased Darnand no more; he thought Colonel de la Rocque "too soft" and too unwilling to take risks, particularly after the unsuccessful attempt to overthrow the Republic on February 6, 1934. Even Doriot and the P.P.F. failed to hold him.

It was in the Cagoule—the C.S.A.R. of Deloncle—that he finally found men of his own type, men who did not wince at the sight of blood and whose hatred of the Popular Front government of Léon Blum and its Communist supporters was as strong as his. Darnand was soon the head of the Cagoule in the region of Nice. After the murder of the anti-Fascist Rosselli brothers by the *cagoulards* at Mussolini's request, it was Darnand and his men who received the payment—a shipment of light arms picked up at night on a stream that crossed the French–Italian border. Arrested in July, 1938, when the C.S.A.R. conspiracy was broken up by the minister of the interior, Marx Dormoy, Darnand was defended in court by Xavier Vallat, whose friendship was to be very helpful during the first years of the occupation. As a result of a strong defense and because war was rapidly approaching, the prosecution dropped the case against the war hero, Darnand. Back in Nice, he satisfied his desire for excitement by secret missions to spy on Italian war preparations, an assignment given him by an army intelligence officer.

When war was declared in September, 1939, Darnand was mobilized as a transport officer in the Chasseurs Alpins. Irked at this reararea assignment, Lieutenant Darnand demanded combat duty and was made second-in-command of a *corps franc*—a commando of raiders whose job was to penetrate the German positions in search of intelligence. It was the same type of work which had gained Darnand so much glory in World War I and the type of dangerous combat in which he reveled.

In a night fight at Forbach (Moselle), when his commanding officer and friend, Agnély, was killed, Darnand returned to the village under fire and brought back the body. For this exploit, he was raised to the grade of officer of the Legion of Honor and given command of the *corps franc*. He continued to distinguish himself during the "Phony War" by his courage and audacity in constant forays into the German lines.

During the Battle of France, he fought untiringly in the rear guard covering the retreat of his regiment and was always the last to leave a position. Taken prisoner on June 19, he escaped from the prison camp at Pithiviers in August and returned to Nice; he quickly gathered about him some of his wartime comrades and began to plot the revenge against the Germans.

In August, 1940, Vichy formed the Légion des Combattants (Legion of War Veterans) to unite the many prewar veterans' organizations into one authoritarian group which would preach the Marshal's words to the people and spy out dissidence. Pétain, as president of the legion, picked Xavier Vallat as its director (and Loustaunau-Lacau as his assistant). It was only natural that Vallat should remember the war hero he had defended at the trial of the *cagoulards* and to select him to head the legion in the region of Nice. The legion was *pétainiste* to a man and rallied around the "Victor of Verdun"; it was also anti-German and dreamed of *revanche* (revenge), which it believed the Marshal with his great cunning was plotting in his famous *double jeu*. It was the small-town notables who were the backbone of the legion, eager to serve the Maréchal by spying on their neighbors to search out any criticism of Vichy or any taint of resistance. Guéhenno described a ceremony of the legion in his hometown in August, 1942: the president was the local pharmacist "who for the past two years has taken his revenge for never having exercised any influence in his life." Those present were there out of fear, self-interest, or vanity: the mayor did not want to jeopardize his Legion of Honor; the teacher was afraid of losing his job; the presidents of the business, political, and social organizations were always happy to parade in public. There was even a sick old man who had hurried to the ceremony out of fear that—when his next crisis occurred—the pharmacist would let him die. Two years before, Guéhenno noted bitterly, they were all Socialists or Radicals.

After Montoire and Pétain's public statement that he had "entered in all honor in the way of collaboration," Darnand sprang to attention like a good soldier and fell into line. Always impressed by authority, he was blinded by the seven stars on the Marshal's sleeve; if Pétain said that collaboration was necessary for the salvation of France, then Darnand could only listen and obey. This blind devotion was intensified when he was summoned to the Marshal's home at Villeneuve-Loubat (near Nice) and told to continue his activity in the legion and to denounce all enemies of the New Order. "I do not like Jews," Pétain told him, "I detest Communists and I hate Freemasons." These were the orders that the Marshal gave to his faithful sergeant.

When the Legion of War Veterans was slow to give up its anti-German sentiment and its hope for *revanche,* the ambitious Darnand decided to form his own party within its ranks. He called it the Service d'Ordre Légionnaire (The Legion Police Force) and recruited not only from among the small-town notables, but also former members of L'Action Française and Croix de Feu. There were also a surprising number of hotheads and young toughs devoted solely to Darnand, who promised them action against the "enemies of the National Revolution," i.e., Communists and Gaullists.

The S.O.L. was to be a military organization, the tightly disciplined advance guard of the "National Revolution." Dressed in their khaki shirts, black ties, and berets, and wearing a badge (Gallic helmet, shield, and sword) on their left shoulders, the legionnaires swore to serve France and Pétain and promised eternal enmity to Gaullism, Bolshevism, Judaism, and Freemasonry.

Since it was considered part of the Légion des Combattants, the S.O.L. was forbidden to recruit in the occupied zone by the Germans, who worried about the persistent idea of "revenge" among the French. Supported as it was by Admiral Darlan and his interior minister, Pucheu, at its inception, the S.O.L. suffered a blow when a year later Pierre Laval returned to power. Laval was suspicious of the S.O.L.; he knew that there were many members of the former Groupes de Protection among them (indeed, Darnand had helped Colonel Groussard form the G.P. in Vichy) and he had never forgiven the G.P. for arresting his staff on the night of December 13, 1940, when Pétain had unceremoniously dismissed him.

Laval's plan was to form a new paramilitary organization, the Légion Tricolore, which would be sent to fight in Russia in German uniforms (thus absorbing the L.V.F.) and would be used in France—fighting in French uniforms—against the Resistance; it could also be useful in Africa to regain those colonies that had gone over to de Gaulle. In this way, not only the ultracollaborators—such as Doriot and Déat, who were backing the L.V.F.—could be controlled, but also Darnand, whose S.O.L. would be absorbed in the new army. Berlin and Rome both vetoed the Légion Tricolore and those volunteers who had been accepted were sent to reinforce the L.V.F. in Russia.

The Allied invasion of North Africa was a turning point for both Vichy and Darnand. Eager to order the S.O.L. to resist the invaders, Darnand wanted to radio his instructions to his troops in North Africa, but was prevented by Laval. While the Paris collaborators screamed for a declaration of war against England and the United States, Vichy hesitated, unable to make up its mind whether to resist or surrender in North Africa; meanwhile, its equivocal instructions to Admiral Darlan continued to flow. Disgusted at this "softness" in his superiors, Darnand tried to resign, but stopped short when the Marshal finally took a strong stand against the Anglo-Americans. On November 19, in a radio broadcast to the nation, Pétain said: "Some generals in the service of a foreign power have refused to obey my orders. Generals, officers, noncommissioned officers, and soldiers of the Army of Africa, do not obey these unworthy leaders. I repeat to you the order to resist the Anglo-Saxon aggression. . . . You have only one duty: to obey."

It was the end of Vichy's hesitation about the North African invasion, the end of its equivocal position with respect to Admiral Darlan, and the end of the idea of the *double jeu.*

Two days later, Darnand made a violent radio speech:

"Without any justification, without any pretext, without any warning . . . English and American troops have flung themselves upon North Africa . . . the soldiers of the Jewish and Anglo-American imperialism have come to look for an easy victory. . . . Some despicable men have agreed to be the invaders' accomplices. . . . Today, I accept the idea of seeing, side by side, Frenchmen, under their own flag and bearing their own arms, and Germans, under their flag and bearing their arms, fighting the same enemy. You will never accomplish your revolution if the Anglo-Americans arrive as conquerers bearing with them democracy, capitalism, and international Jewry. . . ."

With the successful Allied occupation of North Africa, the invasion of France had to be accepted as a realistic prospect. It was from the German concern for the safety of their troops from attack in the rear while resisting an Allied invasion that the Milice was born. In December, 1942, Hitler summoned Laval to his headquarters and demanded the formation of an auxiliary police force to maintain order in France. Not only was the Führer concerned with the growing boldness of the French Resistance, but he planned to demand more forced labor from France, which he knew would lead a number of conscriptees to flee to the Maquis. Laval proposed the creation of a Milice Française to guarantee law and order, the suppression of the Resistance, and the rounding up of the delinquents of the S.T.O. (Compulsory Labor Service Act). Laval himself was to be president of the Milice and the energetic Joseph Darnand its secretary-general. The selection of Darnand was a ploy by the wily premier to prevent a possible joining of the S.O.L. to the ultracollaborationist parties in the occupied zone, in particular, to keep Darnand from joining forces with Déat and Doriot. The Légion Tricolore having failed to absorb the pro-Nazi groups in the northern zone, Laval hoped that Darnand and the Milice could now accomplish this task.

The law establishing the Milice Française was published in the *Journal officiel* on January 31, 1943, and signed by Laval. Article 2 of the statutes stated, "The French Militia is composed of volunteers morally ready and physically capable not only of supporting the new state by their action, but also of cooperating in the maintenance of order." Article 3 required that members of the Milice be French by birth, not Jewish; not belong to any secret society; and be volunteers.

So was born the infamous Milice under the presidency of Pierre Laval and under the effective direction of Joseph Darnand. Openly supported by Pétain, who called them "the advance guard for the maintenance of order inside French territory, in cooperation with the police," it was violently opposed by Doriot, who recognized the threat from Laval—but approved by Déat, who optimistically assumed that he would eventually absorb both Darnand and the Milice.

Laval wanted the Milice to be the Praetorian Guard of the Vichy regime; under Darnand, it became its S.S.

All the trappings, ceremonies, and insignia of the Nazi stormtrooper were lavished on the French Milice. For its uniform, it took the khaki shirt and black tie of the S.O.L., added dark blue pants and jacket and a Chasseur Alpin beret. Army shoes, leggings, and a wide military belt from which a gun holster was suspended completed the outfit. In the beginning, the holster was packed with paper, for Vichy was unable to supply arms. The weapons with which the Milice was later to earn its horrible reputation would be supplied to them by the Germans.

There was also an oath: "I promise on my honor to serve France, if need be at the sacrifice of my life. I swear to dedicate all my strength to make the revolutionary ideal of the Milice Française triumph and I freely accept its discipline. . . ."

The marching song of the S.O.L. was taken over as the *Chant de la Milice:*

> Kneeling, we take the oath,
> *Miliciens*, to die singing
> If need be for the new France.
> In love with glory and grandeur,
> All united by the same fervor,

We swear to remake France:
Kneeling, we take this oath.

Their insignia was a white gamma, the sign of the zodiac signifying the Ram—a symbol of strength and renewal. For the armed groups of the Milice, known as the Franc-Garde, the white gamma was displayed on a black background in a shoulder patch. It was the Franc-Garde, the only armed and paid group, which was to lead the terrible assault on the Resistance and the Maquis.

Among the many sinister men who now gathered about Darnand, there were two whose names the French have good reason to remember: Francis Bout de l'An was an ex-professor of history and geography who in his youth had been a Socialist and a republican. His unusual family name (which means "year's end") was given to his great-grandfather, who had been found as an infant abandoned on New Year's Eve. Francis had taught in high schools in the Middle East and had served in the army during the debacle of 1940. Vice-president of the Legion of War Veterans in Syria, he had fought against the English and the Gaullists. Returning to France in September, 1941, he had become head of propaganda for the legion and had followed Darnand into the S.O.L. and then into the Milice.

Joseph Lécussan was a tall, arrogant ex–naval officer who had been director of Colonel Groussard's resistance network in Toulouse. A fanatical anti-Semite, he had been chosen by Xavier Vallat to run the local office of the Commissariat Général des Questions Juives in the same town. As a token of their esteem, some anti-Semitic medical students from the school in Toulouse gave him a Star of David made of human skin cut from the corpse of a Jew. Lécussan kept this present for several years. From time to time, he would show it and say, "It's from the buttocks." Darnand picked this alcoholic ex-officer to be the regional head of the Milice first in Toulouse, then later in Lyons.

Anxious to lead his new troops into action against Vichy's enemies, Darnand pleaded with Laval to provide them with arms. The cunning premier, who had no wish for an armed group which was more loyal to its leader than it was to him, kept stalling, saying that the Germans would not allow Vichy to arm the Milice.

Once more disgusted at this seeming evidence of weakness and a refusal to fight, Darnand thought momentarily of switching sides. He contacted Colonel Groussard in Switzerland and offered him his support. When the colonel asked him to sign a letter promising to obey him under all circumstances and to fight only against the Germans, Darnand dropped the negotiation. Through ex-*cagoulard* friends of his in the Resistance, he offered his support to de Gaulle. There was no reply.

This was another turning point in the life of Joseph Darnand. If he had received any encouragement from Groussard or de Gaulle, the Milice might have played a role in the French Resistance. To the Milice chief, the road back was closed. There was only one place now in which he could get the arms that he needed: the Nazis in Paris. The refusal to accept Darnand's help in the anti-Nazi struggle was to seal the fate of thousands of *miliciens* and *résistants.*

11
The French Gestapo

Rue Lauriston is a quiet narrow street that branches off the avenue Victor Hugo not far from the Arc de Triomphe, then marches in a straight line for one-half mile before ending near the crowded avenue Raymond-Poincaré. Number 93 rue Lauriston is a four-storied mottled gray building with long narrow windows protected at the bottom by graceful metal railings; it is distinguishable from its neighbors only by the colorful emblem of an insurance company on its glass-paneled doors.

Across the street at the local café, customers chat and laugh over their apéritifs; it is probable that most of them are unaware of the bloody role that 93 rue Lauriston played in the tragic years of the German occupation. Two doors away at No. 97, Hôtel Résidence Kléber, there is a plaque cemented into the wall, dedicated to Louis Moreau, F.F.I.,* who died at that spot on the twenty-fifth of August, 1944. It is a tribute paid by "those he had set free." But there is no commemorative plaque on No. 93; the good people of the *quartier Lauriston* do not want to remember it. It is, in fact, a silent unmarked "memorial" to those thousands of Frenchmen and Frenchwomen who eagerly served the Germans as spies, informers, extortionists, torturers, and murderers. This undistinguished gray stone building was one of the headquarters of the French Gestapo—and a grim monument to one of France's greatest shames.

During the occupation, the Germans found no lack of recruits for the hundreds of "auxiliary services" they so quickly organized, not only in Paris and the occupied zone, but—secretly at first and later openly—in every *préfecture*, *sous-préfecture*, village, and even hamlet. All France was meticulously covered by this *quadrillage*, which had been prepared long in advance of the occupation; it had also been planned that this network for terror should be manned by native agents.

They came forward by the tens of thousands, not only the killers,

* Forces Françaises d'Intérieur—the armed branch of the French Resistance.

thieves, pimps, and prostitutes who could clearly see the advantages of working under German protection, but men and women from every stratum of French society: clerks, housewives, salesmen, policemen, doctors, lawyers, aristocrats, petty functionaries . . . the list is endless. Their motives were as diverse as their origins: greed, ideological conviction, hatred of the Republic, anti-Semitic venom, a need for power over their unfortunate compatriots, the desire to be on what they believed to be the winning side, a taste for cruelty—or simply a chance to live well, dine well, and survive in the midst of hunger and ruin.

As one very shrewd Gestapo official named Bickler* cheerfully said, "There are more than three hundred and sixty types of cheese in France. Our French agents will be more varied than the French cheeses!"

Number 93 rue Lauriston was the comfortable Paris headquarters of one such group of French Gestapists and merely to mention the address was sufficient to send a shiver of fear and horror through Parisians; it was more often whispered in frightened awe than spoken aloud. There were in those days other feared addresses in the French capital: 180 rue de la Pompe, 18 rue Pétarque, 11 rue des Saussaies—but none surpassed the rue Lauriston in its murderous reputation and its ability to terrorize. In all of France, no other gang of killers was better known; none was headed by so powerful, so complex, so brutal a leader as Henri Lafont.

On June 16, 1940, in the face of the German advance, the convicts of the Cépoy prison were evacuated and sent south toward Montargis. The worst fears of the prison officials for the safeguarding of the prisoners were soon realized: trapped on the road by a paralyzing tangle of refugees, carts, trucks, and retreating French troops, the Cépoy convoy was bombed and machine gunned by Stukas. The first to vanish in the *sauve qui peut* were the prison guards, hard pressed in flight by the convicts, who were only too happy to take advantage of this divine intervention in their affairs.

One group of four prisoners quickly made its escape through the nearby woods. Three prisoners were agents of the Abwehr,† captured before the outbreak of the war by French counterespionage; the fourth was a tall, husky Frenchman with an incongruous falsetto voice. Now thirty-eight years old, he had accumulated a long list of convictions for

* Karl Bickler, an Alsatian of uncertain citizenship, was in charge of the recruiting and training of French agents for the S.S. Very popular in Paris society during the occupation, he charmed his audience with his brilliant conversation and his collection of skulls and skeletons.

† German Military Intelligence. Under Admiral Canaris it reported directly to the Army High Command (O.K.W.).

burglary, assault, fraud, swindling, and other criminal offenses. His name was Henri Chamberlin, and it was clear that he was the trusted leader of the group.

Chamberlin was a child of the Paris slums, born in 1902 in a poverty-stricken district. During the 1914–1918 war, he worked in the teeming markets of Les Halles as an errand boy and part-time thief. Assembling a gang of young toughs, he led them in a series of petty thefts, specializing in stealing chairs from sidewalk cafés and reselling them. When the band of young hoodlums was arrested, Henri escaped; this he took to be a propitious sign that his future was to be a brilliant one filled with money, women, and all the luxuries he could see in the shop windows during his cold hungry tours of the *grands boulevards.*

Meanwhile, his fortunes being at their lowest, he lived from the garbage cans on the rue Séguier, especially those at No. 6 and No. 12, inhabited by two rich Jewish families. He never forgot and he never forgave this unwitting humiliation. Years later, he was to remember the rich Jews of the rue Séguier—to their horror.

In 1919, he was sent to a reform school for stealing. After his release, Chamberlin wandered throughout France working at odd jobs. He was in and out of jail mostly for petty thefts, bad checks, and assault. It was in the prison at Aix that his marriage took place, his wife eventually deserting him for a lover.

When the war broke out in 1939, Henri Chamberlin, stirred by an unexpected sense of patriotism, tried to enlist. Despite a blameless two-year record of military service in the 39th Régiment des Tirailleurs Algériens, he was rejected as a confirmed criminal; discouraged, he joined a freelance outfit (organized by a chauvinistic journalist named Perricault)* with the grandiose name of "The Volunteers of Death." But even this chance at redemption was denied him, for two months later the unimaginative authorities dissolved this group of candidates for suicide.

Using the alias of "Henri Normand" (for there were still several warrants out for Henri Chamberlin), he found a job as a car salesman near the Porte des Lilas. In some strange unexplained manner, the fugitive from justice became a friend and patron of the Paris police; on one occasion, he gave them a car as a lottery prize. His police friends found him very *sympathique* and introduced him to their superiors as a true friend of the Force. At the suggestion of Inspector Albert Priolet,† "Normand" became the manager of the canteen of the Ami-

* As Simone de Beauvoir later wrote: "He's launched an appeal to all the cripples and those suffering from incurable diseases who had nothing to lose if they died anyway . . ."

† It was Priolet who in 1917 arrested the famous German spy, Mata Hari. In the early days of the occupation, he tried to organize a resistance group among the Paris police but was caught and deported to Germany.

cale de la Préfecture de Police.* Through the parties that he arranged and the entertainment that he hired, "Normand" became very popular with his new friends.

It was a great shock and a profound embarrassment to Priolet and the other members of the Amicale when "Normand"—Chamberlin—was suddenly arrested on an old charge. This arrest started him on the road to Cépoy and Montargis. . . .

Three days after their escape near Montargis, Henri Chamberlin and the three Abwehr agents were able to enter occupied Paris unmolested. It was a deserted Paris emptied by the exodus, a Paris in mourning under gray skies, silent except for the triumphal blaring of the German military band on its daily parade down the Champs-Elysées. "All had been lost save honor," † and for four terrible years that too was destined to disappear.

One of the Abwehr agents, a Swiss named Max Stocklin, urged Chamberlin to join them at the Hôtel Lutétia.‡ He had grown to like and admire this tall, broad-shouldered fellow with his lively ways and his strong virile appearance; also, he knew him to be energetic, cunning, inventive, and ready for any task that would show a profit. Instinctively, Stocklin felt that this was the ideal recruit for the forces the Abwehr would need to control occupied France.

But Chamberlin was reluctant. Was it a spark of patriotism in this confirmed outlaw, the same spark that led him to enlist at the outbreak of the war, only to be refused because of his criminal record? The memories of his buddies in the 39th Regiment? Or was it the vague stirring of anti-German sentiment at the sight of jackboots on the *grands boulevards*, a feeling of shame for France defeated?

In any case he shook off Stocklin and made his way to the prefecture of police. It was to his friend, Inspector Priolet, that Henri Chamberlin turned in those tragic days, hoping to get back his job as manager of the police canteen.

Priolet, still smarting over the embarrassment Chamberlin's arrest had caused him, kicked him out brutally and threatened him with rearrest.

This was one of those turning points that decide a man's fate. As the historian of the French Gestapo, Philippe Aziz, reported in *Tu trahiras sans vergogne*, Chamberlin had told his captors four years later: "It was really pure chance. Put yourself in my place—penniless

* Fraternal Society of the Paris Police.

† After losing the battle of Pavia (February 25, 1525), François I wrote to his mother: "Of all things, nothing remains to me but honor and life, which is safe."

‡ The Hôtel Lutétia on the boulevard Raspail was the headquarters of the Abwehr during the occupation.

and saddled with this prison record. And then, with the war on, there wasn't much opportunity. I tried my luck with Priolet, but he threw me out like something dirty.... My buddies had all disappeared... no hope of finding a job. So, I made out as best I could. There was the Hôtel Lutétia and Max Stocklin. If the guys on the other side, the resistance men, had offered me something, I would have grabbed at it—no doubt about that. And today I'd be a bloody hero."

Vouched for by an enthusiastic Stocklin, Chamberlin was quickly accepted by the Abwehr. Although the use of French criminals was viewed with distrust and distaste by the commanding officer, Colonel Reile (alias "Rudolph"), a rigid Prussian of the old school, his subordinates, Captain Radecke and Otto Brandl,* immediately grasped that Chamberlin was a prize recruit. Not only was his criminal past an asset—what other choice did he have except to collaborate?—but his energy, his cunning and knowledge of the underworld were invaluable. Also, the Third Reich had a plan—a complete and carefully thought out scheme—for ruling and looting France with the help of French agents, and Chamberlin was to be the test case.

Since there would not be sufficient German manpower to administer and control their European conquests, it would be necessary to use that part of the native population which, either from National Socialist conviction or self-interest, was favorable to the German occupation. To accomplish this, one need not be concerned with the motives or origins of those agents if their cooperation was efficient and freely given. Starting with "collaboration" in the economic sphere, the native agents would be gradually moved to cooperation in police work against the Jews, Freemasons, "terrorists," and all other enemies of the Third Reich.

A directive issued by the heads of the R.S.H.A.† in Berlin set forth the plan; the Paris Abwehr, through Brandl and Radecke, was to test it in the person of their prize recruit, Henri Lafont (as Chamberlin was now known).

They started by putting him in charge of one of the "purchasing offices" through which the German military command was looting France of almost everything that could be bought, confiscated, stolen or extorted from the population. Where purchase rather than confiscation was thought necessary, these *bureaux d'achats* paid with the enormous sums of "occupation francs" provided by Vichy itself. There

* Hermann ("Otto") Brandl, born 1896 in Bavaria. A longtime Abwehr agent, he had served in Belgium and France before the war. He was the head of all Abwehr purchasing offices (Bureau Otto) which effectively looted France using French funds. He was arrested by the American army in Munich on August 6, 1945; the next morning he was found hanged in his cell. The vast part of his loot, jewels, and bullion, worth millions, was never recovered.

† Reichssicherheitshauptamt—the Chief Security Service of the Reich.

was no haggling over the price if the goods were acceptable. What did it matter since the French were paying for it anyway and tomorrow would bring another 400 million francs into the coffers?

This then was the "business" into which Lafont was introduced and in which he quickly starred. Starting with one office on rue Tiguetonne, he specialized in buying clothing, furniture, and objects of gold and silver. Very soon, he had three offices and was traveling widely to purchase huge quantities of food products, including cattle and poultry for his German friends. His native shrewdness and knowledge of where large stocks of materials could be found led him to surpass the highest expectations of Brandl and Radecke. Lafont became the prize pupil of the Hôtel Lutétia, drawing reluctant praise even from Colonel Rudolph, who nevertheless continued to view him with suspicion.

Having passed the first test with honors, Lafont was now to be carefully manipulated toward the second step—and this was an infinitely more delicate process. There had been a shred of legality about these "purchasing" activities, a sense of business as usual, eagerly entered into by French businessmen and farmers anxious to escape the price restrictions with which Vichy was desperately trying to hold down the growing inflation and the exploding black market. That they were in fact draining France of its wealth, substantially aiding the Nazi war effort, and contributing to the misery and hunger of the majority of their countrymen seems to have bothered them as little as it did Lafont and the other French managers of the *bureaux d'achats*. Business is business, and "money has no odor."

But now the game was changing for Lafont. Subtly, Brandl and Radecke suggested an expansion of his activities to something more profitable and inevitably leading to even more power. It is probable that Lafont saw through the hints and suggestions of the two Abwehr officers; everyone who knew him during the years of the occupation testified to his astonishing insight, his sense of strategy and maneuvering, and his ability to grasp the essentials of the most complicated scheme. This side of his complex character, as well as the startling falsetto voice that contrasted so strangely with his strong physique, was remarked upon by all who came in contact with him.

So it can be assumed that the trap was clearly spotted and the bait evaluated. Lafont was no fool; he knew that only the Germans stood between him and the French police. He was still a fugitive from justice, and only the protection of the Abwehr kept him out of prison. That they were capable of throwing him to the wolves was clear enough; it had been done to others. Still, a man should not sell himself too cheaply; there were advantages to be gained before selling one's soul.

It is probable that the unschooled son of the Thirteenth Arrondissement had never heard of Faust; nevertheless, he was magnificently equipped to bargain with the devil.

Quietly, but firmly, he set his conditions: for what the Abwehr had in mind, he did not have the staff. Buying for the German army was one thing, oh, maybe a quiet threat here and there, just pointing out that the Fridolins might confiscate what was not offered for sale . . . but *this* was different. For this job, he would need men who would flinch at nothing, men from the milieu—the French criminal underworld—men handy with a knife. Casually, he mentioned that such men, friends of his from the old days, were presently imprisoned at Fresnes. If they were available . . . Appalled and delighted at this audacity, Brandl and Radecke quickly agreed to his plan.

The next day, a strange drama, probably unique in French penal history, was played out in the well-lit corridors of the Fresnes prison. Lafont—tall, elegant, well-dressed, accompanied by the mesmerized Captain Radecke—sauntered from cell to cell, looking for familiar faces. Here and there, a yelp of surprise from the inmate, a fond embrace, and the magnanimous words, "You are free." Twenty-seven convicts were liberated that day to enter service with "the boss," as Lafont was soon called. Tough, unscrupulous men familiar with theft, assault, blackmail, and murder, men who knew how to inflict pain—these were to be the cadre of the rue Lauriston.

In spite of this astonishing coup, not everything went smoothly for the new gang chief. Learning of the releases from Fresnes, a furious Colonel Rudolph ordered Lafont's arrest. Warned by his friends, Henri slipped out of sight with hastily obtained orders for a new mission from Radecke in his pocket: hidden somewhere in the south of France was the leader of the Belgian resistance, Lambrecht, for whom the Abwehr had been searching in vain for over six months. He was a very important prey, and, if Lafont could uncover his hiding place, all would certainly be forgiven.

As Aziz describes it, Lafont, pretending to be a Belgian refugee, haunted the sleazy bars and nightclubs of Bordeaux, dropping hints of his hatred of the Germans and his desire to serve once again. He drank a lot (but only feigned drunkenness), talked indiscreetly, and soon passed for a poor devil of a Belgian exile drowning his sorrows in wine. But all the time he listened carefully to the conversations at his table and around him. Convinced of his authenticity, his companions talked of sending him to Lambrecht, who was hiding in Toulouse. An address was mentioned, a fatal mistake.

Two days later, just after dawn, a car drew up in front of a house in Toulouse. Five armed men in German uniforms got out; Lafont gave his orders and entered the house alone. Since his reputation with the

Abwehr was at stake, he was not about to share the success of capturing an important resistance leader with four thugs.

Lambrecht was shaving when Lafont burst into the room, quickly knocked him out, tied his arms behind his back, and dragged him down to the waiting car. After the Belgian was bundled into the trunk, the car took off at high speed for Bordeaux.

The last act of *l'affaire Lambrecht* was played out in the cellar of the Bordeaux Gestapo. It was a sordid bloody scene that was to be replayed thousands of times in the next four years. Sometimes the central character was a man (Gaullist, Communist, Jew, "terrorist"), sometimes a woman; the other actors varied in number, three, four, often as many as five. Lafont was frequently present, whip in hand, for the main questioning; if the "star" proved stubborn, the questioners were relieved every four hours; but the play went on, twenty-four hours a day, day after day until all the questions were answered. Whippings, blows with the fist, clubbings, slaps, kicks—everything was used to reduce a stubborn silent *résistant* to a bleeding, helpless lump of humanity anxious to talk just so the torture would stop. Only death—which many prayed for—could save them from eventually talking.

Lambrecht was strong; it took two days to break him. His resistance organization had cells in France, Belgium, Holland, and even Germany, and, with the information that Lafont tore from his bleeding body, the Abwehr was able to arrest over six hundred of the organization's members. It was an incredible feat; an uneducated French criminal had succeeded where the supposedly efficient German counterespionage agencies had so miserably failed. In spite of hurt professional pride, the Abwehr applauded the master stroke. Even the unbending Colonel Rudolph spoke fondly of Lafont; he called him "Monsieur Henri," a name that stuck.

L'affaire Lambrecht sealed a bond of blood between Lafont and the Germans. Phase two had been successful; the transition from "purchasing agent" to fledgling French Gestapist had been made. For Lafont, there now could be no turning back.

Early in 1941, Monsieur Henri moved to 93 rue Lauriston. This gray house with its large rooms and central garden in a quiet wealthy district was to be his headquarters up to the end, and he was to make the name "rue Lauriston" a dreaded synonym for torture, extortion, and murder for the next three and one-half years.* From his office on the second floor, surrounded by fine period furniture and objets d'art (but not neglecting the precautions of steel screens in front of the

* In December, 1942, when it had become necessary to find additional space, Lafont set up an auxiliary office–prison at 3 bis Place des Etats-Unis, the home of an American citizen who had left France at the outbreak of the war.

windows and two armored cabinets), Lafont started another recruiting drive. He picked his staff carefully for a certain background and experience that fitted his new plans and objectives. There were so many anxious to join him (for Monsieur Henri was mentioned respectfully not only in German military circles and in the tawdry Paris underworld, but even in the fashionable salons where society and big business discussed its affairs) that he could afford to select carefully. In the main, he preferred old friends from the *milieu,* men who could be trusted to be loyal to a "boss" who protected them from the police, filled their pockets with money, and let them fulfill that wildest dream of all criminals: to rob, to extort, to beat and stab, to murder in complete safety. What French policeman would dare interfere with a member of the rue Lauriston who was protected by the German police of the avenue Foch and the rue des Saussaies? These addresses struck terror into the hearts of even cabinet ministers. The few policemen who tried to interfere were summoned to Lafont's office and coldly threatened with deportation to Germany—or worse.

The old authority and order which the French had accepted for a hundred years were gone. To the baffled, helpless French police, shouldered from the pavement by gangsters of the milieu, it was the world turned upside down. The rats were ruling the rattrap.

In May, 1941, two events of the greatest importance in the history of the French Gestapo occurred: Lafont quietly switched his allegiance from the Abwehr to the Gestapo and Pierre Bonny joined the rue Lauriston.

It was at a sumptuous dinner to celebrate his new headquarters that Lafont was introduced to Kriminalrat* Carl Boemelburg, one of the political chiefs of the German Gestapo of the rue des Saussaies. According to Aziz, the two men were soon on the warmest of terms, for they both clearly saw the advantages of such a friendship. Alert and perceptive as usual, Lafont was aware of the strained relationship between the German army (especially the Abwehr) and the Gestapo; he also knew that, because of its close ties to Hitler, the Gestapo was winning this surreptitious battle for power. Never a man to tie himself to a losing cause, Monsieur Henri began to shower Boemelburg with expensive presents chosen with the peculiar insight for which *le patron* (the boss) was noted. The finest wines and the best dishes of a famous Paris restaurant appeared daily at Boemelburg's office, for the Gestapo chief prided himself on his appreciation of French cuisine. The day after the first meeting—a master stroke!—two

* Police Councilor. Boemelburg was a veteran police official who—before the war—had belonged to the predecessor of Interpol.

Kabyle* bodyguards in native dress were sent to delight the aging homosexual.

Nor was Boemelburg unaware of the advantages to be gained from tying Monsieur Henri and his men to the rue des Saussaies. Already Lafont's fame had spread in military circles; here then was an ideal recruit for the Paris Gestapo, with its mission of suppressing resistance in occupied France. Boemelburg's superior, Standartenführer (S.S. Colonel) Helmut Knochen, quickly agreed with his enthusiastic subordinate; never reluctant to damage his rivals in the Abwehr, he took immediate steps to secure Lafont's cooperation in Gestapo work.

Slowly and carefully, Lafont began to withdraw from the Hôtel Lutétia and work more closely with his new friends of the rue des Saussaies. From the latter he received guns, police identification cards, three cars and unlimited gasoline, and money to speed up his recruiting; but this surfeit of money, men, and material soon proved to be an embarrassment. The rue Lauriston was no longer a gang; it was an important German service and Gestapo auxiliary and its lack of efficiency was crippling it. Lafont, who was virtually illiterate, did not know how to go about setting up an organization.

It was at this propitious moment that Radecke introduced Pierre Bonny to the boss—Bonny, whom a French minister had once called "the first policeman in France." But that was in 1934, when he had played such a brilliant—if shady—role in the Stavisky scandal.† Since then he had been convicted of accepting bribes and violating professional secrets and had been scratching out a living as a private detective, shadowing unfaithful wives. In 1941, he had tried to get a job with the Abwehr, but Colonel Rudolph had refused to consider such a tainted character; he had to draw the line somewhere. It was Bonny's friend, Captain Radecke, who took him to the rue Lauriston. The thought of the French ex-cop working for the French fugitive from justice must have amused Radecke.

After a testing period in which Bonny was required to perform a number of demeaning tasks, Lafont was ready to accept him as his adjutant; he was impressed by Bonny's silent acceptance of his degradation and his obvious admiration for Monsieur Henri. This admiration was the tribute that failure frequently pays to success.

Installed at a small desk in a corner of Lafont's office, Bonny set to work eagerly. This was the job that he knew best; this was the detail

* Kabyles: Algerian Arab tribesmen.

† Bonny, an agent of the Sûreté générale, was a close friend of the notorious swindler Stavisky. When the financial scandal that threatened to topple the government broke out, Bonny saved the day by recovering Stavisky's check stubs, which had disappeared from his dossier. Stavisky, like Colonel Henry, who forged documents to prove Dreyfus's "guilt," very conveniently "committed suicide," thus saving certain government ministers great embarrassment.

work that he delighted in, among men who were familiar types: criminals of the *milieu*. These included not only the crooks who were also available for other assignments, but the boss's friends among the society and business crowd who so frequently boasted of their powerful friend, Monsieur Henri. Bonny was quite meticulous in his work, for he saw the rare advantage of the *fichier*—his beloved card index—for future blackmail.

He also established a series of regular reports to Knochen and Boemelburg, a display of efficiency that was greatly appreciated by the file-happy Nazi functionaries. Thus the Germans were given not only the latest information on the activities of their new "service," but also were reassured that all profitable activities were contributing their proper share to the German coffers—for, although the Gestapo was very generous in splitting the booty (not all of which was reported to Berlin), they watched Lafont very carefully.

The first activity undertaken by the newly expanded gang of French Gestapists was the recovery of hidden gold coins and bullion plus foreign stocks, bonds, and currency. Under the armistice agreement, Vichy was required to make certain that all valuables were to be deposited in French banks, that they were listed, and that the lists were given to the occupation authorities. Many Frenchmen hid their gold napoleons, American dollars, and British pounds from the Germans and from the Vichy tax inspectors (who were none too eager themselves to reveal the existence of these valuables to the grasping Germans). But, as the occupation went on and on, the high prices and the scarcity of food and other necessities dictated that something of value had to be sold just so one could exist. The problem of disposing of gold or foreign currency without alerting either Vichy or the Gestapo of the avenue Foch sent many desperate people to the black-market bars and restaurants, where it was rumored that such transactions had been safely handled in the past.

Unfortunately, the careful hints dropped in these places very quickly were reported to the rue Lauriston and were filed by Bonny on one of his cards as either a "big deal" or a "little deal," depending on the amount involved. After review by Lafont, certain members of the gang were assigned to the case, their number being that thought appropriate to its importance; where it was deemed necessary because of any unusual circumstances, "specialists" were included.

The customary technique—which varied little from case to case—was for one or two members of the gang disguised as prospective buyers to meet with the would-be seller and inspect the "goods" or a sample. Once the hiding place of the gold or currency was established, police identification cards were produced and the terrifying words "German police! You're under arrest!" pronounced. At the rue Lauriston, the booty was evaluated and sent to the avenue Foch. The prospective seller, terrorized by fear, was questioned closely; if lucky, he escaped with nothing more than a few slaps and kicks—and the loss of his money—but if he were Jewish, his fate was sealed. Invariably, he was sent to the Gestapo with a report on the affair, to be either deported to a death camp in Germany or held as a hostage.

The complexity of Lafont's character, his moodiness and periods of depression, as well as the violence of his temper at any act of disloyalty or disrespect, have been recounted by many of his associates at their interrogations. On the one hand, he adored flowers, particularly dahlias and orchids, going so far as to establish a prize for dahlias which he endowed with one hundred thousand francs. At his lavish parties for Paris society, high government officials, and his Gestapo friends, the tables were covered with the choicest blooms. Every day, fresh flowers were put in his office, for he could not bear to see them die.

Yet he was capable of the worst cruelty. Whip in hand, he was frequently present at the torture sessions in the cellars of the rue Lauriston. Through the haze of pain that enveloped them, his victims could hear that high-pitched girlish voice constantly screaming, "You will talk! Tell me . . ." Then the whip smashing across their faces, the kicks, the blows of the fist, the clubs on their buttocks and kidneys. Some talked, some died silent; it was not even a matter of individual endurance, but rather of temperament, pride, or stubbornness.

Toward any member of his own gang who wavered in his fidelity, Monsieur Henri was merciless. Lesser offenses, such as a killing for personal reasons rather than in the "line of duty," holding out some of the loot from a particular deal, or quarrels between members of the gang were dealt with by a series of fines and admonishments. "We are an important service," Lafont was fond of saying, "we are not petty crooks." But woe to any Gestapist who did not heed the warning, who tried to slip away from the boss's authority or to appeal to the avenue Foch above his head.

When the crook Estebéteguy became a burden, he was sent by Lafont's orders to be "processed" in Doctor Petiot's* furnace. Others who tried to escape the discipline of the rue Lauriston were hunted down and mercilessly killed. The boss was a serious man who ran an important operation, and disloyalty was the unforgivable sin, for it threatened his standing with the Gestapo.

The lesson was quickly learned by the gangsters of the rue Lau-

* During the occupation, Dr. Petiot let it be known that he could guarantee safe passage to South America for a price. Rich clients who came to his office on the rue Le Sueur (with their baggage, gold, and jewels) were asphyxiated and cut into small pieces which were burned in the furnace. He was guillotined in 1946.

riston. Loyalty to a chief was a new idea to them, but they accepted it. After all, *le patron* was very, very generous, and one could really enjoy life in Paris with a German police card in his pocket. It was better than being one of those poor hungry rats with the pinched faces that one could see shivering on the cold streets. Business was good and the Germans would win. . .

Business *was* good, and, for administrative purposes, Bonny had to divide the gang into three departments, the first of which handled all matters relating to gold, stocks, bonds, currency, or black-market activities. The second concerned itself exclusively with "Jewish affairs": denunciations, confiscations, arrests, etc. Although Lafont later claimed that this work had to be done to satisfy the Gestapo and that he himself took no part and no interest in it, the man he chose to head this section was a virulent anti-Semite and notorious for his cruelty to those Jews unfortunate enough to fall into his hands.

The third section of the rue Lauriston was one that *le patron* considered as important—if not as profitable—as the recovery of gold and foreign currency: the infiltration and destruction of resistance networks. Time and again, brave men and women struggling to liberate a stricken France found themselves betrayed by their own countrymen to the enemy. The price in pain and blood was enormous; the captives could hope for nothing but torture in a filthy cellar followed by a firing squad or perhaps deportation to a slower death in a German concentration camp.

Alone, the Germans could not have arrested a fraction of those who finally fell into their hands; it was the cold-blooded efficiency of their French servants—without whom the Gestapo would have been blind—that decimated the Resistance.

With the day-by-day affairs of the rue Lauriston in the hands of an administrative genius like Bonny, Lafont could turn more and more to the cultivation of important contacts in the upper levels of Paris society, business and politics. His social success was astonishing, and invitations to his dinners were eagerly sought after and boasted of in the most exclusive salons in Paris. At these lavish affairs, one could find the most fantastic mixture of black-uniformed Gestapo officers—such as the emaciated sardonic Knochen—obsequious Vichy ministers, and the most elegant of theater and film stars, all skillfully manipulated by this suave gangster from the slums of Paris. Lafont despised them, but he found them useful. He plied them with gifts and granted their requests for favors—a friend released from prison, an *Ausweis* to visit their country place in the unoccupied zone, gasoline coupons, food coupons, clothing coupons. He trusted none of them, but their flattery helped him forget the Thirteenth Arrondissement; it was very heady stuff even for a realist and a cynic.

One of his most frequent guests was the very powerful and useful Jean Luchaire, president of the French Press Corporation and publisher of the pro-Nazi *Nouveaux Temps.* He often visited the rue Lauriston, bringing his film-star daughter, Corinne, and his mistress of the moment; in his relations with women, he was as fickle and inconstant as Lafont, which may explain the great friendship between them. More likely, it was an exchange of important favors: Luchaire had certain friends who had been unfortunate enough to offend the Gestapo and were languishing in jail. In return for their release (which Lafont accomplished very easily), he kept the rue Lauriston informed on the intrigues in collaborationist circles both in Paris and Vichy.

It was Luchaire who introduced Lafont to Pierre Laval during a dinner given by Otto Abetz. "I've heard a lot about you, Monsieur Henri. No formalities please . . . we'll use '*tu*' as compatriots should," said Laval.* This was the beginning of the strange close relationship between this Vautrin of the underworld and the shifty politician in the white necktie who, as Président du Conseil, was determined to secure France's salvation by the closest possible collaboration with the Nazis.

Luchaire let it be known that Lafont had important contacts with the Germans and Laval was impressed. "I like people like you. My door is always open whenever you wish. We have a lot to do together." After that, according to Lafont, they met frequently at dinners or at Laval's office.

During the interrogation following his arrest, Lafont boasted of his influence on Laval, claiming that the president had even asked his advice on a proposed treaty of peace with the Nazis. Once, when Lafont spoke of chucking the whole unsavory business that he was in, Laval quickly ordered him to remain. "There are not too many of us who can save French lives."

Lafont's success in society was matched by his success with many of the most desirable of its women. They fluttered about him, attracted as much by the aura of power that surrounded him as by his ability to do them the little favors that meant so much during the occupation. Also, there was about him that smell of blood that is an irresistible scent to certain women.

At a formal dinner, Lafont met the "countess," an ex-model and ex–film star. It was the *coup de foudre;* the countess moved into 93 rue Lauriston and was Lafont's hostess at the many formal dinners given there for the French and German dignitaries who eagerly came to dine at his table.

* In July, 1942, Chamberlin–Lafont received not only the rank of captain in the S.S., but German citizenship—a strange compatriot for the head of the government!

But *le patron* was not known for his fidelity to any mistress. There was then a quick succession of untitled claimants to the position of Lafont's bed partner, a not unremunerative post. One of the *patron's* most exotic consorts was a genuine French countess, a member of the old nobility. Her life before 1940 reads like a chapter from Restif de La Bretonne.

The countess was an immediate success with the French Gestapo. Her contacts and entry in Paris society enabled her to develop more than one coup in the black market, and she was frequently congratulated on her ability to denounce rich Jews worth robbing. Besides, with her exotic past, she amused people at a time when diversion was hard to find.

Aziz reports that the longest period of service as Lafont's mistress and hostess belongs to an elegant red-headed marquise, an expert horsewoman who taught him to ride and persuaded him to buy a stable of racehorses. In the last few months before the liberation, Lafont was frequently seen at the Paris tracks watching his horses race and playing at the unfamiliar role of millionaire sportsman.* But Lafont eventually became bored with both horses and his demanding mistress; he sold the stables and passed the marquise on to one of his deserving subordinates. After his arrest in 1945, *le patron* ungratefully described her as "a madwoman and a real bitch."

To Lafont, women—even society women with important contacts—were a pleasant diversion, but his chief interest was the accumulation of power and the enjoyment of exercising it. Soon, even the Resistance was forced to acknowledge his enormous prestige and influence in occupied France.

During the summer of 1943, reeling under the terrible blows dealt to their networks by the rue Lauriston, a resistance group composed of ex–army officers tried to neutralize the ferocious Monsieur Henri. Unable to kill him because of ever-present bodyguards (and unwilling to take the risk of provoking the Germans into shooting a large number of hostages), they tried to buy him off, to pay him to turn against his Nazi masters. With appropriate precautions, a rendezvous was arranged at the gang's favorite nightclub, Le Chapiteau, between Lafont and a prominent member of the Resistance. This attempt to "turn around" the French Gestapo chief failed, Lafont refusing the opportunity to extricate himself and his men from complicity with the Nazis. As he bluntly put it: "You can never give me as much money, as many women, or as much power as I now have . . . these are important to me. I won't give them up. . . ."

* Lafont was at Longchamps on April 5, 1943, during an Allied air raid; several bombs exploded in the crowded stands. He watched coolly as the dead and wounded were carried away. The races continued.

He held on to all this wealth and power almost to the end. After the Allied landings in Normandy, his influential friends (but not his aristocratic mistress) quickly dropped him and started to prepare their excuses for the coming purge; Jews and "terrorists" were hidden in the finest Paris homes and money poured into the coffers of the C.N.R.* At last it was clear which would be the winning side and *Tout Paris* sighed in relief as this troublesome dilemma was solved for them by the rapid Anglo-American advance.

For the French Gestapo, with so much blood on its hands, no such self-deception was possible. Not only had the BBC warned them of the coming retribution, but the resistance newspapers had published their names and addresses.† No amount of twisting and turning could save them from the execution post and "*douze balles dans la peau*" ("twelve bullets in their hides").

Maddened by the inexorable doom that was coming closer every day, other French Gestapists flung themselves desperately into their murderous work. Between June 17 and August 17, 1944, the gangsters of the rue de la Pompe were responsible for 110 murders and four hundred deportations of Jews and *résistants;* of those deported to the Nazi concentration camps, less than half returned after the war. Old political scores were settled: on the twentieth of June, 1944, Jean Zay, who had been minister of education in the Popular Front government of Léon Blum, was murdered by hired killers; two weeks later, Georges Mandel, who had worked closely with Clemenceau and who had opposed the 1940 armistice while minister of the interior in the Reynaud cabinet, was taken from his prison cell and machine gunned to death on a sideroad in the forest of Fontainebleau.

In August, 1944, the insurrection that was to free the capital was being desperately prepared. The lack of weapons with which to fight the Germans was obvious to the resistance leaders and frantic attempts were made to secure arms. So critical was the situation that the need for security and caution in their work which had been acquired at such a terrible cost in blood was ignored. Thirty-four young men, members of three resistance groups from the Paris suburbs, were trapped in a garage by a French traitor who had promised them guns; after a short interrogation at the rue des Saussaies, they were turned over to the French Gestapo of the rue de la Pompe for "processing." They were driven to the waterfall in the Bois de Boulogne and shot down, one by one, as they got off the truck; the last ten young men,

* Conseil National de la Résistance—National Council of the Resistance formed in May, 1943, of many different dissident groups.

† "More repulsive than the executioners are those who supply the victims to them . . . those Frenchmen who deliver other Frenchmen to the torturers. So we have decided to publish a list of those who collaborate with the Gestapo." There then followed a list of sixty-four names. (*Combat,* July 10, 1943.)

terror-stricken, refused to step down, huddling in the back and begging for mercy. The Gestapists slaughtered them without hesitation, piled all the bloody bodies in a heap on the red-stained grass, and departed, singing.

The next day, the same group of French traitors started their flight to Germany, leaving a trail of rape and murder in their wake.

As the French Gestapists scattered like scorpions under a descending heel, Lafont resigned himself to his fate. He forced a reluctant Bonny to destroy the files, smashed the bottles in the wine cellar, distributed false papers to the gang members to facilitate their escape, and retired to a small farm near Bazoches about forty-five miles east of Paris. With him when the French police and F.F.I. surrounded the farm was Pierre Bonny and their wives and children. Lafont and Bonny surrendered without a struggle.*

The trial of the "Gestapo of the rue Lauriston" opened before a special tribunal in Paris on December 1, 1944. There were twelve defendants.

Henri Lafont, "with his long nose and the little round eyes of a bird of prey," was the center of attraction during the ten-day trial, but he said little. Resigned to his fate, he accepted the blame even for crimes of which he could not have known. He had been the *patron*, he told the presiding judge, and the boss is responsible for what his subordinates had done. This included the particularly atrocious rape-murder of two elderly women by his dwarfish nephew, Paul Clavié, and the sadistic killer, Louis Engel.

Maître Floriot, Lafont's lawyer, based his defense on the German citizenship that his client had received in 1941 ("with the approval and congratulations of Pierre Laval," a journalist wrote); clearly, a citizen of the Reich could not be tried by a French court for treason to France. But there was too much blood, too much hatred between those in the dock and those in the audience for such legal niceties.

Bonny tried to save his neck by informing on his fellow-Gestapists. No stranger to courtroom strategy, he skillfully played the penitent, laying the blame for all the murders and tortures on the "madness of those [occupation] years"—and on Lafont. This masterful performance of the ex-inspector of the Sûreté availed him nothing; in the end, he was condemned to death with the others. When sentence was pronounced, Bonny burst into tears, railing against the deceitfulness of his interrogators who had promised him his life for his betrayal of his accomplices.

* Lafont was betrayed by his colleague in the Bureau Otto, Joanovici, who had been given the secret of the farm by the indiscreet Bonny. For Joanovici's career in the black market and his contacts with the two Gestapos, see Jacques Delarue, *Trafics et crimes sous l'occupation*, Fayard, 1968, p. 87.

On the morning of December 26, nine condemned French Gestapists (three teen-agers had been sentenced to life imprisonment) were taken in "Black Marias" to the grim Fort de Montrouge. At the far end of the firing range, three smooth posts had been planted.

Lafont was in the first group with his nephew and the unrepentant Engel.

Bonny was in the last group. He died weeping.

Today, no one—except possibly some inquisitive functionary in the damp catacombs of Vincennes where the war ministry archives molder—knows the exact number of French Gestapists. Buried in these files and inaccessible under the "fifty-year law" * are hundreds of reports listing the names and addresses of the thousands of traitors who worked directly for the Nazis; these reports had been assembled at great risk by the Resistance and sent to the Free French military intelligence bureau (B.C.R.A.) in London.

Although most of the Gestapo archives were destroyed in the autumn of 1944, a few were captured during bold attacks by the Resistance on local headquarters in the south and southwest of France. In the town of Saint-Etienne (Loire), Gestapo records containing the names of all German and French agents were seized; for fifteen Germans, there were over three hundred men and women of French origin. In Marseilles, similar captured lists show that some fifty Germans were aided by over a thousand French agents and that many of these had been recruited *after* the Allied invasion of June 6, 1944!

A French historian has estimated that in 1943 there were twenty times as many Frenchmen as Germans in the ranks of the German police. This is consistent with the captured records and the statement by Bickler that the French agents of the Gestapo numbered thirty-two thousand.

It is true that not all of the members of the French Gestapo were French (the infamous "Masuy" who invented the torture of the "bathtub" was a Belgian named Georges Delfanne; Friedrich Berger of the rue de la Pompe was a German who had served in the Foreign Legion; while one notorious band of killers in Paris was Italian); nevertheless, the vast majority of the men and women who sold their birthright for the privilege of killing and torturing their countrymen and who eagerly profited from the degradation of *la patrie*—these were French.

Today, in France, the French Gestapo is dismissed as "a miserable handful of traitors not worth mentioning." There is a general re-

* All state documents are unavailable even to authorized historians for fifty years after they are first issued. For the dampening effect of the "*loi de cinquante ans*" on historical research into recent French history, see the preface to William L. Shirer's *The Collapse of the Third Republic*, Simon and Schuster, 1969.

luctance to discuss even the harm done by such traitors, not all of whom were found after the liberation: some escaped to Spain and South America; some successfully hid from the authorities, coming out in the open only years later when the purge was over; some entered the Resistance with false papers at the last moment and now proudly walk the streets with the black-and-red rosette of the Medaille de la Résistance in their lapel. Former members of the anti-Gestapo teams of the French Sûreté are occasionally startled to see a name or glimpse a picture in the newspapers which evoke memories now almost thirty years old. Still, how much finer it is to sing of the glorious deeds of patriots, of the heroism of *résistants,* to salute those who died and those who bled to liberate France.

"The French Gestapo? A handful of traitors, monsieur, no more!"

12
The Fate of the Jews

The German plan for the total elimination of the European Jews went through several phases. In the beginning, the Nazis had proposed to acquire the island of Madagascar from France, by peace treaty, and four million Jews were to be forcibly transported to the island, where they would be permitted to govern themselves in a sort of apartheid. It was anticipated that they would be allowed their own mayors, policemen, and post offices, while, in the more habitable areas of the island, the Germans would establish military bases and airfields. The German administration would watch over the hostages and thus guarantee a "suitable" attitude on the part of the American Jews. The Germans also proposed to use occupied France, Belgium, and Holland as initial staging areas for expelled German Jews while awaiting the annexation of Madagascar. It had been agreed that the first groups of Jews to be sent to the island to prepare the way for the others would include farmers, manual laborers, carpenters, and artisans of all types, plus a sufficient number of doctors to keep them healthy in an unfamiliar tropical climate. The cost of this forced immigration and settling of European Jews was to be paid for by the confiscation of Jewish possessions in Europe and by the required purchase of land by the Jews.

However, the stubborn English defense and the prolongation of the war killed the elaborate "Madagascar plan"—but, still determined to make the Reich *jüdenrein* (free of Jews) and having won the Battle of France, the Nazis proceeded with the next phase of their program. In October, 1940, not only did they expel all the Jews from Alsace-Lorraine (which had been annexed to the Reich in spite of Vichy protests), but 7,500 German Jews were rounded up with less than one hour's notice and dumped unceremoniously at the demarcation line. Vichy protested, but when they were once again ignored the Pétain government chose to send all 7,500 of the Jewish refugees to the French internment camps at Gurs and Rivesaltes. In these camps, at the foot of the Pyrenees, there were already thousands of German and stateless refugees who had been arrested as security risks by the Reynaud government in May, 1940. Also suffering under the filthy conditions and the starvation diet were many foreigners who had fought in the foreign detachments of the French army during the Battle of France; demobilized after the war, they had been hunted down and interned by the Vichy police. The German Jews among the camp inmates must have felt themselves thrice accursed: pursued by the Gestapo because of their religion, they had been arrested by the Third Republic because of their nationality and would soon be turned over to the Nazis once more by Vichy as political pawns. There the mad pursuit would end—at Auschwitz.

The Nazi goal was clear, and they never wavered from it despite the vicissitudes of war. They were determined to eliminate the Jews from Europe—by emigration if possible, by extermination if necessary—but in dealing with the Jews of Western Europe they knew that they were being watched by the rest of the world and therefore could not apply the murderous tactics which had been so successful in Poland and the other eastern territories of the Reich. However, the conditions were quite different; the French Jews were scattered among the population, and it was not possible to distinguish them from other Frenchmen. Since the early nineteenth century, the French Jews had enjoyed equal civil rights, and any direct German action against them threatened to have a very bad reaction from the French people, who were fundamentally anti-German. The Nazis quickly realized that an anti-Semitic approach based on religion would find no favor among the French; another method had to be found. In February, 1941, S.S. Colonel Doctor Knochen wrote to the head of the German military administration: "It seems almost impossible to develop in the French an ideological anti-Jewish feeling, whereas the offer of economic advantages would more easily produce sympathy for the anti-Jewish struggle (the internment of nearly 100,000 foreign Jews living in Paris would give many Frenchmen a chance to lift themselves into the middle classes.)" It was therefore to the economic advantages to be derived from the spoliation of their fellow citizens, as well as to the well-known xenophobia of the French, that the Germans would appeal in their anti-Jewish propaganda campaigns.

So that the rounding up and internment of the French Jews should not appear as an act of German oppression, the Nazis were anxious that it be carried out by Vichy. To encourage the Pétain government to take such action against both the foreign and French Jews, a carrot was dangled before them: hints at changes in the armistice terms, particularly with respect to the release of French prisoners of war and the occupation costs. In Vichy, whose anti-Semitism was a mixture of xenophobia and reactionary clerical doctrine, the Nazi overtures found a willing listener. Since it was first necessary to isolate the Jews from the rest of the French population, Vichy quickly passed laws requiring a Jewish census and excluding Jews from participation in the press, radio, and cinema; the number of Jewish doctors was limited and the enrollment of Jewish students was never to be more than three percent of the total.

As mentioned in Chapter 4, the General Commission for Jewish Questions was formed in March, 1941, to serve Vichy's anti-Semitic policy. The first commissioner, Xavier Vallat, was personally picked by Pétain, who remembered that, as a deputy, Vallat had once attacked Léon Blum, then premier, as "a subtle Talmudist who does not have the right to head an ancient Gallo-Roman country." Although under the armistice terms Vichy's decrees applied to all of France, the Nazis still promulgated and carried out their own anti-Semitic measures in the occupied zone.

To promote the segregation of the Jews from the rest of the French populace, a "General Union of French Israelites" (U.G.I.F.) was set up by the Germans. Similar to the *Jüdenrat* (Jewish Council) which had been used so successfully by the Nazis in Poland, the U.G.I.F. was to represent the French Jews to the German military administration. It was to be responsible for all social and charity functions and was required to take its own census of all Jews in the occupied zone. Funded by aryanization of Jewish businesses, the U.G.I.F. was controversial from the beginning. Its directors thought that they would be able to shield French Jews from the Nazi excesses, but others warned them that this hope was futile. There were men in the U.G.I.F. who risked their lives to warn Jews when a roundup for deportation was imminent; but in the end the Nazi purpose was served. Even the U.G.I.F. files neatly classifying French Jews, foreign Jews, and Jewish institutions and children's homes fell into the Nazi hands and were used in their massive roundups. Many directors of the U.G.I.F. and their families were deported and died in the Nazi extermination camps.

The first *rafle* or roundup took place on May 14, 1941, when 3,600 Jews—mostly Polish, but including Czechs, Germans, and Austrians—were summoned by the French police to appear at the Japy Gymnasium. Thinking that it was another census (such as they had undergone the previous September), they arrived unsuspecting at the gymnasium and were immediately arrested and sent to the internment camp at Beaune-la-Rolande. A collaborationist newspaper boasted the following day, "Five thousand Jews are gone. Five thousand foreign Jews have slept their first night in a concentration camp. Five thousand parasites less in Greater Paris which had contracted a mortal disease from them. The first puncture has been made. Others will follow."

> To trace the history of the Jews in France, it is necessary to go back to the time of the Roman conquest. It is known that a great number of traders and peddlers accompanied the Roman legions. The Jews were numerous among them. And so it is that they came into the Gaul of that day and that part of them stayed in these regions, probably because they foresaw the future which awaited them in this country. They settled in the principal cities of Gaul. . . .

Thus began the report that on July 1, 1941, S.S. Obersturmführer (Lieutenant) Theodor Dannecker submitted to his superior, Adolf Eichmann, in Berlin. Entitled "The Jewish Question in France and Its Treatment," it was intended as a "scientific" and "impartial" survey of the current situation of the French Jews. Since his arrival in Paris in December, 1940, as the Gestapo representative concerned with the solution of the Jewish problem (Section IV-J of the Reichssicherheitshauptamt or R.S.H.A.), Dannecker had applied himself assiduously to the study of the historic role of Jews in French society, the attitude of the Vichy government toward its Jewish citizens, the strength of the anti-Semitic French Fascist groups, and the willingness of the French population to protect not only the French Jews, but the foreign Jews in their midst. In his report, Dannecker listed those French allies the Nazis could count on to help them in their plan to deport all the European Jews.

He pointed out a very helpful precedent: the expulsion of all the Jews from the kingdom of France by Charles VI in 1394. Dannecker charged that Louis XVI had been swayed by the Freemasons ("under Jewish influence") to annul the order of expulsion in 1776. He traced the growth of the Jewish communities in Alsace-Lorraine and the influx of Spanish and Portuguese Jews into the south of France, fulminating against the civil rights granted to them during the French Revolution. Although Napoleon did not like the Jews, he had called the Grand Sanhedrin together and, in 1808, officially recognized the Jewish religion. All Jewish influence in the French state was attributed by Dannecker to the rise of the Rothschilds, but he was strangely silent about the Dreyfus Affair.

The report went on to say: "The Jewish apogee certainly took place when the Jew Blum became president of the council of ministers while Mandel-Jeroboam Rothschild* was a minister and Jean Zay be-

* Georges Mandel was born Louis Rothschild, but changed his name in 1902 when the Socialist newspapers for which he was writing complained that Rothschild sounded too rich.

came minister of national education." Blum's successors, Daladier and Reynaud, were certainly excellent friends of the Jews and through Jewish influence turned French policies against the new National Socialist state in Germany. "By the French declaration of war on Germany, Judaism thought it had defeated its most important and most formidable enemy. But it turned out otherwise."

After a discussion of the cultural and charitable Jewish organizations in France (stressing the importance of the American Joint Distribution Committee, funded by American Jews), Dannecker discussed the work to date of the Gestapo against Jewish groups in France. Following a résumé of the German and Vichy anti-Jewish laws then in effect (see Chapter 4), he discussed the formation of the Commissariat Général aux Questions Juives (General Commission for Jewish Questions—C.G.Q.J.), which had been set up by Vichy with the task of: (1) formulating plans to carry out the anti-Jewish laws and to present these plans to Pétain; (2) watch over all political, economic, and social activities of the Jews in both occupied and unoccupied France; and (3) take a census of all the Jews in France. The first commissioner general, Xavier Vallat, was discussed by Dannecker in great detail—and in none too complimentary a fashion.

Xavier Vallat, born October 23, 1891, was a former teacher who, in 1919, had taken his seat in the Chamber of Deputies called the "*chambre bleu horizon*" (because of the large number of deputies attired in sky-blue uniforms). A man of the extreme Right and a militant Catholic—he was president of the Fédération Nationale Catholique—Vallat considered the Jewish problem from a nationalist and not the Nazi racist point of view. He stressed that exceptions must be made for those Jews, principally of Alsatian origin, who had lived in France for centuries and had been thoroughly assimilated. It was this willingness to distinguish between Jews whose families had lived in France for hundreds of years and the recently naturalized and foreign Jews which enraged Dannecker. Also, Vallat was known to be strongly anti-German, and in November, 1939, he had declared in the Chamber of Deputies, "One of the conditions of a durable peace is the reconstitution of the several Germanies and the destruction of the present unity of the Reich." In addition, he had infuriated the S.S. lieutenant by declaring condescendingly, "I am an older anti-Semite than you. I could be your father in these matters." In his report, Dannecker pointed out the shortcomings of Vallat as head of the C.G.Q.J.; later, pressure would be applied on Vichy to replace Vallat with a "stronger" candidate.

Dannecker's report concluded with a statistical study of the Jews in the occupied zone, pointing out that 160,000 Jews had been counted in the recent census, ninety percent of whom lived in the area of

Greater Paris. Since the population of the occupied zone was over twenty-six million and that of Greater Paris was over two million, the percentage of Jews was 0.61 percent of the total population of the occupied zone and eight percent of the population of Greater Paris. In the unoccupied zone, it was impossible to determine the total number of Jews, since the census recently ordered by Vichy had not yet been completed; Dannecker guessed that it was somewhere between 400,000 and 800,000—a grossly exaggerated figure. To emphasize the "scientific" nature of his report, Dannecker included diagrams showing the Jews of Greater Paris classified by age, nationality, and social condition.

"The attached photographs taken in May, 1940, give an idea of the Jewish districts of Paris, close to the islands of the Seine and of the Fleamarket, since closed. There are also some photographs showing scenes of the roundup of May 14, 1941. On that day, the French police arrested a total of 3,600 Jews, Polish for the most part." Dannecker ended by apologizing for the length of the report (it consisted of seventy typewritten pages), saying that he hoped it would be useful and suggestive for the work of other teams. "If in the future I am given the same task in another part of Europe, it can serve as a general directive for the future treatment of the Jewish question in France."

The fanatical S.S. lieutenant (whom Laval described as a "real madman") then signed the report.

Vichy's role in the arrest and deportation of the Jews, both foreign and French, was clear. Not only did it willingly help the Germans to isolate the Jews from the rest of the population by a census, by requiring that the word "Jew" be stamped on their identity and ration cards, and by banishing them from all official posts and certain professions, but it also proposed the denationalization of those Jews who had been granted French citizenship after 1932 (the Germans held out for 1927). Vichy's definition of a Jew, based as it was on religious grounds, was more inclusive than Berlin's, which was based on racial grounds. The interpretation of these laws by the directors of the C.G.Q.J. (especially by Vallat's successor, the fanatical Louis Darquier de Pellepoix) was stricter still: for example, a small group of Georgians who still adhered to the Jewish faith were considered Jews by Vichy, but Aryans by the Nazis.

It is true that each of Vichy's anti-Jewish laws allowed for exceptions. Mitigating circumstances which supposedly shielded a Jew from Vichy's anti-Semitic legislation included war exploits such as having been decorated with the Military Medal or the Legion of Honor for military deeds, or having received a certain number of citations in army orders. Residence of his family in France for five generations or more, or unusual civic services were also grounds for exemption; but the Nazis and Darquier ignored this evidence of Vichy's "softness."

In addition, high Vichy officials all had Jewish friends for whom an exception to a specific law could be found—a deed that they carefully stored away against the day their German friends lost the war. De Brinon's wife was exempted from wearing the yellow star inscribed "Juif" (although she had been born Jeanne-Louise Frank), "until there has been a definitive clarification of her origin." The Marshal himself intervened for two aristocratic Jewish women, the Countess d'Aramon and the Marquise de Chasseloup-Laubat. In addition to these three women, eight Jews who worked for the *bureaux d'achats* and thirteen employed by the Abwehr and the Gestapo were also exempted from wearing the yellow star.

The General Commission for Jewish Questions was the instrument of Vichy anti-Semitism. After the Nazis had ordered the removal of Xavier Vallat and had forced Vichy to accept the half-mad fanatical Darquier (who had added the phony aristocratic "de Pellepoix" to his name), the pursuit of French and foreign Jews by the C.G.Q.J. was intensified. Darquier, who assumed the office on May 6, 1942, shortly after Laval's return to power, was wholeheartedly behind the German anti-Jewish measures. A letter dated September 9, 1942, from his office ordered that, "A Jew must be called a Jew and not described in writing as 'Mr. Levy' or 'Mr. Dreyfus,' but as 'the Jew Levy' and 'the Jew Dreyfus.'" On the status of a converted Jew who had become a priest, the C.G.Q.J. said, "If Pontius Pilate had ordered a census of the Jews, Jesus Christ himself would have obeyed; the humblest of his representatives on earth must therefore submit to the obligation of the law, especially when these obligations are in no way harassing, and also because humility is a Christian virtue."

But more than any other man, Pierre Laval was the final arbiter of the fate of the Jews. Although he considered himself free of anti-Semitic prejudice ("Why should I hate Jews? We have none in the Auvergne. We have ruined all of them"), he saw the Jews not as French citizens, helpless individuals, or even human beings, but as pawns to be used in his struggle with the never-ending German demands for labor, food, and raw materials. In the beginning he protected the French Jews by sacrificing foreign Jews; in the end, he was willing to abandon the French Jews as well, for political concessions.

In a letter to Berlin dated July 6, 1942, Dannecker wrote: "President Laval has proposed the inclusion of children under sixteen at the time of the deportation of Jewish families from the unoccupied zone. The question of Jewish children remaining in the occupied zone does not concern him."

Several days after the frightful roundup of Jews, known as the "*rafle du Vel d'Hiv*," the head of the French Protestant Church, Pastor

Marc Boegner, wrote a strong protest to the Marshal, openly displaying his hostility to Vichy's anti-Jewish legislation; shortly after that, he had a private meeting with Laval. To all of Boegner's bitter criticisms of the treatment of the Jews, Laval gave only evasive answers. "I can't do otherwise," he said. And of his anti-Jewish policy: "I'm carrying out preventive medicine" ("*Je fais de la prophylaxie*").

Pastor Boegner was horrified. "Do you intend to carry out a manhunt?" he asked.

"They will be searched for everywhere that they are hidden."

"Will you allow us to save the children?"

"The children must remain with their parents."

"But you must know that they will be separated from them?"

"No."

"I tell you that it is so."

"What do you want to do with the children?"

"French families will adopt them."

"I don't want that. Not one must remain in France!"*

Laval's willingness to sacrifice even the French Jews in return for an amelioration of the armistice terms soon became known to the Nazis. S.S. Colonel Knochen wrote to R.S.H.A. in Berlin on February 12, 1943, that "Laval himself will approve the measures against the Jews if in return he can obtain political promises . . . whatever form they may take."

One of the problems facing the Nazi police was how to track down a Jew in a modern city if he did not declare himself. The Nazis tried to make a science of identifying Semitic characteristics and one of their many "experts" was the phony professor Georges Alexis Montandon, a recently naturalized French citizen who had been born in Switzerland. A self-proclaimed anthropologist and ethnologist, he was also a member of Doriot's P.P.F. and a prestigious member of Dannecker's Anti-Jewish Institute. "Professor" Montandon gave the following guidelines for the identification of Semites:

> Blood Type AB. Feet poorly arched. Septum slightly depressed at extremity. Lips very prominent. Something Jewish about the total facial cast. Gestures Jewish. Circumcision: very short mucous sheath, but with the fraenum intact.

In addition to being well paid by the Nazis for this dubious advice, Montandon was able to build a considerable fortune by selling certificates of Aryan origin to Jews for two hundred dollars each. Frantic

* Any American reader who might be horrified at Laval's callousness should read *While Six Million Died* by Arthur D. Morse (Random House, 1967, p. 259) to learn the attitude of such groups as the American Legion, Veterans of Foreign Wars, Daughters of the American Revolution, etc., to the admission of the endangered Jewish children to the United States.

with fear, those Jews who had the means paid large sums for false papers declaring them Aryan. With identification papers that did not label them as Jews, they could disappear in a large city or go into hiding in the country. So many attempted to escape to Switzerland and Spain that arranging for escapes soon became a large industry. There were organizations which, for an often exorbitant price, would take these desperate people to the Swiss frontier or across the mountain passes to Spain. Clutching frantically at these meager hopes for safety, the Jewish refugees were sometimes subjected to the cruelest form of blackmail by those who pretended to aid them. Often the guides refused to continue unless they were paid a premium for their work. In this way, many of the fugitives were stripped of all their money and valuables; and there are several authenticated cases in which elderly Jews, unable to continue the arduous climb through the Pyrenees, were murdered and robbed by those they had paid to guide them to safety. In addition, no one knows the exact number of Jews who, having heard that passage to South America could be guaranteed for a considerable sum, knocked at the door of the murderous Dr. Petiot on the rue Le Sueur (see Chapter 11) and were never heard from again.

The Resistance helped as much as it could to allow the Jews to escape the Nazi roundups, but the *résistants* were few in number compared to the tens of thousands of fugitives and there was little they could do without jeopardizing their own existence. A police inspector, who also worked for a Lyons resistance group, was asked to provide false identity papers for hunted Jews. He refused, saying, "If a single one of them is taken, say a foreign Jew, noticeable by his accent, and if he is carrying papers with the stamp of my police station, that would blow my whole network." The requester had to agree that he was right.

Simply crossing the demarcation line into the unoccupied zone did not make the refugees safe. In the first two years of the occupation, Vichy's policy was to ward off any German demand for the delivery of the French Jews by voluntarily turning over to them all foreign and stateless Jews, with whom their internment camps were bulging. French police in the unoccupied zone hunted down all those who tried to cross the demarcation line surreptitiously, all those whose papers were suspect, all those who "looked Jewish." After interrogation and verification of their status, the unfortunate suspects were sent to a holding camp until the time came for them to be delivered to the Germans. After November 11, 1942, with the total occupation of France, the Germans no longer needed Vichy assistance in arresting Jews, but the Vichy government, in a desperate attempt to maintain its "sovereignty," still insisted that the foreign Jews be arrested by French, and not German, police. This insistence by Pétain's government that the rounding up of Jews in both zones was to be done only by the French police—although frequently under German supervision—is one of the blackest marks against Vichy of the whole occupation period. All later attempts to show that Vichy's anti-Semitic policies were forced on them by German pressures have been proved false. In many respects (for example, in the definition of a Jew) Vichy went beyond the German measures or demands. It was Pétain who insisted upon the expulsion of all Jews from the ministries of justice and education and their elimination as officers in the army. He was even careful enough to make sure that there would be no protest to his anti-Jewish legislation from the Vatican. A report dated September 7, 1941, to Pétain from Léon Bérard, the French ambassador to the Holy See, reported, "Never has anything been said to me in the Vatican which might suggest on the part of the Holy See criticism or disapproval of the legislation and ordinances in question." The Vatican insisted, however, that a Jewish convert to Catholicism be considered a Catholic and that the marriage of a Jew to a Catholic be valid.

Although the hierarchy of the French Catholic Church was careful not to criticize Pétain or Vichy policy directly, it was outspoken in its denunciation of the treatment of Jews by both the German and French police. The French Catholic and Protestant Churches together were in the forefront of the struggle to save as many of those endangered by deportation as possible, especially the Jewish children.

It was only in its insistence that foreign rather than French Jews be turned over to the Germans for deportation that Vichy in any way resisted the ever-increasing German demands. Driven by an anti-Semitic fervor based in part on a requirement for cultural assimilation, Vichy was always willing to consider the unassimiliated foreign Jews, recently arrived in France, as a subhuman species which could be sacrificed to protect those Jews whose ancestors had lived in France for generations. This policy was doomed to failure in the light of the inexorable Nazi determination to exterminate all European Jews. In a letter that Knochen sent to Berlin dated February 12, 1943, he reports with a satisfied air:

> Jews of French nationality, arrested for not wearing the star or for other infractions, should be deported. Bousquet [Vichy undersecretary of police] stated . . . that the French police will not cooperate in this. To our reply that this would be carried out by German forces, the French police answered by organizing a raid and arresting 1,300 foreign Jews. These Jews were handed over to the German police with a request to deport them instead of French Jews. It goes without saying that both categories of Jews are going to be deported.

Pursued relentlessly by the Nazis, hunted down by the Vichy police, the Jews fled to the only refuge open to them. By one of the strangest paradoxes of that time, the only place of safety for the hunted Jews was in the zone occupied by Hitler's Axis partner. Initially, under the armistice terms, the Italian occupation zone was simply an extension of the Franco–Italian frontier by about thirty-five miles, but after November, 1942, it was extended to eight French *départements,** which included the city of Nice. In this zone, the Italian army refused to recognize either the Nazi or the Vichy anti-Semitic measures. It protected not only the Italian Jews, but even foreign and French Jews who were able to reach their occupation zone. By 1944, there were over 30,000 Jewish refugees crowded into these eight *départements.* When the French prefects arrested and imprisoned and prepared to deliver the foreign Jews to the Gestapo, the Italian military authorities demanded that these orders be canceled and the imprisoned Jews released; they even threatened to back up their demands with armed force. Their ingenious excuse was that foreigners who might be guilty of anti-Italian propaganda could not be allowed to escape from their authority. Vichy protests at this infringement of their "national sovereignty" and violation of the Franco–Italian armistice terms were ignored. Upset at their failure to get their hands on this reservoir of human material (needed to satisfy the ever-increasing German demands for Jews to be turned over for deportation), Vichy protested the Italian attitude to the Gestapo which in turn reported to R.S.H.A. in Berlin. The German foreign minister, Ribbentrop, flew to Rome to put pressure on the vacillating Mussolini and the Italian military to comply with the Vichy demand. Il Duce hesitated, claiming that the whole business was a Vichy plot to separate the Axis partners. After the departure of the German foreign minister, a report from the Italian foreign ministry detailing the German atrocities in Poland was placed on Mussolini's desk. This was enough to sway the Fascist leader to consent tacitly to the protection of the Jews in the Italian occupation zone.

The Italian army, the foreign ministry, and the ministry of the interior were united in their determination not to permit either Vichy or the Gestapo to get their hands on the Jews in their zone—whether these were Italian, French, or stateless Jews. Led by the foreign minister, Count Galeazzo Ciano (and his director general, Vitetti, and assistant director general, Vidau), the foreign ministry devised scheme after scheme to thwart and delay the Nazi and Vichy demands for their intended victims. As a member of the Italian High Command put it, "We must keep the Italian army from dirtying its hands with this busi-

* Var, Alpes-Maritimes, Hautes-Alpes, Basses-Alpes, Isère, Drôme, Savoie, and Haute-Savoie.

ness. . . . It is already painful enough for the army of a great country to permit crimes of this sort, not to speak of taking part in them."

Fascist Italy stood firmly against Nazi Germany and the Vichy government of the "National Revolution" to protect the helpless Jews in their occupation zone against deportation to the death camps in Poland. This anomalous situation lasted until the fall of Mussolini and the Italian armistice with the Allies in September, 1943. The plans of the Italian army to evacuate the Jews with their retreating troops were thwarted by the premature announcement of the armistice by the Americans. The Wehrmacht and the Gestapo poured into the former Italian occupation zone, and many of the Jews were trapped, particularly in Nice. Those who were able to follow the Italian army through the passes of the Alps into northern Italy got no farther than the small villages on the other side. There, exhausted from the long march and hungry, they were rounded up by the rapidly advancing German army and shipped to Drancy.

Three miles northeast of Paris on the Saint-Denis road, five tall concrete buildings surrounded by barbed-wire fences and watchtowers loomed over the town of Drancy. Originally intended for low-cost housing, it had been used by the Third Republic for its Communist prisoners, by the Germans for French prisoners of war, and—finally—by Vichy for the helpless mass of Jews they had arrested.

The internment camp itself was not in the very tall buildings, but in a large U-shaped four-storied building in the center. Here—throughout the occupation—under filthy, humiliating conditions, guarded by the coldly efficient French police, the Jewish victims of Vichy waited for the deportation convoys that would take them to "forced labor in the east." To keep the remaining prisoners unaware of their fate, the Nazis had arranged for the first deportation convoys to be filled with young men who were really capable of doing hard labor. Francs had been exchanged for Polish zlotys by the Germans and, later, postcards had come back to Drancy from the deportees praising the "working conditions" in Poland. The children in Drancy had a name for the mysterious unknown destination of the convoys—they called it "Pitchipoi."

Its real name was Auschwitz.

In June, 1942, in a further attempt to isolate the Jews from the general population, the German military command in France decreed that all Jews in the occupied zone must wear the "yellow star." This was a six-pointed star, the size of the palm of one's hand, edged in black, of yellow cloth with "JUIF" (JEW) embroidered in black. It had to be worn securely sewn on the left side of the chest by all Jews older than six years. The yellow stars were distributed at the police station and the Jews were required to give up one point of their textile ration card to acquire this humiliating distinction.

As with all the anti-Semitic regulations, there were exceptions: English, American, South American Jews, and Jews from neutral countries were exempt from the regulation (as were Jewish citizens of countries allied with Germany). Surprisingly, Jews in the unoccupied zone were never required to wear the yellow star, even after November, 1942, when the Germans overran the whole of France. This exception did not represent any special sensitivity or protection for the Jews on the part of Vichy, but rather the Pétain government's unwillingness to allow purely German measures to apply to the area of Vichy "national sovereignty."

The regulation was strictly enforced, however, in the occupied zone, and any attempt to cover up the star, either under the lapel of a jacket or by carrying a coat slung over the left shoulder, or by failing to wear it at all times in public, was punished by immediate arrest and transportation to Drancy. In this, the German police were backed by the French police, who stopped anyone on the streets who spoke with an accent or who "looked Jewish" and who did not have the regulation yellow star clearly displayed. The Jews soon learned that the star had to be very securely stitched to their clothing for if there were gaps along the edges (which the police would investigate with the point of a pencil), and if it had been put on with snaps, the penalty was arrest, an internment camp, and deportation. A six-year-old child hurrying to school or to the bakery for a loaf of bread who had neglected to put on his jacket with the yellow star—or had grabbed a sweater whose star had some loose stitches holding it—could be arrested and deported to Auschwitz.

The fanatical anti-Semites were delighted at this new humiliation, but many among the "Aryan" French population were aghast at this new evidence of Nazi brutality. The sight of a Jewish veteran walking down the street with his Croix de Guerre and Médaille Militaire proudly pinned above the yellow star made them ashamed. Very quickly many non-Jews appeared in public wearing yellow stars that carried the inscription "ZULU" or "AUVERGNAT" or had a Christian cross; one woman sewed one to her dog's collar with the inscription "POODLE." This mocking of the occupation authorities was not without danger; with their notorious lack of humor, the Germans arrested those who flaunted their regulation and shipped them, too, to the camp at Drancy. Several later died after deportation to Poland.

But for every brave soul who tried to show his solidarity with the persecuted, even those who simply raised their hats to salute a wearer of the yellow star, there were hundreds who from jealousy, greed, or the most virulent hatred denounced the Jews in their midst to the Nazis.

Tens of thousands of letters—some signed, some anonymous— poured into the Kommandantur. Jews in hiding, those with false papers, or those who in any other way had tried to disappear into the "Aryan" population were betrayed by their fellow Frenchmen and Frenchwomen.

"Three Russian Jews are hiding in a villa: 238 Avenue des Grands-Ports, at Aix-les-Bains [Savoie]. The three are brothers." This letter, typically, was unsigned.

The huge volume of denunciations to the German occupation authorities was often intercepted by post-office workers, who destroyed the letters and warned the person threatened. Even the German officers of the Kommandantur were disgusted by the eagerness with which the French betrayed each other.

No segment of French society was free of the virulent desire to denounce the helpless Jews. Doctors denounced their Jewish colleagues; lawyers denounced those whose practice they coveted; grocers denounced their competitors; a gravedigger at the Pére-Lachaise cemetery denounced another gravedigger.

The anti-Semitic newspapers such as *Au Pilori* and *Je suis partout* published the hiding places of fugitive Jews and complained bitterly to the occupation authorities when they were slow in arresting prominent Jews. They bitterly attacked the Catholic and Protestant churches for attempting to hide Jewish children, denounced "baptisms at the last minute," demanded the expulsion of all Jewish students from the schools and universities, and tried to infect the French population with a racial anti-Semitism that had always been foreign to it.

Disapproval of love affairs also played a role in the denunciations: When a young "Aryan" Frenchman told his parents of his plans to marry a Jewish girl, his father wrote to the Kommandantur and the girl was arrested. To save her, the boy renounced the marriage plans, but it was too late; his fiancée was deported.

Outside of those who risked their own safety to save the Jews and those who were fanatical anti-Semites and entered all too willingly into the Nazi game, the mass of the French population in both zones showed an indifference to the suffering of the Jews in their midst. Out of fear (or perhaps from a traditional anti-Semitism) they stood by in the streets while the Jews were rounded up and started on their way to the extermination camps. As a historian of the holocaust wrote:

> For the ordinary man, pity and commiseration are excited by sudden disaster, but the contemplation of prolonged suffering tires and finally irritates him. Imperceptibly, people tend to draw away from the outcast marked with the obvious signs of punishment and misfortune. Ancestral hostilities revive in an atmosphere where defamation is relentless. . . .

It was not only the skins of the Jews that the Nazis coveted, but their property as well. Spoliation of Jewish goods went on at the same time as the roundup of their owners, who, since they were marked for death, would have no further use for their earthly possessions. The booty was various and enormous: the famous art collections of the absent Rothschilds were plundered from their châteaux near Bordeaux; the apartments of the middle-class and even the poor Jews who had been arrested were emptied of anything that could be of value to the Third Reich. In the bulging warehouses that the Germans requisitioned for this plunder, before shipment to Germany, could be found many works of the Old Masters, historic furniture, sculpture, cameras, clothing, jewelry, furs. Nothing was neglected; there were large boxes of china, sweaters, eyeglasses, blankets, silverware, even shoes and hats. The Germans were methodical as usual and kept exact lists of their booty. In July, 1944, they were able to report proudly to Hitler that he now possessed almost 6,000 paintings by such masters as Rubens, Rembrandt, Watteau, Fragonard, Van Dyck, Renoir, and Picasso.

July 16, 1942–4 A.M.

In a fifth-floor apartment on the rue de Poitou in Paris, a young mother sat in the darkness, listening to the quiet breathing of her two sleeping children. Alone and friendless (her husband was in the internment camp at Pithiviers), she sat silently waiting for what she feared most—a knock on the door. Outside in the blackness that enveloped the narrow crowded district, which had been the Jewish quarter of Paris since the Middle Ages, thousands of other Jews living on streets with such peaceful names as the "Rose Trees" (*Des Rosiers*), the "Parchment Factory" (*De la Parcheminerie*), the "White Cloaks" (*Des Blancs-Manteaux*), waited fearfully. The thousands of foreign and stateless Jews who had fled to France seeking political asylum and the respect for human rights, for which the French were famous, now trembled in their little apartments.

Suddenly they heard the sound they dreaded most. In the darkness, trucks were rolling through the streets of the Jewish quarter; soon they could hear the stomping of boots across the sidewalks and into the buildings—and then the clatter as they came up the stairs.

The young mother leaned back in her chair, pressed her fist against her mouth, and waited. There was a pounding at the door.

"Open up! Police!"

Silence. The deathly silence of the quarry as the beaters approach its hiding place.

The pounding continued, insistent, demanding. Outside in the night, the streets were blocked as the French police poured out of the trucks and into the buildings which had been assigned to them. People were screaming and weeping as the three-man teams—two police officers and one civilian—told them to dress quickly, to take a few belongings, and to follow them to the collection centers. Although their instructions did not specifically require it, many of the French policemen felt frustrated when there was no answer to their knock, and they forced the doors open. After all, one has his duty. . . .

On the rue de Poitou, the young mother waited until the police began smashing against the door, then, rising from the chair, she went to the bed and picked up her sleepy children. When the police finally broke into the room, she leaped from the window with the children in her arms. They were killed instantly.

"Operation Spring Wind" had begun.

It had started in Eichmann's office on the Grossen Wannseestrasse in Berlin in January, 1942. Before an attentive audience of Gestapo and other officials, Reinhardt Heydrich had given a speech on the "final solution" of the Jewish problem. He had told them that the *Endlosung* —the final solution—concerned only about eleven million Jews in Europe and that Germany was determined to carry it out regardless of the effect on the war effort. After the meeting he, Eichmann, and Heinrich Müller had sat around cozily chatting in front of the fireplace, drinking brandy. Among such dedicated Gestapo men, there was no need for euphemism, and it was clearly understood that the "final solution" meant the extermination of the European Jews.

Heydrich, who had received orders directly from Goering to plan this final solution, worked out the details of arrest and deportation with his two associates.

When Heydrich arrived at Paris on May 5, 1942, to be present at Oberg's installation as supreme police chief in France, he met with Dannecker and Dannecker's assistant, Heinz Röthke, to go over the plans concerning deportation of the French Jews. (According to Dannecker's inflated figures, there were about 180,000 Jews in the occupied zone and some 260,000 in the unoccupied zone.) No trouble from Vichy was foreseen; if Laval or Pétain raised any problems about the deportation of French Jews, it would be sufficient to offer them some minor improvement in the armistice terms to still their consciences.

When Heydrich, the protector of Bohemia and Moravia, was assassinated by Czech paratroopers sent from England, the giant roundup of all Jews in occupied Europe who were doomed to extermination was given the code name "Operation Reinhardt" in his honor. It was divided into two parts: "Operation Sea Spray" for the occupied eastern territories and "Operation Spring Wind" for western Europe. It is not known what poetic Gestapo officer was responsible for these names.

On July 7, 1942, in his office at Gestapo headquarters on the avenue Foch, Dannecker met with Darquier and other French officials to work out the final details of Operation Spring Wind. Darquier was enthusiastic about this opportunity "to rid the French nation of its Jews." The plan called for the arrest of 28,000 foreign and stateless Jews to take place in Paris from Monday, July 13, to Wednesday, July 15. Dannecker pointed out that there might be some difficulty because of the different French and German definitions of a Jew, but allowed magnanimously that, "since the French definition of Jew is less restrictive than the German, it shall be used for the determination of doubtful cases."

In the following week there was feverish activity at French police headquarters. The elaborate card index on Jews in Greater Paris, which had been taken from the September, 1940, census (conducted by order of General de la Laurencie and Dannecker) was scrutinized carefully and 27,388 cards taken out for action; on each card, the intended victim was identified by name, address, district, occupation, and nationality. Nothing had been left to chance, and the French police were so proud of their thoroughness that they had supplied copies of their master index to the Gestapo.

The operation was planned with the precision of a military campaign: 9,000 French policemen—gendarmes, Gardes Mobiles, cadets from the police academy, and the special anti-Jewish police force of the C.G.Q.J.—were mobilized. They were assisted by four hundred of Doriot's young Fascist toughs of the P.P.F., who showed up in their dark blue shirts, wide leather belts, and P.P.F. armbands, eager to help. Secret instructions were issued in a military manner, outlining the objective of the operation—namely, that the occupation forces had decided to arrest and intern a certain number of foreign Jews. The categories to which the instructions applied were then given: German, Austrian, Polish, Czech, Russian (both "White" and "Red"), and stateless Jews; only those between sixteen and sixty years (sixteen and sixty-five for women) were affected. There were, of course, a number of exceptions: pregnant women about to give birth; those who were still breast-feeding their infants; those with a child less than two years old; the wives of prisoners of war; widows or widowers who had been married to non-Jews.

There were warnings about the gigantic roundup which had been originally planned for July 13–15, but postponed to July 16 because the fourteenth of July was Bastille Day and it was felt that the French population in its patriotic, festive mood might become ugly when the raids began. People working in the police stations on the preparation for the "*grande rafle*" had left warning messages in the mailboxes of some of the threatened Jews; phone calls had been made to a few friends and the peril outlined in a few guarded words. The Resistance had hurriedly distributed pamphlets warning of the coming roundup, but very few had been able to take advantage of the warnings since the difficulties of escaping were almost insurmountable: not only were the foreign Jews marked with the yellow star and with the stamp "Jew" on their identification papers, but frequently they had a distinct accent and were strangers and friendless in Paris. Where could they go? The railroad stations were carefully watched; there were roadblocks at all the exits from the city, and the danger of being picked up with false papers seemed even greater than the danger of being sent to what some thought was forced labor in Poland. To find someone to help them cross the demarcation line into the unoccupied zone was difficult and the cost often prohibitive. In many cases, the passer stripped the desperate fugitives of all their money and then turned them over to the Germans at the demarcation line for the one-hundred-franc bounty that had been offered.

There were other reasons why they were unable to persuade themselves that their only safety lay in flight. Those who had served as foreign volunteers in the French army thought that their military service would save them. Those whose children had been born in France, and were therefore French citizens, thought themselves safe. Since, in the past, only the men had been taken in the roundups, it was felt that the women and children, in any case, were in no danger. But the Jews had underestimated both the insanity of the Nazis and the French capacity for betrayal.

Those who had non-Jewish friends willing to take the risk hid in their apartments; some found empty rooms in their own or in other buildings and crowded in to spend the night. Some refused to go to bed and stayed awake, close to an open window that led to the rooftops or a back door that led to "safety"; mostly it was the men who took the precautions, for no one dreamed that France would arrest women and children and turn them over to the Gestapo for deportation. The more resigned simply packed their bags and waited for the knock on the door.

The young mother on the rue de Poitou was not the only one to seek safety in suicide. Another woman leaped to her death in the rue de Belleville; there were deaths from poison, from throat-cutting—and one doctor killed himself and his family with injections of strychnine. Ironically, on several occasions the police, who had broken down doors at which there had been no answer, revived Jews, half dead from having taken the gaspipe; this timely intervention saved the police the embarrassment of filling out long reports and permitted these same Jews to be deported and gassed at Auschwitz.

There were heartrending scenes as children who had been born in France and therefore were safe from arrest were separated from their parents; some of them refused to stay behind and accompanied their agonized parents to Drancy—and to death. Men who had gone into hiding, thinking that they alone were threatened, gave themselves up when they saw their families being arrested. Several families that had found a refuge in an empty apartment were betrayed to the police by their neighbors or by the concierge. The letters of denunciation that had poured into the Kommandantur had not been an isolated phenomenon; even some of the French police were disgusted at the willingness of Frenchmen and Frenchwomen to point out the hiding places of the fugitive Jews.

On the sidewalks were the other French, up early in the morning on their way to work, who looked on helplessly with tears in their eyes as Jewish families, with their pitiful bundles, were hurried along to the waiting trucks. Murmurs of dismay mingled with the insults hurled at the police, who continued to drive their prey before them, ignoring the sounds behind their backs. By 11 A.M., almost all the arrests had been made and the police returned to the apartments that they had found empty the first time, hoping to catch some of the missing Jews returning for some of their possessions. In their natty blue uniforms, kepis, jodhpurs, and white leggings, the police formed a line at the end of the street and moved forward slowly, checking the papers of everyone caught in their net. Anyone whose identity card was not in order or was marked "Jew," who had an accent, or was in any other way suspicious, was hurried into a waiting truck.

At the collection centers, usually a large auditorium, gymnasium, or school in the district, the first sorting out took place. Those Jews who were single and those families without children were sent directly to the concentration camp at Drancy. The others were loaded into city buses and taken to the Vélodrome d'Hiver.

The Vélodrome d'Hiver, popularly called the "Vel d'Hiv," was on the rue Nélaton near the Seine, just south of the Eiffel Tower. It was a sports stadium dedicated to cycle racing and political meetings. Under the huge glass roof (which had been painted blue as an air-raid precaution), the light from naked bulbs and small projectors illuminated the oval track; from the arena floor, tiers of benches rose to a height of thirty feet. Normally, the Vel d'Hiv could hold 15,000 spectators, but now 7,000 Jews (including over 4,000 children) with their bundles and luggage were jammed into the stadium. The dust raised by the crowd made the air unbreathable. There was no room to move, no room to stretch out; people were jammed shoulder to shoulder on the benches and on the arena floor, leaning helplessly against each other. There were only five lavatories available, the other five having been closed because their windows offered convenient escape routes.

These were soon unusable and people were forced to relieve themselves in any convenient corner. Soon, the odor of urine and fecal matter filled the air.

For eight days, 7,000 people were locked in the Vel d'Hiv without water or toilets. The only food and medical aid they received were given by the selfless and devoted Quakers, the French Red Cross, and the few doctors and nurses who were permitted to enter. Their nerves rubbed raw by the brutal treatment and the uncertainty of their fate, the trapped Jews gave way to hysteria: women ran screaming through the arena, begging for death. There were several who committed suicide by leaping from the top tier of the benches.

There was no escape. The policemen at the gates were at best indifferent and cynical, at worst, brutal. An appeal by a mother to be allowed to go out and find food and water for her children was treated with contempt. The actions of the French police in this and other anti-Jewish actions, and their indifference to the suffering that was taking place under their eyes, were noted and commented upon by many observers. If they felt the slightest remorse at the pain and suffering they were inflicting upon their innocent victims by German orders, they displayed not the slightest hint of it; of the 9,000 French policemen who took part in this savage roundup, only one resigned as a result.

In 1965, a commemorative plaque was placed in a school at Saint-Ouen to commemorate the six hundred Jews who had been arrested there during the "*grande rafle*" by the French police. The text of the plaque stated that the victims had been arrested by "German occupation troops," for the truth was too painful to be admitted even twenty-three years later.

In a report dated July 18, Dannecker's assistant, Obersturmführer Heinz Röthke, detailed the final results of the roundup: 3,031 men, 5,802 women, and 4,051 children, for a total of 12,884 Jews. The high percentage of women and children was explained by the fact that previous roundups had taken only the men and therefore more men than women had hidden themselves. He complained that, according to his informers, several officials of the French police had warned the intended victims of the coming roundup, advising them not to remain in their apartments during the night of July 16–17. Unfortunately, his informers had not been able to give him the names of those police officials who had been so derelict in their duty. "The French population repeatedly expressed pity for the arrested Jews, especially for the children. Often the movement of the Jews was not done in a discreet manner, so that part of the non-Jewish population had the chance to form in little groups and talk about the arrests," complained Röthke. The collaborationist press had received its orders to intimate that the Jews, having conducted themselves in their usual impertinent manner, had been subject to necessary severe measures and that those who had been arrested had been black-market profiteers, had held false papers, or had been guilty of corruption and other crimes.

Reporting on a meeting that he had had with Darquier "de Pellepoix" and other French officials, Röthke pointed out that "the representatives of the French police have on several occasions expressed a desire to see the children deported with their parents to the Reich." The troublesome problem of the children had been referred to Berlin for a decision and in the meantime it was decided that they would be transported with their parents from the Vel d'Hiv to the camps at Pithiviers and Beaune-la-Rolande; the French police were charged with the organization of the move. The adult Jews presently in these two camps were to be transferred to Drancy in trains of 1,000 each; there would be room for them at Drancy since the 6,000 childless Jews now there were about to be deported to Auschwitz.

It has been argued by unrepentant Vichy supporters that the French Jews suffered less than the Jews in other Nazi-occupied countries; and, indeed, the statistics bear out this claim: only three percent of Jews holding French citizenship were deported. Out of a total Jewish population in France of 300,000, about one-third were deported, compared to over half for Belgium and more than three-quarters for the Netherlands (where most of the Jews clustered in Amsterdam).

What the apologists for Laval and Pétain fail to point out is the distinction that Vichy made between "foreign" and "French" Jews, and that it was Vichy law that helped isolate both categories; that it was the French police who arrested the foreigners, and French guards who kept them in filthy camps such as Drancy until it was time to load them into sealed freight cars for the fatal voyage to Poland. That Vichy's anti-Semitic policy was based on xenophobia, religious prejudice, and political considerations rather than the blind fanatical "racism" of their Nazi masters excuses nothing. The end result was the same.

Of the 12,884 Jews arrested during the *grande rafle* of July 16–17, 1942, less than four hundred returned from the death camps.

Of the 4,051 children, not one survived.

13
The Civil War

The French dictionary *Nouveau Petit Larousse* for 1970 carries the entry: "FRESNES, a town in the department of Val-de-Marne (Créteil district); population 26,847 (the townspeople are called *fresnais*). The town contains a prison which the Germans used as a jail for political prisoners during World War II."

Seven miles south of Paris, near the road to Orly, the cold gray stones of the prison stand as a monument to pain and suffering. Here French *résistants*—both men and women—suffered the long imprisonments, the months of solitary confinement, the endless interrogations, the beatings, the tortures, and, finally, either execution or deportation to a slow death in a concentration camp. Crowded seven or eight into a cell intended for one, sleeping on filthy straw mattresses filled with vermin, slowly starved on a diet that never exceeded six hundred calories a day, they suffered in silence. But there was a terrible need not to disappear without a final word to those who would survive them, a last farewell to those they loved, a last warning to their comrades, an avowal of faith both political and religious, and in the end—stripped of all bombast and pretentiousness—a concession of their fears before the unknown. On the plaster walls of their cells, with a nail, the edge of a spoon or a sharpened bit of wood, they laboriously carved their last messages. Dampness and cold have long since destroyed their pitiful testaments and, except for the happy intervention of a French writer who copied the inscriptions shortly after the liberation of Paris, their last words would have been lost.

Love, patriotism, loneliness, pride, hatred of the Germans, Vichy, and the collaborationists, all these were scribbled on the flaking plaster walls. From the edge of the grave they called for vengeance on those who had betrayed them:

> Laurent, Pierre—shot
> Professor of Philosophy
> Denounced by Trinquely, Pierre
> 36 rue Laborde IX, 2nd courtyard on the left

(at Barnier's), Manager of the Volcan Company,
Algiers, rue Sadi Carnot

The Czech Lieutenant Milos Sliva wrote that he had been arrested for espionage on September 11, 1943, "denounced by his own chief, Paul Gauthier."

Time and again the rage at betrayal was carved into the wall: ". . . Left December 16 for an unknown destination . . . betrayed by a buddy."

"All my life I will remember the suffering that I endured in Cell 85 because of the denunciation by a cow of a woman who sold me to the Germans. But I'll have her skin if I get out . . ." This last message, signed R.L., started with a frantic plea for help: "You're doing nothing for me. I beg you to come to my aid for I am going to die. . . . Perhaps they will have pity on my four innocent children and my poor little wife, Raymonde, who cries night and day for me."

Madeleine Grador de Perier was already resigned to her fate and scratched only the essentials on the wall: "Thirty years old, three little girls, condemned to death on June 22, 1944."

The Francs-Tireurs et Partisans died courageously, obedient to the end to Communist discipline. They listed their names in a column on the wall: "Robert Doissy, André Bries, Baillon, André Léon Lucien Robert, Marcel Lamar, Dupont . . . all of us F.T.P. of the Alsace-Lorraine group . . . condemned to death March 28, 1944." Doomed by the Germans as Communists and "terrorists," they proudly proclaimed their political allegiance before marching out to the execution grounds singing *La Marseillaise* and the *L'Internationale.*

"Long live de Gaulle!" "Long live Stalin!" "Long live the Red army!" numerous representations of the Cross of Lorraine, the hammer and sickle, "*Vive la France,*" or simply the V-for-Victory: all these filled the walls of Fresnes and testified that the vanished had believed in the cause they died for.

Nor were their enemies forgotten:

"Death to Pétain. Laval to Fresnes."

"Death to Darnand, Laval, Déat, Henriot, and the whole Vichy crew."

On the wall of another cell was a mother's desperate cry: "Where are you, Yvonne, my little doll? Your mama Yolande"; a lover's plea for strength to endure: "Popaye, I love you. Give me courage. Second day in solitary. Cric, August 4, 1944"; "Christmas, today is Christmas; an occupation Christmas, a sad Christmas, with no Christmas Eve party. December 25, 1943." Directly beneath this wistful message, "Marcel" brought the prisoners back to the grim reality of existence with the exhortation: "Never admit anything!"

Besides Cric, Marcel, the plaintive R.L., and the silent F.T.P.'s, who were of the people, there were notables who passed through Fresnes prison. "Yvon Delbos, minister, slept here"—minister of foreign affairs in the Popular Front government of 1936, in Reynaud's cabinet in 1940, Delbos was deported to Germany in May, 1943.

On another wall was scratched, "Madame de Rothschild/Madame Pierre [the last name was undecipherable], wife of the former ambassador to Ankara." De Rothschild is a famous name in France, and it is probable that this was the non-Jewish wife of Baron Philippe de Rothschild; ironically, she was the only member of the wealthy Jewish banking family to die at the hands of the Nazis. The unfortunate Baroness Elisabeth de Rothschild had been involved in an affair concerning a false identity card made out in her maiden name and had appealed to de Brinon for help. The ambassador had arranged an interview with the Gestapo chief Boemelburg. Madame de Rothschild had flattered the head of the German police, emphasizing not only her Aryan background but the fact that she was about to divorce her husband. Released, the baroness was rearrested in 1944 for organizing a charity drive to aid the Jews in Drancy and died in a German concentration camp.

Fresnes was not only a prison for political suspects and "terrorists" but was used as a transit depot for downed Allied fliers; they were kept there before being sent to prisoner-of-war camps. The Americans were particularly active in recording their presence:

S/Sgt John P. Watson
Blairsville, Pennsylvania
7-19-44

S/Sgt. Edward Vallee
8-3-44 Brockton, Mass. U.S.A.

T/Sgt. S. Joe Marshall 20932531
USAAF
Arrived at Fresne [sic] Prison
June 22–44 Still here July 25–44
Anybody got a match. I have one
butt left. Had 100 in a month.

Some of the fliers were bitter at their reception by supposedly "friendly" Frenchmen:

Donald C. Schumann
Lt USARAF 27-2-44
Betrayed by a Frenchman
William Koenig Ohio USA

Delivered into German hands
by a traitor 18-1-43
Toughincki

[The French writer who copied these wall inscriptions was puzzled by the last word. "What does 'Toughincki' mean? It is a name?" Unfortunately he copied it incorrectly; the word is "Toughnicki" and in American slang it means—in its polite form—"Too damned bad."]

One constant complaint of the Allied fliers was the food:

"If they took the bugs out of the soup—we would all starve to death, and dry up and blow out the window."

One ambitious Yank pilot calculated the pay that he was saving and wrote:

"If you are a First Lieut. in the USAAF and the war lasts two years, you will have saved approximately $7,500." Underneath, an admiring British hand had added, "18 £ per week—cor!!!"

There were mysteries in Fresnes prison too. Who was the "Sir John Granwett/24b Downing Street, London" who scratched his name and address on a plaster wall? Why was he there? What became of him?

Who was the "Franz Feuerlich, Austrian" who was "to be shot August 18, 1944"? Was he a member of the Wehrmacht? What act of resistance brought him in front of a German firing squad?

Amid the terror of the daily executions and the uncertainty of the date of deportation to a death camp, the terrible need to write went on. To mark one's existence before dying, to be remembered by those who had loved and been loved, to survive if only in a crude design—the graffiti of the doomed filled the cell walls of Fresnes. Confessions, good-byes, defiance, pride—they were all there like stones in a cemetery:

". . . jailed as patriots who committed the crime of being French."

An English pilot boasted, "Took 'em over three months to get me."

"Important warning, Dr. Paul was here—Philippe and the lieutenant are from the Gestapo . . ."

Crosses, Stars of David, "*In hoc signo vinces*" and the religious credo of a disillusioned Englishman: "Everything is bunkum but God."

Even in the searching room where they were brought upon their entry into the prison, standing naked in closets without lights, they filled the walls with their pleas, exhortations, patriotic and political avowals—all in response to some overwhelming human need not to disappear without a last outcry.

The autumn of 1943 was a turning point in the war. As the Allied army stormed the beaches in Sicily, it was clear that Italy—the weakest of the Axis powers—was close to collapse. On July 25 Mussolini fell; in September the Allies landed, and the Badoglio government asked for an armistice. As Vichy clung more and more to its weakening powers, as the German pressures increased and the resistance attacks became bolder, the leaders of the Milice began to dream of a bigger role in the state than that of a Praetorian Guard.

It had been clear from the beginning that the announced aim of this armed Vichy police, to maintain order and fight Communism, was to be extended to the battle against "Gaullist supporters, officers who dream of revenge against the Germans and all the admirers of a democracy that leads to disaster," as Darnand put it. In the rapidly weakening nature of Pétain's government and its dependence on the strength and action of the Milice, Darnand and his subordinates saw a chance to play not only a military role but a political one as well. With Francis Bout de l'An as their chief theorist, they dreamed of becoming the *parti unique,* the sole political party in the neo-Fascist France of the New Order. To attain this, they were prepared to turn the Milice into the Brownshirts of Hitler or the Blackshirts of Mussolini.

Recruitment for the Milice had been very difficult and very slow. The nationalist and traditional S.O.L., with its adoration of the Marshal and its anti-German sentiments, had looked with suspicion on its offspring as it turned more and more to the Nazis and aped all the ceremonies and symbolism of the S.S. Although an ardent attempt was made to make the Milice a broadly representative group, it drew the overwhelming percentage of its support from the Right and the far Right. The leaders and the rank and file were conservative Catholic veterans of World War I—confirmed anti-Communists and anti-Semites. Originally the idea of an authoritarian group under Pétain had drawn a large number of young middle-class sons of good families, but as the aims and goals of the Milice moved closer and closer to those of Nazi Germany and farther and farther away from the National Revolution of Vichy, these young men quietly resigned. A large number of the regional and district leaders came from the French petty nobility—bearers of noble names and small-château owners without a great deal of political sense, but violent in their opposition to the Republic. Counts, marquis, barons—it was their ancestors who had led the revolt in the Vendée during the Great Revolution, who had led the bloody suppression of the Commune, who had filled the streets shouting "Death to the traitor!" during the Dreyfus Affair, and whose hatred of the Popular Front government of Léon Blum had so blinded them that they had almost welcomed the defeat by the Nazis.

By autumn of 1943, there were some 29,000 adherents of both sexes in the Milice, but of these only 10,000 were active. Whole families joined, families in which father, mother, son, and daughter all belonged to different *milicien* groups. Other families were bitterly divided between the Milice and the Resistance; in the town of Brive, a young *milicien* denounced his father and brother to the German police as members of the Secret Army of the Resistance.

The Resistance was quick to recognize the danger of the Milice, an armed German auxiliary dedicated to the repression of "terrorism." By the fall of 1943, the French Resistance had overcome its terrible growing pains, had learned from the losses suffered through their earlier naïveté and inexperience, and had hardened into an almost professional underground clandestine organization. Their reaction to the actions of the Milice against them was violent but predictable.

As early as April, 1943, the savage murders of the local heads of the Milice began when the assistant *département* head in the Bouches-du-Rhône was cut down by machine-gun fire in Marseilles. This was the first of a long series of assassinations that marked the fratricidal war between the Milice and the Resistance. Very often it could not be determined who was really responsible for a particular murder; local and regional Milice chiefs acted like feudal barons and were jealous of their prerogatives. The rivalry between them often led to a violent settling of accounts through assassination. Also some of them had attempted to contact local resistance groups (which they knew or believed to be anti-Communist) in an effort to subvert them into joining the general anti-Bolshevik crusade. Murder could in that case simply have been a way of breaking off negotiations or an effort by an F.T.P. group to end this approach. In any case, the assassination of the Milice leaders and even many of the rank and file continued and was quickly answered by the retaliatory assassination of men suspected either of being *résistants* or of having pro-Gaullist sympathies.

It was in the autumn of 1943, as Italy sought an armistice and as Vichy trembled for its faltering power, that the French civil war, in numbers one of the most terrible in its history, began.

Although Pétain and Laval both ardently supported the Milice as a new Vichy army against "terrorism" and a bolster to their shaky regime, neither of them was able to satisfy Darnand's insistent demand for arms. Worried about an invasion by the Anglo-American armies and concerned only about the protection of their troops, the Germans were determined that they would have effective control of any armed French force pledged to fight the Resistance, just in case it should harbor any ideas of revenge (as did the S.O.L.). Sooner or later, Darnand, committed to action and determined to take the field against the "terrorists," would have to come to them and pledge his allegiance to Germany on the Nazis' terms.

In August, 1943, frustrated by Vichy's vacillations and the spurning of his overtures to the Resistance, Darnand took the irrevocable and fatal step. At the German embassy, in private, he swore an oath to Adolf Hitler: "I swear to you, Adolf Hitler, Führer of Germany and reformer of Europe, to be loyal and brave. I swear to obey unto death both you and those leaders that you will designate. So help me God." By accepting the rank of Sturmbannführer in the Waffen-S.S., Darnand had put his last stake on an ultimate German victory.

The quid pro quo was quickly paid: the Nazis supplied the Milice with fifty submachineguns. A public appeal for enlistment of the *miliciens* in the Waffen-S.S. was published by Darnand in the Milice newspaper, *Combat*. The response was negligible. Although by a law passed on July 22, 1943, Vichy had approved enlistment in the Waffen-S.S. "to fight Bolshevism outside of the national territory," and, although Darnand toured the country speaking before mass meetings of the Milice, only a few of the leaders put on the German uniform. Stubbornly adhering to the idea that only a French army devoted to the Marshal could properly fight the Communists and "terrorists" in France, the younger sons of the bourgeoisie who had been initially attracted by the authoritarian and military milieu of the Milice now left. To fill the depleted ranks, the dregs of the French underworld were recruited: petty thieves, murderers, swindlers, pimps, and their ilk gladly put on the navy blue uniform and the beret of the Milice to gain not only the protection it offered against the regular police, but also the opportunities that they foresaw for booty and loot, chiefly at the expense of the Jews. Many a petty black marketeer was offered a choice by the courts of a prison term or enlistment in the Milice. Those who made the wrong choice and became *miliciens* almost invariably paid for some minor transgression of the rationing laws with their lives. Spurred on by the London radio, which daily proclaimed "*Miliciens*, today's murderers will be shot tomorrow," the Resistance showed no mercy to its enemies.

The assassination of both Milice chiefs and the rank and file continued at a rapidly increasing rate. With machine guns, pistols, and grenades, they were cut down one by one on the streets in front of their headquarters, in their homes, wherever they could be found; the recruiting offices and headquarters of the Milice in a dozen French towns were blown apart by grenade attack. The resistance newspapers printed lists of local *miliciens* who had been condemned to death by clandestine court-martials. Driven to a wild fury by these attacks, the regional chiefs of the Milice decided on a bloody reprisal. To avenge six of their men who had been killed in the southeast of France, six suspected Gaullists had been designated to be murdered in reprisal.

Joseph Lécussan, the alcoholic ex–naval officer who was the regional head of the Milice in Lyons, selected his victim from the list. It was the seventy-year-old Elie Dreyfus, a Jew hiding in Annecy. As the violently anti-Semitic Lécussan later described it:

> I knocked on the door. This guy opened it. I went in. I said to him, "Sir, our comrade Jacquemin was cowardly murdered by your friends. The Milice has condemned you to death. If you have any religious faith, say your prayers. You have three minutes to prepare yourself for death."
>
> I held a large watch in one hand and my pistol in the other. When the three minutes were past, I fired several times, then turned on my heel and left.
>
> I had sworn to empty my gun. Once outside, I saw that there was still one bullet left in it. I went back. This guy was on the ground and there were a lot of people around him. I said to them, "Pardon me," pushed them aside, and fired my last bullet. Then I left.

Three dead, three seriously wounded: these were the reprisals exacted for the murder of six *miliciens*. Of the victims, only two belonged to the Resistance.

The round of deaths continued—*miliciens* crumpled under machine-gun fire from the shadows, and Gaullists and Jews perished in bloody reprisals. At a mass meeting of the Milice in Nice (November 28, 1943), Darnand stormed from the podium, "It is a question of life or death! You will be hanged along with me, we will all be hanged if we do not know how to fight! Be resolute, together we will win!" There was a storm of applause in the auditorium, cries of "Long live Darnand!" The whole room rose to its feet and shouted its approval. In the front row the German officers who had been listening politely stood up and applauded. They could only approve such sentiments.

That same night, in front of a Milice restaurant, someone threw a grenade into a crowd of *milicens,* killing two and wounding nine. The war went on.

The murder of relatively unknown resistance men, suspected Gaullists, and refugee Jews having failed to stem the murderous attacks, the Milice now selected notables as their victims.

Maurice Sarraut was the editor of the newspaper *La Dépêche de Toulouse* and a power in the Radical Socialist party (which in France is neither radical nor socialist, but rather lukewarm republican). With his brother Albert (minister of the interior in Daladier's 1938 cabinet), Sarraut had been influential in the maneuvering of the Third Republic in the chaotic prewar days. When Vichy, feeling its power slipping from it with each German retreat, sought support in the old parliamentary circles, it was with Sarraut among others that they had opened conversations. Fearful that the victory of Gaullism and the Resistance would mean the end of all political parties—and possibly the triumph of their implacable enemies, the Communists—the Radicals had been listening to Vichy's approaches. Hated by the ultracollaborationists for their role under the Third Republic, the brothers Sarraut were viewed with great suspicion by the Resistance for listening to Vichy's siren songs. In fact, the clandestine newspaper *Bir Hakeim* had recently announced that the Sarrauts had been condemned to death by the Resistance, while in Paris Doriot and the P.P.F. newspapers were fulminating against Albert and Maurice Sarraut.

At seven o'clock on the evening of Thursday, December 2, 1943, Maurice Sarraut's car arrived at his home in a Toulouse suburb; the chauffeur sounded the horn as a signal that the gates were to be opened. At that moment, a man stepped out of the shadows and—poking his machine gun through the rear window of the car—fired at point-blank range. Maurice Sarraut, alone in the rear seat, toppled over dead.

For several days the murder remained a mystery. Who had been responsible: the *doriotistes*, the Resistance, or the Milice? An inquiry conducted by the Vichy secretary general for police, René Bousquet, was pushed vigorously in spite of threats by Darnand and Oberg. Bousquet, who had been for many years an editor of Sarraut's newspaper, finally discovered that the murder had been jointly planned by the Milice and the Gestapo. The assassin, Dossuet, was an L.V.F. officer who had been armed by the local Milice chief, who also supplied him with Maurice Sarraut's daily schedule. After the murder Dossuet fled to Paris and placed himself under the protection of the Germans. He was killed by the Resistance in February, 1944.

The year 1943 ended with yet another demonstration of Vichy's helplessness before German pressure. On December 4, Otto Abetz handed the Marshal an ultimatum from Hitler demanding stronger action against the Resistance; the inclusion of Déat, Darnand, and Doriot into the government; and the submission of all future Vichy laws to Hitler for his approval before they were announced. Pétain grumbled and hedged as long as he could. Déat, whose attacks on Vichy in *L'Oeuvre* made the Marshal furious, was unacceptable, and he was able to have the head of the R.N.P. removed from the list; Doriot was away fighting in Russia and it was easy to ignore him (the Germans later substituted the name of Philippe Henriot). Finally, after the terms of the ultimatum had been restated in the most brutal manner, Pétain bowed. On January 1, 1944, Joseph Darnand was made secretary general for the maintenance of order, with control over the regular police, the Gardes Mobiles, the gendarmerie, even the firemen. In this powerful post he was responsible only to a figurehead minister of the interior and to Laval as the head of government. Philippe Henriot was named minister of information and propaganda, a post for which he was eminently suited and which he had unofficially filled for some time.

Marcel Déat had to wait until the following March to see his dream fulfilled. He entered the cabinet at that time with the portfolio of minister of labor and of national solidarity.

New Year's Day, 1944, was a beginning and an end. It was the beginning of the year in which both Resistance and Collaboration knew that the decisive battles would be fought. The Resistance dreamed of the coming Allied invasion which would sweep the invader out of France, and the collaborationists dreamed of the bloody repulse that would drive the Anglo-Americans back into the sea and ensure, if not a German victory, at least a compromise peace that would save their necks. And New Year's Day brought an end to the thought that Vichy was an independent government dedicated to the salvation of the French rather than a puppet pushed this way and that by German pressures; an end to the idea of Pétain's *double jeu;* an end to the German façade of "correctness" (which they had attempted to maintain in spite of the shooting of hostages and the torturing of *résistants* by the Gestapo). It ended what du Moulin de Labarthète called "the time of illusions," those terrible illusions which had been so necessary to the French, peering fearfully at the Nazi New Order from behind the Marshal's cloak.

So fearful was Vichy of losing even the little authority it still held that it had contemplated appealing to the detested deputies of the National Assembly (which had led to the death of Maurice Sarraut); now they depended totally on Darnand and the Milice to protect them from the increasing attacks by the Resistance. Laval said: "Democracy is the antechamber of bolshevism. . . . I march in full accord, in total accord with Darnand." Pétain complimented the head of the Milice on his "success" in repressing resistance. Recalling his own success in quelling the mutinies in the French army in the spring of 1917, the Marshal advised the secretary general for the maintenance of order to set stern examples (i.e., executions) to cow the *résistants.* The old man still remembered the glorious deeds in his past.

Under tremendous pressure from the Germans to crush all resistance and to secure the rear of the German army in expectation of the Allied invasion, Pétain and Laval gave Darnand complete power over all the police forces of the Vichy government. They urged him to use the severest measures against the "terrorists" and Darnand was not reluctant to do so.

Now it was to be war, brutal bloody civil war—the most terrible of all conflicts, a battle to the death between brothers.

There were warnings, first from the collaborationists:

> Dear Sir: We have the honor to inform you that we know you are overly sympathetic to the Communist–Gaullist terrorists who are responsible for murder and other crimes against France.
>
> This sympathy is only cowardly complicity on your part and if you hope in the future to satisfy your fratricidal hatred against Frenchmen . . . you must from now on understand that one should never count one's chickens before they're hatched. Fortunately for France, unfortunately for you, the Bolsheviks are not yet the masters of our country. So, with this letter, we wish to advise you that you are henceforth responsible to us for your acts, for your words and for those of your friends. . . . We are ready to publish this warning if necessary and regardless of the risks you would then incur; we are also ready to make you pay when the time comes for the crimes that you conceal by your good will. . . .

An underground newspaper published a warning to the "murderers of the Milice and of the P.P.F."

> In several towns the *miliciens* and the P.P.F. have shot down men who did not fight in our ranks but who, because they were known to be republicans and patriots, offered an easy target. But that's enough. When a traitor falls, when a French mercenary of the Gestapo is executed, France applauds. . . . To each new murder that they commit, the *milicien* and the P.P.F. must expect immediate and merciless reprisals. . . . To this whole miserable band, the French Resistance sends a warning . . . "For an eye, both eyes; for a tooth, the whole jaw!"

There were other warnings. Known collaborators received little packages in the mail containing a small coffin or a miniature noose. Sometimes, there was a letter advising them to make their wills, for they had been condemned to death by a resistance court-martial. Swastikas were painted on their doors and there were ominous phone calls in the middle of the night cursing them as "*vendus*" (those who have sold out to the Germans) or "*mouchards*" (informers). Judges, policemen, and minor Vichy officials were shot down for showing too much zeal in the pursuit and prosecution of "patriots." Every day bodies were found in the streets and on country roads; sometimes there would be a slip of paper pinned to the corpse saying "Death to collaborators" or "Terror for terror—this Jew has paid for the murder of a national." In the great majority of the cases the perpetrators of the crime were never discovered.

Every crime called for a reprisal which in turn provoked new bloodshed; the dance of death went on and on.

Before the war, Victor Basch had been president of the League for the Rights of Man, an organization dedicated to protecting the principles of the Revolution of 1789 and a pillar of support for the Republic. He was also a Jew pursued by the Gestapo and had been in hiding for many months. On January 10, 1943, Lécussan, then the regional chief of the Milice in the Lyons area, learned that Basch and his wife were hiding in a nearby suburb. With the help of his friend Klaus Barbie (the Lyons Gestapo chief), Lécussan and his men were able to ferret out the hiding place. That night they arrested Victor Basch and his wife, who refused to leave her husband. The next morning, the bodies of the two elderly people (Victor Basch was eighty years old; his wife was seventy-nine) were found at the edge of a little-traveled country road. Each had been killed with several shots in the head.

Ten days after this brutal crime, Pierre Laval signed the law establishing special court-martials under Darnand's authority. The measure had been urged by the judiciary who—frightened by the murders of judges and prosecutors—had wanted to rid themselves of the dangerous job of judging the "terrorists." Under the new law, any resistance member taken during an attempted sabotage, attack on German or French units, or during any other anti-German or anti-French act, was to be tried immediately by a three-judge panel chosen by the secretary general for the maintenance of order (Darnand). The proceedings were to be closed; the accused was to have no defense counsel; the verdict could not be appealed and the sentence—invariably death—was to be carried out immediately. There was to be no written transcript and the verdict was either unsigned or signed with an illegible scrawl so that the judges (who entered late at night with their faces covered) were never identified. Sometimes they were officers of the regular police or Gardes Mobiles who were now under Darnand's orders, but most frequently they were leaders of the Milice. This parody of justice was carried out with almost complete anonymity.

In prisons all over France, late at night, the same charade was played out time and again. Muffled in their overcoats, the three judges would enter and take their places in a guarded room. One by one, the accused—who were already the condemned—were brought from their cells to face the inquisitors. The questioning was brief; there seemed to be no point in prolonging the proceedings since the accused had been taken in *flagrante delicto*. Invariably the verdict was guilty and the sentence was always carried out immediately.

The other prisoners knew that the court was sitting from the sounds they could hear through the doors of their cells. As one later wrote:

> A truck entered, stopped in the courtyard and we could hear the dull thud of coffins laid on the ground.
>
> The great gate squeaked once more. . . .

A word of command, the sound of rifle butts echoing on the flagstones. . . .

A vague murmur arose. . . .

A cry of rage or despair quickly stifled. . . .

A salvo which echoed horribly rolled between the high walls, clung to it, bounced off the corners of the prison and echoed in our heads. The sharp report, pathetic after this thunder—the coup de grâce.

It was over . . . Darnand's justice had passed us by.

Even before the executions—usually by a squad of Gardes Mobiles or *miliciens*—the judges had sneaked away into the night. Only their victims had seen them and it was certain that the dead would not talk. After the Liberation, the Resistance attempted to identify these murderous judges, but failed. Usually they had arrived from out of town and were unknown to the few prison officials who glimpsed them. Except for one or two well-known Milice leaders (who were slated for the firing squad in any case), not one of the judges on these "Bloody Assizes" was ever identified.

The blind hatred that the Milice excited in the breasts of the *résistants* led to terrible reprisals, some of which the Resistance later wished to forget. Shooting down a *milicien* or blowing up one of their recruiting offices was a patriotic act, but what happened at Voiron was to leave a stain on the magnificent record of the French Resistance.

The hated and greatly feared Milice chief in Voiron (near Grenoble) was one Jourdan. Fearful for his life, he was constantly surrounded by bodyguards and his home patrolled by armed *miliciens* day and night. Determined to strike a patriotic blow by killing him, four students—aged eighteen and nineteen—enrolled in the Milice and quickly gained Jourdan's confidence. On the night of April 20, 1944, the students approached Jourdan's house while he was being protected only by two members of the Milice. While two of the students watched the outside of the house, the other two entered, quickly pulled submachine guns from under their coats, and shot down Jourdan and his two guards. Then—and this was the unforgivable crime—they killed his wife, his eighty-two-year-old mother, his ten-year-old son, and his daughter, aged fifteen months.

The two students who had butchered the Jourdan family, and their supervisor from the technical school (who had helped them plan the crime), were shot in the back by a Milice firing squad in the presence of twenty students and teachers from the school. The unwilling audience was later deported to Germany; almost all died in concentration camps.

The Allied landing in Normandy (June 6, 1944) brought wildly conflicting advice to the bewildered French populace from both sides of the Channel. From London, de Gaulle called for insurrection, proclaiming that the final battle had begun. "It is France's battle and it is the battle for France."

From Vichy, Marshal Pétain warned against any rash acts which would bring down terrible German reprisals: "Do not aggravate our misfortunes by acts which may bring down on you tragic reprisals.... France can save herself only by observing the strictest discipline."

Laval followed with a speech in which he pleaded with the French to remain calm, for "France is not in the war." He begged them not to aggravate a foreign war by the horror of a civil war; he reminded the French that the armistice had been ratified by all Frenchmen and by the National Assembly.

It was to Vichy rather than to London that the majority of the French listened. Still *attentistes* in their sympathies, exhausted by the deprivations of four years of occupation, they wanted the Germans swept out of the country but were unwilling to do anything active to accomplish this. Unarmed, with only a strong instinct for survival, they were eager for an Allied victory at no risk to themselves.

For the ultracollaborators, there was no choice. Since an Allied victory was a victory for de Gaulle and meant the firing squad for them, they called for an end to "waiting" and for total war against the Anglo-American "invaders." Doriot and the P.P.F. called for cooperation with the security forces of the "European" armies to maintain internal order. They denounced the Anglo-American attack against "Europe." Darnand mobilized the Milice against the F.T.P., the Secret Army, and other groups of the Resistance. Marcel Déat sent the militants of the R.N.P. to join the Milice, and de Brinon, president of the L.V.F., pleaded with the legionnaires to join the ranks of the Milice.

Now, with the collaborationists terrorized by impending doom and the Resistance exulting in its new strength, the civil war degenerated into a murderous orgy.

Jean Zay had been in prison for almost four years. In June, 1940, the former minister of national education in the Popular Front government and then deputy had sailed on the *Massilia* for North Africa in the hope of continuing the war. Upon his arrival, he had been arrested along with two other prominent Jews,* Georges Mandel and Pierre Mendès-France, returned to France, and brought to trial for "desertion." Condemned to deportation for life by Vichy, Zay had benefited by the isolation of France; obviously he could not be sent

* Jean Zay's father was Jewish and his mother Protestant. He had been raised as a Christian, had married one, and had raised his children as Protestants. To his enemies, he was a Jew who in 1924 had rashly compared the French flag to toilet paper.

to an overseas penal colony. So—for four years—he was confined to a prison cell under the strict regime reserved for common criminals.

On June 20, 1944, three *miliciens* showed up at the prison in Riom to transfer Zay to Melun near Paris. One of them signed the required release papers with a false name and then the three of them pushed Zay into a black Citroën and drove away. In the car, they told him that they were *résistants* and that he was being taken to a Maquis in the mountains where he would be safe.

Upon arriving at the foothills, they all got out of the car and started to climb to where the "Maquis" would be waiting. When they arrived at a deep crevasse, ominously known as Devil's Well, they stopped to catch their breath. Zay sat down on a rock and, taking off his glasses, started to wipe them. Behind him one of the *miliciens* took out a rubber truncheon.

The blow behind Zay's ear knocked him off the rock onto the ground, where he was killed instantly by a volley from a submachine gun. His body was stripped to destroy any possibility of identification and then thrown into the crevasse. To make discovery of the crime even more difficult, the *miliciens* went back down to the car and brought up explosives; they blew up an overhanging rock ledge, thus burying the body under a pile of shattered rock.

Alarmed at the news that her husband had been moved from Riom, Jean Zay's wife went to Laval and demanded an explanation. The astonished Laval ordered an inquiry to be made. Later that day, Darnand reported to him that the car in which Zay was being transferred to Melun had been attacked on the road by the Maquis and, wounded in the skirmish, Jean Zay had been carried off; there was even a cock-and-bull story about a wounded *milicien* who had been taken to the hospital in Versailles. It is doubtful that Pierre Laval was taken in by this story, but no further inquiries were made and the killers—who belonged to the Milice Deuxième Bureau (Intelligence Service) in Vichy—were never punished.

Jean Zay's body was found accidentally by two hunters in September, 1946. His murderer is today safely in South America.

At the end of May, 1944, a coded message from the B.C.R.A. (Gaullist military intelligence) in Algiers was received by the resistance group known as C.O.M.A.C. (Commission for Military Action). The orders were imperative and categorical, leaving no room for discussion or possible misinterpretation: "Kidnap Philippe Henriot! If you cannot kidnap him, kill him!" Henriot, the "man with the golden voice," had been a thorn in the side of Fighting French propaganda for years. Now, with his new prestige as the Vichy minister of information, he had succeeded in confusing the wavering French public, who, applauding the German defeats in Russia and North Africa and convinced of the weakness of the Vichy government and of the imminence of an Allied landing, were moving closer to the Resistance. Henriot's pro-German radio broadcasts had caused public opinion to hesitate before taking the final step. It was time that the golden voice was silenced.

The assignment had been given to Morlot, a twenty-two-year-old lieutenant colonel in charge of C.O.M.A.C. commandos who had distinguished himself in the last four years by his daring attacks on both the Germans and the collaborators. Knowing that Henriot was heavily guarded, Morlot set his plans carefully. He chose the men for this special job himself and rounded up three automobiles and the necessary weapons. The ministry of information building (at the corner of the rue de Solférino and the rue de Lille) was scouted and the plans of its layout obtained. Soon all was in readiness—only the intended victim was absent.

On June 27, summoned by Laval to an important meeting of the council of ministers, Philippe Henriot arrived in Paris. The ultracollaborationists had started a violent press campaign for a government of "public safety" which would fight alongside the German army against the Anglo-Americans. To offset this threat, Laval needed his two *milicien* ministers, Henriot and Darnand, to support him against the ambitions of Déat, Doriot, and the other French Fascist leaders.

On his arrival from Vichy, Henriot learned that the meeting had been postponed until the next day, so he decided to spend the night in Paris. That afternoon, he and his wife saw their son—a volunteer driver in the Nazi Motorized Supply Corps (N.S.K.K.)—to the railroad station, where young Henriot left to rejoin his unit in Italy. That evening on the Paris radio, the minister answered the Gaullist "Lesage," a speech which is quoted on page 58. Then he and his wife went to the movies, returning to the ministry of information about 11 P.M.

In addition to the three night watchmen who patrolled inside the building and three policemen on sentry duty outside, there were usually two or three *miliciens* present as a personal guard for the minister. That night there was only one, and, when Henriot learned that he had not yet dined, he sent him to eat, telling him not to return that night. "If I were sensitive to threats, I would have been silenced a long time ago. . . ." Henriot had said on the radio that evening, and he meant it. The man was no coward.

Twice during the night the telephone rang in Henriot's bedroom. When he picked up the receiver, there was only an ominous silence at the other end. It was very disturbing, for this was a private line with a number known only to very few people. Upset by the incident, Henriot's wife asked him to call the Milice for extra guards, but he refused: incredibly, he did not know the telephone number of the Milice in Paris.

Dawn on June 28, 1944, came at 5:30 A.M. At first light, three cars stopped a short distance from the ministry of information. From the first car, five men got out and quickly disarmed the three policemen. The leader of the second group rang the bell and ordered the concierge to open the door. Terrified, the concierge refused, even after a Milice card had been shown to him through the half-opened door. Finally a revolver was shoved under his nose; reluctantly he opened the door. While one group disarmed the watchmen and another cut the telephone wires, the third commando raced upstairs to Henriot's apartment—which was pointed out to them by the frightened concierge.

Morlot knocked on the door. "Milice! Special brigade! Some terrorists want to kidnap the minister. We have come to protect him."

Half asleep, Henriot got out of bed and walked toward the door. Despite the pleas by his terrified wife not to unlock it, he half-opened the door. Morlot and two others pushed their way into the room as Madame Henriot screamed.

"Be quiet, madame!" Morlot ordered. "No one will do you any harm. We have nothing against you."

Then turning toward the minister, "Are you really Philippe Henriot?"

"Yes, I am."

Morlot fired immediately. Henriot staggered, then leaped forward and struggled with the younger man. Morlot fired again at point-blank range through the chest. Philippe Henriot crumpled groaning to the floor and was finished off with a burst from a submachine gun by a man named Desmoulin. Under the shattering sound of the volley in the small bedroom, a framed collection of pinned butterflies fell to the ground; the dead man had been a passionate collector of butterflies.

Five minutes later, the C.O.M.A.C. commando drove away and the ministry of information building was silent except for the weeping of the frantic Madame Henriot, kneeling at the side of her dead husband in the little bedroom on the second floor.

For four days the crowds walked silently past the bier of Philippe Henriot, first in the ministry of information and later in the Hôtel de Ville. Pétain sent a note of sympathy to the widow, and Laval praised Henriot in a radio speech as a great patriot and Christian. The Milice swore revenge.

Many of the killers in the C.O.M.A.C. commandos (and indeed in the entire Resistance) had been recruited in the "milieu," and the inducement to serve had been money rather than an appeal to patriotism. Desmoulin—who had finished off Henriot—was one of these paid assassins. On July 15, he was killed by the Milice during an attempted robbery. It had been a trap.

But a hoodlum like Desmoulin could not pay for a star like Philippe Henriot. Someone more important, someone better known would have to pay—someone whose death would cause a shudder through the ranks of the Resistance.

At the end of June, 1944, the Germans informed Vichy that three leading members of the Third Republic—Paul Reynaud, Léon Blum, and Georges Mandel—were to be returned to France from German concentration camps to be tried by special court-martials and shot in retaliation for the executions carried out by the Gaullists in Algiers. Saying that shooting hostages was not a French policy, Laval refused to accept the three politicians and instructed Darnand (whom he had made minister of the interior on June 14) not to receive the three men in any French prison. General Oberg and Colonel Knochen of the Paris S.S. put pressure on Darnand to take custody of the three men, try them under the law of January 20, 1944, and execute them. Darnand refused and sent word to his subordinates that the three hostages were not to be received if delivered by the Germans.

When, on July 6, Oberg informed Max Knipping, head of the Paris Milice, that Georges Mandel had just arrived by plane from Germany, Knipping refused to take custody of the ex-minister of the interior and asked for time to receive new orders from Vichy. Twenty-four hours later the exasperated Gestapo chief had Mandel delivered to the prison of La Santé, where he was reluctantly registered and locked in a cell. Knipping, worried about the safety of his prisoner and unable to communicate with Vichy, decided to transfer Mandel by car to the prison camp at La Brosses near Vichy. Fearful of a resistance attack during the transfer, he telephoned the Deuxième Bureau of the Paris Milice and asked that a guard be provided.

Georges Mandel was probably the most hated of the prominent figures of the Third Republic by the ultracollaborationists and the Milice. Not only had he been minister of the interior in Paul Reynaud's cabinet, but he had vigorously opposed both the armistice and Pétain's taking power. He had sailed on the *Massilia* to Casablanca, where he had been arrested, returned to France, and imprisoned by Vichy. After November, 1942, Pétain had handed him over to the Germans, who had imprisoned him in the Buchenwald concentration camp.

After Knipping had signed his release, Georges Mandel was taken to a car driven by the *milicien* Mansuy and in which there were three other men: Boero, Néroni, and Lambert. Followed by another car containing *miliciens* (but not Knipping, who returned to his office), they left Paris by the Porte d'Italie.

There was a short halt during an air alert, but soon the two cars were rolling through the forests of Fontainebleau. During the trip, Mandel talked with Néroni about his love for France and how he had forced Marshal Pétain in June, 1940, to write a letter apologizing for having had the ex-minister of the interior arrested by mistake. He took the letter from his pocket and read it to the silent *miliciens.* Georges Mandel, a realist in life as well as in politics, was probably fully aware of the fate that awaited him.

After passing the Obelisk and turning toward Nemours, Mansuy suddenly pulled into a side road and stopped.

"Something's wrong with the carburetor," he said.

"It's the gasoline," Mandel suggested.

While Boero worked on the car, Mandel and Néroni got out and walked about. The second car had stopped some fifty yards back and was waiting.

Néroni was pointing out various parts of the forest to Mandel, explaining that they had stopped at the foot of Mont Morillon where one could see the curious rocks Les Demoiselles.

While they were standing quietly chatting, Mansuy had sneaked up and, standing only a few yards behind them, suddenly fired on Mandel with a submachine gun. In his haste, he barely missed Néroni.

Hit in the chest by seven bullets, Mandel fell to the ground. Mansuy walked up to him and fired two more shots at point-blank range. One of them pierced Mandel's skull.

Boero yelled at Mansuy, "You're mad! What's gotten into you?"

Mansuy shrugged, "Both sides have agreed on this; you're not in charge here!"

Then the killer turned and fired a long burst on the car as "evidence" of a Maquis attack. Mandel's body was taken to the prefecture in Versailles and later to a hospital where an autopsy was performed.

No one knows who gave Mansuy his orders to kill Mandel, but certainly it was neither Laval nor Darnand, both of whom were ignorant of the arrival of Mandel in France until after his "death in a Maquis ambush" was reported to them. As for the *miliciens* who were present, Boero and Néroni were executed by a French firing squad on October 25, 1944, still denying any role in the murder. Mansuy himself switched sides in August, 1944, and was killed fighting the Germans near the barricades on the Boulevard Saint-Michel on August 26.

With the eventual defeat of the Germans in France becoming more likely every day, Laval played his last card. To prevent de Gaulle (and the Communists in his cabinet) from taking power, he decided to reconvene the National Assembly. By calling back the deputies and senators who had given power to Pétain on July 10, 1940, and who had been dispersed by the Marshal in 1941, he hoped to present de Gaulle with a fait accompli. On arriving in Paris, the Gaullists would find the National Assembly in session, holding all constitutional powers which the Marshal would have returned to them.

Laval, with the agreement of Abetz and the connivance of Knochen, drove to the psychiatric hospital at Maréville near Nancy, where Edouard Herriot and his wife were kept under house arrest. There he persuaded the former president of the Chamber of Deputies (who himself feared that a de Gaulle in power would prevent the return of the prewar parliamentary parties) to come to Paris and preside over the coming meetings of the National Assembly. Laval was less successful with Jeanneney, the ex-president of the Senate, who remained at his home in spite of the premier's fervent pleas; Jeanneney, like most politicians of the Third Republic, had good reason to be suspicious of Laval.

The arrival of Laval and Herriot did not go unnoticed by the ultracollaborationists; Laval's scheme to bring back the National Assembly was looked on as a renunciation of "collaboration." It was also an opportunity to overthrow the head of the government and replace him with an ultracollaborationist. Marcel Déat and Fernand de Brinon hurried to S.S. Colonel Knochen and persuaded him that Laval was acting without Pétain's authorization (which was true) and that Berlin's wrath would fall heavily on the Paris Gestapo when the truth was known. Worried, Knochen telephoned Berlin for instructions and was told that Herriot was to be rearrested and returned to Maréville. A new French government headed by Déat and containing de Brinon, Darnand, and Doriot was to be set up, and the seat of government was to be moved to Belfort in the east of France.

Learning that the Gestapo had arrested Herriot again, Laval vigorously denounced the action, telling Abetz that under the circumstances he refused to exercise his powers as head of the government and considered himself a prisoner of the Germans. He also refused to move the seat of the government to Belfort, knowing this was just a stopping place on the road to Germany. Abetz coldly informed him that the decision of the German government was irrevocable and—if necessary—force would be used.

On the night of August 17, Pierre Laval signed his last decree, turning power over to the secretary general of each ministry to act in the absence of the minister until the arrival of a successor. Then, taking his leather briefcase, his cane, and his hat, he walked down to the front of the Hôtel Matignon, and kissed his daughter good-bye. With his wife, he entered a car, and at midnight the convoy left for exile.

In Vichy the same drama was played out. Determined that the Marshal would not fall into Allied hands, the Germans presented him with an ultimatum: either leave voluntarily for Belfort or be taken by force. After writing a last letter to Hitler denouncing this kidnaping as a betrayal of the armistice and of Montoire, Pétain declared himself a prisoner and submitted to avoid reprisals.

At eight o'clock in the morning of August 20, 1944, in a pouring rain, Pétain left the Hôtel du Parc amid a crowd which cheered him for the last time. He entered the car with his wife, his doctor (Ménétrel), and several aides. Preceded by six motorcyclists and surrounded by armed Germans, the Marshal left Vichy forever.

L'Etat français had ceased to exist.

14
Sigmaringen

Belfort—near the Swiss–German frontier—was to be the staging area for the Vichy government and the ultracollaborationists prior to their transfer to Germany. Pierre Laval—who had been removed from Paris under protest by armed German police—arrived with his wife and several ministers on Friday, August 18, followed the next day by Darnand, de Brinon, and Déat (minister of the interior, minister without portfolio, and minister of labor respectively).

Under a German threat to use force if necessary, Pétain had left Vichy on Sunday; as the convoy carrying him to exile passed through the occupied zone, mimeographed copies of Pétain's protest to Hitler against his forcible removal and his last message to the French people were surreptitiously scattered along the roads. The armed convoy reached Belfort on Monday evening with the Marshal, his wife, his physician, the ministers of war and navy, six other officials, and five of Pétain's personal servants.

Prefecture of the *département* of Vosges, the town was soon crowded with several thousand weary Vichy officials, collaborationists, members of the Milice and the Fascist parties, who had followed the government in its retreat to Alsace out of loyalty to the Marshal or fear of their fate at the hands of the victorious Gaullists. Most of them had brought their families, not daring to leave them behind to the mercies of their enemies. The *miliciens* from southern France who had retreated at Darnand's order had been forced to fight their way through areas held by armed resistance groups. Hampered by their wives, children, and parents, and with no illusions as to their fate if they should fall into the hands of the Communist F.T.P., they had battled desperately to keep the roads open for the long automobile and truck convoys. On several occasions, they suffered heavy losses when they were attacked suddenly by heavy machine-gun and rifle fire. At Tronçais (Allier), the F.T.P. attacked a train carrying the wives and children of *miliciens*, many of whom were killed.

It was in Belfort that both Pétain and Laval showed that they considered themselves prisoners of the Germans and would refuse to exercise any governmental functions. To avoid the formation of an ultra-collaborationist government by de Brinon, Doriot, and Déat, Laval informed the Marshal that he would not resign as premier but under no circumstances would he continue to act as the head of the Vichy government. Agreeing that this was the only attitude to take under the circumstances, Pétain withdrew completely, declining to receive any official visitors or communications. The Vichy government was "on strike" against their German abductors.

But not all of the Vichy ministers followed the example of the head of state and the chief of the government. Believing that their time had finally come and that Vichy—which they had always believed to be too "soft" and too hesitant in its support of the New Order—was outdated, de Brinon (and later Darnand, Déat, and Doriot) flew to Hitler's headquarters to push his own views on the makeup of a new collaborationist government manned by French pro-Nazis deeply committed to the New Order. It was only a question of who would get the Führer's nod to head this new regime.

Hitler's headquarters in August, 1944, was in an area of thick pine forests broken by numerous small black lakes near Rastenburg in East Prussia. Called the "*Wolfsschanze*"—or "Wolf's Lair"—it was an armed camp: mine fields, barbed wire, bunkers with machine guns mounted in them, antiaircraft guns, all manned by fanatical S.S. troops. Since the unsuccessful attempt on Hitler's life by the army on July 20, the security in the area had become drastically increased. To reach the highly restricted center zone where Hitler lived and worked, one had to pass through a series of control zones and checkpoints, each guarded by heavily armed, suspicious Nazi troops.

The preliminary conversations between the French ultracollaborationists and the German foreign minister were held in the latter's luxurious railroad car at a siding near the outskirts of the restricted zone. It was here that Ribbentrop met with de Brinon and Otto Abetz on Wednesday, August 23, for the first of the separate meetings that he held. The ex-champagne salesman, now German foreign minister, was in a highly undiplomatic mood: Ribbentrop denounced Pétain's last message to the French people, calling it a betrayal of "collaboration" and an invitation to the French to unite with de Gaulle. He threatened reprisals on those Frenchmen now in Germany—prisoners of war, those in forced-labor camps, and deportees—and demanded the formation of a government that would unhesitatingly work for German victory. With the Marshal's approval or without it (and in any case excluding Laval), a "national and revolutionary" French government containing men like Doriot, Déat, and Darnand was needed. He allowed that de Brinon could probably play a role in the new regime, but he made it clear that, in his opinion, Doriot was the only man who could head it.

During this tirade by his superior, Otto Abetz squirmed in his chair and tried to efface himself. It was obvious that his policy to bring about Franco-German collaboration (which he had based on his support of Laval) was now in ruins. In addition, he had shown in the past his dislike and distrust of Jacques Doriot, now the rising star in the coming French government-in-exile. As he listened to Ribbentrop fulminate against Laval and praise the leader of the P.P.F., Abetz could feel the floor being cut out from under him and knew that his days close to the seat of power were numbered.

While Abetz was unhappily contemplating his future, de Brinon was thinking furiously. It was clear to him that a Doriot government could only be imposed forcibly by the Germans, for Pétain would never agree to it. The last thing de Brinon wanted was to see Doriot as the head of the new government: not only were the two men personal enemies and not only did de Brinon covet the power for himself, but he knew that once in power it would be impossible either to influence or remove the energetic, spellbinding Doriot. Even without the Marshal's consent, Doriot was capable of (and certainly willing to set up) a "national and revolutionary" government and of mercilessly eliminating his old enemies. For de Brinon, it was a question of delaying that day as long as possible.

When Ribbentrop had finished speaking, de Brinon pointed out suavely that nothing could be done without Pétain's approval, since the Marshal embodied the very principle of legitimacy. Because, he said, it would be extremely difficult to obtain Pétain's consent to a Doriot government, might not it be better to set up a "delegation," a committee of men devoted to the Nazi cause, to safeguard French national interests, such as the welfare of the French prisoners of war, workers in Germany, and deportees? The wily count pointed out that as Vichy ambassador to the German occupation authorities, he could head such a "delegation" without having to ask for additional powers. The delegation would simply be a mechanism for providing a smooth transition to a Doriot government, which would be set up after the Marshal's approval had been obtained.

Marcel Déat also met with Ribbentrop and was subjected to the same demands for a Doriot government. Like de Brinon, Déat was dead set against giving power to his most implacable enemy. After private discussions with de Brinon, he agreed to the idea of the formation of a delegation as a temporary measure to smooth the transition to a Doriot government, but as usual he had one more trick up his sleeve —he planned to absorb de Brinon and the delegation, eliminate Doriot, and seize the highest power for himself.

After talking to Ribbentrop, de Brinon, Déat, and Doriot, Joseph Darnand was hopelessly bewildered and confused. Somewhere in this mass of would-be leaders, there had to be a real "chief," someone who would give him orders. Completely beyond his depth and worried about his beloved *miliciens* being absorbed by the P.P.F., the good soldier Darnand agreed to support the delegation.

Not a man to be used without getting his price, Doriot had set certain conditions to his acceptance of the top post in a new government. One had been that the new capital would be either at Nancy or Belfort—which implied that Alsace-Lorraine would be French. This demand Ribbentrop vigorously rejected. The German government was prepared to guarantee the territorial integrity of France and its empire—even against the demands of Italy and Spain—but Alsace-Lorraine was and would remain German. To soften this harsh blow to French pride, he announced that Adolf Hitler had graciously consented to speak with the French collaborationists.

The Führer's bunker was in the most restricted zone of the Wolf's Lair, covered with camouflage netting and tree branches so that from the air it looked like part of the forest floor. It was ostentatiously bare: unpainted work tables and chairs, limed walls with no pictures or maps, all of it coldly illuminated by bulbs covered with plain green metal shades. It was intended to impress the front-line soldiers who came here to be decorated with the fact that the Führer was sharing their hard life and their sacrifices.

The cold damp conference room in which the French awaited Hitler was horribly depressing. Windowless and illuminated by a bright hard light, the only sound was the hissing of oxygen being pumped into the closed room. When Hitler entered, the after-effect of Claus Graf von Stauffenberg's bomb on July 20 was apparent to the startled French collaborationists. This was not the energetic, hypnotic leader of the "Thousand-Year Reich," but an old man: white-haired, bent, dragging his right leg, his puffy face yellow from jaundice. His right hand trembled constantly and he had to grip it tightly with his other hand. Only his eyes were bright, probably as a result of the massive injections of vitamins that Dr. Morell gave him daily.

Hitler sank wearily into an armchair and greeted the visitors in a low voice. He spoke in a rambling fashion of the Bolshevik menace, the army plot and the purge that had followed it, his regret at having to make war against England and France, and his strong pacifist sentiments. Finally turning to the subject of the meeting, he called for a new French government "national and revolutionary," but he wanted Pétain to approve it. Strangely enough, the principle of legitimacy was firmly implanted in his mind; he told his visitors that it had worked wonders for him in 1933 and had enabled him to accomplish more than he had hoped in a very short period of time. He boasted of the new weapons which would shortly be in the field and which would drive the Anglo-Americans back into the sea. He promised to spare France as much as possible, particularly Paris and other open cities.

To Darnand, who was standing modestly in the rear, Hitler said, "The men of the Milice died for a great cause, and, like those at Stalingrad, they did not die in vain." After listening to the translation, Darnand could only stammer his gratitude. Hitler turned to Doriot and complimented him on his military valor, as evidenced by the Iron Cross with which the Führer himself had decorated the leader of the P.P.F., and wished him every success in the formation of the new government. Then Hitler quickly left the room, his head nodding uncontrollably.

So it was that, while Pétain and Laval refused to exercise their official functions and considered themselves as prisoners of the Germans in Belfort, Hitler and Ribbentrop had decided that Doriot would head the new government, sanctified by the Marshal's blessing if possible—but without it if necessary. Until that blessing could be obtained, it was agreed that de Brinon would set up his "delegation for the defense of national interests" to act as a transition to a "national and revolutionary" government headed by Doriot.

But de Brinon had his own idea as to who a suitable head of government would be. Upon his return to Belfort, he wrote to the Marshal, asking his permission to aid French nationals in Germany (prisoners of war, workers, deportees), an obvious extension of his duties as Vichy ambassador to German-occupied territories. Nothing was said about a possible Doriot government or de Brinon's promise to obtain Pétain's consent to it. Concerned about the treatment of Frenchmen in Germany, the Marshal agreed. This was all the wedge that the ambitious count needed.

Meanwhile, events were moving rapidly. On September 6, the American 7th Army and the French troops of General Jean de Lattre de Tassigny were advancing on the approaches to Belfort. Determined not to let the Vichy government escape from its grasp, the Germans informed Pétain and Laval that they were being moved to Germany—once again, by force if necessary. Crushed by the thought of being taken into exile, the Marshal wrote to Hitler:

> On August 20, 1944, I was forced to leave Vichy which I had freely chosen as the seat of government according to the articles of the Armistice; the government of the Reich gave me, on August 19, 1944, the assurance that in all circumstances, I would remain on French soil.
>
> Today, in spite of that solemn pledge, I am being led into captivity in Germany. . . .

The same day, Pierre Laval, tears in his eyes and his voice breaking with emotion, read a stinging letter to Otto Abetz protesting against this forcible exile. Both men knew that "one does not carry the soil of the Fatherland on the soles of one's shoes."

At 11 A.M. on September 7, 1944, the long convoy carrying the last leaders of the Vichy government into captivity in Germany crossed the Rhine River on a pontoon bridge northeast of Mulhouse. Two days later, they reached Sigmaringen.

The ancestral castle of the Hohenzollern-Sigmaringen stands on a craggy cliff overlooking the Swabian Danube at its beginnings where it flows out of the Black Forest in southwestern Germany. It is a forbidding mass of towers, turrets, and parapets containing a conglomeration of huge apartments decorated in the worst taste of the nineteenth century. Crowded with the loot of the robber barons who had dominated this area for hundreds of years, the apartments are connected by long cold corridors filled with the portraits, armor, and weapons of former owners. The writer–doctor Céline (who had fled France a full two months before the other collaborators, packing his bags only eight days after the Allied landing) probably described it best in his staccato, sometimes frantic style:

> Stucco, bric-a-brac, gingerbread turrets, chimneys, gargoyles ... super-Hollywood ... every period from the melting of the ice cap ... to Kaiser Wilhelm II and Goering ... Wormeaten battlements and drawbridges ... that goddam cradle of the Hohenzollerns! Perched on its rock ... out of kilter! Lopsided ... all ready to topple into the water for the last fourteen centuries! ... Cradle and den of the worst pack of rapacious wolves in Europe! Ten, twenty mountains of trees! Black Forest, descending pine trees ... waterfalls ... the stage is the city, so pretty–pretty, pink and green, semi-pistachio, assorted pastry, cabarets, hotels, shops ... all in "baroque Boche" ... the most amazing is the castle ... like a wedding cake on top of the town. ...

This was the setting for the "French government-in-exile," the "last stand" of the collaboration. Hitler had picked it himself from a list submitted to him by Ribbentrop, and the Führer had probably been amused by the fact that it was Leopold von Hohenzollern-Sigmaringen's candidature to the throne of Spain that had been the trigger for the Franco–Prussian War of 1870. It was to prevent a Prussian prince from becoming king of Spain that Napoleon III had flung his armies into that disastrous adventure. The Führer was also not reluctant to punish the present princely family whom—related as they were to the royal family of Rumania—he held responsible for the pro-Allied attitude of young King Michael. So the remaining Hohenzollern-Sigmaringens were unceremoniously dispossessed to make way for the crowd of Vichy officials and ultracollaborationists who started to arrive the night of September 8, 1944. They had come from Belfort, following Pétain and Laval in what most had believed to be a temporary detour before their triumphal return to Paris. Now they waited for the "secret weapons" that Hitler had promised would inevitably turn the tide of the war.

The personal apartments of Prince von Hohenzollern-Sigmaringen were given to Marshal Pétain and his wife; his aides, the one-armed General Victor Debeney and Admiral Henri Bléhaut, were nearby, as was his doctor, Bernard Ménétrel. It was in this "atmosphere of heavy grandeur and faded ostentation," surrounded by statues and portraits of his hereditary enemy, that Pétain was to spend the nine months of exile.

Having divorced himself from any official function, he refused to receive any of his ministers and no communication from de Brinon's "delegation" was ever answered. The Maréchal spent most of his time reading the volumes on nineteenth-century French history (at least up to 1870) with which the castle library was well stocked and never touched the copies of the collaborationist newspapers which were placed on his desk. He listened to the Paris radio on which the victorious Gaullists continued to insult him and was depressed to learn of the arrest of men whose sole crime was to have been loyal to him. Convinced that very soon he would have to defend himself before a French court on a charge of treason, he worked assiduously, preparing his defense. A summary was later found among his papers after his return to France: seventeen handwritten pages covering his role in the request for the armistice in June, 1940, his part in the crucial decisions of the Supreme War Council in the 1930s, and his response to the Allied landings in North Africa.

Sometimes he would motor out into the countryside and then walk along the banks of the Danube with his wife and Dr. Ménétrel. At its beginnings in the Swabian Jura, the Danube is little more than a swift stream littered with white rocks that plunges between steep banks lined with birch and beech trees. At age eighty-eight, the Marshal was still capable of a rapid pace on these promenades, which quickly tired the younger men on his staff.

On the floor below the Marshal, in an "apartment of honor" which had been used by Cardinal Pacelli, the Papal Nuncio who became Pope Pius XII, Pierre Laval and his wife were housed. Madame Laval was horrified at the pseudo–First Empire decor and thoroughly detested "the false luxury and bad taste" of their surroundings, but the ex-head of the Vichy government was more concerned about the menu: he had ulcers and suffered from the unsuitable food.

To emphasize their withdrawal from political affairs, Pétain and Laval saw each other only infrequently. Like the Marshal, Laval spent much of his time reading in his little office (which was elegantly papered in blue silk) and took long walks with his wife. Unlike the Marshal, the Germans had given him no car and his promenades were followed by two armed Gestapo agents. (Hitler had never forgiven him for his refusal to come to the Wolf's Lair to discuss the future French government.) During these walks Laval took a great interest in the farming in the immediate vicinity of the castle and lost no opportunity to speak to the French workers in the fields. The peasant from the Auvergne reappeared in him, and he would spend hours discussing new methods of agriculture, the crops, and the weather.

The Germans never failed to inform him of any bad news from France. One of them hurried to his office to inform him maliciously that he had just been condemned to death in absentia by a court of justice in Marseilles (this was in connection with the trial of two newspaper editors, an affair with which he had only the slightest connection); the charge had been "intelligence with the enemy." Without bothering to remove the ever-present cigarette from the corner of his mouth, Laval remarked quietly, "It is better to be intelligent with the enemy than to be stupid with him." This witticism and sarcasm did not increase Laval's popularity with his Nazi captors.

The Germans never stopped trying to convince Laval of the inevitability of a Nazi victory. S.S. Sturmbannführer Boemelburg (who had been so friendly with Henri Lafont; see page 213) was in charge of the surveillance of Pétain and Laval in Sigmaringen—a role he had performed as head of the Gestapo in Vichy. One day he approached Laval on one of his walks and began an enthusiastic report on the new German secret weapon—"a cloud that will pulverize everything." This was probably the first hint of the German research effort toward a uranium bomb, but Laval refused to be impressed. Irritated, the Gestapist complained, "You do not seem to believe this, Mr. President." Throwing aside the butt of his cigarette, Laval said, "Listen, Boemelburg. In cases like this, we French like to quote a proverb which I believe is Italian: 'Even if it's not true, it's well put.'" Followed by Boemelburg's grim look, Laval walked away smiling, murmuring, "*Se non è vero, è bene trovato.*"

Knowing Laval's devotion to his daughter, the Nazis hastened to inform him of her arrest—along with her husband—in Paris. Prostrated by the news, the ex-premier retreated to his apartment and refused to leave. He was heard to mutter, tears in his eyes, "Josée! . . . They're going to kill her! . . . Why? . . . Why Josée?" It was only a week later that the news was proved to be false and it was learned that the Count and Countess de Chambrun had been saved from arrest by the intervention of the American authorities. With no illusions as to his own fate if he fell into the hands of the Gaullists, Laval feared that the sins of the father might fall upon the head of his only child.

Sigmaringen was crowded with a frantic mass of refugees, huddled in fear at the foot of the forbidding castle which contained the last remnants of legitimate power. The leading members of the Milice, of Doriot's P.P.F., and of Déat's R.N.P. competed for rooms with the other French Fascist militants. Wives, mistresses, nurses, babies, generals, admirals, bodyguards—even ambassadors—filled the narrow sloping streets that converged on the castle or crowded around the buildings on the *Platz* which housed the ministries of de Brinon's "French governmental delegation for the defense of national interests." The town (which normally contained seven thousand inhabitants) was overwhelmed by the French, notoriously ungrateful for this safe haven from Allied bombs. The brightly painted one- and two-story houses, their windows decorated with flowers, had a certain comic opera air about them for the disdainful sophisticated Parisians. As miserable as the crowded housing was, however, the food was even worse: kohlrabi, red cabbage, potatoes, and sour beer were the most frequent items on the menu, and delicate French palates protested in vain against this diet.

In the castle itself, two mutually antagonistic groups lived among the enormous salons, the grand ornate staircases, and the secret passages. Those ministers like Jean Bichelonne (communications and industrial production) and Paul Marion (information) who followed the example of the Marshal and Laval and refused to participate in the new "governmental delegation" avoided all contact with the "active" ministers, such as Déat, Luchaire, Bonnard, General Bridoux, and especially Count de Brinon (whose office door bore the sign "Graf von Brinon"). This was all the easier since the "passive" ministers were housed in apartments on the same floor as Laval, while the others lived in a far wing of the castle; when they met on one of the huge staircases or in one of the endless corridors, recognition was reduced to the briefest of nods and no words of greeting were exchanged. To the "prisoners of Sigmaringen," de Brinon and his cabal were no longer Frenchmen but German stooges, and to the members of the "governmental delegation" the Marshal and his followers were traitors to "collaboration" and the New Order. There could be no reconciliation between the two groups, and the castle teemed with intrigue, scheming, maneuvering, and denunciation. Meanwhile, the Allied armies continued their inexorable advance.

In the midst of this Cloud Cuckoo Land, the French sense of history—especially the ability to relate the past to present difficulties—reasserted itself: the intellectuals in the castle debated whether there had ever been a clique or a caste as hated as they were or as furiously pursued. To satisfy themselves, they pored over the books in the huge library and came up with an answer: the Spanish collaborators who had supported Napoleon's brother, Joseph, on the throne of Spain in 1808. They had fled to France after the popular Spanish uprising supported by Wellington's army had forced the French troops out of Spain. These Spanish collaborators had been called the *"josefins"*; thus the French collaborators in Sigmaringen became the *"adolfins."*

Having secured the Marshal's approval to continue to serve the interests of those Frenchmen now in Germany, de Brinon was ready to make his next move in his struggle with Doriot. With the help of Otto Abetz, he obtained Ribbentrop's consent that Sigmaringen Castle be declared French territory. This concession of extraterritoriality was communicated to Pétain by the German embassy, and the Marshal was requested to be present the next day when the French flag would be raised over the castle. Pétain refused, and neither he, Laval, nor any of the "passive" ministers took part in the ceremony.

The next morning, October 1, 1944, at 11 A.M., an honor guard of *miliciens* and German soldiers stood at attention before the flagpole in front of the castle door. In the presence of all the ultracollaborationists, accompanied by Abetz and the German diplomats as well as the wolfish Boemelburg, the *tricolore* was raised to the top of the mast over the French enclave in the midst of a dying Germany.

De Brinon made a speech:

"My first words will express our gratitude to the Führer, who has permitted Frenchmen working for their Fatherland to live in a bit of France, even on the soil of the great German Reich.... We are here at the Marshal's side, the only legitimate head of the French state... our only goal is to continue to serve the policy that the Marshal embodied... in that way, we serve French interests.... *Vive la France! Vive le Maréchal!*"

Pushed by Dr. Ménétrel, who, more and more, was assuming the role of political adviser to the isolated Marshal, Pétain wrote a letter protesting furiously de Brinon's presumption. He denied ever having authorized a "governmental delegation for the defense of national interests" and also denied de Brinon's right to exercise his authority as the Vichy ambassador in the occupied zone under the present circumstances—especially since he, Pétain, had refused any political role. The letter ended with an appeal to de Brinon's "sense of honor and of discipline." On its way to de Brinon, this angry message crossed a letter to the Marshal from de Brinon himself, asking Pétain to draw up a civil list for his staff and household, the money for which would be provided from funds that the Germans had placed at the count's disposal. Pétain returned this letter unanswered and, when de Brinon continued to claim authority for the "delegation" in the Marshal's name, Pétain ordered him to return his *francisque* (the blue-and-gold enameled badge in the shape of a double-headed Gallic battle ax which served as a lapel pin for the Vichy elite).

The Marshal's protests were muffled by the thick castle walls. Only the members of his entourage, de Brinon and his coterie, and the German diplomats at Sigmaringen knew of them; Hitler's desire that the governmental delegation be sanctioned by Pétain was satisfied by the Marshal's failure to make his objections public.

The members of the delegation gathered around a large conference table in one of the ornate salons of the castle, prepared to carry out their ministerial duties under de Brinon's chairmanship. Marcel Déat was to protect the French workers in Germany; General Bridoux was concerned with the war prisoners; Jean Luchaire was in charge of information and propaganda (press, radio, etc.); Joseph Darnand was to weld the Milice, L.V.F., and French Waffen-S.S. into a single Waffen-S.S. division to be called "Charlemagne." This ludicrous "committee for the protection of French national interests" was to be nothing more than a rubber stamp by which the Nazis would seize the maximum number of French citizens for their armed forces and their factories. The German war machine was desperately short of both cannon fodder and labor.

From the Paris radio and the Swiss newspapers, the French in Sigmaringen received the news from France. It was frightening: as more and more of the national territory was liberated, a gigantic purge of all Vichy and collaborationist elements was taking place, sometimes under illegal conditions. Maquis and resistance court-martials had sprung up everywhere and were dealing out summary punishments to their enemies; Communists of the F.T.P. were settling old scores with their political foes; denunciations abounded as the provisional government of General de Gaulle raced to set up proper courts of justice to head off the popular vengeance. After four terrible years of occupation, the festering hatred had burst forth and was sinking France in blood and terror.*

* The number of summary executions that took place in France in the autumn of 1944 is still a matter of bitter dispute. While official accounts tend to belittle the arbitrary killings and the collaborators and Vichy apologists inevitably exaggerate them, even supposedly objective scholars of the Liberation period disagree widely. The French historian, Robert Aron, has estimated the toll at 30,000–40,000, but this is an extrapolation from a gendarmerie report that is clearly in-

Admiral Jean Platon, who had been a Vichy minister and an implacable enemy of the Freemasons, had been arrested at his home (he had been under house arrest since Pétain had dismissed him from the government for his ultracollaborationist views). Brought before a military tribunal of the F.F.I. sitting at Limoges, he had been condemned to death on July 24, 1944, and shot on August 18. The news of this summary execution did not reach Sigmaringen until October 17, when it sent a shiver of horror and fright through the colony of French expatriates. Now there could be no doubt that the fate with which they had been threatened daily during the last four years by the BBC had not been idle mouthings; it was only a question of whether it would be the rope, the guillotine, or a firing squad.

On October 23, the first condemnation to death by a legally constituted court of justice was pronounced against Georges Suarez, editor of the collaborationist daily *Aujourd'hui.* The trial lasted only four hours and the jury needed only twenty minutes to arrive at its verdict. Among the six hundred editorials that Suarez published above his name during the occupation, the most damaging were those in which he called for brutal reprisals against the Resistance, Gaullist sympathizers, and Maquis. He had shrilly demanded that relatives of Free French leaders who were being held as hostages be shot in reprisal. He also proposed that Jews and Allied prisoners be used as hostages against the murderous air raids. The most lavish praise of Hitler and the Nazi New Order was mixed with the most vicious invectives against the adversaries of the Führer. One wonders what de Gaulle—going through Suarez's dossier while considering his plea for mercy—thought when he found himself described in the editorials as a "vulgar mercenary in the pay of the English—responsible for the German reprisals and the English aggressions. . . . If after being the torturer of his country, he still hopes to be the chief of it, it is only because stupidity with him is stronger than ambition." De Gaulle refused the pardon. To have made the wrong choice in politics, and especially to have published these mistaken convictions in the press or proclaimed them over the radio was punishable by death.

Georges Suarez died bravely. A guard at Fresnes prison told how the condemned man stood before the truck that was to take him to the

---

complete (Peter Novick has pointed out the inconsistencies in Aron's treatment of the official data).

It is probable that at this late date no one will be able to determine with any degree of certainty just how many Frenchmen and Frenchwomen were summarily shot not only as "collaborators," but because of political differences, class hatreds, and private quarrels. Some were even killed by criminals disguised as *résistants.*

What is clear is that the fear and hatred that accumulated during the occupation years exploded in the fall of 1944 in a bloody Terror whose toll exceeded that of the Great Revolution.

execution grounds at the Fort Montrouge: "He looked at the weather as if he were going away for a weekend. 'Well, now,' I said to him, '*au revoir,* Monsieur Suarez.'—'No,' he said to me, 'Today, it is not *au revoir,* Monsieur Pin, it's good-bye.' "

When they tied him to the execution post, he refused to allow them to blindfold him.

"Oh, no! Let me see this farce to the very end."

The firing squad was made up of nervous recruits, and their first volley only wounded their target. Their second salvo left him still gasping, a death rattle in his throat. It then took two pistol shots in the head to finish the bungled job.*

In Sigmaringen the news of Suarez's execution brought panic. If they were going to shoot the journalists, where would they stop?

As abject fear gripped the ultracollaborationists, they flung themselves into a frenzy of denunciations, calling for the heads of their enemies and frantically maneuvering for the empty vestiges of power. Convinced that Dr. Ménétrel was plotting with Doriot's people to obtain the Marshal's approval of a Doriot government, de Brinon had the hapless doctor arrested by the Gestapo on November 22 and placed under house arrest in a small village not too far from Sigmaringen. Pétain stormed and raged at the arrest of his faithful Bernard, pleaded illness and the necessity of having his physician at hand, and demanded that Ménétrel be returned to the château. The Germans calmly informed him that they considered the doctor one of their worst enemies and offered to supply a qualified German physician to the Marshal.

"You will find my corpse," the furious Pétain shouted, "but no German doctor will ever get close to me."

De Brinon offered the services of a French doctor: Céline. Clearly shocked at the thought of being treated by a "pornographer," the Marshal said, "I'd rather be dead."

* In December, Suarez's colleague on *Aujourd'hui,* Paul Chack, was condemned and shot; his final words were "I am dying for my opinions!"

Robert Brasillach appeared before the Cour de Justice in Paris on January 19, 1945; his trial lasted one day. The discussion between the judges and the defendant was calm and dignified; the only thing in dispute was whether the charge of "intelligence with the enemy"—collaboration—could be considered a crime until after Pétain and his ministers had been tried. But a plea to postpone the trial was quickly rejected by the court and the young writer was condemned to death.

Sixty French intellectuals (including Anouilh, Cocteau, and Colette) signed a petition for mercy that was presented to de Gaulle. The general's answer was: "Brasillach gambled and lost. Now he will pay."

On February 6, 1945—the eleventh anniversary of the bloody riots that he had for so long extolled as "the dawn of Fascism in France"—Robert Brasillach was tied to the execution post at Fort de Montrouge. Pale, proud, and erect, he shouted "Courage!" to the firing squad just before they fired.

One month later, Pierre Drieu La Rochelle, who had been hiding since the liberation of Paris, took an overdose of Gardenal and opened the gas jets. To his cook (who had saved his life after an earlier suicide attempt), he left a pathetic note: "Gabrielle, this time let me sleep."

De Brinon's sneaky triumph over his enemy, Ménétrel, was short lived. On December 13, de Brinon's ally, Otto Abetz, was ordered by Berlin to leave Sigmaringen with the least possible delay and without having any further contact with the French "governmental delegation" or with the Marshal and his entourage. This stunning revocation of his staunch supporter was a severe blow to the ambitious de Brinon—and it seemed even more threatening when he learned that it had been ordered by Hitler himself at the request of Jacques Doriot.

At dawn on December 16, 1944, the snow-filled hills and ravines of the Ardennes were shattered by the thunder of almost two thousand heavy guns. It was the beginning of what the British would later call the "Ardennes offensive," the Americans the "Battle of the Bulge," and the Germans the "*von Rundstedtschlacht*." As planned by Hitler himself, two Panzer armies (a quarter of a million men and a thousand tanks) were being flung across an eighty-five-mile front weakly held by six American divisions—three of them untested in battle. The objective was to capture Antwerp, cut the British army off from its supply base, and force it to evacuate the continent in another Dunkerque. The winter offensive was a desperate gamble, Hitler's last throw of the dice, but because of the element of complete surprise it achieved a series of initial victories. As the panic-stricken, disorganized Americans fell back, the 6th Panzer Army under General Sepp Dietrich rushed for the Meuse crossings south of Namur; once across the Meuse, its goal was to push toward Brussels and then on to Antwerp.

For a week Berlin was silent about the magnitude of its offensive, reporting only increased activity on the Ardennes front. When at last it proclaimed a great victory in Belgium and Luxembourg, there was unrestrained joy among the French expatriates in Sigmaringen. The "ultras" congratulated each other on having bet on the right card and on having believed that Hitler's secret weapons would turn the tide of the war (the first German jet fighters—the *Messerschmidt 262*—appeared during the battle in the Ardennes). The pall of fear that had enveloped the little colony at the news of the executions of Platon and Suarez was dissipated by the series of triumphal communiqués over the Berlin radio. Now faces were smiling and there was feverish activity in the castle and in the town as numerous new cabinets were planned, lists of new ministers drawn up, and posts in the "new regime" distributed among the faithful. There were eager guesses as to when they would be back in the seats of power: the optimists thought it would be two weeks; the pessimists thought it might take as long as two months.

After having been afraid for so long, the collaborationists allowed themselves to indulge in dreams of vengeance on their Gaullist enemies. A very complete and thorough list of those to be purged was drawn up by de Brinon's clique and the composition of this list—who should be executed, who jailed, and who exiled—was the subject of numerous conversations in what passed for salons in Sigmaringen.

There was even a theatrical event, complete with poetry readings, dances, and an original musical composition entitled *Celebration of the Retaking of the Ardennes.* Pleased at their political acuity in choosing the German side, the "ultras" indulged in an orgy of self-congratulation. Now, at last, they would hold all the top posts and send their enemies before a firing squad. As they rushed down the long corridors of the castle to exchange the latest good news with their friends, they passed the portrait of Kaiser Wilhelm II, who, in 1914, had also believed that early successes in Belgium and Luxembourg had spelled victory for his armies.

As the German armored spearheads thrust toward the Meuse, protected from Allied air attack by the bad weather, the *adolfins* cheered and celebrated. But it was only the last fluttering of the moth before it plunged into the flame.

In the midst of this hysterical revelry, the mysterious death of the minister of industrial production sent a new shiver of apprehension through the small French colony. Once again they realized how completely they were at the mercy of their brutal Nazi masters.

Jean Bichelonne had been a constant amazement to his less talented colleagues. First in his graduating class (1923) at the Ecole Polytechnique, his marks had shattered the hundred-year-old record set by the physicist François Arago—which had for so long been thought unbeatable. A mathematical economist, Bichelonne was a living encyclopedia, a man with a phenomenal memory, who could quote the most obscure statistics, identify the capital and chief cities of any country no matter how small and give its export and import figures for the last ten years plus its industrial capacity and population. Laval, who had no great love for polytechnicians, had nevertheless made Bichelonne the minister for industrial production and communication in the Vichy government; he would frequently call him in to confound the German experts by having him quote a long table of statistics which had the Germans frantically searching their books and reports for verification. Abel Bonnard, who was trying to establish a reputation as the resident wit and had a description for everyone, called the very tall Bichelonne "a giant such as the Flemish exhibit at their fairs."

At Sigmaringen, Bichelonne had still been suffering from the effects of an automobile accident that had left him with a fractured leg. The leg had failed to heal properly and the minister was limping badly and was in great pain. He consulted Céline as to the advisability of an operation. The writer-doctor said that the leg would have to be broken and reset and advised against having it done in Germany in the middle of the war. Unhappy with this advice, Bichelonne consulted with S.S. Doktor Gebhardt, who agreed to do the operation, but only in the S.S. hospital in Hohenlychen. The minister agreed.

As Céline furiously described the operation: "... he died at Hohenlychen in East Prussia ... pure coquetry ... lunacy ... went up there to be operated, have a fracture fixed ... He had visions of himself going back to Paris on the double beside Laval, triumphant ... Arch of Triumph, Champs-Elysées, the Unknown Soldier . . . he was obsessed by his leg ... it doesn't bother him any more ... the way they operated on him up there at Hohenlychen, I'll tell you about it ... the witnesses have gone out of existence ... so has the surgeon ... Gebhardt, war criminal, hanged! ... not for the way he operated on Bichelonne! ... for all sorts of genocides, little intimate Hiroshimas ..."

The cause of Bichelonne's death on the operating table was never officially determined. When the mourning party arrived at Hohenlychen for the last rites, the coffin had been sealed and Gebhardt was gone. What was known was Bichelonne's deep interest in uranium research; he had learned before the war of the discovery of uranium fission and on several occasions had spoken to Laval about the importance of this research, even pointing out the crucial part that would be played by heavy water. It is possible that, in his obsessive curiosity, he had made some indiscreet inquiries about the German work on a nuclear bomb.

As the year 1944 ended, hope died and naked fear returned to Sigmaringen. The Nazi communiqués on the fighting in the Ardennes had become cautious, predicting a long struggle in that area. The mysterious death of Bichelonne, the continuing purge of their friends who had remained in France, the uncertainty as to their own fate, all these combined to make the customary good wishes and resolutions for the new year seem empty and futile. Isolated in a Germany that was being systematically shattered by Allied air raids and crushed between the advances of the Soviet and Anglo-American armies, the fearful expatriates at Sigmaringen were aware of only one terrible certainty: General Leclerc and his Senegalese troops were approaching ever closer and closer.

Thursday, February 22, 1945; 12:15 P.M.

A large black Mercedes was speeding along the tree-lined road ten miles southeast of Sigmaringen; on the pyramidal *gazogène* strapped to its back was a freshly painted French *tricolore*. Next to the German driver, a tall, stocky, bushy-haired Frenchman in horn-rimmed glasses was talking vivaciously with the attractive young woman sitting alone in the seat directly behind him. As he talked, his eyes darted nervously across the skies above; at 9:30 that morning, an air alert had been sounded to warn of Allied fighters over the area. Although the alert had ended three-quarters of an hour earlier, the possibility of attack was always present. For many months now, Allied planes had been strafing anything that moved along the German roads.

Jacques Doriot was in an excellent mood. He was on his way to Mengen to have lunch with Marcel Déat, who had agreed to give his support to Doriot's newly formed "Committee for French Liberation." Backed by Hitler and Ribbentrop, the committee headed by Doriot would put an end to de Brinon's pretensions of heading the French government-in-exile, write *finis* to the count's "delegation," and put all power into the hands of the leader of the P.P.F.—in spite of the Marshal's stubborn refusal to recognize him. There were still a few trouble spots: Doriot had incurred the enmity of the R.S.H.A. through his refusal to permit the P.P.F. men enlisted in the French Waffen-S.S. (*Charlemagne*) division to be used on the western front. He had insisted that the only enemy that they recognized was Bolshevism and that the French volunteers could be used only against the Russians. In addition, he had put an end to the parachute missions in which *doriotistes* had been dropped behind the Allied lines in French territory to carry out sabotage missions. With the backing of the Führer, Doriot felt that he had nothing to fear, even from such powerful men as Heinrich Himmler and Martin Bormann.

Suddenly, out of nowhere, two planes roared over the car at a very low altitude. The driver braked violently and brought the car to a stop at the right-hand edge of the road. He said something to Doriot in German. Madame Jacqueline Normand (a secretary in the P.P.F. and the wife of an officer serving in the L.V.F.) did not understand German, but she caught the word "*Jäger*" (fighter plane) and what sounded like a number. Doriot repeated the word and turning to the young woman, he said soothingly, "Don't be alarmed, madame, they're German planes."

The driver put the car in gear and started off again down the middle of the road. Two or three minutes later, Madame Normand saw a plane approaching quickly from the right. It passed over the car, turned, and opened fire.

The machine-gun fusillade that ripped into the car wounded the driver in the knee and Doriot in the thigh, but the car continued to speed along the road; Doriot tried to reassure the terrified young woman in the rear that his wound was not severe.

The plane circled and returned to the attack. As it again opened fire, the driver tried to bring the car to a halt and Doriot struggled to open the door. Madame Normand screamed in terror as a third volley struck the two men. The driver, hit in the chest, crumpled on the seat, and Doriot, whose chest and heart had been ripped by two bullets, fell on top of him. His left eye torn from its socket, his cheek and jaw broken, the leader of the P.P.F. died instantly.

Miraculously unscathed, the young secretary ran screaming from the car toward the houses on the outskirts of Mengen, about a quarter of a mile away. The planes had disappeared; after the terrible roar of the motors and the staccato hammering of the machine guns, there was silence.

So died Jacques Doriot, ex-Communist and would-be Führer of a Nazi France. But had he really been killed by Allied fighter planes? The official German report on the incident claimed so, even identifying the attacking planes as "British *Mosquitoes.*" But Jacques Doriot had always been enthusiastic about flying, and it had been only his age which had kept him from being a pilot in the French air force. How then was it possible for him to mistake the planes that he had seen and to reassure Madame Normand that they were German? How could the German driver have made the same mistake? And "*Jäger*" followed by a number? Only German fighters are identified by numbers (*ME-110, Focke-Wulf 109,* etc.); American and British fighters are given names, such as *Mustang, Thunderbolt, Spitfire,* or *Mosquito.*

The air alert had ended three-quarters of an hour before the attack; if there had still been Allied fighters in the area, the alert would have been given again. Also, Doriot's death was worth a medal to the Allied pilot who killed him, but it was never claimed. The operation orders and flight reports of all British, American, and French planes that could have been in the area of Mengen at the time of the attack were searched; no report of an attack on a car was found. When Doriot's assistant, Sabiani, rushed to the spot after receiving a telephone call from the hysterical Madame Normand, he found a Gestapo man holding Doriot's briefcase, standing next to the riddled car. The wounded driver was quickly taken away and an attempt by the P.P.F. staff to question him was in vain; he had been moved from the hospital. The exact circumstances of Jacques Doriot's death were to remain a mystery.

They buried Jacques Doriot in Mengen after his body had lain in state in the town hall. The elite of the collaboration had gathered to pay their last respects to the man who, as head of the Committee for French Liberation, had pledged to bring them triumphantly back to France. Their hopes, dreams, and plans were now dead, along with the man in the flag-draped coffin. On a cushion were displayed his decorations, including the Iron Cross that he had won fighting with the L.V.F. in Russia.

In the presence of Doriot's mother, wife, and daughter, de Brinon eulogized his dead enemy: "I knew Jacques Doriot, but I knew too little of him. I knew, to be sure, his magnetism, his courage, his tenacity. I felt a real attraction toward him. I had often met him, which is not enough to really know him well. It happens that we had a few differences ... when we spoke frankly, we saw that basically nothing separated us. . . ."

As the flag-draped coffin was lowered into the ground and a P.P.F. bugler sounded the *Salut aux morts,* the mournful notes of the French version of *Taps* must have underscored the desperate situation of many of the men crowded around the open grave. All illusions had disappeared; they knew that they too were dead, condemned by the denunciations of the BBC and Radio-Paris. They had fled France just ahead of their would-be executioners, and now, with the American and French troops advancing rapidly on Sigmaringen, it was time to flee again.

But where could they go?

Céline was the first to leave. Detecting the danger earlier than the others (as he had shortly after the Normandy landings), he left Sigmaringen at the beginning of March with his wife and his cat. Permission to travel across war-wracked Germany was unusual, while permission to leave the country was almost unheard of; nevertheless, Céline had obtained an *Ausweis* to do exactly that (no doubt his services as a doctor to the many German officials in Sigmaringen was the source of this good fortune). He managed to reach what he thought was safety in Denmark, but, when the British liberated the country, the anti-Nazi Danes threw him in jail for two years.

Several days after Céline's departure, Joseph Darnand left suddenly to join his *miliciens* fighting the partisans in northern Italy. Disgusted and discouraged, Darnand hurried to the battlefront, hoping for nothing better than an honorable death in combat.

On April 5, Marshal Pétain wrote a letter to Adolf Hitler asking permission to return to France to defend himself at his coming trial:

> I have just learned that the French authorities are about to try me in absentia before a high court. The trial should open April 24. . . . I cannot without forfeiting honor let it be believed, as certain malicious rumors have it, that I have sought refuge on foreign soil to hide from my responsibilities. Only in France can I answer for my acts and I am the only one who can judge the risk that this attitude might entail. . . . You will certainly understand the decision that I have taken to defend my honor and to protect by my presence those who followed me. That is my only goal. . . . At my age only one thing is to be feared: not to have done one's entire duty. . . . I wish to do mine. . . .

Hitler's answer came two weeks later: Boemelburg brutally informed the Marshal that he was to be moved to a "new place of safety." It was made quite clear that the transfer would be made by force if necessary. At the Château de Zeil, where they stopped for the night, the Marshal and his staff knew that they were being taken to the redoubt in Bavaria where a last stand against the Allies was being planned. To avoid being taken any further away from the Swiss frontier (only thirty miles away), Pétain went on strike, got into bed and refused to leave. He scolded the two German diplomats who had replaced Boemelburg as his guard for their bad faith and insisted he would go only to Switzerland and then only when accompanied by a Swiss official. Frantic at the old man's stubbornness and desiring above all to see that he did not fall into Allied hands, the two Germans agreed and hurried out to get the consent of the Swiss government for the Marshal to cross the frontier and to find a Swiss diplomat to accompany him across the border.

At nine o'clock in the morning of April 24, a convoy of automobiles crossed the Swiss frontier at Sainte-Marguerite. In the leading car, the Marshal smiled and waved to the crowd of soldiers and customs officials standing nearby. It was his eighty-ninth birthday.

Two days later, the same convoy brought Pétain across the Swiss–French frontier near Vallorbe. Waiting to receive him was the hero of the famous Free French defense of Bir Hakeim, General Pierre Koenig. Standing rigidly at attention, the General watched coldly as Pétain (dressed in the uniform of a Marshal of France) stepped from his car and saluted the company. The soldiers and customs officials rendered no military honors, but watched curiously as the Marshal moved forward, offering his hand to the general.

General Koenig refused the proffered hand and motioned Pétain to a nearby car.

The masquerade was over: this was no Marshal of France, no "Victor of Verdun"—this was Philippe Pétain, accused traitor.

15
The Trial of Pétain

"*Accusé, levez-vous!*" ("Prisoner at the bar, stand up!")

From behind the massive oak table, the old man in the khaki summer uniform of the French army, the Military Medal pinned to his chest, rose to face the three judges. Behind him the crowded audience in the first chamber of the Palais de Justice held its breath. That noble grandfatherly face was one that they had seen so many times during the four years of the occupation, on posters, lithographs, dishes, stamps; the busts of "Saint Philippe" had been everywhere. But now the pink skin was furrowed, the bright blue eyes had a look of weariness; only the edge of white hair and the broad mustache were the same. Above the stiff white collar and black necktie, the folds of the neck hung loosely; but still it was the Maréchal, the "Victor of Verdun," the savior of a defeated France. To this man they had given loyalty and devotion for four grim years; to see him they had thronged the streets of so many towns and had sung fervently "Marshal, we are here . . ." It seemed strange to hear him addressed as "prisoner at the bar"; it made them uneasy and a little sad. When he had entered the crowded courtroom, they had all risen, embarrassed. After all, he *was* a Marshal of France.

Mongibeaux, the first president of the High Court of Justice, had little time or sympathy for regrets or sadness. Resplendent in his red ermine-trimmed robes, impressively tall, with a little pointed beard, he was determined to proceed normally with the business at hand in spite of the anguish that he sensed in the courtroom. At the moment there was the accused to be interrogated.

"What is your name, first name, age, and occupation?"

"Pétain, Philippe, Marshal of France."

It was the same voice—only firmer—they had heard so many times over the radio, first telling them that the battle was lost, then exhorting them to follow him, "in the honorable path of collaboration." It was the voice that had cajoled, scolded, denounced their enemies, pleaded

DEATH OF A *MILICIEN*: The ropes which bound him to the stake have just been cut by the bullets which are ripping through his uniform and the post. (*Wide World.*)

DEATH OF A *RESISTANT*: Placed at the corner of the building so that the ricochets would not endanger his executioners, he smiles at the firing squad. (*Roger Viollet.*)

PUNISHING A "HORIZONTAL" COLLABORATOR: Her head shaved, the swastika smeared on her forehead, she is paraded through the streets, clutching her German baby. (*Wide World.*)

Opposite: SIGMARINGEN CASTLE: "Turrets, chimneys, gargoyles . . . battlements and drawbridges . . . perched on its rock . . . that goddam cradle of the Hohenzollerns." (*Roger Viollet.*)

MARSHAL PETAIN ON TRIAL: "It is the French people who entrusted power to me. . . . It is to them I have come to give an accounting. . . . I put my trust in France!" (*Wide World.*)

PIERRE LAVAL FACES HIS JUDGES: "You can condemn me, you can kill me, but you do not have the right to insult me. . . . I am a Frenchman; I love my country; I have served only her. . . ." (*Wide World.*)

for a greater effort under the National Revolution, a comforting fatherly tone that had told them, "I hate the lies that have done you so much harm." Was it vanity that made him forget to give his age? He was eighty-nine years old.

With cunning insight into the psychology of his accusers both inside and outside the courtroom, the Marshal had said simply "Philippe," rather than "Henri Philippe Bénoni Omer." Three months earlier, at the little customs house on the Swiss–French frontier where he had been taken for the formal verification of identity, he had given his name in full, but had insisted that the "Philippe" be underlined—which was done. He wanted to remind the jury of another Philippe, Philippe de Gaulle, son of the rebel general who now held the reins of power that had been pulled from Pétain's hands. Perhaps the sly old man was sending a subtle message from the stifling courtroom on the Ile de la Cité across Paris to de Gaulle in the Elysées Palace: "You may try me here, condemn me, perhaps even shoot me, but always remember that once you loved me."

Before President Mongibeaux could proceed with the questioning, Pétain's chief defense counsel, Bâtonnier* Payen, rose and in his high squeaky voice demanded that the court disqualify itself from sitting in judgment on the Marshal. Under the 1875 Constitution (which was still in effect since Pétain had failed to have his proposed constitution ratified by the country), only the Senate could try the head of state on a charge of treason.

His sunken cheeks puffed by the force of his argument, Payen also pointed out the inherent unfairness of the jury selection. Picked by lot from lists submitted by commissions of the National Assembly were twelve former members of parliament (from among those who had voted "No" to Pétain on July 10, 1940) and twelve former *résistants.* It was true that the defense had a limited number of challenges and had used these to eliminate several Communist resistance members who were implacably hostile to Pétain; one of these was Lucie Aubrac, the wife of Raymond Aubrac of *l'affaire Jean Moulin* (see page 157), whose daring rescue of her husband after Caluire had made her a popular heroine of the Resistance. Both the Resistance and parliamentary jurors were enemies of the Marshal, Payen argued, and therefore could not judge his case impartially.

In addition, the elderly *bâtonnier* pointed out, the three judges and the prosecutor had taken the oath of loyalty to Pétain and had tried cases in the special courts which Pétain was accused of setting up.

Attorney General Mornet leaped to his feet to answer the charge. His Roman nose pointed belligerently toward the *bâtonnier*, he denied

* President of the local bar association. Past presidents retain the honorary title.

having taken the oath of fidelity to Pétain in September, 1941, since he had been retired for over eighteen months at that time. Then he proceeded to fall neatly into the trap that the defense had laid.

"Would I have taken the oath? Perhaps. I say 'perhaps' without hesitation because I consider that an oath forced on public officials by their superiors, whose authority is being exercised under the enemy's control, has absolutely no value. . . ."

There were murmurs of protest from the lawyers gathered in the back of the courtroom.

Monsieur le premier président: "No demonstrations!"

Monsieur le procureur général Mornet: "I invite the fifth column to stop its demonstrations. We are not at a public meeting here."

New protests were heard. After the angry whispers subsided, the attorney general argued that Pétain was not a president of the Republic, since the National Assembly on July 10, 1940, had not elected him president (which they had no power to do) but had simply confided the Republic to his care. Therefore, there could be no question of a trial before the Senate. The three judges retired, returning a half-hour later to reject the defense's argument that the High Court could not try Marshal Pétain.

While the clerk droned through the boring, monotonous indictment, the defendant chatted with his lawyers. Outside the Palais de Justice, Paris was suffering the aftereffects of the war and the occupation. Food was still rationed and the allowance of certain staples was even less than it had been under the Germans. The black market was as active as ever and officials still turned a blind eye to it. People grumbled that nothing had changed except the names of the rulers. The meager one- and two-page newspapers carried the story of the trial, some even giving a stenographic report of parts of it, but the public was apathetic. They had cheered the Marshal at the height of his glory, then they had cheered de Gaulle as he marched down the Champs-Elysées after the liberation of Paris. Pétain had lost; de Gaulle had won. It was normal that the loser should pay. There were no angry crowds outside the weather-darkened walls of the Palais de Justice calling for the Marshal's head, but his political enemies were determined to have that head nonetheless. There were posters on the walls of Paris showing Pétain's hand grasping Hitler's over a mountain of French corpses.

Inside the first chamber, crude wooden stands had been erected for distinguished guests. The reporters and photographers were crowded behind a long narrow table in the center near the accused, while the jury sat in two boxes separated by the judges' bench. The audience sweltered in the stifling heat. The army doctor who watched over Pétain's health ordered a window opened; this task was not simple, for the window had been sealed back in the seventeenth century by a magistrate frightened of drafts.

The clerk droned on. . . . "The above-named is accused of having, during a period of time which is not specified: (1) committed crimes against the internal security of the state; (2) had dealings with the enemy with a view to promoting their aims as well as his own; crimes which are covered by Articles 87 and 75 of the penal code."

At this point in the proceedings, the usher called the roll of the witnesses, who then withdrew from the courtroom. They had sat quietly on the benches behind the accused—the discredited leaders of the Third Republic (such as Paul Reynaud and Edouard Daladier) trying to set themselves apart from the discredited officials and generals of Vichy who already had the smell of the High Court upon them and who were promised to future trials.

Bâtonnier Payen requested permission for the accused to make a brief statement; it was granted. The Marshal stood erect and proud; from beneath the gold-braid-encrusted kepi which he had placed on the oak table in front of him he withdrew several sheets of paper and began to read:

"It is the French people who, through their representatives in the National Assembly, entrusted power to me on July 10, 1940. It is to them that I have come to give an accounting.

"The High Court . . . does not represent the French people. . . .

"I will make no other statement.

"I will answer no more questions.

"I have spent my life in the service of France . . . I led her armies to victory in 1918. . . . On the most tragic day of her history, again it was to me that she turned. . . . I asked for and desired nothing. They begged me to come: I came. Thus I inherited a catastrophe that I did not cause. Those truly responsible hid behind me to escape the people's anger."

Firmly, without the slightest hesitation, he denied the charges. The armistice had been a "necessary act and an act of deliverance" which he had negotiated with the agreement of the military leaders. In any case, the armistice had not only saved France but had been responsible for the Allied victory by assuring that the Mediterranean remained free and the French empire untouched. The National Assembly had given him power legally and it had been recognized as such by every country in the world, from the Vatican to the Soviet Union. This power he had used as a shield to protect the French people; for them he had sacrificed his prestige by remaining at the head of an occupied country. Did the court wish to understand the difficulty of ruling under such conditions? "Every day, a knife at my throat, I fought against the enemy's demands. History will tell of everything that I protected you from, while my adversaries think only of reproaching me for what was inevitable."

The occupation had forced him "against my will and against my heart" to do certain things because of the implacable and unceasing German pressure, but he had never abandoned anything that was essential to France's existence. De Gaulle had been the sword and Pétain had been the shield, preparing the way to liberation by keeping France alive although in agony. "What good would it have done to liberate ruins and cemeteries?

"My life matters little. I have given France the gift of my person . . . if you must condemn me, let my condemnation be the last . . . but I say to you—in front of the world—you would condemn an innocent man. . . . After your judgment comes that of God and of posterity. They will suffice for my conscience and for my name.

"I put my trust in France!"

There was absolute silence when the Marshal finished and sat down. The cadence of the simple sentences, so powerfully felt and so vigorously presented, stunned the audience. There was anguish in the people's minds, a question had been raised, an uncertainty had appeared: had Vichy been no more than an agonizing choice between equally evil solutions? Could nothing be reproached the Marshal except that he had stayed to make those choices? The black market had saved many Frenchmen from starvation, but it had permitted the looting of France and had destroyed the solidarity of the French people: was it good or evil? The Marshal had saved many from the worst effects of the occupation, particularly those in the unoccupied zone, but would the Jews and the *résistants* have suffered more under a Gauleiter? The man who was so stingy with his soldiers' blood in the furnace of World War I—did he under entirely different circumstances think too much of the French and not enough of France?

As President Mongibeaux protested against the impossibility of interrogating an accused who refused to speak, the defense returned to the attack. Maître Jacques Isorni was young, tall, and handsome; his voice rang out loud and compelling among the scratchy, reedy voices of the old men who dominated the courtroom. It was he who had cycled each day to Fort de Montrouge (where the Marshal had been imprisoned prior to the opening of the trial) to shake the old man out of his apathy. It was he who had composed the stirring appeal to posterity that Pétain had just read to the startled audience. It was he who had fought so vigorously against Bâtonnier Payen's decision to base the defense on a plea of diminished responsibility due to senility. In February, Isorni had seen his condemned client, Robert Brasillach, crumple under a volley from a French firing squad, and he was prepared to see the Marshal die the same way—but only after the courts,

France, and the world had been made to understand that what they were executing was not a traitor but a man who had done his best in an impossible task. France under Louis XVIII had shot the brave Marshal Ney, yet it was before the honored statue of Ney in Metz that Pétain had been presented with his Marshal's baton by the president of the Republic. At eighty-nine, Isorni pleaded, Pétain should not fear death, only dishonor. Still suffering from the agonizing train trip from the Swiss border where angry crowds had gathered at every stop crying "Pétain to the gallows!" and had spat on the windows of his car,* and from the long fatiguing interrogation, the Marshal had sunk into a deep apathetic depression from which he was slowly pulled by the incessant pleas of his youthful lawyer. The statement he had just read had been Isorni's idea, but Pétain had roused himself long enough to correct it meticulously, point by point, and to finally copy it out in his large childish handwriting so that he could read it without his glasses.

Having bolstered his elderly client for the attack, Isorni now proceeded to challenge the impartiality of the court; in particular, he pointed out two statements which had been made to the press by the first president and the attorney general. Mornet was quoted as saying, "When it is a question of the gravest acts, it is obvious that the judicial power must ask for the death penalty, and I will do so." Mongibeaux had told a reporter, "Before anything else, it is important to destroy the idea that Pétain was a man who tried to save what he could of our unfortunate country, and to show, on the contrary, that he was the one who—to satisfy his personal ambition and his political goals—wallowed in degradation to the point of treason."

When the attorney general tried to evade this clear indication of the court's prejudice against the defendant, once again there were murmurs of protest from the young lawyers in the audience. His gray beard bristling, Mornet blustered, "Really, there are too many Germans in this hall." This was too much—a storm of protests and shouts filled the courtroom until President Mongibeaux hastily suspended the proceedings.

When the trial resumed a half hour later, the anger had been dissipated. To calm whatever antagonism had been left by Mornet's outburst, the president of the Paris bar assured his young colleagues that the attorney general had meant no offense to them and, at the same time, assured the president of the court that there would be no further outbursts from the group of young lawyers in the courtroom. After a vain attempt by the third of Pétain's lawyers, Maître Lemaire,

* "Is this where we are to be murdered?" Madame Pétain coldly asked the guards at one such halt.

to force the court to acknowledge the newspaper reports of their prejudice, Mongibeaux called for the first witness.

Paul Reynaud, the next-to-last premier of the Third Republic, had escaped the ravages of time that had so drastically touched the other actors in this courtroom drama. Very short, with wavy black hair that shone with pomade, and jutting ears, at sixty-six he looked twenty years younger. It was he who had called Pétain from the French embassy at Madrid to become vice-premier in those chaotic June days of 1940. At the same time he had summoned General Weygand from Syria to take over the supreme military command from the faltering hands of General Gamelin. When Weygand had refused to capitulate in the field and demanded that the government ask for an armistice (in which he was strongly backed by the Marshal), Reynaud had resigned rather than break France's pledge to England to negotiate no separate armistice or peace with the enemy. At the same time, he had recommended to President Lebrun that Pétain form a new cabinet, since the Marshal headed the majority of ministers who wanted to request an armistice. Later, Pétain had offered him the post of ambassador to the United States and Reynaud had almost accepted it; it was Laval who forced the Marshal to withdraw the offer. Imprisoned in Fort du Portalet, Reynaud had been forgotten until 1944 when Vichy handed him over to the Germans.

Reynaud started his testimony with a pious avowal of its impartiality. "I hope, gentlemen, that the High Court will do me the honor of believing that the wrongs that Marshal Pétain has done me will in no way influence the testimony that I am going to give. When he was at the height of his power, I despised him, and from the depths of my prison, I let him know it. Today I pity him. . . . It is true—a fact which is without precedent in our history—that he delivered me to the enemy and it is by a miracle that I am here. My comrade, Georges Mandel, is not here. . . ."

In his clear solemn voice, he spoke of the Marshal's tremendous prestige and how it had been important to have him in the cabinet when things were going so badly (but he had also told de Gaulle that it was better to have Pétain in the cabinet where he could watch him than plotting outside). He spoke of his plans to move the government to North Africa and continue the war from there, and how Weygand and Pétain had opposed him step by step. He talked of his meetings with Churchill and of the English prime minister's concern with the fate of the French fleet; of Weygand's incessant demands for an armistice so that an army would be left "to preserve order in the country." He repeated with relish his words to the wavering cabinet: "You believe that you're going to come to an understanding with Hitler? You think that he's an old 'gentleman' like Wilhelm I who took two provinces from you and then life began again? You're mistaken. Hitler is Genghis Khan."

He developed his case against the Marshal and the general with the consummate skill of the true parliamentarian. Behind him, the bored audience began to get restless. When the weary first president closed the proceedings for the day at 6:30 P.M., Reynaud had finally arrived at the critical meeting of the council of ministers at which the armistice had first been discussed.

The next day he returned to what was obviously a defense of Paul Reynaud rather than testimony at the trial of Marshal Pétain. In boring detail, he emphasized his own courageous determination to continue the war from North Africa and the cowardice of those ministers who had opposed him by demanding an immediate armistice. Later, when Pétain had him thrown into prison, Reynaud had studied the causes of the defeat—and particularly the Marshal's role in it. He quoted from the memoirs of Marshals Joffre and Foch—and of the then president of the Republic, Raymond Poincaré—to show that even in 1918 Pétain had been known for his hesitant, indecisive character and had not truly merited the glory given him during World War I. (When Pétain had received his Marshal's baton, Weygand had whispered to his friend, "And to think that we have shoved him to such an eminence by untiringly kicking his buttocks!")

Behind the tiny witness testifying so ardently, Pétain, pretending to scratch the back of his neck, cupped his hand behind his deaf ear to hear better. Then, bored by a familiar attack, he turned to the nearby press table and openly admired the bosom of a pretty young woman reporter.

After a heated exchange with the defense lawyers over his role in the cabinet that had accepted the Munich agreement and his initial acceptance of the post of ambassador to the United States from Pétain, Paul Reynaud gave way to the man he had succeeded as premier in 1939, Edouard Daladier. The stocky, bald "Bull of the Vaucluse" defended himself vigorously as he had done before the Vichy court at Riom. He dragged out a long list of statistics to show that in May, 1940, the French army had been supplied with 3,600 tanks and 2,500 combat planes. It had been the inability of the French High Command to appreciate the importance of armored divisions and dive-bombers, plus their failure to train a sufficient number of technicians to man these new weapons, which had led to the 1940 defeat by a Germany that employed only 3,200 tanks and approximately 3,000 planes. Daladier explained how, as premier in 1939, he had appointed Pétain ambassador to Madrid and had later offered him a seat in the cabinet. When the Marshal had insisted upon the inclusion of Laval in the government, Daladier had refused. Then came the same dreary story of the German attack, the dissensions in the cabinet over the request for an armistice, Reynaud's resignation, and Pétain's assumption of power. Nothing was said about Daladier's political struggles with his enemy, Paul Reynaud, or the role which had been played during those tragic days by their respective mistresses, Madame de Crussol and Countess Hélène de Portes. It was the countess who had drained Reynaud of his strength by her hysterical behavior while France was being torn apart by German armor.

After the two-and-a-half hour exposition—which added little new, other than the fact that France had not suffered defeat through lack of arms—Bâtonnier Payen rose to question the witness:

"Do you believe that he [Pétain] betrayed his country?"

"In all conscience, I will answer that in my opinion Marshal Pétain betrayed the duties of his office."

The Bâtonnier was not satisfied with the answer: "That's not the same thing."

". . . The word treason has many different meanings. There are men who betray their country for money; there are men who betray it sometimes out of pure incompetence. . . . As for Marshal Pétain I will state frankly—even though it pains me—that he betrayed his duties as a Frenchman. . . ."

At the end of Daladier's testimony, one of the jurors asked that the Marshal admit or deny the authenticity of a telegram he was supposed to have sent to the German military authorities congratulating them on their successful defense against the Canadian landing at Dieppe. Isorni protested that the question and the answer were in the record of the preliminary interrogation, but Mongibeaux insisted that they were now in the presence of the accused and only he could answer. The Marshal refused to be baited into changing his stand against answering questions. "How can I answer? . . . I didn't even hear the question. . . . I don't know what it's all about." There were murmurs of protest in the audience at this obvious evasion.

The next witness was the last president of the Third Republic, Albert Lebrun—seventy-three years old, bald, with bulging eyes, a broad gray mustache, and a weak mouth—a man who had taken seriously the purely ceremonial duties of the French president, never trying to exercise any authority and allowing himself to be pushed and pulled from all directions. After Reynaud's resignation, he had summoned Pétain and had said, "Form a government."

"Immediately, the Marshal with a familiar gesture opened his briefcase, showed me a list, and said to me, 'Here is my government.'

"I must say that even in the great sadness of the moment, all the same I felt a little relieved. During my eight years [in office], I recall the difficult formation of ministries which lasted, you remember, three or four days . . . whereas I had it immediately. . . . I found that wonderful."

With wet eyes, the man who was called "the Wailing Wall of the Third Republic" complained bitterly that he had wanted to go to North Africa to continue the war, but had been bullied by Laval and forced to remain. When the Marshal had dismissed him curtly as one might discharge a dishonest butler, Lebrun had submitted weakly. He had never held a grudge against the Marshal and each year sent him a laudatory New Year's telegram. The ex-president ended with a tearful recollection of Pétain at the height of his glory: receiving his Marshal's baton in the autumn of 1918, marching alongside Joffre and Foch down the Champs-Elysées on July 14, 1919, in the great victory parade, admired and respected by all of Europe.

"To have climbed so high! To have fallen so low! What baneful and diabolic fate had clung to his heels! What mistakes had falsified his judgment! What evil passions had troubled his soldier's soul!" There was a sob in the witness's voice.

A juror requested that the Marshal be asked when the list of ministers that he had given President Lebrun had been prepared, but when Mongibeaux put the question to him Pétain claimed he could not understand it because he could not hear. The first president ordered the question repeated to the accused by his counsel, but Pétain persisted in pretending not to understand. Finally, with a gesture of weariness, he grumbled, "In the beginning I was able to think of a few names, but the list that I proposed had not been the one . . . that is to say, that the list that I had in my pocket was not the one that was used. I have answered."

The juror complained that the question that he had asked had not really been answered, but Mongibeaux wearily said that he could not obtain any more from the accused.

On this exasperating note, the third day of the trial ended.

The trial dragged on for another seventeen days under the high gilded ceiling of the first chamber of the Palais de Justice. From the little office just off the courtroom which had been sparsely furnished for him and for his wife, the Marshal entered every day to sit in the high-backed armchair, occasionally listening to the venomous attacks, the legalistic squabbles, and the frightened self-serving statements. Most of the time he maintained his self-imposed silence, but occasionally, under the urgings of the first president or on the advice of Payen, he would offer a brief statement or a criticism of the testimony. His chief diversion was ogling the breasts of a well-endowed young lady at the reporters' table and the day that she was absent he pouted. Most of the time, he dozed.

Over sixty witnesses came forward to denounce or defend the accused. There were the former officials of the Third Republic who chose to forget the lavish praise that they had poured on the Marshal when they had begged him to assume the highest office and to protect them from the people's wrath; there were the frightened Vichy officials and generals hiding behind the khaki uniform with its seven stars, fearful of drawing down on themselves the wrath of the new rulers by too ardent a defense of Vichy.

At age eighty-one, with a gaunt face, pointed beard and white hair, looking like an "El Greco figure," Jules Jeanneney, the former president of the Senate, denounced the armistice as an unforgivable error into which he had been tricked by Laval and Pétain (the Marshal slept in his armchair through this testimony). Léon Blum defined the Marshal's treason as his failure to make the enemy respect the armistice which had "created in favor of the French people a certain number of guarantees and protections," which Vichy had yielded "point by point, bit by bit." Also, Pétain had been given a mandate to revise and reform republican institutions, not to destroy them.

Edouard Herriot, who, in July, 1940, had been president of the Chamber of Deputies, retold in great detail the story of the demand for the armistice, the resignation of Paul Reynaud, and how the decision to transfer the government to North Africa had been thwarted by Laval's cabal. He insisted that the National Assembly had given power to Pétain to head a republican government. Herriot boasted of his later refusal to turn over to Vichy a list of the Jewish deputies. When several officers of the L.V.F. had been decorated with the Legion of Honor, he had returned his own to Vichy. Bâtonnier Payen gleefully read part of a speech that Herriot had made two weeks after the armistice: "Our nation in its distress has gathered around Monsieur le Maréchal Pétain with the veneration that his name inspires in all of us. Let us take care not to disturb the accord which has thus been established by his authority."

There was Louis Marin, who had been vice-premier in the 1940 Vichy cabinet and had remained close to the Marshal until April, 1944, when (perhaps because he was disappointed in his ambitions) he had gone to London. A former attaché in the French embassy in Madrid tried to assure a post in the new government by peddling rumors, gossip, and innuendo: Pétain had once shown him a list of ministers for a future cabinet on which Laval's name had figured prominently. The head of the French delegation to the armistice commission at Wiesbaden, General Doyen, tried to clear himself of having zealously served Vichy. He managed to stumble through his testimony without damaging the Marshal.

Caous (who had served as president of the Supreme Court of Justice at the Riom trials) came forward to defend the court against the charges that it had been "a political purge trial under Pétain's domination in which the prisoners had been condemned beforehand." When he had finished and Attorney General Mornet had paid tribute to the judges of the Riom court, Isorni exploded a bombshell:

Maître Isorni: "I am convinced, Monsieur le Président, having heard what the attorney general has just said about the Riom court, that he will take advantage of this exceptional circumstance to publicly deny the rumor that has circulated through all of Paris, according to which he had begged to be part of that court."

Attorney General Mornet: "That's infamous!"

President Caous: "I have never heard it said that Monsieur Mornet—at that time the honorary president of the court of appeals—had asked to be part of the High Court. What is correct is that I offered him a place on the court at the beginning of August, 1940, but he never asked me for a seat. . . . He accepted the post, but was not picked. That was beyond his control and mine."

Isorni sat down with a smile. He had made his point.

On the seventh day of the trial, a ghost came into the courtroom—a ghost supported by two canes, painfully swinging its legs forward. Gaunt, deathly pale, his hair just beginning to grow in again, Major Georges Loustaunau-Lacau, once the head of the resistance network Alliance and a former aide to Marshal Pétain (who had made him vice-president of the Legion of War Veterans) had been called to testify to the Marshal's contacts with the Cagoule and his prewar contacts with Laval. Although just returned from the hell of a German concentration camp (Mauthausen), the major had lost none of his fight and contempt for officialdom. In a "fierce toneless voice," he gave a résumé of his career: his services in World War I, duty at the War College "in the class which was honored to count in its ranks General de Gaulle, which was less honored to include General Bridoux." He talked about his service on Pétain's staff, how he had been dismissed from the army by Daladier but had returned to service after the declaration of war; he discussed his wounds and escape from the hospital and how he had reestablished contact with Pétain at Vichy and had accepted a position in the Legion of War Veterans, which "unfortunately included Vallat."

When he spoke of his resistance group, there was a visible softening, a tone of pride in his voice. "This network held together through the whole war. It now counts three hundred and three executed and five hundred and twenty deportees who did not return [from the concentration camps]."

On General Weygand's order, he had been arrested in Africa in

May, 1941,"for dissidence"; he had escaped, joined the Maquis, been recaptured and sentenced "by a perfectly dishonest tribunal" to two years in prison and the confiscation of his possessions. After fifteen months in a cell in Clermont-Ferrand, he had been turned over to the Gestapo by the Vichy government. "Fifty yards from the Hôtel du Parc [in Vichy], I suffered six months on bread and water without light in the dungeons of Major Geissler . . . condemned to death. . . . I was sent to Mauthausen with the label N.N. [Nacht und Nebel—to disappear without a trace]. . . .

"I owe Marshal Pétain nothing, but that does not prevent me from being disgusted by the sight of those in this courtroom who tried to load the burden of all their mistakes onto a man who is almost one hundred years old."

Loustaunau-Lacau cleared the Marshal of any connection with the Cagoule and asked the court to spare the Marshal's life, "although he let me down in the most despicable way."

The next witness was a mother whose son, obedient to the commands of Marshal Pétain and Admiral Darlan, had gone down in a French submarine while attacking American shipping off Oran. In an emotionally charged speech "in the name of eleven thousand mothers whose sons died fighting the Allies in North Africa at the orders of Marshal Pétain," she denounced the Marshal for sacrificing her son and so many others "in the service of Germany."

She was followed by Pastor Marc Boegner, the president of the French Protestant Federation (who had quarreled with Pierre Laval over the fate of the Jewish children; see page 231). No one in high office in Vichy seemed to be aware of the terrible things that were taking place in both the occupied and unoccupied zones, the pastor related; when he had brought them personally to the Marshal's attention, Pétain had been horrified, but pleaded tearfully that there was nothing he could do.

General Maxime Weygand walked into the courtroom leaning on his cane, a little man with Oriental eyes who had never forgotten that he at one time was the guardian of the "honor" of the French army. Although himself facing a future trial for treason, he refused to be discreet. He told the court that he had refused to capitulate in the field in spite of Reynaud's insistence because it would have dishonored the French army, which had fought well in spite of overwhelming odds. He also told the court that it was Paul Reynaud who had first mentioned the word "armistice."

Reynaud leaped to his feet to protest, and the two men, so alike in appearance that they could have been brothers, engaged in a bitter controversy over who had been responsible for the armistice request.

Four years and their common suffering at the hands of the Nazis had not lessened one iota their bitter hatred of each other. As the quarrel went on, the audience became increasingly bored and restless; there seemed to be no point in these vitriolic excursions into antiquity and certainly they had very little to do with the trial of Pétain.

After the two intransigent gamecocks had yielded the arena, a letter to Pétain from Admiral William D. Leahy (who had served as United States ambassador to Vichy from January, 1941, to April, 1942) was read to the court. It was a very careful letter in which the admiral pointed out that he could not become implicated in a purely internal French affair, but that he paid tribute to the Marshal's total devotion to the French people.

> You have often expressed to me your fervent desire to see the Nazi invaders destroyed . . . you have, at my request, on different occasions acted against the desires of the Axis and favorably to the Allied cause. In all the cases in which you did not accept my recommendations to oppose the Axis powers by refusing their demands, the reason given was that such a positive action would only end in an additional oppression of your country by the invaders. I was then and I am now convinced that your principal goal was the well-being and the protection of the abandoned people of France. . . . However, I must in all honesty repeat my opinion, which I expressed to you at that time, that a positive refusal to make the slightest concession to the Axis demands—which could have led quickly to greater suffering for your people—would, nevertheless, in the long run have been advantageous for France.

Admiral Leahy closed his letter with the desire that the Marshal's activity during the occupation would be justly evaluated by the French people.

After a eulogy of the Marshal by General Héring came a denunciation by a resistance man (known as Lieutenant Colonel Grégoire) who emphasized to the court that, when Maître Pierre Massé (who had written the stinging letter to the Marshal quoted on pages 86–87) had been arrested as a Jew by the French police, he had been turned over to the Germans. When his brother-in-law had asked Pétain to prevent his deportation, the Marshal had refused to intervene. Pierre Massé never returned from the German concentration camp.

There then followed a series of other generals, Vichy ministers, and minor officials who cautiously praised the Marshal and tried to justify their zeal for the National Revolution in terms of fidelity to the "Victor of Verdun" and to the orders of their superiors. Only General Bernard Serrigny refused to compromise his loyalty. Just as almost thirty years earlier, Serrigny had tactfully pulled Pétain from his amorous rendezvous at the Hôtel du Gare du Nord (see page 23) and hurried him to his glorious destiny at Verdun, so today Serrigny proclaimed to a hostile court his devotion to Philippe Pétain. Among the clippers and shavers who had shuffled forward with self-serving statements that corrupted the coin of loyalty, his was the only fresh honest voice. When he left the witness stand, he insisted on shaking the Marshal's hand.

No one paid much attention to Charles Trochu—who had been president of the Paris municipal council during the occupation—as he denied that the Marshal had ever been a member of the Cagoule; word had just been received that Pierre Laval was back in Paris and locked up in Fresnes prison. The Marshal's defense lawyers had hurriedly insisted that Laval not be heard before a new preliminary examination of his testimony had been made, but the court rejected this plea and ordered that the former premier (whom many considered to be the Marshal's evil genius) be brought to the Palais de Justice the next day to testify. The audience hummed with excitement: after the long list of Vichy officials and generals who had stuttered so lengthily about tactics, strategy, armistice, North Africa, and *double jeu,* here at last was a man who could tell them the truth about Vichy. Now they would hear from the man who had uttered those infamous words, "I hope for Germany's victory . . ." and who for so long had been the scapegoat for those Frenchmen unwilling to blame the Marshal for the mistakes of "collaboration."

At last, tomorrow would bring Laval—and a break in this long boring trial.

The next day, August 3, 1945—the eleventh day of the trial—the courtroom was jammed as never before. For fear of an assassination attempt on Laval, armed police were everywhere; photographers crowded into the room, overflowing even into the section reserved for witnesses. There was an air of expectancy. Laval, the cunning parliamentarian, a man who was a magician with words, "Black Peter" himself, was about to make his entrance into the drama.

On leaving Sigmaringen, Laval had requested political asylum from Switzerland, Lichtenstein, and Spain. The first two refused, but the Spanish foreign minister, de Lequerica, persuaded Franco to permit Laval and his wife to remain in Spain three months, provided the ex-premier agreed to internment in a fortress near Barcelona. Franco pledged that he would not turn the fugitive over to the French, but to the Americans "if it becomes absolutely necessary." An airplane to take Laval, his wife, and Abel Bonnard to Barcelona was provided by a German friend, Rahn, in Merona, Italy.

News of the approaching trial of Marshal Pétain had reached the restless Laval in the Montjuich fortress. Fearful that the Marshal's friends would use his absence as an excuse to make him the scapegoat for Vichy's actions, Laval determined to return to France and explain his policy under the occupation.

From Spain, Laval had been flown in Franco's personal *Junker* plane to Linz, Austria, where he had surrendered to the American army authorities, hoping that his son-in-law's dual citizenship would protect him. The Americans promptly turned him over to the French army.

His guard pushing a path for him through the hostile crowd, Pierre Laval, looking very tired and haggard, entered the courtroom, darting worried glances to the right and to the left. The photographers crowded around him and there was an explosion of flashbulbs as the white-haired ex-premier (dressed in a wrinkled gray-striped suit and wearing his famous white necktie) came forward clutching a black briefcase. First President Mongibeaux disdainfully told him that he would not be required to take an oath and that no questions would be asked of him which might be regarded as the preliminary examination of an accused person. They both knew that Laval was under indictment and that his own trial for treason was not too far off. He was warned against any long digressions, a back-handed compliment to his parliamentary skill at debate. The first question asked of Laval was quite simple: when did your political relations with Marshal Pétain begin?

Nervous and uncertain as to what attitude to strike before the obvious hostility of the court, Laval started a long rambling discourse on his prewar diplomacy and French relations with Italy. He boasted at length of his skill at obtaining concessions from Mussolini and giving little or nothing in return. In spite of irritated interruptions by the first president and the reiterated demand that he answer the question, he continued to muddy the waters: Ethiopia, relations with England, his talk with the Prince of Wales, etc. "Men of good will reproach me and have reproached me for not having declared a preventive war in 1935, which would have saved France the suffering from the stronger weapons of Germany. I ask their pardon for that, but I am against war. I hate war. I am against violence. I know that war even when it is victorious does not pay . . . and then, I have a respect for human life." (Protests were heard in the courtroom.)

As he spoke, Laval's voice became stronger, he stood straighter, and there was now a new confidence about his gestures and in his tone. The air of fatigue disappeared, and he seemed to be enjoying the battle against overwhelming odds in which he was engaged. Without deceiving himself as to the inevitable outcome in his own case, he could imagine that he was back in the tribune of the Chamber of Deputies instructing the people's representatives in their duties. As he spoke, weaving his web of denials and insisting on his patriotism, he was testing the audience—and they, fascinated, listened attentively to this master of the spoken word.

Still, in spite of the strength of his voice and his confident air, he was tired and he made several mistakes which would have been unthinkable for the old Pierre Laval. When Mongibeaux interrupted once again to try to bring him back to the original question, saying that it was Pétain's trial that was being judged, Laval slipped:

Monsieur Pierre Laval: I do not know what's been said in the Pétain trial, because I was not there. I do not have newspapers and I know exactly nothing. . . .

Monsieur le premier président: I asked you a precise question. I asked you, when did your relations with Marshal Pétain begin . . . ?

Monsieur Pierre Laval: I apologize for having been too lengthy. If the things that I said are not important and do not interest the public, I apologize for them. . . .

Monsieur le premier président: I am convinced that they interest the public, but . . .

Monsieur Pierre Laval: In any case, they interest the French. . . .

There was a violent storm of protests and boos.

". . . I did not say that you were not French," Laval apologized hastily to the audience, "I said that they would interest the *other* French people. I am not in the habit of being insolent; it is neither my nature nor my intention."

In spite of this unexpected and uncustomary humility, the audience was antagonized. Laval had blundered.

He was deliberately vague concerning his prewar conversations with Loustaunau-Lacau about the possibility of Pétain's taking power—"after four years, I cannot remember." He spoke in great detail about the fatal day of July 10, 1940, disclaimed responsibility for Vichy's repressive laws and emphasized that only an accommodation with Nazi Germany, by the name of "collaboration," prevented France from suffering an even worse fate. "Do you believe that, in 1940, any reasonable man could imagine anything except a German victory?" Again there were protests from the audience. Laval's insolence was becoming insupportable.

At Mongibeaux's request, Laval's testimony was interrupted to allow the ex–secretary general of the Senate, de la Pommeraye, to describe an incident which had purportedly taken place in Pétain's office; after the Marshal had affixed his signature to several constitutional acts, Laval was supposed to have turned to de la Pommeraye and said sarcastically, "And that is how one overthrows the Republic!"

I don't remember the incident, Laval insisted, and, if it did take place, it was only a bad joke told to a man with whom my personal relations were not particularly friendly. "Overthrow the Republic? I am not a Fascist. I am not a Nazi.... I love liberty, the Republic... [There was loud laughter in the audience.] ... You may laugh, the Republic..."

"I did not ask you if you loved the Republic," Mongibeaux said sharply. "I asked you if you made that remark."

"I know nothing about it. It's impossible after four years for me to remember...."

As for his famous statement (made during a radio broadcast on the first anniversary of the German attack on the Soviet Union),"I hope for Germany's victory, because without it Communism would tomorrow control all of Europe," he insisted that it had been necessary in order that he have "a minimum of authority in speaking to the Germans" and so that they (the Germans) might believe that he was dealing honestly with them—"because if they became suspicious of me, then the demands would become much rougher...." Besides, Laval pointed out, the Marshal had approved the statement with only one minor change: originally Laval had said "I *believe* in Germany's victory..."; but the Marshal had pointed out that—since he was not a soldier—he could not say that he "believed" in a victory. So Laval had willingly changed it to "hope for."

A little later, the weary ex-premier stumbled again: "And when the attack on Normandy took place..."

A roar of laughter from the audience alerted him to his blunder and he hastily corrected it.

"When the *landing* in Normandy took place—I beg your pardon, but I've been speaking a long time..." When the Nazis had demanded that the L.V.F. and the French Waffen-S.S. be sent to fight on the western front, Laval had refused.

The next day he continued his testimony, disclaiming responsibility wherever possible, associating himself with the Marshal in everything that he did; boasting of his skill in negotiating with Gauleiter Sauckel, Hitler's emissary for foreign labor, on the problem of French labor for German factories (for every three Frenchmen sent to work in Germany, Laval had forced the Germans to release one French prisoner of war); and speaking of Vichy's powerlessness in the face of the Nazi determination to eliminate the Jews. When the Nazis had demanded the denaturalization of all Jews, Laval had refused; but he did permit the setting up of a commission to examine the case of foreign Jews who had been naturalized since 1927 (his logic was unfathomable: "If they had been given citizenship, it was because they were foreigners before becoming French"). He had admitted Déat to the cabinet after having fought against the nomination for a long time, and only after the severest German pressures. Joseph Darnand had also been forced on him against his will.

He told of his shock at the news of the murder of Georges Mandel —"Monsieur Mandel was my friend . . . we were not always in agreement on political questions, but I had the friendliest feelings toward him, which he shared. I was all the more affected by his murder." He was vague about the disappearance of Jean Zay—"I fear that he was murdered under the same conditions." Questioned by one of the jurors about the bloody repression of the Maquis, Laval said: "We were forced into that. We reduced to a minimum the extent of those measures." At this point Mornet interrupted to read a letter from Pétain to Laval: "I said to you a long time ago that I was not adverse to creating court-martials to judge men who had killed. Better some spectacular executions than turmoil and riot." Laval shrugged his shoulders and pointed out that there were many men who were presently occupying high positions in the new provisional government whom he could have had arrested during the occupation years. He had not done so, for these men were working for France, as he—Laval—also was doing.

When Laval had finished and left, clutching his briefcase under his arm and bowing to the court and to the Marshal (who pointedly ignored the gesture), there was a feeling of disappointment in the audience. They had expected more fireworks, something more spectacular from the magician, but he had succeeded only in pulling a very skinny, unhealthy rabbit out of the hat. Still, with his departure, a sense of excitement left the first chamber and the trial sank back into its wearying routine.

Monday, August 6, 1945.

The parade of witnesses continued: each praising Pétain, each disclaiming his own responsibility and publicly preparing the excuses that would be needed for his trial. The only explosion took place when General Picquendar boasted of the war matériel that he had hidden from the Germans at Pétain's request—"enough to arm twenty-four divisions." The resistance jurors were furious that, at a time when the underground and the Maquis were desperately short of weapons, when Allied planes were being shot down during parachute missions to supply them with arms, the armistice army had been sitting on these large caches of guns and explosives—most of which were seized by the Germans when they overran the unoccupied zone in November, 1942.

The testimony of the five Vichy generals who were heard that day was almost crowded off the skimpy pages of the newspapers by the startling report of the destruction of the Japanese town of Hiroshima by a new type of bomb called "atomic." If the news penetrated Laval's cell in Fresnes prison, he may have remembered some of his conversation with the scientifically curious and perceptive Jean Bichelonne, the late minister of industrial production and communication. There were also the ominous words of Boemelburg at Sigmaringen (see page 273), and Laval might have mused over the possibility that, if Hitler had achieved the new weapon first, he (Laval) would be in the Elysées Palace and de Gaulle would be sitting in a cell.

One by one, the former Vichy ministers were brought under armed guard from their prisons to the Palais de Justice. Their testimony was not very important, but they made the most of the opportunity to explain in public their zeal for the Marshal's service. Peyrouton boasted of arresting Laval on December 13, 1940; Jacques Chevalier talked of his secret conversations with the Canadian attaché and of his friendship with Lord Halifax; Yves Bouthillier vaunted his skillful handling of finances during the occupation, which brought from the first president the shrewd observation that "a minister of finance always can show the taxpayers that the burden which he imposes on them is extremely light."

Even the testimony of de Brinon and Darnand failed to shake the audience from its lethargy. Treated contemptuously by Mongibeaux, who refused to permit them to take the oath or to identify themselves—"Your identities are well known"—they made no startling revelations, and the defense was happy that their testimony was short.

The trial dragged on for four more days through a long closing speech by Attorney General Mornet and the *plaidoirie* (closing statement) of the three defense counsels. Bâtonnier Payen's was long and dull, and he only succeeded in making the Marshal furious by hinting at his client's senility; Maître Lemaire's was belligerent and continued to attack the impartiality of the court; only Isorni's plea struck a spark, ending with the stirring words: "Magistrates of the High Court—listen to me, hear my appeal. You are only judges; you are judging a mere man. But you carry in your hands the destiny of France." It was very effective, but the audience still carried in its ears the words of Mornet's closing speech: "I ask the High Court to pronounce sentence of death on the man who was once Marshal Pétain." Isorni's oratory was in the finest tradition of French justice, but it was time to be done with oratory.

The trial had dragged on too long. The public wanted an end to it.

After another final plea by Payen, which almost undid the effectiveness of Isorni's, the judges and the jurors retired to consider the verdict (in French courts, the judges vote with the jurors). Their deliberations lasted seven hours, and it was only at four o'clock in the morning that the verdict was announced:

". . . since there can be no doubt that he is guilty of dealings with Germany, a nation at war with France, with a view to promoting the enemy's enterprises; crimes covered . . . by Articles 75 and 87 of the Penal Code—

"For these reasons—

"The High Court condemns Pétain to the penalty of death, to national indignity, and to the confiscation of his goods.

"Taking account of the great age of the accused, the High Court of Justice expresses the wish that the condemnation to death not be carried out."

The condemned man was returned to Fort de Montrouge to pack his bags and then taken to the airfield at Villacoublay, where General de Gaulle's personal plane was waiting for him. He was flown to Fort du Portalet in southern France and put into a cell which had formerly been occupied by Georges Mandel; it is not known whether this bizarre touch had also been ordered by his considerate ex-protégé, de Gaulle.

Two days later, his sentence was commuted to life imprisonment by the president of the provisional government of the Republic, Charles de Gaulle, who later designated the Ile d'Yeu in the Bay of Biscay off the west coast of France as the place where the sentence was to be served.

On this lonely rock in the Atlantic, closely watched by his guards and visited only by his wife and lawyers, Philippe Pétain, Maréchal de France, spent his last days—ignored and forgotten. When a parliamentary commission investigating the war and the occupation period arrived to question him, the old man babbled, stammered, and wandered in his answers to their questions. The fall from the glory of Verdun to the ignominy of this new Saint Helena had been too much for his aged mind. He was senile.

On July 23, 1951, he died in a private home in Port-Joinville on the Ile d'Yeu. In six years, passions had slowly abated and the government of Premier René Pleven, thinking to please the unrepentant *maréchalistes* without angering the *résistants*, allowed him to die outside the prison; however, his wish to be buried among his soldiers at Douaumont near Verdun was not granted.

He was interred under a massive granite slab in the little cemetery of the Ile d'Yeu, surrounded by the white stone tombs of the native fishermen drowned at sea.

He was ninety-five years old.

16
Vichy Condemned

After sentencing Marshal Pétain, the High Court considered the cases of Jean Bichelonne and Admiral Platon just long enough to note for the record that the accused men had died before being brought to trial. The peculiar circumstances under which the admiral had perished (see Chapter 14) were not commented upon. Then, the High Court turned to the case of a living defendant: Joseph Darnand.

After leaving Sigmaringen, Darnand had rejoined the remnants of the Milice fighting Italian partisans in northern Italy near Lake Como. On April 24, he commanded the last five hundred of his men in a battle at Tirano against a superior force of Italian anti-Fascists. On the day that Pétain entered Switzerland and celebrated his eighty-ninth birthday, Darnand and his men, holed up in a house in the center of the town, fought off attack after attack. Finally the partisans offered them terms: safe passage to Switzerland and the honors of war if they would surrender and give up their arms. Knowing the fight to be hopeless, Darnand accepted.

"Why have I once again escaped death?" Darnand wrote at this time. "Twenty-five comrades fell at my side, more than sixty were wounded. I moved around ceaselessly. I commanded in the open as it was my duty to do. . . . I would have liked to have fallen leading them, but God willed that I live to answer before the French for the Milice—and perhaps to save our comrades by my attitude before the High Court."

The Swiss, who had been so considerate of the old Marshal, refused to allow the *miliciens* to cross the frontier. Their attitude seems to have been determined by Walter Stucki, the Swiss minister to Vichy, who had admired Pétain and had despised Laval, Darnand, de Brinon, and most of the other Vichy collaborationists. Unable to cross into neutral territory and be interned, the *miliciens* were soon rounded up by Allied troops and turned over to the French army.

Unwilling to submit docilely to arrest, Darnand fled into the mountains disguised as a priest. He was arrested at Edolo on June 25 by pure chance. English troops came looking for an Italian priest, who happened to be talking to the Milice chief at the time. Taken to Milan, Darnand was questioned by French Army Security concerning the whereabouts of his subordinates, such as Bout de l'An. Stubbornly, he refused to answer any questions about the hiding place of those who had been under his orders and for whom he felt responsible. Tiring of the game, the French officers demanded that he reveal the whereabouts of the "Milice treasure"—the money which Darnand's men had taken at gunpoint from French banks during their retreat in August, 1944. Darnand took them to a monastery near Tirano where he had hidden the loot months ago. The Father Superior stubbornly denied any knowledge of a treasure cache until Darnand remembered the password: "May Our Lady of Puy and Our Lady of Tirano bless you!"

In the basement of the monastery were over two hundred million francs in bank notes, gold coins, gold bars, and platinum wire. In the strongbox there was a note signed by Darnand as secretary general for the maintenance of order: "These funds belong to the French State (*L'Etat français*—i.e., Vichy), and can only be returned to the custody of the French State."

From Milan, the leader of the Milice was taken to Nice, where he was beaten up by the soldiers in the local jail. On July 2, he was flown to Paris and locked up in Fresnes, where at least no unscheduled brutality was permitted.

On October 3, 1945, Joseph Darnand appeared before the High Court on a charge of treason. The first president once again was Mongibeaux, but the vindictive Mornet had yielded his place to Attorney General Carrive. The trial was almost a model of judicial calm and respect for law and justice. Darnand refused to defend himself, seeking rather to assume responsibility for all the actions of the Milice (even those which he obviously could not have known about in advance), to protect his men and to defend not his life but his honor as a soldier. There was no anger or hatred in the courtroom; the accused did not argue or dispute and neither did his lawyers—apparently at his request.

There was only one witness for the defense, the accused's wartime comrade in the commandos (later a resistance chaplain), the Dominican, Father Bruckberger. However, he could only stress Darnand's military virtues, which were not in dispute, for even the judges and the prosecutor repeatedly referred to the military glory that Darnand had earned in two world wars.

Only once did Joseph Darnand show any bitterness. Near the end of the questioning, he referred to a letter that Pétain had written to Laval on August 6, 1944; in it, the Marshal had said bitter things about the Milice and had personally attacked Darnand for their crimes. This blow from the man he had worshiped rankled in Darnand's mind, and he told the court he had written to the Marshal that: "For four years I received compliments and congratulations from you. You encouraged me. And today, because the Americans are at the doors of Paris, you say to me that I will be a stain on the history of France? You might have pointed that out to me a little earlier."

After listening to this recital of Darnand's disillusionment with his hero Pétain, President Mongibeaux observed, "Democracies are not the only ones guilty of ingratitude."

The closing speech by Attorney General Carrive was long and tedious. He went through a detailed list of the crimes of the Milice as though they were news to the jurors and the audience, laying each crime in turn at Darnand's feet. Finally, he closed with the expected demand:

"Ladies and gentlemen of the jury, it is not without emotion . . . nor without sadness in thinking of Darnand's military past, but very firmly, in the name of our country, in the name of justice, that I ask you to pronounce the supreme penalty against this traitor and this murderer who is Darnand."

Seven hours after the trial began, Joseph Darnand was sentenced to death.

From his cell in Fresnes, Darnand wrote to General de Gaulle:

> . . . It is not my own pardon that I am asking, but that of my comrades in the Milice.
>
> I swear to you as a soldier and as a commando veteran in both wars that the very great majority of these men are real Frenchmen with all the warrior qualities of their race and are animated by a patriotism that makes them capable even of the supreme sacrifice.
>
> The only mistake they made was to be faithful to a great soldier, and they are almost the only ones who did not betray their oath by abandoning a lost cause. I can testify, since I know them best, that even those who wore the German uniform are in their hearts truly French. Many of them died on the field of battle crying "*Vive la France!*" Others were shot with this same cry of devotion on their lips. Many of them—the most numerous—are in your prisons waiting to be condemned by partisan judges. The rest are still in Germany or in Italy, prisoners of war or in hiding. Their families are suffering. The hatred is growing and could become ferocious. What will become of these thousands of men?
>
> . . . I would die with an easier conscience if I knew that my blood was being spilled to bring my men back into the honor of being French once more.

The chief of the provisional government, General de Gaulle, did not answer. Since there had been no request for mercy, the execution could proceed.

On the morning of October 10, 1945, Joseph Darnand got out of the prison truck on the firing range at the Fort de Châtillon. Breathing deeply, he said to Father Bruckberger, "What a beautiful day it is, Bruck. How happy I am that it is a beautiful day. Look at the trees . . ." After receiving absolution and kissing the crucifix, he walked calmly to the stake. He refused to let them blindfold him and started to sing the *Chant de la Milice*: "Kneeling we take the oath, as *miliciens* to die singing . . ."

At the very last minute he turned toward the Dominican priest and shouted "Good-bye, Father! Good-bye, my friends! Good-bye, my *miliciens! Vive Dieu! Vive la France!*"

The salvo of the firing squad cut short his cries.

The coup de grâce was a needless formality. Joseph Darnand was dead.

The trial of Pierre Laval took place in the same high-ceilinged courtroom, (the first chamber of the Palais de Justice) in which Marshal Pétain had been tried, and once again the team of Mongibeaux and Mornet was present; however, there the resemblance between the two proceedings ended. Although the prejudices of the jurors and the judges in the Marshal's trial had been obvious, the proceedings had at least taken place in an atmosphere of decorum and respect for the forms of law. Laval, however, was to stand alone in the pit surrounded by the open hatred and bitterness of jurors and audience, an animal being hunted to the end.

Even his lawyers refused to appear, but for another reason. Aware of the nature of the trial which was about to take place, they sent a letter to the first president which he indignantly read at the opening of the second session:

"A prior *instruction* [interrogation] was necessary, even indispensable; we were told and promised that we would have it; it was suddenly terminated in spite of our protests.

"We fear that the haste to open the proceedings may be inspired, not by judicial reasons, but by political ones.

"The declarations you made yesterday and which are published by the press leave us in no doubt. In fact, you said that you had decided to keep the court in session, if need be, morning, noon, and night in order that the trial be finished before the election."

The preliminary interrogation (which began on August 16) had been unreasonably short. There had been only seven sessions in which to question Laval on his actions and policies, not only during the four years of the occupation—the years in which he had been in power at Vichy—but also on the accusations deriving from his supposed prewar conspiracy with Pétain to overthrow the Republic. A number of documents in the possession of the prosecution had not been made available to the defense lawyers—a clear violation of the rights of the accused. Although the defense had been informed that a supplemental interrogation would take place, this promise had been broken and the trial suddenly set for October 9, 1945. The provisional government of the Republic had ordered elections for the new legislature to take place on October 21, and it was felt necessary for the peace of mind not only of the electors but of their new representatives to try and execute Laval before that time. The Gaullists were being hurt by the Communist claims that they were "soft" on the purge, and they were offering the electorate Laval's head as a token of their determination to punish Vichy and its collaborators.

Pierre Laval was not reluctant to approve the decision of his two young lawyers, Maître Naud and Maître Baraduc, to retire from the case. Confident of his ability to sway audiences, an acknowledged master of parliamentary debate, he preferred to fight alone and to share the spotlight with no one. In this, the supreme spectacle of his life, indeed for his life, Pierre Laval was fighting barehanded against his enemies. He relished the coming combat.

After Mongibeaux had protested that he was not responsible for what newspapers published, Attorney General Mornet rose to pooh-pooh the defense lawyers' claims that the preliminary interrogation had been cut short:

"Pierre Laval's case is one that could have come to trial without any need for a prior judicial interrogation, for the interrogation began the day Pétain and Laval, his second-in-command, came to power; it continued the day of the coup d'état on July 11 [1940], when they suppressed the Republic or the basic laws of the Republic.

"It then continued with those abominable racial laws which excluded from the French community a whole category of Frenchmen.

"It continued with Montoire. . . ."

The attorney general continued to beat the accused with those crimes that he called so obvious that a long preliminary interrogation would have made them no clearer: the workers sent to Germany, Vichy's attitude toward the landings in North Africa, the hunting down of the men of the Resistance, the Milice, and the court-martials. Irritated by this one-sided attack, the swarthy Laval leaped to his feet:

Monsieur Pierre Laval: But you were all under the government's orders at that time, all of you who are judging me, and you too, Monsieur le procurer général. . . .

Monsieur le premier président: I tell you once more . . .

Monsieur Pierre Laval: You can condemn me, you can kill me, but you do not have the right to insult me. . . .

Monsieur le premier président: . . . that, if you say anything which is insulting toward the judges, we will disregard the disputed point. . . .

Monsieur Pierre Laval: I am a Frenchman, I love my country, I have served only her and when . . . [commotion in the courtroom]. I will prove it to you! . . .

The official transcript notes that at that moment there was turmoil among the nonparliamentary jurors (i.e., those chosen from the list of resistance members).

Monsieur Demussois, juror: A little more modesty, you fraud!

Thus the tone of the trial was set early. Laval was not to be permitted to strike any noble attitudes or to offer any explanations of his policy. Try as he might, summoning the superb skill at debate that had always distinguished his career, Pierre Laval could not sway the executioners who surrounded him. Hatred filled the courtroom. Finally, shrugging his shoulders in despair, he announced that he would not participate in a judicial murder and would retire from the proceedings.

Before refusing to answer any more questions or take any further part in the trial, Laval threw one last taunt at the judges and the jurors.

Monsieur Pierre Laval: . . . There is something which is higher than all of us, higher than you, higher than me: the truth and the justice that you are supposed to embody. . . .

Monsieur Bedin, juror: Justice will be done!

Another juror: Justice will be done!

Monsieur Pierre Laval: It will be done, yes! . . . But the truth will remain.

Laval sat down.

Monsieur le premier président: You do not wish to answer?

Monsieur Pierre Laval: No!

Mongibeaux hastily suspended the proceedings and ordered the accused taken away. As he was being taken from the courtroom, the jurors stood and shouted at him. Amid the confusion and uproar, the stenographers could not identify who said what, but they carefully noted that the following was hurled at the accused:

"You are the provocateur!"

"Bastard!"

"Twelve bullets in his hide!"

"He hasn't changed a bit!"

Monsieur Pierre Laval: No, and I will not change now.

Monsieur le premier président (standing by his chair): I beg you, we are not at a public meeting!

Monsieur Pierre Laval: The jurors! . . . Even before judging me! *C'est formidable!* . . .

A parliamentary juror: You have already been judged, and France has judged you, too!

The guards took Pierre Laval away.

On the fifth day of his trial, in the absence of the accused and his lawyers, the High Court sentenced Pierre Laval to death, national degradation, and the confiscation of his worldly goods.

De Gaulle—on the advice of his ministers—refused to order a new trial. A request for pardon was rejected.

Fresnes Prison, October 15, 1945, 8:15 A.M.

The large black curtain that covered the entry to "death row" was raised so that the small party of men—all somberly dressed—could enter. Preceded by two guards, they walked solemnly down the empty main corridor. The sliding panels of the judases in the cell doors were quickly closed so that the condemned men could not see what was going on. The footsteps resounded loudly on the cement floor.

Behind the locked doors, the condemned men held their breath and prayed silently.

Someone was going to die.

The official party was led by Attorney General Mornet, who had lost the vulturish aspect that had distinguished him in his ermine robes before the High Court. Now, dressed entirely in black, he was pale and nervous at the thought of the task that lay ahead of him. Aware that the trial of the man that he must now lead out to execution had been a disgraceful insult to French justice, he waited anxiously while the door of the condemned man's cell was opened by a guard. Then, stepping into the doorway, he pronounced the traditional words:

"Pierre Laval, have courage."

Stretched out on the bed, his head buried under the sheet and blanket, Laval seemed to be asleep. Clearing his throat nervously, Mornet shook the sleeping man by the shoulder and said, "Pierre Laval, the time has come. Prepare to die courageously."

There was no reply. Laval did not move.

Thinking that his client had lost his nerve in the face of death, Maître Naud entered the cell and said roughly, "Come, sir, get up!"

Laval seemed to bury himself deeper under the covers.

"For yourself, for your lawyer, for history, be brave."

The form under the blanket twitched convulsively.

"I beg you, monsieur," Naud pleaded, "a little dignity! The only thing left is for you to die well."

Moaning, Laval turned, his face twisted with pain, a light foam on his lips. His left hand opened involuntarily and a small glass vial fell to the floor. Around his neck he wore a tricolor scarf, for the ex-mayor of Aubervilliers had determined to die a republican.

Pierre Laval had taken poison.

The small cell was in a turmoil as people crowded in. The doctor who had been present to certify the condemned man's death before a firing squad picked up the vial and sniffed it carefully. "Cyanide," he declared. He examined the stricken man and checked his reflexes and his pulse; then, turning to the audience, he declared solemnly, "He has only a few minutes to live."

On a shelf, Laval had left his last letters to his wife, his daughter, and his lawyers. In the latter he had written, "I refuse to fall under French bullets. I don't want the soldiers to be the accomplices of a judicial murder. I have chosen my death: the poison of the Romans. I had hidden it in my overcoat." This was the same vial of poison that Laval had had sewn into the lining of his coat in November, 1942, when, uncertain of his fate, he had been summoned to Munich by an angry Hitler. Now, three years later, he used it to try to escape the indignity of an execution by his fellow countrymen. But the poison had failed him. In three years it had deteriorated to the point where it was not immediately fatal.

Mornet rushed to a nearby office and called de Gaulle's office for instructions. The response was brutal: "If Laval is not yet dead, the sentence must be carried out as soon as possible."

Hurrying back to the cell where Pierre Laval lay twitching convulsively, his eyes glazed, a horrible gurgling sound in his throat, the attorney general demanded that the doctor try to revive him. Dr. Paul refused; his job was to certify the death of a condemned traitor, not to bring a dying man back to life. The prison doctor and his assistants were hastily summoned to attempt to save Laval's life. Several injections of camphor to promote vomiting were given, the soles of the dying man's feet were slashed to promote circulation, and large amounts of water were forced down his throat. Seventeen times his stomach was washed out.

For two hours the doctors fought desperately to save Pierre Laval. The odor in the small crowded cell soon became unbearable, but finally their frantic efforts were rewarded. The condemned man began to revive.

Frantic at the delay, Mornet proposed that the semiconscious Laval be carried to the execution grounds on a stretcher and shot. Maître Naud protested that the condemned man could only be shot if he were lucid and in control of himself; it was pointed out to the nervous attorney general that the penal code forbade the execution of a man who was not in a state to make a final statement. Mornet mumbled that he only proposed it out of humanity.

"On my client's behalf, I am very touched by your concern," Naud sneered.

It was 11:30 when the doctors triumphantly issued a communiqué which for its ineptness and irony—considering the situation—is probably unequaled in medical history: "Pierre Laval is no longer in danger of dying."

While they were dressing the half-conscious ex-premier, the director of penal institutions, Amor ("*à mort,*" Pétain had said on learning the name of his chief jailor, "just like me—'to death' "), entered the cell and shouted "Come on now! Let's get this over with quickly! And no more nonsense!"

"Are you in a hurry for lunch, monsieur?" Laval asked weakly.

The flustered Amor withdrew while Laval finished dressing with the help of a nun. He knelt with the priest for his last confession; rising, he turned to the men in the doorway and said firmly, "There are others who should ask pardon of God."

At noon the cortege began. Refusing to be carried in a chair, Laval stumbled painfully down the corridor, supported by his two lawyers. Every twenty steps he had to stop and rest; in spite of the large amount of water that he had been forced to swallow, he still suffered from a terrible thirst and a guard stood nearby with a bottle of water for him. Most of the time he could not keep it down.

The "Black Maria" was waiting in the courtyard of the prison. Helped by his lawyers, Laval hoisted himself into the back and sat on a chair. "Is it far?" he asked. They assured him it was not. "So much the better," Laval said dully. "I don't mind dying, but I feel grief for my wife and my daughter."

Although the execution had originally been set for the Fort de Montrouge, the firing squad had been hurriedly called to Fresnes; it was clear that Pierre Laval could not have managed the long trip. Back of the prison, on a small plot that the guards' wives used to dry their laundry, the stake had been quickly planted.

As Laval stepped slowly from the van, he looked about at the assembled witnesses. "Where are the court officials?" he demanded.

From their hiding place behind the van, Attorney General Mornet and Magistrate Bouchardon* (who had conducted the preliminary interrogation) came forward, nervous and trembling.

"I am sorry," Laval said to them, "that you have to do a job like this. You wanted this spectacle; you'll have it to the very end. Stand there."

Then turning, he walked alone toward the execution post. Fearful that he might be too weak to stand, the guards had placed a stool at the foot of the stake. Laval ordered them to take it away. "A premier of France dies standing. . . ."

* In 1917, Mornet had been the prosecutor and Bouchardon had conducted the preliminary interrogation in the Mata Hari case.

After they had tied his hands, he refused the blindfold. His lawyers stepped forward and embraced him. He smiled and said softly, "Don't go too far away. I want to see you while dying. You have fine faces."

The officer commanding the firing squad raised his saber. "Ready!"

Laval, who had been staring steadily at his lawyers, turned to look at the muzzles leveled at his chest. The squad was wearing British helmets and perhaps—for a moment—he might have deceived himself into believing that it was not the French who were shooting him.

"*Vive la France!*" he cried.

The saber whipped downward.

"*Vive la Fr—!*" This last cry was cut off by the volley.

His body bent forward, then slipped to the ground. The officer ran forward and fired his revolver into the dead man's brain.

With the red, white, and blue scarf still wrapped tightly around his neck, the body of Pierre Laval, the last premier of Vichy France, lay huddled on the ground.

Fernand de Brinon was becoming desperate. His attempts to cross into Switzerland with the cars containing his secretaries, his voluminous baggage, and his numerous documents had repeatedly failed. The Swiss—ungrateful for past "favors"—had refused sanctuary to the bony, hawk-faced Vichy ex-minister. His attempts to enter Italy had been equally fruitless; the Gauleiter in Innsbruck had not only refused him a pass but had ordered him out of the military zone.

When everything else failed, de Brinon decided a little blackmail was in order. He sent a message to the Swiss that he wished to return to France (probably the last thing in the world he really wanted) and that he was in possession of a large number of important documents which the Swiss foreign office and the French ambassador would be most happy to see. He suggested they allow him to come and discuss it with them.

The Swiss authorities did not even bother to answer. Finally, realizing that his bluff had failed, de Brinon surrendered to the American army, who promptly turned him over to the French at Lindau. Ten days later, he was driven in an open truck to Paris, in handcuffs.

For almost two years de Brinon remained in prison—or in the prison hospital, following two serious operations that left him a pain-ridden, broken man. While he suffered in his hospital bed (intermittently questioned by the magistrates), Darnand, Laval, and Luchaire fell before French firing squads. The "radio traitors," Hérold-Paquis and Ferdonnet, as well as a thousand informers, French Gestapists, torturers, and *miliciens* had also been executed. The purge went on inexorably, but by the time de Brinon was brought to trial in March,

1947, the composition of the High Court had changed. Disturbed by the unseemly procedures—particularly in Laval's trial—and aware of the prejudices of the resistance jurors, the government had revised the procedures for selecting the judges and jury of the new political tribunal. Mongibeaux had been replaced by Louis Noguères, a man with a better sense of the defendant's rights; Mornet no longer appeared at the prosecutor's desk, and the jurors were selected from among the new deputies to the National Assembly in proportion to the strength of their parties.

The even-handedness of the new court and the calm in which the proceedings were now carried out could not save Fernand de Brinon. The act of accusation was long and detailed: his prewar activities in the Franco-German committee, his ardent procollaborationist attitude as the Vichy representative to the occupation authorities, his role as president of the L.V.F., his struggle to align France militarily with Nazi Germany, his position as head of the "French Committee for the Protection of National Interests" in Sigmaringen—all these condemned him. He was in fact convicted out of his own mouth; at Doriot's fueral, he had said:

"It is clear that the French had never suffered so much as since the American liberation. Our only hope is the triumph of the ideas that we represent and that is why we particularly honor those of our men who—as volunteers in the L.V.F., the Waffen-S.S., and all the other groups which are fighting against Bolshevism—have taken up arms for a cause which is that of France. . . . The army of the democracies led by General Eisenhower sees the tide of French blood which is flowing and is silent on everything which is going on in France. . . . England and the United States have already delivered a part of Europe to the Soviets. Only a wonderful and amazing Germany is defending civilization today."

The accused used every trick in his bag in an effort to avoid the inevitable verdict. He tried to have the first president removed because he had sat in on the *instruction* of previous defendants (in his memoirs, de Brinon claimed that Noguères had a grudge against him that went back to the time that they were law students together); he demanded a longer preliminary interrogation and claimed that important documents in the dossier had been kept from him. When all these demands were rejected by the court on good and sufficient grounds, the wily de Brinon tried the ploy that Laval had used (and that had so clearly failed). He refused to appear in the courtroom and persisted in this attitude until finally the first president sent a bailiff to his cell and warned him that the trial would proceed whether he appeared or not. Returning to the courtroom, de Brinon maintained a silence which was broken only by one speech defending his past and his policies during the occupation.

During his absence, the court went to the ministry of information on the avenue Friedland to see a Wehrmacht film of de Brinon reviewing the L.V.F. on the eastern front. The sight of the Vichy representative saluting column after column of Frenchmen in German uniform had a powerful effect on the jurors.

The witnesses for the prosecution included General Doyen, who had been head of the French delegation to the armistice commission at Wiesbaden. He complained that, when he had sought de Brinon's aid in saving a group of French peasants condemned to death by the Germans, he had been horrified that the Vichy representative in Paris had failed to supply him with the needed information in time. On another occasion he told de Brinon about the bitter struggle that the French delegation was waging at Wiesbaden against German arrogance; de Brinon had replied: "... Here in Paris we get along very well with the Germans. They are so kind! ..."

General de la Laurencie stomped into the courtroom to complain bitterly about the man who had replaced him as Vichy representative to the occupation authorities (after the fiasco of the return of the ashes of L'Aiglon). He did not seem to have much in the way of facts to offer, except some secondhand gossip—an ambassador of France had said on his deathbed that de Brinon was a spy in the pay of Germany; Marshal Pétain had told his wife that the Germans had forced him to name de Brinon to Paris. At the end, the angry General repeated the statement he had made earlier: "I swear under oath and after carefully weighing all my words, that in all conscience I am not afraid to say that I consider Monsieur de Brinon to be the complete traitor [*le traître intégral*]."

An accountant testified that, after examining de Brinon's income and expenses, he had concluded that the ex-minister could not possibly have lived in the expensive fashion that he did during the occupation on the money which had been paid him by the government. The accused had insisted that the money had come from the sale of stocks and bonds belonging to his wife; his wife denied this. There was also the question of large sums of money turned over to de Brinon by various organizations to be used for French prisoners of war in Germany. Much of this seems to have ended up in the accused's pocket.

The court was surprised when the suave Otto Abetz asked for an interpreter, for it was well known that the ex–German ambassador to Vichy spoke fluent French. The witness finally agreed coyly to speak in that language, asking only that the court excuse any mistakes that he might make.

Abetz stressed de Brinon's desire for a closer relationship between France and Germany before the war and his concern for endangered Frenchmen during the occupation. He blamed Darlan (now safely dead) for the attempt to align France militarily with Germany and spoke of de Brinon's protest at the murder of Georges Mandel. On this latter point, he was very careful to plead his own innocence as well, for he knew it would be a charge against him at his coming trial that he had demanded the executions of Mandel, Reynaud, and Blum.

During most of the testimony, de Brinon was in the courtroom, listening attentively. He heard Edouard Daladier tell of the report that he (de Brinon) had made on his conversations with Hitler in the thirties and of how Daladier had "accidentally" met Ribbentrop at de Brinon's villa. None of this seemed very relevant to the small audience, which was only waiting to applaud the inevitable verdict.

There is a photograph of the accused standing by his chair, answering a question from one of the jurors; next to him, his guard is staring at him with a look of such utter contempt that not for one moment could anyone imagine any other verdict but death.

On April 15, 1947, supported by two canes, he limped painfully to the execution post. His last words were, "History will prove me right."

His devoted secretary, Simone Mittre, who had served him slavishly since 1920, during his years in power at Sigmaringen and during the arduous flight through Austria, tried to explain to the *juge d'instruction* her steadfast affection for the man whom everyone held to be "*le traître intégral.*" The magistrate threw up his hands in despair and said, "Women are mad!"

With the French 1st Army only twenty miles behind them and advancing rapidly, the Luchaire family (Jean, his wife, their son, and three daughters—with one of the latter about to give birth), accompanied by Marcel Déat and his wife, drove around Lake Constance and up into the Vorarlberg Mountains of the Austrian Tyrol. They spent the night of May 2 at an inn in Sankt Anton discussing in frightened tones their escape plans. It was here that they learned from a radio flash of Hitler's death (which had occurred on April 30). Immediately, the mood of the many guests in the inn changed; French, Germans, Austrians, and Italians all became gay and excited. There was a tremendous sense of relief, and the drinking and dancing went on all night.

The next day the Luchaires and the Déats separated to reach Italy by different routes. For three weeks Luchaire and his family hid in the Italian town of Merano, undisturbed by the American army when it arrived there, even after Luchaire had identified himself to the authorities. Thinking himself temporarily safe, Luchaire sent a telegram to the Italian ambassador in Washington reminding him of their old friendship and asking that the ambassador please see that he was not turned over to the French authorities and that he be permitted to remain either in Italy or be admitted to the United States. He pointed out that he could always claim Italian citizenship, having been born in Italy, and made mention of his "anti-Fascist" past.

Harassed by the large number of French, German, and Italian collaborationists with whom they had to deal, the American counter-intelligence unit in Merano had recruited three Frenchmen from a German concentration camp to help them, not knowing that they were notorious Gestapo agents. These three arrested Luchaire and his daughter Corinne (the film actress) and turned them over to a French security unit. They were transferred to Milan, then Nice (where Jean Luchaire received the same brutal reception as had Darnand), and were finally imprisoned in Paris on July 5.

It took the High Court two days to condemn Luchaire. Like de Brinon, he was convicted by his words in print and by the damaging evidence of his extravagant living during the occupation when so many of his fellow countrymen had suffered from hunger and cold. The verdict was announced on January 22, 1946, and one month later, after his plea for pardon had been turned down, he was shot.

He went to his death calmly and without saying a word, a cigarette dangling from the corner of his mouth. Perhaps he failed to utter the usual "*Vive la France!*" since—as he had told the High Court—he was "Italian in his heart and Italian under the law."

His daughter, Corinne, was convicted of "national unworthiness" and was sentenced to ten years of "national degradation" * by a Paris court for her alleged "horizontal collaboration" (sexual relations) with Otto Abetz and Count Ciano.

After leaving the Luchaires at Sankt Anton, Marcel Déat and his wife tried to enter Switzerland; turned back at the border, they finally drove into Italy by the Resia Pass. There, a village priest advised them to hide on the mountain; they abandoned the car and started the long climb, burdened with valises filled with money and documents. Pursued by French security troops and Italian police, they climbed higher and higher, always one step ahead of the searchers. Claiming to be political refugees, they received help from the village priests and fi-

* *L'indignité nationale* (national unworthiness) is a crime which carries the punishment of national degradation—the civil equivalent of ripping off an officer's epaulets and buttons and breaking his sword. For the specified term, the prisoner condemned to national unworthiness loses all civic and political rights: he cannot vote, be elected to or hold public office, teach, practice law, hold any rank in the armed services, wear any decorations, be a juror or a witness under oath, hold a job in press, radio, or cinema, or be a corporation director.

nally reached Genoa, where—according to Madame Déat—they hid "in a shady hotel filled with black Americans and whores."

Déat grew a little beard and wore glasses; by now his hair was all white and there was little chance of his being recognized. They used the name Leroux (which had been his mother's name), avoided the neighbors, and stayed off the streets as much as possible.

In November, 1954, they were living in Turin, when a doctor found a serious lesion in Déat's lung. A sanitarium was recommended, but the ex-Vichy minister of labor refused; he was afraid that his identity might be revealed. The disease took hold quickly and on January 5, 1955, Marcel Déat died in the forgiving arms of the Roman Catholic Church. Known before the war as a rabid anticleric, he had become a practicing Catholic in 1947 and asked for extreme unction before he died.

This was his last betrayal: his prewar pacifism, Socialism, and patriotism he had all denied during the occupation. His lifelong anticlericalism was the last thing to vanish.

The trial of the Vichy ministers before the High Court continued, but de Brinon's was the last death sentence that was followed by an execution. The others who were condemned to the supreme penalty avoided it either by having it pronounced in absentia or by having the sentence commuted, usually to life imprisonment. Abel Bonnard, Darquier de Pellepoix, General Bridoux, and Raphaël Alibert were safely out of the country when sentenced to death. General Fernand Dentz—who had had the sad duty of surrendering Paris to the Germans and who had made the mistake of too vigorously defending Syria against the Allies—had his sentence of death commuted, but died in chains in prison.

The other ministers received various sentences: Yves Bouthillier, who had led the conspiracy against Laval in December, 1940, received a prison term of three years; Paul Marion was sentenced to ten years for following the Marshal to Sigmaringen; General Weygand—who had been arrested and imprisoned by the Germans since November, 1942—received a "*non-lieu*" (no prosecution), as did General Colson (who in 1940 had ordered de Gaulle sentenced to death). The list of recipients of *non-lieux* is long: Carcopino, the ineffectual minister of education; Ripert, who had been innocently dismissed with Laval; Georges Lamirand, the exuberant minister for youth (who attempted to explain his past in the documentary *The Sorrow and the Pity*); and even Darquier's successor, du Paty de Clam, who was able to prove that he had only accepted the job as head of the Commissariat Général aux Questions Juives (C.G.Q.J.) after consulting the Resistance and then only to introduce the maximum of confusion in its operations.

The first head of the C.G.Q.J., Xavier Vallat, was sentenced to ten years imprisonment (and pardoned in 1960); he spent his years in jail in a voluminous correspondence with his fellow prisoner, Charles Maurras. Paul Baudouin, ex-minister of foreign affairs, received five years at hard labor, but Jacques Chevalier, ex-Vichy minister of national education, was stunned by twenty years at hard labor (because of several letters urging strong action against the Maquis). Ybarnegaray, who had been a minister so briefly in 1940, had his sentence of national degradation suspended for "contributions to the Resistance," as did Pierre-Etienne Flandin, who had been minister of foreign affairs for two months in 1940. Jacques Benoist-Méchin, a great admirer of the German army, who had as an undersecretary of state worked for military cooperation with the Nazis, had his death sentence commuted to life imprisonment and was released five years later. (He is the author of one of the best books on the military and political drama of the Battle of France [May–June, 1940], called *Sixty Days that Shook the West.*)

Admiral Gabriel-Paul Auphan had been sent by Marshal Pétain in August, 1944, to contact General de Gaulle and arrange a peaceful turnover of power from Vichy to the victorious Fighting French. But the general would have none of it; his victory was to be "pure," unsullied by any gift from Vichy. He had refused to receive Auphan or to accept the message. In August, 1946, Admiral Auphan was sentenced to life imprisonment at hard labor by the High Court—in absentia. He was later granted amnesty.

The High Court tried the Vichy leaders and passed eight death sentences (only three of which resulted in executions: Darnand, Laval, and de Brinon). The vast majority of the cases resulting from collaboration with the enemy were tried in the *cours de justice* (for serious crimes) and the *chambres civiques* (for offenses likely to be punished only by national degradation).

Of the almost 125,000 men and women who were tried by these courts, 2,853 were sentenced to death and, of these, 767 were executed. France sent more of its errant citizens before a firing squad than any other occupied country in western Europe (although the ratio of those shot to the total population is smaller than that of Belgium). The percentage of French imprisoned for collaboration is approximately one-fourth that of Denmark and Holland, and one-sixth that of Belgium and Norway.

De Gaulle, sitting late at night in his office, alone with his conscience, carefully studied the dossiers of all those condemned to death. Without exception, he commuted the sentences of all women (even the torturers and the auxiliaries of the Gestapo); in almost every case, he refused to send a minor to the execution post. France, he knew, was weary of the purge. France, he insisted, needed all her sons.

Amnesty began as early as 1947 for those who had been sentenced to national degradation. In March, 1954, all sentences in absentia were canceled and those who had fled returned to stand trial before understanding judges; in almost every case, they received either an acquittal or a suspended sentence.

Jail sentences were revised downward and prisoners released long before their terms had ended.

By 1964, twenty years after the liberation, not one collaborator remained in jail.

Epilogue

Monday, February 19, 1973.

In the little cemetery overlooking the wharves of Port-Joinville on the Ile d'Yeu, the gravedigger–guardian, Jean Taraud, stood staring at the gravel path leading to the grave of Philippe Pétain. He scratched his head, puzzled.

In spite of the crowd of unrepentant *pétainistes,* veterans of Verdun, ex–Vichy officials, and pious elderly women who still worshiped Pétain, who every Sunday crowded around his tomb on the wooded slope, the gravel was undisturbed. Clearly, someone had raked it. But who—and why?

Taraud carefully examined the heavy slab with its simple inscription "Philippe Pétain, Maréchal de France." In two corners, it had been slightly chipped, and it was clear that the seal had been chiseled away and then recemented. Someone had tried to conceal the fact that the Marshal's tomb had been opened.

Informed of the desecration, the public prosecutor at Sables-d'Olonne on the mainland hurriedly called the ministry of the interior in Paris, then flew to Port-Joinville to supervise the investigation.

At 3:30 P.M., the nine-ton marble slab was slowly shifted to permit an electric torch to be shone into the *caveau.* It was empty. Marshal Pétain's body had been stolen!

When the news was flashed to Paris, there was tremendous excitement. The political implications to the government were clear, but who was responsible: the admirers or the enemies of Vichy? From President Pompidou to Premier Messmer to Minister of the Interior Marcellin down to the harassed *police judiciare* at the rue des Saussaies the word was passed: find the Marshal's body and *quickly!*

Back on the Ile d'Yeu meanwhile, the gendarmerie, traditionally jealous of their prerogatives, had started their investigation. An old woman had put some flowers on the tomb at 6:30 Sunday night. At two o'clock Monday morning, an islander living near the cemetery had heard his dog bark and the muffled sound of an auto starting up. Since Taraud had discovered the desecration at eight in the morning, and the only ferry to the mainland after two and before eight had been at 2:45 A.M., the evidence was clear: sometime after 6:30 Sunday night and before two Monday morning, a team of men had chiseled off the seal around the heavy slab, moved it aside (chipping it in the process), removed Pétain's coffin to a nearby station wagon, and driven to the ferry.

Ten miles from the ferry landing on the mainland, the *police judiciare* located an unoccupied château owned by an ex-Croix de Feu, a deputy who had voted for Pétain in July, 1940, and who had served under the occupation as the departmental head for the Vichy ministry of information. He was presently the local head of Les Amis du Maréchal (The Marshal's Friends). On the day of the kidnaping, he was in Paris.

What intrigued the police were the wide-open garage doors and the muddy tracks of a heavy car that could be seen on the asphalt. No doubt, this is where the station wagon had come from the ferry. But where was it now? And—more important—was the coffin still in it?

In Paris, Monsieur de Casson, the owner of the château, denied any knowledge of the kidnapping. The garage doors? Oh, he had lent the keys to some stranger who needed a garage for a few days. No, he had not seen the man since and the keys had not been returned.

Meanwhile, Jean-Louis Tixier-Vignancourt (who had been head of the Vichy radio and who had recently polled one million votes in his unsuccessful bid for the presidency of the Republic) received an anonymous phone call: "We have taken the Marshal's body and we have transferred it to Douaumont!"

The government rushed police squads to guard the vast cemetery near Verdun, where sixteen thousand *poilus* rest near what had once been the embattled Fort de Douaumont. In the dense fog and biting snow, they stood—where their fathers and grandfathers had stood to stop the armies of the Crown Prince—to stop a dead man.

Il ne passera pas! (He shall not pass!)

The next day was the anniversary of the opening of the German attack on Verdun.

In Paris, Maître Isorni (who had defended Pétain at his trial) and Tixier-Vignancourt negotiated on their own with the government: if not Douaumont, let the old Marshal rest in the Invalides. Messmer refused: Foch was buried in that citadel of military glory and everyone knew that Foch had despised Pétain. Besides, Vichy was still anathema to many Frenchmen; no government could permit the Marshal entry to the Invalides and survive.

In the face of this categorical refusal, the kidnapers capitulated.

Their leader had no memories of Verdun or Vichy to justify his desecration of the tomb. Only thirty-six years old, he had been taught by his grandfathers (both veterans of 1914–1918) to revere the Marshal; his unstable temperament had done the rest. In a hastily called press conference, he tried to explain his motives. Arrested, he led the police to a rented garage in Saint-Ouen, where—under a pile of soiled mattresses and grimy tarpaulins—rested the coffin of Philippe Pétain.

Covered with a *tricolore* edged with gold, the coffin was flown by helicopter to the Ile d'Yeu. In the little church of Notre-Dame du Port, before the island fishermen and sailors and a few nervous officials, the village priest said the mass for the dead. Surrounded by four large candles on metal tripods, his Marshal's kepi resting on the flag that covered his coffin, Pétain was once again prayed into eternal rest.

Conscious of the vindictiveness that still pursued the dead man, the *abbé* took his text from Paul's Epistle to the Corinthians on the difficulty of discerning good from evil.

In the presence of the prefect of the Vendée, the coffin was returned to its tomb near the four small cypresses on the windswept hill. As the marble slab was slowly pushed into place and carefully sealed, the words of Abbé Gindreau seemed to linger softly in the air:

"God gave us brothers and—alas!—we invented hate."

Chronology

Events that occurred inside France are set in italic type.

1940

March: 20 — *Daladier government falls. Paul Reynaud new premier.*
28 — *France and Britain pledge no separate peace or armistice without mutual consent.*

April: 9 — Germany invades Norway and Denmark.
20 — French expeditionary force lands in Norway. Withdraws two weeks later.

May: 10 — Germany invades Belgium, Holland, and Luxembourg. Neville Chamberlain resigns; Winston Churchill becomes prime minister.
14 — *German army crosses Meuse near Sedan and starts race to the sea.*
15 — Dutch army surrenders.
17 — *Reynaud reshuffles cabinet: Pétain vice-premier, Mandel minister of the interior.*
19 — *General Weygand replaces Gamelin as commander in chief.*
27 — Belgian army surrenders.
28 — *Evacuation of British and French troops begins at Dunkirk.*

June: 5 — *Battle of France. Germans smash the Somme line. Daladier dropped from Reynaud's cabinet; de Gaulle undersecretary of defense.*
10 — Italy declares war on France and England.
11 — *Paris declared open city.*
14 — *German army enters Paris.*
16 — *Reynaud resigns; Pétain new premier.*
17 — *Pétain broadcasts that he has asked for armistice terms.*

18 – General de Gaulle's first call for resistance on BBC.
22 – *Franco–German armistice signed at Rethondes.*
24 – Franco–Italian armistice signed in Rome.

July: 2 – *French government transferred to Vichy.*
3 – British warships attack French fleet at Mers-el-Kebir.
10 – *Pétain voted full powers by National Assembly.* First large-scale German air raids on Great Britain.

August: 2 – *De Gaulle condemned to death by Vichy court-martial.*
29 – Chad, French Equatorial Africa, Cameroons, and French Oceania join the Free French movement.

September: 8 – *Reynaud, Daladier, and Gamelin under house arrest.*
10 – *First Nazi anti-Jewish law in occupied zone.*
23 – Anglo–Free French attack on Dakar fails.

October: 3 – *First Vichy law excluding Jews from public office, press, radio, and cinema.*
7 – *Vichy deprives Algerian Jews of French citizenship.*
24 – *Meeting of Pétain and Hitler at Montoire.*
28 – Italy attacks Greece.

November: 11 – *Demonstration by students at the Arc de Triomphe.*
23 – *Admiral Leahy arrives in Vichy as the U.S. ambassador.*
30 – *Alsace-Lorraine annexed to the Reich in spite of French protests.*

December: 13 – *Laval dismissed as vice-premier and placed under house arrest.*
15 – *Ashes of Napoleon's son interred in the Invalides.*
25 – Admiral Darlan confers with Hitler in Germany.

1941

January: 3 – *Bread ration reduced to ten ounces a day.*
27 – *All public officials required to take oath of loyalty to Pétain.*

February: 1 – *Marcel Déat announces formation of the Reassemblement National Populaire in Paris.*
9 – *Flandin resigns and is succeeded by Darlan as vice-premier.*

March: 11 – Lend-Lease Bill passed by U.S. Congress.
29 – *Xavier Vallat named Commissioner General for Jewish Affairs.*

April: 6 – *Vichy allows German planes passage through Syria to attack British in Iraq.* Germany invades Greece and Yugoslavia.

May: 10 – Rudolf Hess lands in Scotland.
14 – *Five thousand foreign Jews arrested in Paris.*
20 – Germans invade Crete.
27 – German battleship *Bismarck* sunk.

June: 15 – *Vichy publishes new anti-Semitic decree.*
17 – *Pétain's radio broadcast on the first anniversary of his request for an armistice:* "Français, *you really have a short memory!*"
22 – Germany invades U.S.S.R.
30 – *Vichy breaks diplomatic relations with U.S.S.R.*

July: 8 – *Formation of the L.V.F.–French volunteers to fight with the Germans in Russia.*
24 – *French cardinals and archbishops pledge loyalty to Vichy government.*
26 – *Marx Dormoy, former minister of the interior in Popular Front government, murdered by followers of Doriot.*
31 – *Occupation costs total three billion dollars.*

August: 14 – Churchill and Roosevelt sign Atlantic Charter.
21 – *German naval officer Moser killed by Communist special action squad in Barbès subway station.*
27 – *Laval and Déat wounded at L.V.F. ceremony in Versailles.*
29 – *Free French Navy Lieutenant-Commander d'Estienne d'Orves and two comrades shot by German firing squads for espionage.*

September: 10 – *Germans start shooting ten French hostages for every German soldier killed by the Resistance.*
19 – Kiev falls to Germans.
23 – *Anti-Jewish exposition in Paris.*
26 – *Germans demand the recall of General Weygand from North Africa.*

October: 3 – *Six Paris synagogues dynamited by French Fascists with the help of the Gestapo.*
12 – *L.V.F. takes oath of loyalty to Hitler.*
16 – *Twenty-seven Communists (including seventeen-year old Guy Môquet) shot as hostages at Châteaubriant.* General Tojo forms new cabinet in Japan.

November: 12 – *General Huntziger, Vichy minister of war, killed in a plane crash.*
18 – *Weygand forcibly retired.*
27 – *Jewish deputies to National Assembly dismissed.*

December: 1 – *Pétain meets Hermann Goering at St. Florentin.*
5 – Battle of Moscow.

7 – Japanese planes attack U.S. fleet in Hawaii. Japan declares war on U.S. and Great Britain.
9 – Darlan meets Count Ciano in Turin.
11 – Germany and Italy declare war on U.S.
22 – Japanese attack Philippines.
25 – Hong Kong falls.
31 – *Jean Moulin leaves London with orders from de Gaulle to unite Resistance. Parachutes into France the following morning.*

1942

January:
1 – *First F.T.P. Maquis formed near Grenoble.*
10 – Japan invades Dutch East Indies.
23 – *Boris Vildé and six other résistants from the Musée de l'Homme executed by the Germans.*

February:
9 – *Beginning of the Riom trial of Daladier, Gamelin, Blum, and other ministers of the Third Republic.*
15 – Singapore falls.
27 – Battle of the Java Sea.
28 – *Joseph Darnand forms the S.O.L. General Otto von Stülpnagel is named German military commander in France.*

March:
3 – *R.A.F. bombs Paris suburb of Boulogne-Billancourt; 623 dead and 1,500 wounded.*

April:
9 – American forces on Bataan surrender.
11 – *Riom trial suspended "for further inquiry."*
17 – *Laval returns as head of the Vichy government.* General Giraud escapes from German prison camp.
18 – Tokyo bombed by U.S. planes.

May:
4 – Battle of the Coral Sea. American garrison on Corregidor surrenders.
5 – British occupy Madagascar.
6 – *Darquier de Pellepoix replaces Vallat as head of the Commissariat Général aux Questions Juives.*
27 – Defense of Bir Hakeim by Free French under General Koenig.
29 – *Jews in occupied zone required to wear yellow star.*

June:
1 – *Gauleiter Sauckel, head of Nazi forced labor, arrives in Paris.*
4 – Battle of Midway.
22 – *On first anniversary of the German attack on the Soviet Union, Laval broadcasts: "I desire Germany's victory. . . ."*

July: 16 — *Roundup of the Vel d'Hiv: 12,884 foreign Jews arrested in Paris.*
19 — *Nazi General Oberg publishes "Family Hostage" law.*

August: 9 — *Ninety-three "terrorists" executed.*
15 — *Four thousand stateless Jews arrested by Vichy in the unoccupied zone and turned over to the Germans.*
19 — *Anglo-Canadian raid on Dieppe fails with many casualties.*

September: 4 — *Forced labor law demanded of Vichy by Sauckel.*
19 — *113 "terrorists" shot.*
30 — *Edouard Herriot under house arrest.*

October: 4 — *Vichy passes law on S.T.O. (forced labor).*
23 — Battle of El Alamein.

November: 8 — Allied landings in North Africa. *Vichy breaks diplomatic relations with the U.S. in protest.*
11 — *Germans invade unoccupied zone.*
12 — *General Weygand arrested by the Germans.*
18 — *Laval given power to issue laws and decrees.*
22 — Russians counterattack at Stalingrad.
27 — *At Toulon, the French fleet scuttles itself to escape seizure by the German army.*
29 — *French armistice army of 100,000 men dissolved.*

December: 1 — *Admiral Platon broadcasts to French troops in North Africa to resist their leaders and the Allies.*
13 — *Pétain protests violation of the armistice in letter to Hitler. Laval tells Paris press conference that he still desires a German victory.*
24 — Admiral Darlan assassinated in Algiers.

1943

January: 11 — *Thirty subway stations closed to conserve electricity.*
14 — Churchill and Roosevelt meet in Casablanca. De Gaulle and Giraud also present.
18 — Siege of Leningrad lifted.
30 — *Law creating the Milice passed by Vichy. Darnand named secretary general for maintenance of order.*

February: 2 — German army surrenders at Stalingrad.
9 — *L.V.F. recognized as an official organization by Vichy.*
16 — *All Frenchmen from twenty-one to thirty required to register for S.T.O.*

March: 2 — Battle of the Bismarck Sea.
6 — *Formation of Maquis in Savoy, made up of young men escaping from the S.T.O.*

8 – *Rennes bombarded by Allied planes.*
12 – *Rouen hit by American air raid.*

April: 5 – Daladier, Blum, and Gamelin deported to Germany, where they join Mandel and Reynaud in concentration camps.
29 – Laval meets with Hitler to discuss the common defense of Europe.

May: 7 – Capture of Tunis and Bizerte by Allies.
27 – *First meeting of the C.N.R. (National Council of the Resistance) in Paris with Jean Moulin as president.*

June: 3 – French Committee for National Liberation under de Gaulle and Giraud announced in Algiers.
9 – *General Delestraint, head of the Secret Army of the Resistance, arrested in Paris.*
21 – *Jean Moulin and other resistance leaders arrested at Caluire near Lyons.*

July: 9 – Allies invade Sicily.
14 – *On Bastille Day, the suburbs of Paris are heavily hit by an Allied air raid.*
25 – Mussolini arrested; Marshal Badoglio forms anti-Fascist government.
31 – Germans take over the Italian occupation zone.

August: 7 – American landings on Guadalcanal in the Solomons.
13 – Pierre Pucheu, ex–Vichy minister of the interior, arrested in Morocco.
20 – *President Lebrun put under house arrest.*

September: 3 – *Allied air raids on Paris.* Allies land on Italian mainland.
8 – Italy surrenders.
12 – Mussolini freed by German paratroops.
17 – *Darnand enlists in the Waffen-S.S.*
29 – *Ritter, head of the Nazi forced labor organization in France, is killed by the F.T.P.*

October: 5 – Corsica is liberated by the Free French.
13 – Italy declares war on Germany.

November: 22 – Churchill, Roosevelt, Chiang Kai-shek meet in Cairo.
25 – *Students and faculty of the University of Strasbourg, which had retreated to Clermont-Ferrand in 1940, deported to Germany.*
28 – Teheran Conference: Roosevelt, Churchill, Stalin.

December: 2 – *Maurice Sarraut murdered by the Milice.*
19 – *Mass meeting of the ultracollaborationists at the Vel*

d'Hiv in Paris, calling for a seizure of power through a Fascist coup d'état.

30 – *Darnand named secretary general for the maintenance of order. Henriot named minister of information and propaganda.*

1944

January:
8 – *The ex-chief of the Cagoule, Eugène Deloncle, and his son murdered by the Gestapo.*
20 – *Vichy law sets up Milice court-martials.*
22 – Allies land at Anzio.
30 – *Pétain signs final proposal for a new Constitution.*

February:
1 – *All Frenchmen aged sixteen to sixty subject to S.T.O.*
18 – *Twenty-three F.T.P. of the Manouchian group condemned to death and executed.*

March:
16 – *Marcel Déat named Vichy minister of labor.*
20 – Pierre Pucheu executed by a French firing squad in Algiers.
25 – *Milice and German troops attack the Maquis on the plateau of Glières.*

April:
10 – Odessa retaken by Soviets.
20 – *Milicien family murdered in Voiron.*
21 – *Bombing of Paris: 650 dead.*
28 – *Pétain visits Paris, calls liberation "a mirage."*

May:
9 – Russians capture Sebastopol.
17 – French Committee for National Liberation (Algiers) becomes Provisional Government of the Republic.
19 – Monte Cassino taken by Allies in Italy.

June:
4 – Rome captured by Allies.
6 – *Allied landings in Normandy.*
8 – *Bayeux liberated by English troops.*
10 – *642 French civilians massacred by S.S. troops at Oradour.*
12 – *Milice and Germans attack Maquis on Vercors.*
13 – *Darnand named minister of the interior.*
15 – B-29's begin raids on Japan.
20 – *Jean Zay murdered by the Milice.*
28 – *Philippe Henriot killed by the Resistance.*

July:
8 – *Georges Mandel murdered by Milice.*
20 – Assassination of Hitler by German officers fails.
30 – *Disappearance of Saint-Exupéry on reconnaissance mission over southern France.*
31 – *American army breaks through German lines at Avranches.*

August: 15 – *Allies land on southern coast of France.*
16 – *Laval taken to Belfort by Germans.*
19 – *Insurrection breaks out in Paris.*
20 – *Pétain removed from Vichy to Belfort by the Germans.*
23 – Rumania surrenders to Soviets.
25 – *Paris liberated.*
26 – *De Gaulle arrives in Paris amid last fighting.*

September: 3 – British liberate Brussels.
8 – Pétain and Laval transferred to Sigmaringen.
17 – Allied airborne invasion of Holland: Battle of Arnhem.

October: 14 – Rommel forced to commit suicide because of his role in plot against Hitler.
23 – Battle of Leyte Gulf.

November: 18 – *High Court of Justice created to try Vichy ministers.*

December: 11 – Franco-Soviet pact signed.
16 – German attack in the Ardennes (Battle of the Bulge).
21 – Bichelonne, Vichy minister, dies mysteriously.

1945

January: 6 – Doriot heads "Committee for French Liberation."
9 – U.S. army lands in the Philippines.
12 – Budapest captured by Russian troops.
16 – Warsaw captured by Russian troops.
22 – Jacques Doriot killed in strafing attack.

February: 4 – Yalta Conference begins: Churchill, Roosevelt, Stalin.

March: 6 – Remagen Bridge captured.
23 – British cross Rhine near Wesel.

April: 1 – Landings on Okinawa.
12 – President Roosevelt dies. Harry Truman becomes president.
13 – Vienna captured by Russian troops.
25 – Meeting of American and Russian troops on the Elbe.
26 – *Pétain returns to France.*
28 – Mussolini killed by Italian partisans.
30 – Hitler commits suicide.

May: 2 – Berlin captured by Soviet armies. Laval flees to Spain.
7 – Germany surrenders.

Dramatis Personae

ABETZ, OTTO—German ambassador to occupied France. Sentenced by French military tribunal to twenty years' imprisonment in 1949. Released in 1954. Killed in car crash 1958.

ALBRECHT, BERTIE—Assistant to Henri Frenay in the Combat resistance network. Believed to have died and to have been buried in Fresnes prison in June, 1943.

ALIBERT, RAPHAËL—Vichy minister of justice. Responsible for the first anti-Jewish legislation. Sentenced to death in absentia.

ASTIER DE LA VIGERIE, EMMANUEL D'—Head of Liberation resistance network. Later joined de Gaulle's cabinet in London and Algiers.

AUPHAN, GABRIEL-PAUL, ADMIRAL—Advisor and confidant of Marshal Pétain. Named to seven-man directory to govern in case of his incapacity. Attempted unsuccessfully to contact de Gaulle in August, 1944, for legal transfer of power. Sentenced to life imprisonment at hard labor in absentia.

BAUDOUIN, PAUL—Vichy minister of foreign affairs. Resigned January, 1941. Sentenced to five years' hard labor.

BENOIST-MÉCHIN, JACQUES—Vichy undersecretary of state. Advocate of French military collaboration with the Nazis. Sentenced to death (commuted to life, later amnestied).

BICHELONNE, JEAN—Vichy minister of production and communications. Fled to Sigmaringen. Died mysteriously during operation in S.S. hospital in December, 1944 .

BIDAULT, GEORGES—History professor, member of Combat, Jean Moulin's successor as head of C.N.R. Twice premier after the war, he led resistance to de Gaulle over Algeria.

BILLOUX, FRANÇOIS—Communist deputy, imprisoned by Daladier and Vichy. Asked Pétain (December, 1940) for better prison conditions if he testified at Riom. Later served as minister in de Gaulle's government.

BLUM, LÉON—Head of the French Socialist party (S.F.I.O.) and of the Popular Front government (1936). Imprisoned by Vichy and turned over to the Germans. Returned from a concentration camp. Premier (December, 1946–January, 1947).

BOEMELBURG, CARL, S.S. STURMBANNFÜHRER—Member of the Gestapo in Paris and Vichy. Fate unknown.

BONHOMME, MAJOR—Pétain's aide-de-camp. Died in ambush 1944.

BONNARD, ABEL—Vichy minister of education. Fled to Sigmaringen. Expelled from the Academie Française. Fled to Spain. Sentenced to death in absentia. Returned and was sentenced in 1960 to ten years' banishment (which he had already served).

BOUSQUET, RENÉ—Vichy secretary general of police. Deported to Germany in 1944. Sentenced to five years' national degradation; sentence suspended.

BOUTHILLIER, YVES—Vichy minister of finance. Sentenced to three years' imprisonment.

BRASILLACH, ROBERT—Author and journalist. Wrote for the collaborationist newspaper *Je suis partout*. Shot February 6, 1945.

BRIDOUX, EUGÈNE, GENERAL—Vichy minister of war. Member of de Brinon's "National Committee" in Sigmaringen. Sentenced to death in absentia.

BRINON, FERNAND DE—Vichy ambassador to the occupation authorities. Head of "National Committee for the Protection of French Interests" in Sigmaringen. Executed.

CARCOPINO, JÉRÔME—Vichy minister of education. Not prosecuted.

CÉLINE, LOUIS-FERDINAND—Pro-Fascist author. Fled to Sigmaringen and later Denmark—where he was jailed for two years. Returned to France. Died 1961.

CHAMBRUN, COUNT RENÉ DE—Descendant of Lafayette; Laval's son-in-law.

CHÂTEAUBRIANT, ALPHONSE DE—Pro-Fascist writer. Died in hiding in Italy after the war.

CHAUTEMPS, CAMILLE—French statesman. Four times premier, he was vice-premier in Reynaud and Pétain cabinets. Left Vichy government after ten days. Condemned to five years' imprisonment in absentia. Died 1963.

CHEVALIER, JACQUES—Vichy minister of education. Sentenced to twenty years' hard labor.

CHURCHILL, WINSTON—British prime minister during World War II. Died 1965.

CLEMENCEAU, GEORGES—Premier of France (1917–1918), he was known as "the Tiger" for his ruthless prosecution of the war and "Old Man Victory" for his role in winning it.

COLSON, LOUIS, GENERAL—Vichy minister of war. Not prosecuted.

DALADIER, EDOUARD—French premier. Imprisoned by Vichy, tried at Riom, then turned over to the Nazis, who put him in a concentration camp. Returned after the war to testify at Pétain's trial. Died 1970.

DANNECKER, THEODOR (Captain—S.S.)—Eichmann's man in Paris. Removed for corruption, he is believed to have committed suicide in 1945.

DARLAN, FRANÇOIS, ADMIRAL—Navy minister, vice-premier, and head of all armed forces under Vichy. Assassinated in Algiers, December 24, 1942.

DARNAND, JOSEPH—Combat hero of both world wars. Head of the Milice and Vichy secretary of the interior. Executed.

DARQUIER "DE PELLEPOIX," LOUIS—Fanatical anti-Semite. Head of the General Commission for Jewish Questions. Sentenced to death in absentia.

DÉAT, MARCEL—Pro-Nazi head of R.N.P. and editor of *L'Oeuvre*. Fled to Sigmaringen and later Italy. Died in hiding in Italy.

DE GAULLE, CHARLES, GENERAL—Leader of the Fighting French, he made the first call for resistance on June 18, 1940. President of the Provisional Government, he resigned in January, 1946. Returned to power in May, 1958, during the Algerian crisis. Elected President of the Fifth Republic twice, he resigned again in 1969. Died 1970.

DENTZ, HENRI-FERNAND, GENERAL—Surrendered Paris to the Germans in June, 1940. Defended Syria against the Allies, for which he was sentenced to death in 1945. His sentence was commuted, but he died in prison.

DORIOT, JACQUES—Ex-Communist. Head of Fascist P.P.F. Fled to Sigmaringen. Killed in a strafing attack in Germany, February 22, 1945.

DORMOY, MARX—Minister of the interior in the Popular Front government (1936). Killed by a bomb set by Doriot's men in July, 1941.

DRIEU LA ROCHELLE, PIERRE—Well-known author and pro-Nazi editor of the N.R.F. Committed suicide shortly before the liberation of Paris.

ESTIENNE D'ORVES, HENRI D', COMMANDANT—Free French naval officer. Shot as a spy by the Germans in August, 1941.

EICHMANN, ADOLF, S.S. OBERSTURMBANNFÜHRER—Head of Amt IVB4 of R.S.H.A., concerned with the extermination of European Jews. Fled to South America after the war. Tracked down and kidnaped by Israeli agents, he was tried and hanged in Israel in 1961.

FLANDIN, PIERRE-ETIENNE—French statesman. Succeeded Laval as vice-premier in December, 1940, and was ousted by Darlan in January, 1941. Sentenced to five years' national degradation, which was suspended.

FOCH, FERDINAND, MARSHAL—Generalissimo of the Allied armies in 1918. Died 1929.

FONCK, RENÉ, COLONEL—French ace of aces in World War I (seventy-five victories). Pétain's liaison with Goering during the occupation. Died 1953.

FONTENOY, JEAN—Fascist journalist. Served with L.V.F. in Russia. Died fighting in Berlin, May, 1945.

FRANCHET D'ESPEREY, LOUIS, MARSHAL—Commanded a French army in World War I. Dabbled in Rightist politics and had contact with the C.S.A.R. Died 1942.

FRANCO, FRANCISCO, GENERAL—Leader of the nationalist forces in the Spanish Civil War and present Spanish dictator.

FRENAY, HENRI, CAPTAIN—Head of the resistance network Combat and later minister in the Provisional Government. Recently published his memoirs of the occupation.

GAMELIN, MAURICE, GENERAL—Aide to Joffre in World War I. Commander in chief of French armies at outbreak of war. Replaced by Weygand May, 1940. Tried at Riom. Deported to Germany and returned after the war. Died 1958.

GEORGES, PIERRE ("COLONEL FABIEN")—Leader of Communist action squad in Paris. Shot German naval officer at Barbès subway station in August, 1941. Killed serving with the French army in Alsace, December, 1944.

GIRAUD, HENRI, GENERAL—Army commander during the Battle of France. Escaped from German prison camp. De Gaulle's rival for the leadership of the Fighting French, he was maneuvered from power. Died 1949.

GOERING, HERMANN, MARSHAL—Hitler's chosen successor and head of the Nazi Air Force in World War II. Tried and condemned at Nüremburg in 1946, he poisoned himself in his cell.

GUITRY, SACHA—Actor, playwright, and friend of Pétain's. Imprisoned for two months after the Liberation for "collaboration." Died 1957.

HENRIOT, PHILIPPE—Vichy minister of propaganda and information. The "star" of Radio-Paris. Killed by the Resistance, June, 1944.

HÉROLD-PAQUIS, JEAN—French Fascist. Broadcast German propaganda on Radio-Paris. Executed.

HERRIOT, EDOUARD—French statesman, president of the Chamber of Deputies and leader of the Radical Socialist party. Voted for Pétain. Died 1957.

HEYDRICH, REINHARDT, S.S. GENERAL—Himmler's second in command. Assassinated in June, 1942, by Czech paratroopers sent from England.

HIMMLER, HEINRICH—Reichsführer and head of the S.S.; committed suicide when arrested by English troops, May, 1945.

HITLER, ADOLF—Führer of the Third Reich. Committed suicide in Berlin, April 30, 1944.

ISORNI, JACQUES—French lawyer. Defended Pétain and Brasillach at their trials.

JOFFRE, JOSEPH CÉSAR, MARSHAL—Commander in chief of the French armies at the outbreak of World War I. Victor of the Marne. Dismissed in 1916. Died 1931.

KNOCHEN, HELMUT, S.S. Colonel—Head of the Paris Gestapo. Condemned to death by a French military tribunal in September, 1945. Sentence commuted to life imprisonment, then twenty years' hard labor. Released November, 1962.

KOENIG, MARIE PIERRE, GENERAL—Hero of the Fighting French defense of Bir Hakeim. Head of F.F.I. (1944).

LAURENCIE, BENOIT LÉON FORNEL DE LA, GENERAL—Vichy ambassador to the occupied zone until December, 1940. Later joined the Resistance, for which he was interned by Pétain.

LAVAL, PIERRE—French statesman, twice premier. Vichy vice-premier (1940). Head of government (1942). Actively pursued policy of collaboration with Nazi Germany. Taken to Belfort, then Sigmaringen by the Germans. Fled to Spain, but returned to France, 1945. Tried and condemned to death by the high court. Executed October, 1945.

LEAHY, WILLIAM D., ADMIRAL—American ambassador to Vichy (January, 1941–April, 1942).

LEBRUN, ALBERT—Last President of the Third Republic. Dismissed by Pétain in July, 1940. Died 1950.

LOUSTAUNAU-LACAU, GEORGES, MAJOR—Former aide to Pétain. Leader of resistance network Alliance. Captured by Vichy and turned over to the Gestapo, he was sent to a concentration camp. Returned in 1945 to testify at Pétain's trial. Died a deputy in 1953.

LUCHAIRE, JEAN—French pro-Nazi head of the Paris press. Fled to Sigmaringen, then to Italy. Executed February, 1946.

MANDEL, GEORGES—French statesman. Clemenceau's *chef de cabinet.* Reynaud's minister of the interior, he opposed the armistice and Pétain. Arrested and imprisoned by Vichy, he was turned over to the Nazis. Returned to France by the Germans in July, 1944, he was murdered by the Milice.

MARION, PAUL—Ex-Communist, later member of Doriot's P.P.F. Vichy minister of information. Fled to Sigmaringen. Sentenced to ten years in prison.

MAURRAS, CHARLES—Head of the royalist L'Action Française and editor of its newspaper. Expelled from the Academy and sentenced to life imprisonment in 1945. Died 1952.

MENDÈS-FRANCE, PIERRE—French statesman. A deputy in 1940, he voted against Pétain. Arrested and sentenced to prison, he escaped and joined de Gaulle. He was premier in 1954–55.

MÉNÉTREL, BERNARD, DR.—Pétain's physician and later his political advisor. Killed in auto accident in 1947, shortly after his release from prison.

MOULIN, JEAN—Prefect of Eure-et-Loir in 1940. As de Gaulle's representative to the metropolitan resistance, he founded the C.N.R. Betrayed at Caluire in June, 1943, he was tortured to death by the Germans. Eulogized by Malraux and inhumed in the Panthéon in December, 1964.

MOULIN DE LABARTHÈTE, HENRI DU—Head of Pétain's civil cabinet in 1940–1942. Dismissed when Laval returned in April, 1942, he went to Switzerland as financial attaché.

OBERG, KARL ALBRECHT, GENERAL S.S.—Supreme head of the S.S. and Police in France 1942–1944. Condemned to death by a French tribunal in 1954, reprieved and sentenced to twenty years' hard labor. Freed in November, 1962.

PÉTAIN, PHILIPPE, MARSHAL—Victor of Verdun. Commander in chief of French armies, 1918. Head of Vichy government July, 1940–August, 1944. Taken to Sigmaringen by Germans. Returned to France to stand trial for treason. Condemned to death; sentence changed to life imprisonment on the Ile d'Yeu, where he died 1951.

PLATON, JEAN, ADMIRAL—Vichy minister for colonies and an ultracollaborationist; he was shot after an F.F.I. court-martial August, 1944.

POMPIDOU, GEORGES—Eighteenth president of the French Republic (1969–1974). No record of resistance or collaboration activity. Died April 2, 1974.

PUCHEU, PIERRE—Vichy minister of the interior. Left government after Laval's return and went to Algiers. Arrested, tried, and condemned by a Gaullist court, he was shot March, 1944.

REBATET, LUCIEN—French pro-Nazi writer on *Je suis partout*. Author of *Les Décombres*. Fled to Sigmaringen.

RIBBENTROP, JOACHIM VON—Nazi minister of foreign affairs. Tried at Nüremburg, he was condemned to death and hanged in 1946.

RIPERT, GEORGES—Vichy minister of education until December, 1940. Not prosecuted.

SAUCKEL, FRITZ—Nazi Gauleiter of Thuringia. Head of the roundup of slave labor in occupied Europe. Tried at Nüremburg and hanged.

SCAPINI, GEORGES—Prewar deputy and blind veteran of World War I. Became Pétain's delegate for French prisoners in Germany. Not prosecuted.

SCHMIDT, PAUL, DR.—Hitler's interpreter at Montoire.

STÜLPNAGEL, HEINRICH VON, GENERAL—Succeeded his cousin Otto as military commander in France. Attempted to commit suicide at Verdun after the failure of the plot to kill Hitler, but only blinded himself. Was hanged later by the Gestapo.

SUAREZ, GEORGES—Pro-Nazi editor of *Aujourd'hui*. Executed in October, 1944.

THOREZ, MAURICE—Member of the central committee of the French Communist party. Deserted from the army in October, 1939, and spent the war years in Moscow. Returned to France in 1945 to become a minister in de Gaulle's government.

TIXIER-VIGNANCOURT, JEAN-LOUIS—Director of Vichy radio (1940); he received one million votes as presidential candidate in December, 1965.

WEYGAND, MAXIME, GENERAL—On Foch's staff in World War I. Replaced Gamelin as commander in chief of French armies in 1940; he refused to surrender in the field and demanded an armistice. Minister of war in Pétain's first cabinet. Arrested and deported by the Germans in November, 1942. Not prosecuted. Died 1965.

ZAY, JEAN—Minister in the Popular Front government (1936), he voted against Pétain in July, 1940, and sailed on the *Massilia* for North Africa. Arrested and imprisoned by Vichy, he was murdered by the Milice in June, 1944.

Bibliography

(All books, periodicals, and official documents listed were published in Paris unless otherwise noted.)

Abel, Jean Pierre: *L'Age de Caïn*, Editions Nouvelles, 1948.

Abetz, Otto: *Histoire d'une politique franco-allemande*, Stock, 1953.

Achard, Paul: *La Queue, ce qui s'y disait, ce qu'on y pensait*, Editions de la Belle Fontaine, 1945.

Albert-Sorel, Jean: *Le Calvaire, 1940–44*, Julliard, 1944.

Ambrière, Francis: *Les Grandes Vacances (1939–45)*, Editions de la Nouvelle France, 1946.

——— et al.: *Vie et mort des français*, Hachette, 1971.

Ambroise-Colin, Charles: *Un Procès de l'épuration: Robert Brasillach*, Mame (Tours), 1971.

Amoretti, Henri: *Lyon capitale, 1940–1944*, Editions France Empire, 1964.

Amouroux, Henri: *La Vie des français sous l'occupation*, Fayard, 1961.

———: *Pétain avant Vichy*, Fayard, 1967.

———: *Quatre Ans d'histoire de France*, Hachette, 1966.

———: *La France et les français de 1939 à 1945*, A. Colin, 1970.

Angeli, C., and Gillet, P.: *Debout, partisans!*, Fayard, 1970.

Aragon, Louis: *Les Martyrs* (clandestine publication), 1942.

Argenson, Marquis d': *Pétain et le pétainisme*, Creator, 1953.

Armand, Chanoine: *La Dure Epreuve du loyalisme français*, Edition I.G.C. (Saint-Etienne), 1950.

Arnoult, P., et al.: *La France sous l'occupation*, Presses Universitaires de France, 1959.

Aron, Robert: *The Vichy Regime*, Beacon Press (Boston), 1969.

———: *Les Grands Dossiers de l'histoire contemporaine*, Perrin, 1963.

———: *Le Piège où nous a pris l'histoire*, Michel, 1950.

———: *Histoire de l'épuration* (2 vols.), Fayard, 1967.

Assaily, G. d': S.S.A., Julliard, 1946.

Assemblée Nationale de France, *Commission d'enquête parlementaire: Les Evénements survenus en France de 1939 à 1945* (11 vols.), Presses Universitaires de France, 1951.

Astier de la Vigerie, Emmanuel d': *De la chute à la libération de Paris*, Gallimard, 1965.
Audiat, Pierre: *Paris pendant la guerre*, Hachette, 1946.
Auphan, Gabriel: *Histoire élémentaire de Vichy*, Editions France Empire, 1971.
Auriol, Vincent: *Hier . . . demain*, Charlot (Tunis), 1944.
Aziz, Philippe: *Tu trahiras sans vergogne*, Fayard, 1969.
Bankwitz, Philip C. F.: *Maxime Weygand and Civil-Military Relations in Modern France*, Harvard University Press (Cambridge, Mass.), 1967.
Baraduc, Jacques: *Dans la cellule de Pierre Laval*, Editions SELF, 1948.
Bardoux, Jacques: *La Délivrance de Paris*, Fayard, 1958.
Barrillon, Raymond: *Le Cas Paris-Soir*, A. Colin, 1959.
Baudot, Marcel: *L'Opinion publique sous l'occupation*, Presses Universitaires de France, 1960.
Baudouin, Paul: *The Private Diaries (March 1940–January 1941)*, translated by Sir Charles Petrie, Eyre (London), 1948.
Beauvoir, Simone de: *The Prime of Life*, World (Cleveland), 1962.
Bechtel, Guy: *Laval, vingt ans après*, Laffont, 1963.
Benoist-Méchin, Jacques: *La Moisson de quarante*, Albin Michel, 1941.
Bénouville, Guillain de: *Le Sacrifice du matin*, Laffont, 1948.
Billig, Joseph: *Le Commissariat général aux questions juives*, Editions du Centre, 1955.
Black, Rowland W.: *Histoire et crimes de la Gestapo parisienne*, Exclusivités en Vente (Brussels), 1945.
Bloch, Marc: *Strange Defeat*, Norton (New York), 1968.
Bloch-Michel, Jean: *Les Grands Circonstances*, Gallimard, 1948.
Borwicz, Michel: *Ecrits des condamnés à mort sous l'occupation allemande*, P.U.F., 1954.
Bourget, Pierre: *Histoires secrètes de l'occupation de Paris*, vol. 1, Hachette, 1970.
———: *Sur les murs de Paris (1940–1944)*, Hachette, 1959.
Boutang, Pierre: *La République de Joinovici*, Amiot-Dumont, 1949.
Bouthillier, Yves: *Le Drame de Vichy*, Plon, 1950.
Boveri, Margret: *Treason in the Twentieth Century*, Putnam (New York), 1963.
Braibant, Charles: *La Guerre à Paris*, Correa, 1945.
Brasillach, Robert: *Journal d'un homme occupé* (Collected Works, vol. 6), Les Sept Couleurs, 1955.
Brée, Germaine, and Brenauer, George, eds.: *Defeat and Beyond: An Anthology of French Wartime Writing, 1940–1945*, Random House (New York), 1970.
Brinon, Fernand de: *Mémoires*, L.L.C., 1948.
Brissaud, André: *Pétain à Sigmaringen*, Perrin, 1966.
———: *La Dernière Année de Vichy*, Fayard, 1965.
Calet, Henri: *Les Murs de Fresnes*, Editions des Quatre-Vents, 1955.
Carcopino, Jérôme: *Souvenirs de sept ans*, Flammarion, 1953.

Céline, Louis Ferdinand: *Les Beaux Draps*, Nouvelles Editions Françaises, 1941.

———: *Castle to Castle*, Dell (New York), 1968.

Charles-Roux, François: *Cinq Mois tragiques aux affaires étrangères*, Plon, 1949.

Chastenet, Jacques: *De Pétain à de Gaulle*, Fayard, 1970.

Chautemps, Camille: *Cahiers secrets de l'armistice*, Plon, 1963.

Churchill, Winston S.: *War Speeches* (2 vols.), Cassell (London), 1952.

Cotta, Michèle: *La Collaboration 1940–1944*, A. Colin, 1964.

Crémieux-Dunand, Jean: *La Vie à Drancy*, Gedalge, 1948.

Debû-Bridel, Jacques: *Histoire du marché noir*, La Jeune Parque, 1947.

De Gaulle, Charles: *The Complete War Memoirs*, Simon & Schuster (New York), 1964.

Delarue, Jacques: *Trafics et crimes sous l'occupation*, Fayard, 1968.

———: *Histoire de la Gestapo*, Fayard, 1962.

Délégation française auprès de la commission allemande d'armistice (5 vols.), Imprimerie Nationale, 1947–1959.

Delperrie de Bayac, J.: *Histoire de la Milice*, Fayard, 1969.

Dieter-Wolf: *Doriot: Du communisme à la collaboration*, Fayard, 1970.

Drieu la Rochelle, Pierre: *Chronique politique: 1939–1942*, Gallimard, 1943.

Dubois, Edmond: *Paris sans lumière*, Payot (Lausanne), 1946.

Ducloux, Louis: *From Blackmail to Treason*, Deutsch (London), 1958.

Du Moulin de Labarthète, Henri: *Le Temps des illusions*, Editions du Cheval Ailé (Geneva), 1946.

Duquesne, Jacques: *Les Catholiques français sous l'occupation*, Grasset, 1966.

Eparvier, Jean: *A Paris sous la botte des nazis*, Schall, 1944.

Evrard, Jacques: *La déportation des travailleurs français dans le Troisième Reich*, Fayard, 1972.

Fabre-Luce, Alfred: *Journal de la France, 1939–1944*, Editions du Cheval Ailé (Geneva), 1946.

Fourcade, Marie-Madeleine: *Noah's Ark*, Dutton (New York), 1974.

Foville, Jean Marc de: *L'Entrée des allemands à Paris*, Calmann-Levy, 1965.

Frenay, Henri: *La Nuit finira*, Laffont, 1973.

Galtier-Boissière, Jean: *Mon Journal pendant l'occupation*, La Jeune Parque, 1946.

Garcon, Maurice: *Plaidoyer pour René Hardy*, Fayard, 1950.

Girard, André: *Bataille secrète en France*, Brentano's, 1944.

Girard, Louis Dominique: *Montoire, Verdun diplomatique*, André Bonne, 1948.

Godefroy, Louis: *Le Havre sous l'occupation, 1940–1944*, Hachette, 1958.

Gounelle, Claude: *De Vichy à Montoire*, Presses de la Cité, 1966.

Granet, Marie, and Michel, Henri: *Combat, histoire d'un mouvement de résistance*, Presses Universitaires de France, 1957.

Grenier, Fernand: *Ceux de Châteaubriant*, Editions Sociales (n.d.).
Groussard, Georges: *Service secret*, Table Ronde, 1964.
Guéhenno, Jean: *Journal des années noires*, Gallimard, 1947.
Guitry, Sacha: *Quatre Ans d'occupation*, Perrin, 1964.
Hérold-Paquis, Jean: *Mémoires*, Bourgoin, 1948.
Hoover Library: *France During the German Occupation, 1940–1944: A Collection of 292 Statements on the Government of Maréchal Pétain and Pierre Laval* (3 vols.), Stanford University Press (Stanford, Calif.), 1959.
Huddleston, Sisley: *France, the Tragic Years*, Devin-Adair (New York), 1955.
Isorni, Jacques: *Le Procès de Robert Brasillach*, Flammarion, 1946.
Jäckel, Eberhard: *Frankreich in Hitlers Europa*, Stuttgart, 1966 (*La France dans l'Europe de Hitler*, Fayard, 1968).
Journal Officiel de l'Etat Français.
Jünger, Ernst: *Journal (1941–1943)*, Julliard, 1952.
Kernan, Thomas: *France on Berlin Time*, L'Arbre (Montreal), 1942.
La Mazière, Christian de: *Le Rêveur casqué*, Laffont, 1972.
Langer, Walter: *Le Jeu américain à Vichy*, Plon, 1948.
Langeron, Roger: *Paris, juin 1940*, Flammarion, 1946.
Latour, Anny: *La Résistance juive en France*, Stock, 1970.
Laval, Pierre: *Laval parle*, Editions du Cheval Ailé (Geneva), 1947.
LeClère, Marcel: *Le six février*, Hachette, 1967.
Lévy, Claude: *La Grande Rafle du Vel d'Hiv*, Laffont, 1967 (translated as *Betrayal at the Vel d'Hiv*, Hill & Wang [New York], 1969).
———: *Les Parias de la résistance*, Calmann-Levy, 1970.
Limagne, Pierre: *Ephémérides de quatre années tragiques* (4 vols.), Plon, 1945–1948.
Littlejohn, David: *The Patriotic Traitors*, Heinemann (London), 1972.
Loustaunau-Lacau, Georges: *Mémoires d'un français rebelle*, Hachette, 1948.
Luchaire, Corinne: *Ma Drôle de vie*, Editions Sun, 1948.
Martin du Gard, Maurice: *Chronique de Vichy*, Flammarion, 1948.
Maze, Pierre, and Genebrier, Robert: *Les Grandes Journées du procès de Riom*, La Jeune Parque, 1945.
Michel, Henri: *Jean Moulin, l'unificateur*, Hachette, 1964.
———: *Vichy: Année 40*, Hachette, 1966.
———: *La France sous l'occupation*, Presses Universitaires de France, 1968.
———: *La Guerre de l'ombre*, La Cercle du Nouveau Livre d'Histoire, 1970.
———: *Histoire de la résistance*, Presses Universitaires de France, 1950.
Monneray, Henri: *La Persécution des juifs en France*, Editions du Centre, 1947.
Moulin, Jean: *Premier Combat*, Editions de Minuit, 1947.
Moulin, Laure: *Jean Moulin*, Presses de la Cité, 1969.

Moussinac, Léon: *Le Radeau de la Méduse*, Editions Hier et Aujourd'hui, 1945.
Naud, Albert: *Pourquoi je n'ai pas défendu Pierre Laval*, Fayard, 1948.
Nobécourt, R. G.: *Les Secrets de la propagande en France occupée*, Fayard, 1962.
Noguères, Henri: *Histoire de la résistance en France* (3 vols.), Laffont, 1967.
Noguères, Louis: *La Haute Cour de la libération*, Laffont, 1965.
———: *La Dernière Etape: Sigmaringen*, Fayard, 1956.
———: *Le Véritable Procès du Maréchal Pétain*, Laffont, 1955.
Novick, Peter: *The Resistance Versus Vichy*, Macmillan (New York), 1968.
Ollier, Nicole: *L'Exode sur les routes de l'an 40*, Laffont, 1969.
Paulhan, Jean, and Aury, Dominique: *La Patrie se fait tous les jours*, Editions de Minuit, 1947.
Paxton, Robert: *Vichy France: Old Guard and New Order, 1940–1944*, Knopf (New York), 1972.
"Pertinax" (André Géraud): *The Gravediggers of France*, Doubleday (New York), 1944.
Pétain, Philippe: *Quatre Années au pouvoir*, La Couronne Littéraire, 1949.
Pineau, Christian: *La Simple Verité*, Julliard, 1969.
Plimyène, J., and Lasierra, R.: *Les Fascismes français, 1923–1963*, Editions du Seuil, 1963.
Poliakov, L.: *La Bréviaire de la haine*, Calmann-Levy, 1955 (*Harvest of Hate*, Syracuse University Press [Syracuse, New York], 1954).
Polonski, Jacques: *La Presse, la propagande et l'opinion publique sous l'occupation*, Editions du Centre, 1946.
Procès de Charles Maurras, Albin Michel, 1945.
Procès Laval, Albin Michel, 1946.
Procès de la collaboration: Brinon, Luchaire, Darnand, Albin Michel, 1948.
Procès du Maréchal Pétain, Journal Officiel, 1945.
Procès de Xavier Vallat, Editions du Conquistador, 1948.
Pucheu, Pierre: *Ma Vie*, Amiot-Dumont, 1946.
Queval, Jean: *Première Page, cinquième colonne*, Fayard, 1945.
Rebatet, Lucien: *Les Décombres*, Editions Denoël, 1942.
Revue d'Histoire de la Deuxième Guerre Mondiale, Presses Universitaires de France, 1950–.
Ribet, Maurice: *Le Procès de Riom*, Flammarion, 1945.
Rougeron, Georges: *Le Département de l'Allier sous l'Etat Français (1940–1944)*, Laffont, 1969.
Roy, Jules: *Le Grand Naufrage*, Julliard, 1966 (*The Trial of Marshal Pétain*, Harper and Row [New York], 1968).
Saint-Loup (Marc Augier): *Les Volontaires*, Presses de la Cité, 1963.
Saint-Paulien (Maurice Yvan Sicard): *Histoire de la collaboration*, L'Esprit Nouveau, 1964.

———: *Les Maudits*, Plon, 1958.
Serrigny, Bernard: *Trente Ans avec Pétain*, Plon, 1959.
Shirer, William L.: *The Collapse of the Third Republic*, Simon & Schuster (New York), 1969.
Texcier, Jean: *Un Homme libre*, Albin Michel, 1960.
Tillion, Germaine: "Première Résistance en zone occupée," *Revue d'Histoire de la Deuxième Guerre Mondiale*, No. 30, 1958.
Tillon, Charles: *Les F.T.P.*, Julliard, 1967.
Tournoux, Jean-Raymond: *Sons of France: Pétain and de Gaulle*, Viking (New York), 1966.
Trouille, Pierre: *Journal d'un préfet pendant l'occupation*, Gallimard, 1964.
Schmidt, Paul: *Statist auf diplomatischer Bühne (1923–1945)*, Bonn, 1949.
Sérant, Paul: *Les Vaincus de la libération*, Laffont, 1964.
Umbreit, Hans: *Der Militärbefehlshaber in Frankreich 1940–1944*, H. Boldt (Boppard am Rhein), 1968.
Vallat, Xavier: *Le Nez de Cléopâtre*, Les Quatre Fils Aymon, 1957.
Vanino, Maurice: *De Rethondes à l'Ile d'Yeu*, Laffont, 1952.
Vidalenc, Jean: *L'Exode de mai–juin 1940*, Presses Universitaires de France, 1957.
Walter, Gérard: *La Vie à Paris sous l'occupation*, A. Colin, 1960.
Wellers, Georges: *De Drancy à Auschwitz*, Editions du Centre, 1946.
Werth, Alexander: *France: 1940–1955*, Beacon Press (Boston), 1966.
Weygand, Jacques: *Weygand, mon père*, Flammarion, 1970.
Wormser, O.: *Les Françaises à Ravensbrück*, Gallimard, 1965.
"X," Général: *Le Drame de la gendarmerie française sous l'occupation allemande* (Private, Toulouse), 1953.

Reference Notes

The books quoted will be found in the bibliography. Short forms of titles are given in these notes after the first mention.

PROLOGUE

PAGE

12 "All right, get out your money": d'Assaily, p. 165.

13 Events at Blanc and Poitiers: Vidalenc, p. 316.
Pétain's broadcast: Amouroux, *La Vie des français sous l'occupation,* I, p. 64.

CHAPTER 1 *"Maréchal, Nous Voilà!"*

17 "In the darkness": Moulin, Jean, p. 107.

17–18 Chartres in June, 1940: Moulin, Laure, p. 187.

18 "Run away? Impossible.": Moulin, Jean, pp. 107–8.

20 "To have seen sadder": du Moulin de Labarthète, p. 15.

22 Description of Pétain: *Ibid.,* p. 89.

23 "Outside the door": Serrigny, p. 44.
In 1920, the young lady became Madame Pétain: Amouroux, *Pétain avant Vichy,* p. 140.
"What I love best": Martin du Gard, p. 88.

24 "I trust no one": du Moulin de Labarthète, p. 16.
"I sacrifice no one": *Ibid.,* p. 94.

24–25 For the relationship between de Gaulle and Pétain, see Tournoux.

25 Pétain's note on the condemnation of de Gaulle is in Noguères, L., *Le Veritable Procès du Maréchal Pétain,* p. 678.
"Old age is a shipwreck": Tournoux, p. 112.

26 Those who begged for jobs: du Moulin de Labarthète, p. 21.

27 "They have given me power": *Ibid.,* p. 17.
The legality of Vichy: Novick, p. 191.

29 The mystery of Weygand's birth: Bankwitz, p. 4, and Weygand, Chapter 1.

31 "Millions of dead bodies": Hoover Library, p. 1249.
"This Chamber has spewed me out": Baudouin, p. 148.

32 "All the same, long live the Republic": Aron, *The Vichy Regime,* p. 115.
"During those two days": *Procès du Maréchal Pétain,* testimony of Léon Blum.
33 "I never expected": Charles-Roux, p. 164.
35 *"Ah! Merde!* . . . pale with pride and with pleasure": Martin du Gard, p. 103.
"I know all about that": Gounelle, p. 79.
36 "Laval told me": du Moulin de Labarthète, p. 47.
37 "A Marshal talking to a corporal": Gounelle, p. 129.
Sawada's warning: Aron, *Vichy,* p. 213.
37–40 The conversations at Montoire are based on Schmidt, p. 514 (an interview by Pierre Bourget, *L'Aurore,* October 21–23, 1960); Gounelle, p. 129; Aron, *Vichy,* p. 218; and Noguères, L., *Pétain,* p. 634.
38 "Sitting very erect": Gounelle, p. 131.
40 "An alert?": du Moulin de Labarthète, p. 52.
42 Pétain's letter to Weygand: Noguères, L., *Pétain,* p. 261.

CHAPTER 2 *The Face of Collaboration*

45–47 The riot of February 6, 1934: LeClère, pp. 129–65.
47 "Divine surprise": Werth, p. 6.
48–53 For Doriot and the P.P.F., see Saint-Paulien as well as Plumyène and Lasierra.
53 For the C.S.A.R., see Ducloux.
54 "Which otherwise he would never have been able to afford": Luchaire, p. 124.
55 "He wants to be a leader": Guéhenno, p. 122.
"We were alone": Brasillach, p. 400.
56 "The price of his liberation": Guéhenno, p. 169.
58 Broadcasts by Lesage and Henriot: Aron, *Histoire de l'épuration,* p. 360.
59 "Passed from truth to error": *Ibid.,* p. 362.
"Some Germans who do not believe enough": *Ibid.,* p. 285.
60 Churchill's speech: Churchill, II, p. 379.
61 "I am today": Aron, *Vichy,* p. 225.

CHAPTER 3 *The First Resistance*

65–66 The complete French text of "Advice to the Occupied" is in Noguères, H., I, p. 468.
67 "I consider that our first job": Bénouville, p. 155.
68 "War and prison": Loustaunau-Lacau, p. 9.
69 "There are no designs": *Ibid.,* p. 41.
"Here's what I want": *Ibid.,* p. 52.
71 "A dunghill and a bastard": *Procès Pétain,* testimony of Loustaunau-Lacau.
"Closed due to old age": Loustaunau-Lacau, p. 97.
72 "Soldiers are not made for crying": *Ibid.,* p. 196.
73 An "honorable *résistant*": Groussard, p. 81.
74 "So many homosexuals": Guéhenno, pp. 178, 199.
"To resist!": Noguères, H., I, p. 482.

PAGE

78 "They have just told me": Bourget, *Histoires secrètes de l'occupation de Paris,* p. 274.

Cochet's speech: Noguères, H., I, p. 23.

79 "Talked a lot . . . about a certain general": *Ibid.,* p. 27.

CHAPTER 4 *Vichy Plays Its Role*

84 "The Alibert law": Hoover Library, p. 626.

"Germany was not the cause": du Moulin de Labarthète, p. 280.

"In French law": Aron, *Vichy,* p. 169.

85 "Wish to defend the French organism": *Ibid.,* p. 166.

86 Census of Jews in Paris: Audiat, p. 79.

Purge of the administration: Aron, *Vichy,* p. 172.

Letter of Pierre Massé: Amouroux, *Vie,* II, p. 171.

87 "My subordinates yesterday": Martin du Gard, p. 259.

88 "If we had remained victorious": Werth, p. 58.

89 "Pétain is France": "Pertinax," p. 545.

93 "I was neither for nor against": Hoover Library, p. 1579.

95 Pétain-Laval confrontation: du Moulin de Labarthète, p. 69.

97–99 Reburial of L'Aiglon: *L'Illustration,* December 21, 1940, p. 417.

99 Hitler's wreath burned: Bourget, *Histoires,* p. 264.

CHAPTER 5 *Francs-Tireurs et Partisans*

101 "The atmosphere grows heavier": Guéhenno, p. 205.

103 Assassination of Moser: Noguères, H., II, p. 77.

105 For the treatment of the imprisoned Communists, see Moussinac.

107 Billoux's letter: *Procès Pétain,* Isorni's plea to the jury.

108 "You will have an adjutant": Angeli and Gillet, p. 312.

109 "At this moment": Noguères, H., II, p. 73.

111 Falling, and falling: Angeli and Gillet, p. 343.

112 "We followed them rapidly": Article by Brustlein in *L'Humanité Dimanche,* August 20, 1950.

113 For the events at Châteaubriant, see Aragon and Grenier.

115 "Forty *good* Frenchmen": du Moulin de Labarthète, p. 354.

116 "We have put down our arms": Bourget, *Sur les murs de Paris,* p. 75.

"It is absolutely natural": de Gaulle, p. 263.

CHAPTER 6 *The Resistance Unites*

119–20 Moulin's instructions: Moulin, Laure, p. 267*n.*

123 "Among the Resistance in 1940": Tillion, p. 11.

"Serene sunburnt face": Bénouville, p. 364.

125 "Give him an amnesty": de Gaulle, p. 314.

126–27 Frenay-Pucheu conversations: Noguères, H., II, p. 339, and Frenay, p. 155.

130 *"Ein Jude ist kein Mensch!"*: Ambrière *et al., Vie et mort des français,* p. 137.

131 Family Hostage Law: Bourget, *Murs,* p. 95.

132 "Gentlemen, think of France!": Moulin, Jean, preface by Moulin, Laure.
133 "A military and revolutionary tool": Michel, *Jean Moulin, l'unificateur,* p. 127.
De Gaulle to Moulin: Moulin, Laure, end covers.
"I found unimpugnable witnesses": de Gaulle, p. 346.
135–36 Hitler's letter to Pétain: Bourget, *Murs,* p. 117, and Noguères, L., *Pétain,* p. 455.
137 "This young man": de Gaulle, p. 379.
137–38 First meeting of the C.N.R.: Moulin, Laure, pp. 424–30.

CHAPTER 7 *Betrayal*

139 "Multon roamed the streets": Bénouville, p. 371.
141 "If I am arrested": Amoretti, p. 162.
143 "An oath to Hitler": Garcon, p. 19.
147 "Let's meet Monday": Amoretti, p. 166.
153 "Well now, *Thomas*": Noguères, H., III, p. 453.
154 "When my guard": Hardy in *France-Soir,* June 3, 1972.
155 "I escaped": *Ibid.*
156 "Imagine my stupefaction": Pineau, p. 122.
"It wasn't a good razor blade": *Ibid.,* p. 123.
"He was stretched out on a sofa": Moulin, Laure, p. 451.
158 "My finest enemy": Barbie interview with Alfredo Serra, cited in *Paris Match,* May 12, 1973.
"Before him, there were *résistants*": Michel, *Moulin,* p. 215.

CHAPTER 8 *The Ersatz Life*

160 "The French people": Baudouin, p. 219.
161 "They preferred [them] wet": *L'Illustration,* March 28, 1942.
164 "The ripened perfume of the camembert": Walter, p. 100.
166 "I wandered through the streets": de Beauvoir, p. 399.
167 "One has the impression": Jünger, p. 175.
167–68 Bicycles in Paris: Amouroux, *Quatre Ans d'histoire de France,* p. 72.

CHAPTER 9 *In Search of Forgetfulness*

174 "Adolf Hitler was born": Cotta, p. 98.
175 "They awaken Fame as best they can": Guéhenno, p. 267.
178 The star excursions: *Ibid.,* p. 232.
"*Homo scribendi*": *Ibid.,* p. 80.
181 Abetz's message: *Procès de la collaboration,* p. 497.
182 "The Berlin Opera": Fabre-Luce, p. 356.
"Only the layman": Audiat, p. 178.
184 "Chevalier did his singing act": Galtier-Boissière, p. 99.
185 "*Cote d'amour*": Audiat, p. 49.
186 "A bit of black humor": Amouroux, *Vie,* II, p. 249.
187 Shakespeare in Paris and Berlin: Kernan, p. 57.

Chapter 10 *The L.V.F. and Milice*

PAGE

188 "The decisive battle": Saint-Paulien, p. 240.

189 "Certain political advantages": Noguères, L., *Pétain,* p. 355.

191 Pompidou's uncle: Galtier-Boissière, p. 355, and *Le Crapouillot,* November–December, 1969.

192 The two Abels and Cains: Galtier-Boissière, p. 33 (translation by the author).

193–94 Laval's wounds: Hoover Library, p. 1296.

195 Pétain's telegram: Noguères, L., *Pétain,* p. 357.

197 "A fine soldier": Boveri, p. 132.

199 Ceremony of the Legion: Guéhenno, p. 190.

201 Pétain and Darnand on radio: Delperrie de Bayac, p. 150.

203 "It's from the buttocks": *Ibid.*, p. 179.

Chapter 11 *The French Gestapo*

Since the transcript of the Bonny-Lafont interrogations contains "serious information on persons still living," the Ministry of War has refused access to it until 1994—even to French historians. Fortunately, Philippe Aziz has managed (by interviewing many of the people involved) to piece together the fascinating story of the French Gestapo of the rue Lauriston (see his *Tu trahiras sans vergogne,* Fayard, 1970). It is on this account that much of the material of this chapter is based. Additional facts can be found in Aron, *Histoire de l'épuration,* I, pages 378–408, and in newspaper accounts of the trial of the Lafont gang, especially *Le Figaro,* December 3–11, 1944.

205–6 French Gestapists: Aron, *L'Epuration,* I, p. 367.

206 Bickler's remark: Aziz, p. 14.
Prison convoy: Aron, *L'Epuration,* p. 381.

207 Chamberlin's youth: Aziz, pp. 29–31, and Aron, *L'Epuration,* I, pp. 380, 381.

208 "It was really pure chance": Aziz, p. 35.

211 A strange drama in Fresnes prison: *Ibid.*, p. 40.

212 Description of 93 rue Lauriston: Aron, *L'Epuration,* I, p. 379.

218–19 For descriptions of Lafont's mistresses, see Aziz, Chapter 9, and Aron, *L'Epuration,* I, pp. 384, 385.

219 "You can never give me": Aziz, p. 233.

221 Capture of Bonny and Lafont: Aron, *L'Epuration,* I, p. 378.
"With his long nose": Article by Georges London in *Carrefour,* December 9, 1944.
"With the approval": *Ibid.*

Chapter 12 *The Fate of the Jews*

225 Knochen's analysis of French anti-Semitism: Poliakov, p. 51*n*.

226 "Five thousand Jews are gone": *Paris-Midi,* May 15, 1941, cited in Latour, p. 48.

227 Dannecker's report: Monneray, p. 84.

228 Vallat on German unity: *Ibid.*, p. 102.
229 A "real madman": Laval, p. 104.
230 "A Jew must be called a Jew": Centre de Documentation Juive Contemporaine (C.D.J.C.), CVI, p. 103.
"If Pontius Pilate": Amouroux, *Vie*, p. 385*n*.
"Why should I hate Jews?": Hoover Library, p. 649.
Dannecker on Laval's attitude: Monneray, p. 142.
231 Pastor Boegner and Laval: Latour, p. 56, and Werth, p. 62.
Knochen to R.S.H.A.: Poliakov, p. 176*n*.
Montandon's analysis: Centre de Documentation Juive Contemporaine (C.D.J.C.), XXXVI, p. 104.
232 "If a single one of them is taken": Latour, p. 11.
233 Vichy anti-Semitism not the result of German pressure: Paxton, pp. 173–85.
Report of the French ambassador to the Vatican: Poliakov, p. 49.
Knochen's letter to Berlin: Centre de Documentation Juive Contemporaine (C.D.J.C.), L. p. 38.
234 "We must keep the Italian army": Poliakov, p. 168.
237 Denunciation of Jews: Amouroux, *Vie*, p. 397.
"For the ordinary man": Poliakov, p. 291.
240 Instructions for the roundup of Jews: Lévy, *Betrayal at the Vel d'Hiv*, p. 279.
243 Commemorative plaque: *Ibid.*, p. 41.
244 Röthke's report: Monneray, p. 148.
The fate of the Jewish children: Lévy, *Betrayal*, p. 210.

Chapter 13 *The Civil War*

245–48 The inscriptions on the walls of Fresnes prison were first published by Calet.
247 Baroness de Rothschild: de Brinon, p. 222.
252 Lécussan kills a Jew: Delperrie de Bayac, p. 216.
Darnand's speech: *Ibid.*, p. 220.
254 "Democracy is the antechamber of bolshevism": *Ibid.*, p. 232.
255 Warning by the collaborationists: Aron, *L'Epuration*, I, p. 453.
Warning by the Resistance: *Franc-Tireur*, December 1, 1943.
256–57 The sounds of Darnand's justice: Delarue, *Histoire de la Gestapo*, p. 538.
263 The murder of Mandel: Aron, *Les Grands Dossiers de l'histoire contemporaine*, pp. 86–90.

Chapter 14 *Sigmaringen*

267–70 Interviews at Hitler's headquarters: Noguères, L., *La Dernière Etape: Sigmaringen*, pp. 41–57, and Saint-Paulien, *Histoire de la collaboration*, pp. 468–74.
270 "The men of the Milice": Noguères, L., *Sigmaringen*, p. 55.
Pétain's letter to Hitler: *Ibid.*, p. 85.
Céline's description of the castle: Céline, *Castle to Castle*, p. 133.
272 "Heavy grandeur": Hoover Library, p. 1177.
"False luxury and bad taste": *Ibid.*

PAGE

273 "Even if it's not true": *Ibid.*, p. 1182.

275 The *"adolfins"*: Céline, *Castle*, p. 136.
De Brinon's speech: Brissaud, *Pétain à Sigmaringen*, p. 232.
"Sense of honor": Noguères, L., *Sigmaringen*, p. 113.

276 Summary executions: Aron, *L'Epuration*, II, p. 557, and Novick, Appendix 2.

277–78 Execution of Georges Suarez: Brissaud, *Sigmaringen*, p. 281.

278 A bungled execution: Aron, *L'Epuration*, II, p. 201.
Execution of Chack: *Ibid.*, p. 342.
For the trial and execution of Brasillach, see Isorni.
Suicide of Drieu La Rochelle: Galtier-Boissière, pp. 249, 274.

281 Bichelonne's death: Céline, *Castle*, p. 135.

282–84 Doriot's death and funeral: Saint-Paulien, *Collaboration*, pp. 505–13.

284 Pétain's letter to Hitler: Noguères, L., *Sigmaringen*, p. 239.

Chapter 15 *The Trial of Pétain*

286 All quotes from the trial proceedings are from *Le Procès du Maréchal Pétain*.

293 "And to think": "Pertinax," p. 324.

296 "El Greco figure": Roy, p. 53.

297 "Fierce toneless voice": *Ibid.*, p. 81.

Chapter 16 *Vichy Condemned*

307 "Why have I once again escaped death?": Brissaud, *Sigmaringen*, p. 503.

308 "May Our Lady of Puy": *Ibid.*, p. 506.

308–9 Pétain's letter to Laval on the Milice: Noguères, L., *Pétain*, p. 653.

309 Darnand's letter to Pétain: *Procès de la Collaboration*, p. 282.
"Democracies are not the only ones": *Ibid.*
"This traitor and this murderer": *Ibid.*, p. 321.
Darnand's letter to de Gaulle: Brissaud, *Sigmaringen*, p. 509.

310–13 All quotes from Laval's trial are in *Procès Laval.*

313 Laval's attempted suicide and subsequent execution: Baraduc, pp. 188–200; Naud, pp. 258–84; Aron, *Grands Dossiers*, p. 191; and Brissaud, *Sigmaringen*, p. 546.

317 De Brinon's speech at Doriot's funeral: *Procès de la Collaboration*, p. 47.

318 "We got along very well with the Germans": *Ibid.*, p. 143.
"The complete traitor": *Ibid.*, p. 153.

319 "Women are mad": de Brinon, preface.
Dancing at the news of Hitler's death: Luchaire, p. 219.

321 "A shady hotel": Brissaud, *Sigmaringen*, p. 520.

322–23 The purge in western Europe: Novick, pp. 184–90.

323 Amnesty of collaborators: *Le Monde*, November 29, 1952.

Epilogue

324–26 The kidnapping and recovery of Pétain's coffin: *Paris Match*, No. 1243, March 3, 1973; also newspaper accounts.

Index